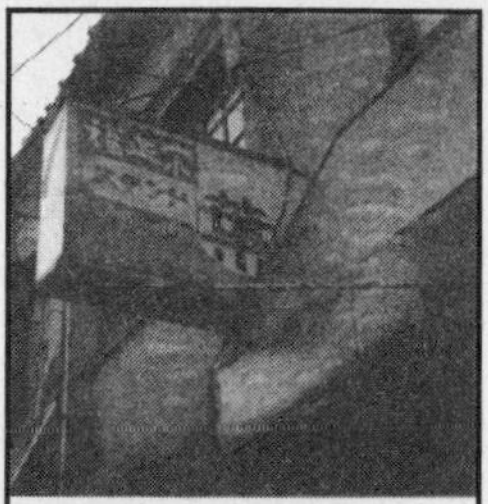

武井宏之

The true meaning of the Tao, or "the Path," is to live simply and freely, bound by nothing. The Chinese word for a fanatic is mī-ren (lost person). While a fanatic may seem to be master of his own path, he is actually lost in the web of life. What a profound concept.

—*Hiroyuki Takei*

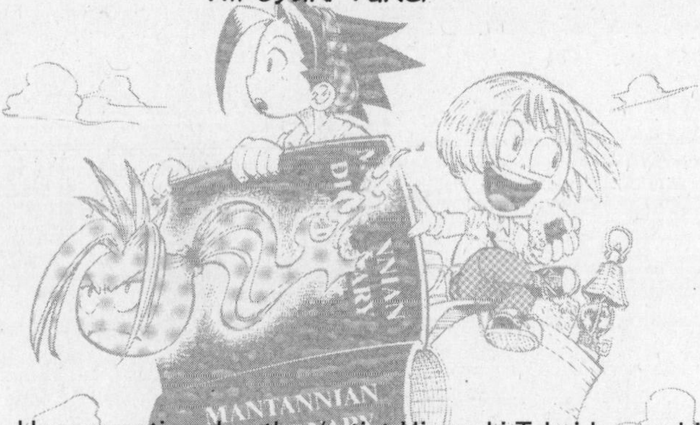
MANTANNIAN

Unconventional author/artist Hiroyuki Takei began his career by winning the coveted Hop Step Award (for new manga artists) and the Osamu Tezuka Award (named after the famous artist of the same name). After working as an assistant to famed artist Nobuhiro Watsuki, Takei debuted in **Weekly Shonen Jump** in 1997 with **Butsu Zone**, an action series based on Buddhist mythology. His multicultural adventure manga **Shaman King**, which debuted in 1998, became a hit and was adapted into an anime TV series. Takei lists Osamu Tezuka, American comics and robot anime among his many influences.

**SHAMAN KING VOL.9**
**The SHONEN JUMP Manga Edition**

This volume contains material that was originally published in English in
**SHONEN JUMP** #36-40.

STORY AND ART BY
HIROYUKI TAKEI

English Adaptation/Lance Caselman
Translation/Lillian Olsen
Touch-up Art & Lettering/Kathryn Renta
Design/Sean Lee
Editor/Pancha Diaz

Managing Editor/Elizabeth Kawasaki
Director of Production/Noboru Watanabe
Vice President of Publishing/Alvin Lu
Vice President & Editor in Chief/ Yumi Hoashi
Sr. Director of Acquisitions/Rika Inouye
VP of Sales & Marketing/Liza Coppola
Publisher/Hyoe Narita

Printed in the U.S.A.

Published by VIZ Media, LLC
P.O. Box 77010
San Francisco, CA 94107

SHONEN JUMP Manga Edition
10 9 8 7 6 5 4 3 2 1
First printing, May 2006

T 252338

www.viz.com

www.shonenjump.com

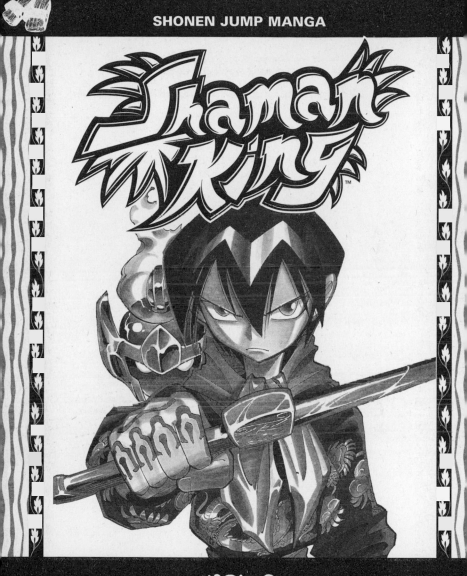

# SHAMAN KING

## VOL. 9
## VOYAGE OF THE SHAMAN

STORY AND ART BY
HIROYUKI TAKEI

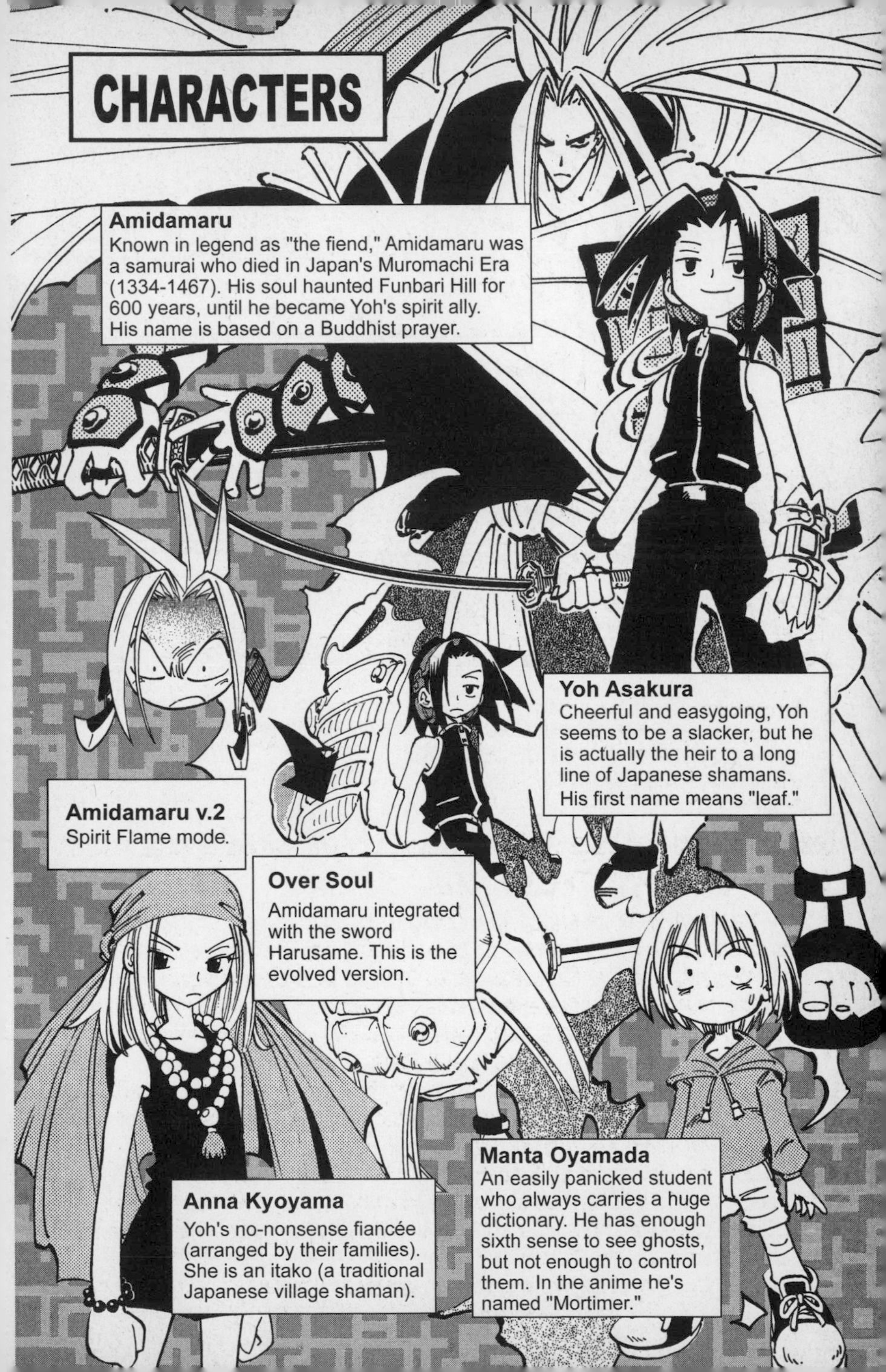
CHARACTERS
Amidamaru
Known in legend as "the fiend," Amidamaru was a samurai who died in Japan's Muromachi Era (1334-1467). His soul haunted Funbari Hill for 600 years, until he became Yoh's spirit ally. His name is based on a Buddhist prayer.
Yoh Asakura
Cheerful and easygoing, Yoh seems to be a slacker, but he is actually the heir to a long line of Japanese shamans. His first name means "leaf."
Amidamaru v.2
Spirit Flame mode.
Over Soul
Amidamaru integrated with the sword Harusame. This is the evolved version.
Manta Oyamada
An easily panicked student who always carries a huge dictionary. He has enough sixth sense to see ghosts, but not enough to control them. In the anime he's named "Mortimer."
Anna Kyoyama
Yoh's no-nonsense fiancée (arranged by their families). She is an itako (a traditional Japanese village shaman).

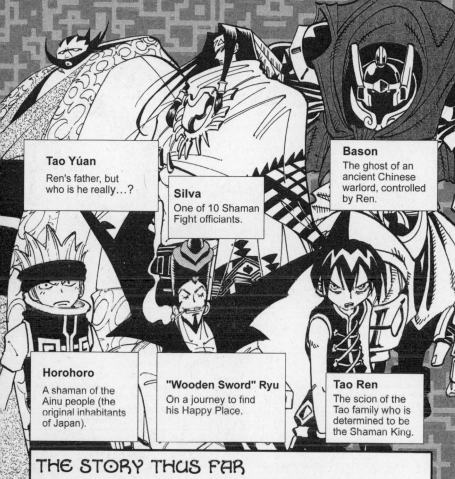

**Tao Yúan**

Ren's father, but who is he really…?

**Silva**

One of 10 Shaman Fight officiants.

**Bason**

The ghost of an ancient Chinese warlord, controlled by Ren.

**Horohoro**

A shaman of the Ainu people (the original inhabitants of Japan).

**"Wooden Sword" Ryu**

On a journey to find his Happy Place.

**Tao Ren**

The scion of the Tao family who is determined to be the Shaman King.

# THE STORY THUS FAR

Yoh Asakura is a shaman, someone who, thanks to training or natural talent, can channel spirits most people can't even see. With the help of his fiancée Anna, Yoh is in training for the ultimate shaman sports event: the "Shaman Fight in Tokyo," the once-every-500-years tournament to decide who will become the Shaman King and shape humanity's future.

Now Yoh has passed the fierce preliminaries and earned the right to advance to the main competition. But his training is interrupted when he learns that Ren has been cast into a dungeon by his sinister father, Tao Yúan! Yoh, Horohoro, "Wooden-Sword" Ryu and Manta journey to the distant wilds of China to free their friend. But what new horrors await them in the Castle of the Tao?

# VOL. 9
# VOYAGE OF THE SHAMAN

# CONTENTS

Reincarnation 72: A Tale of Two Men—Our Teamwork  7

Reincarnation 73: Wrath of the Dao-shi Maiden  25

Reincarnation 74: Tao Yúan: The Immortal Secret  45

Reincarnation 75: Over Soul: Dà Dào Wáng  67

Reincarnation 76: The End of the Tao  87

Reincarnation 77: Voyage of the Shaman  107

Reincarnation 78: The Future King  129

Reincarnation 79: Patch Airlines  148

Reincarnation 80: Sky High  167

Bonus: 3,000 Leagues to Funbari Hill  186

Reincarnation 72: A Tale of Two Men--Our Teamwork

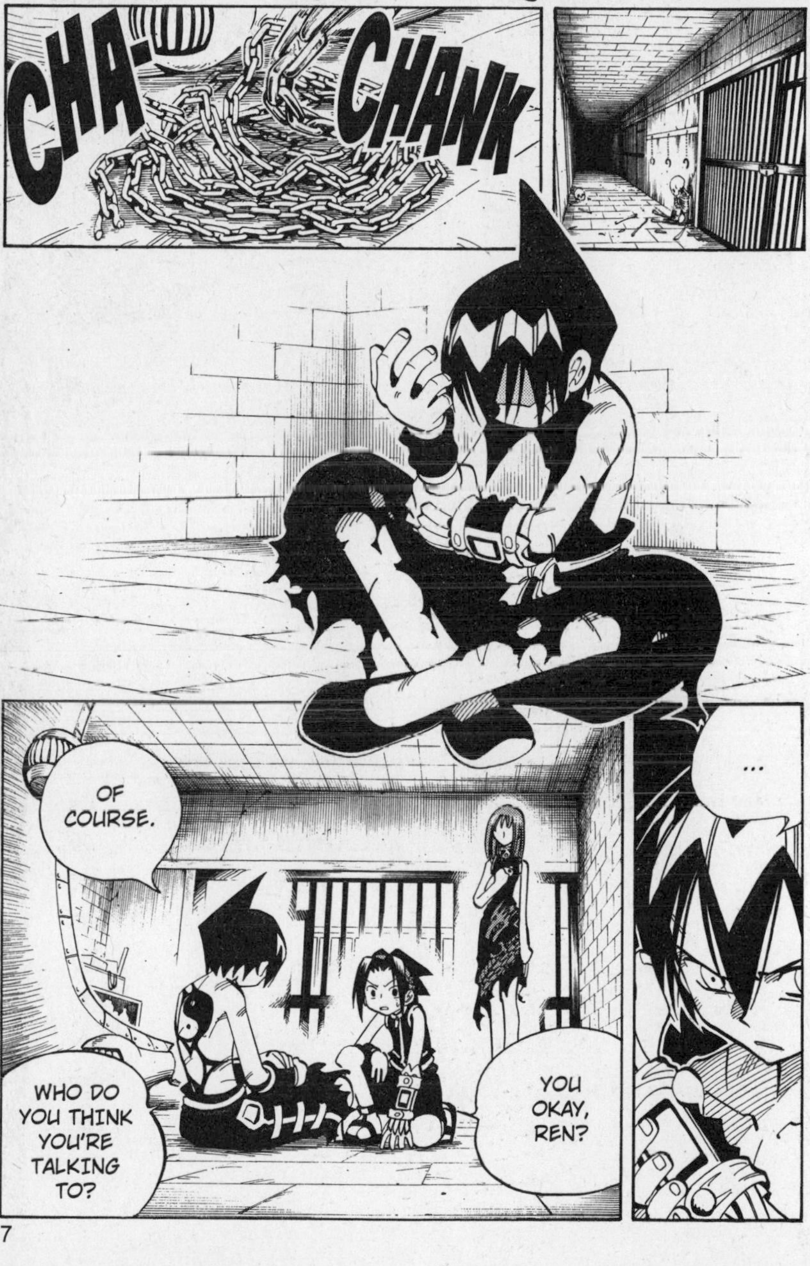
CHA-CHANK
...
YOU OKAY, REN?
OF COURSE.
WHO DO YOU THINK YOU'RE TALKING TO?

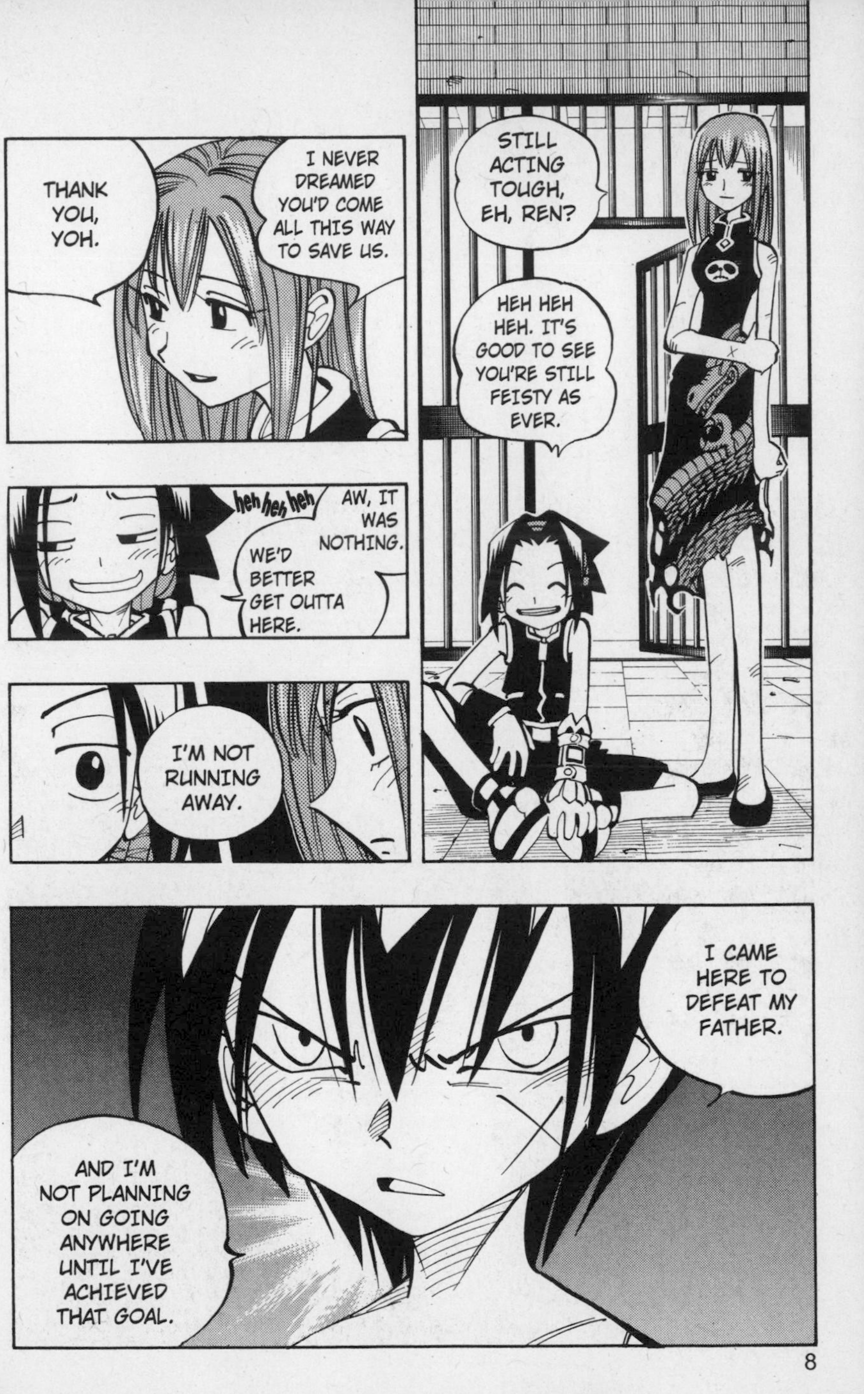
STILL ACTING TOUGH, EH, REN?
HEH HEH HEH. IT'S GOOD TO SEE YOU'RE STILL FEISTY AS EVER.
I NEVER DREAMED YOU'D COME ALL THIS WAY TO SAVE US.
THANK YOU, YOH.
AW, IT WAS NOTHING.
heh heh heh
WE'D BETTER GET OUTTA HERE.
I'M NOT RUNNING AWAY.
I CAME HERE TO DEFEAT MY FATHER.
AND I'M NOT PLANNING ON GOING ANYWHERE UNTIL I'VE ACHIEVED THAT GOAL.

# Reincarnation 72: A Tale of Two Men--Our Teamwork

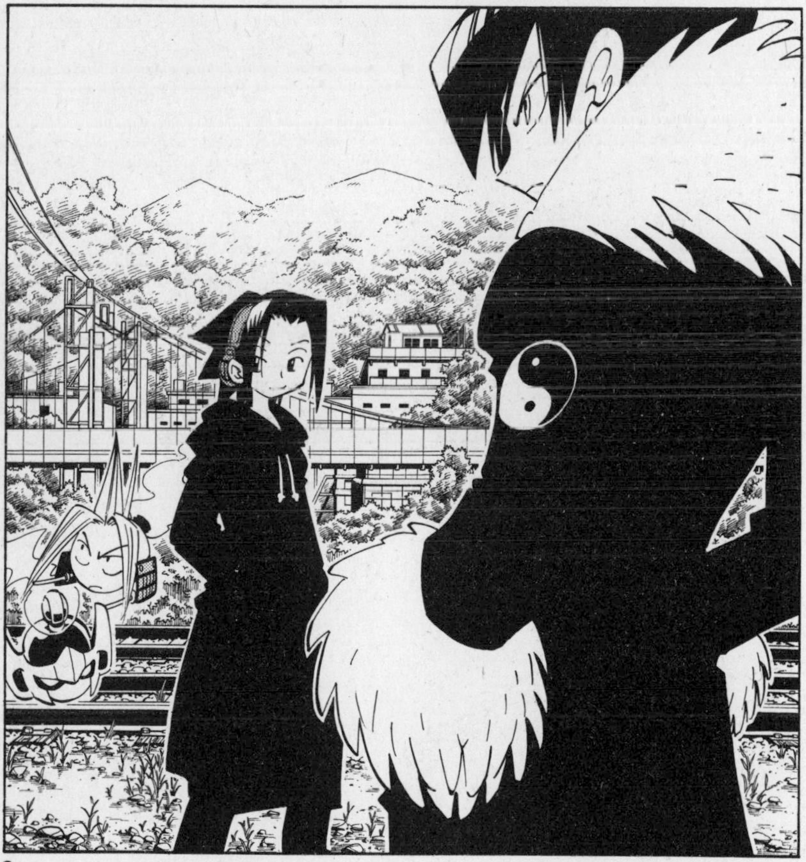

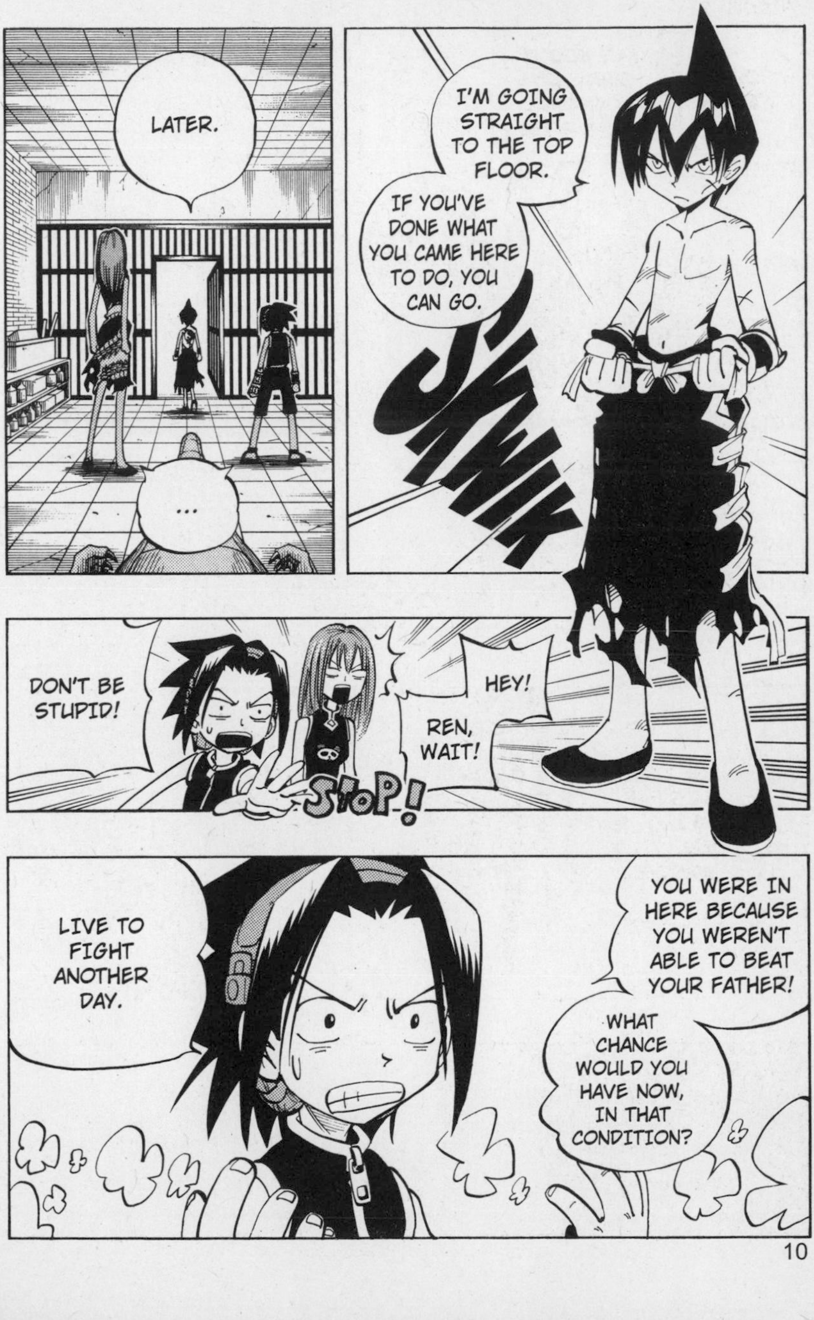
I'M GOING STRAIGHT TO THE TOP FLOOR.
IF YOU'VE DONE WHAT YOU CAME HERE TO DO, YOU CAN GO.
LATER.
...
HEY!
REN, WAIT!
DON'T BE STUPID!
STOP!
YOU WERE IN HERE BECAUSE YOU WEREN'T ABLE TO BEAT YOUR FATHER!
WHAT CHANCE WOULD YOU HAVE NOW, IN THAT CONDITION?
LIVE TO FIGHT ANOTHER DAY.

READ THIS WAY

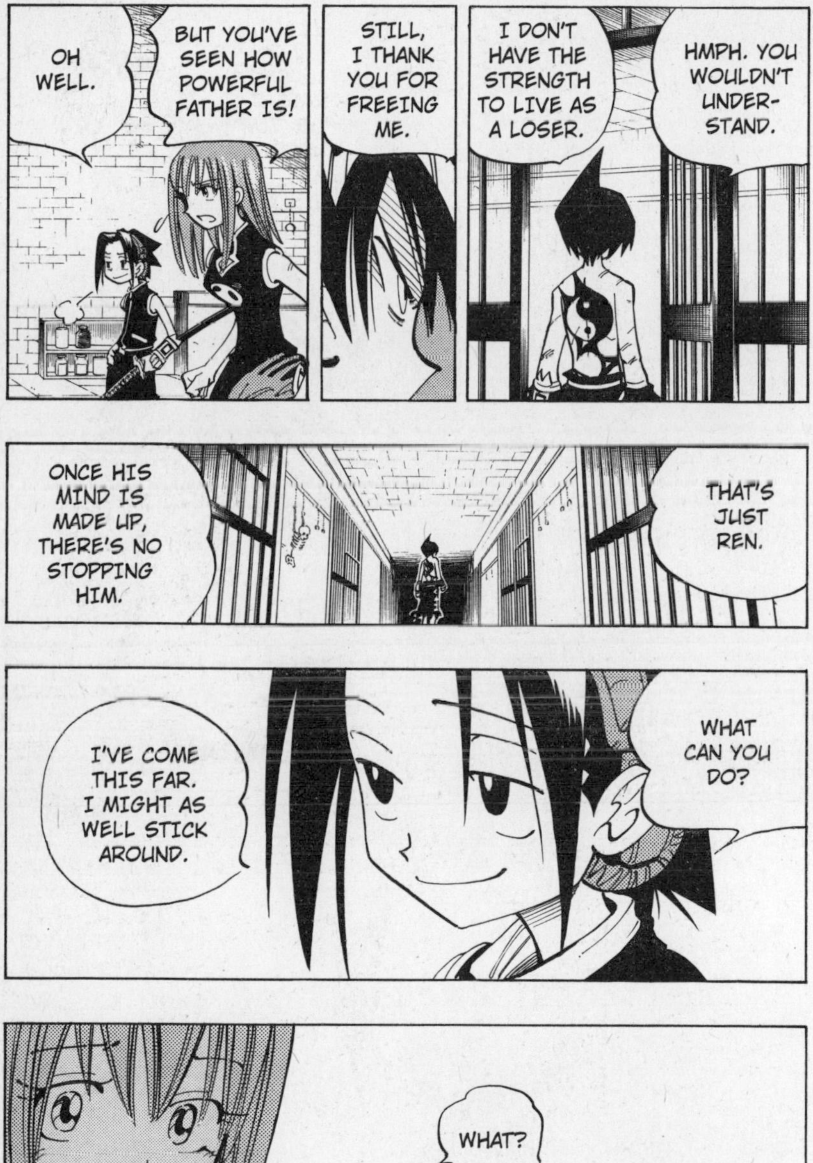
HMPH. YOU WOULDN'T UNDER-STAND.
I DON'T HAVE THE STRENGTH TO LIVE AS A LOSER.
STILL, I THANK YOU FOR FREEING ME.
BUT YOU'VE SEEN HOW POWERFUL FATHER IS!
OH WELL.
THAT'S JUST REN.
ONCE HIS MIND IS MADE UP, THERE'S NO STOPPING HIM.
WHAT CAN YOU DO?
I'VE COME THIS FAR. I MIGHT AS WELL STICK AROUND.
WHAT?

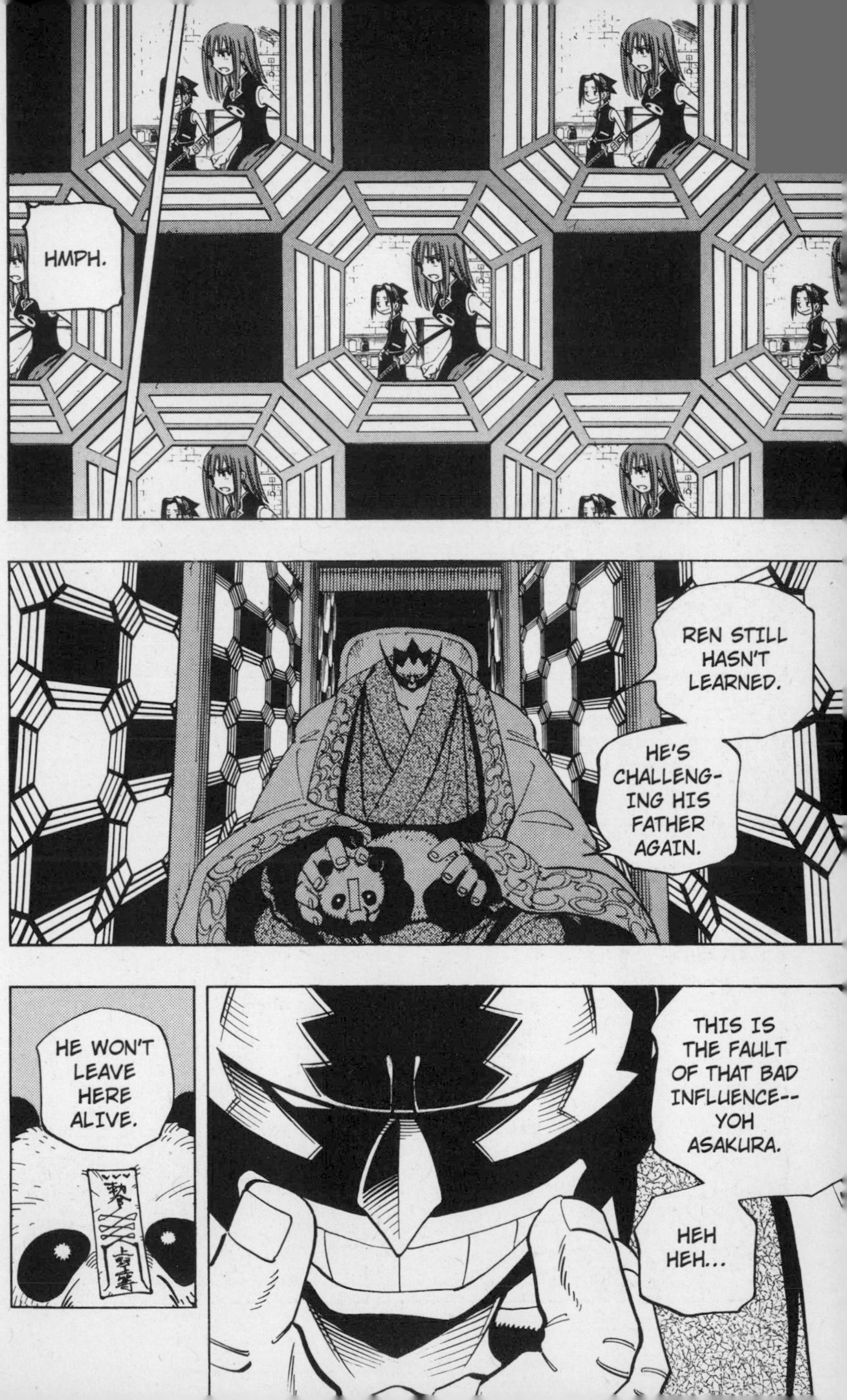
HMPH.
REN STILL HASN'T LEARNED.
HE'S CHALLENG-ING HIS FATHER AGAIN.
THIS IS THE FAULT OF THAT BAD INFLUENCE-- YOH ASAKURA.
HEH HEH...
HE WON'T LEAVE HERE ALIVE.

READ THIS WAY

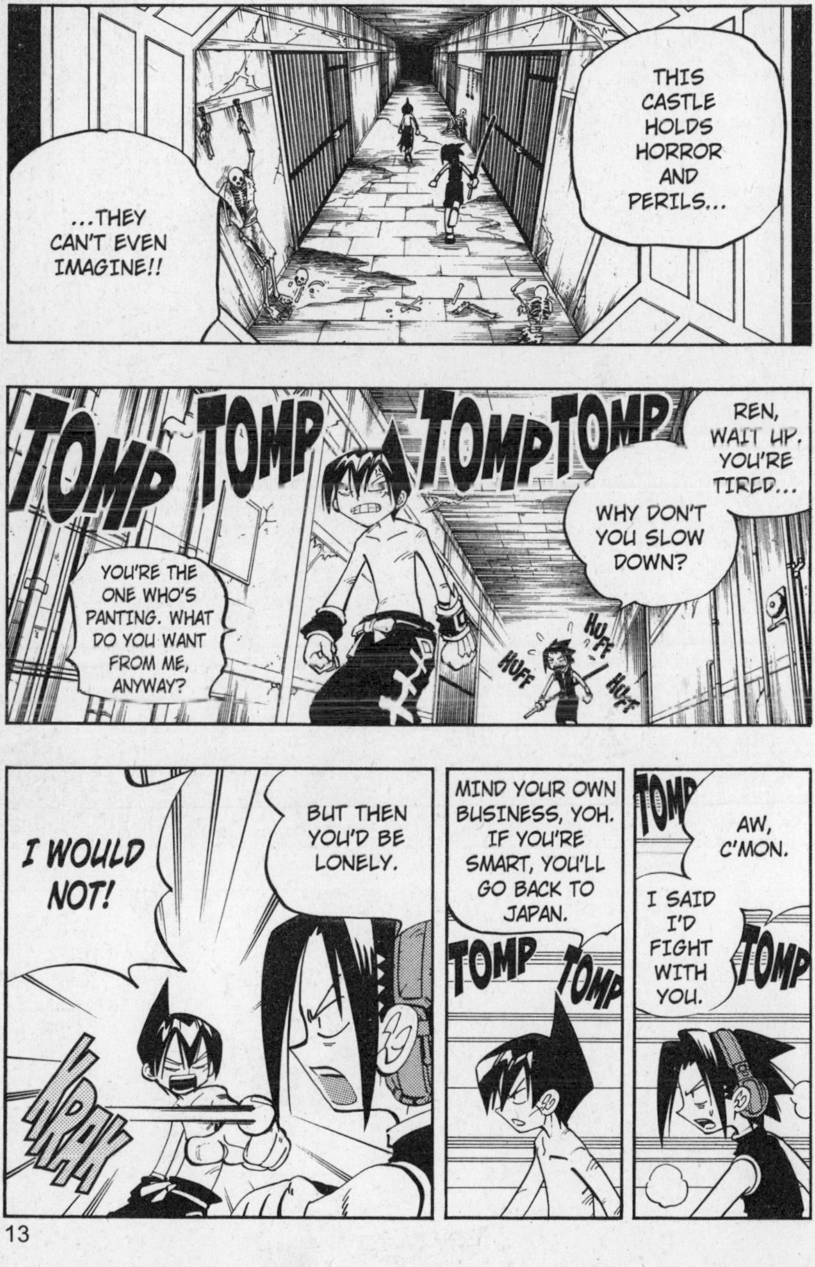

THIS CASTLE HOLDS HORROR AND PERILS...
...THEY CAN'T EVEN IMAGINE!!
TOMP TOMP
REN, WAIT UP. YOU'RE TIRED...
WHY DON'T YOU SLOW DOWN?
HUFF HUFF
HUFF HUFF
TOMP TOMP
YOU'RE THE ONE WHO'S PANTING. WHAT DO YOU WANT FROM ME, ANYWAY?
TOMP
AW, C'MON.
I SAID I'D FIGHT WITH YOU.
TOMP
MIND YOUR OWN BUSINESS, YOH. IF YOU'RE SMART, YOU'LL GO BACK TO JAPAN.
TOMP TOMP
BUT THEN YOU'D BE LONELY.
I WOULD NOT!

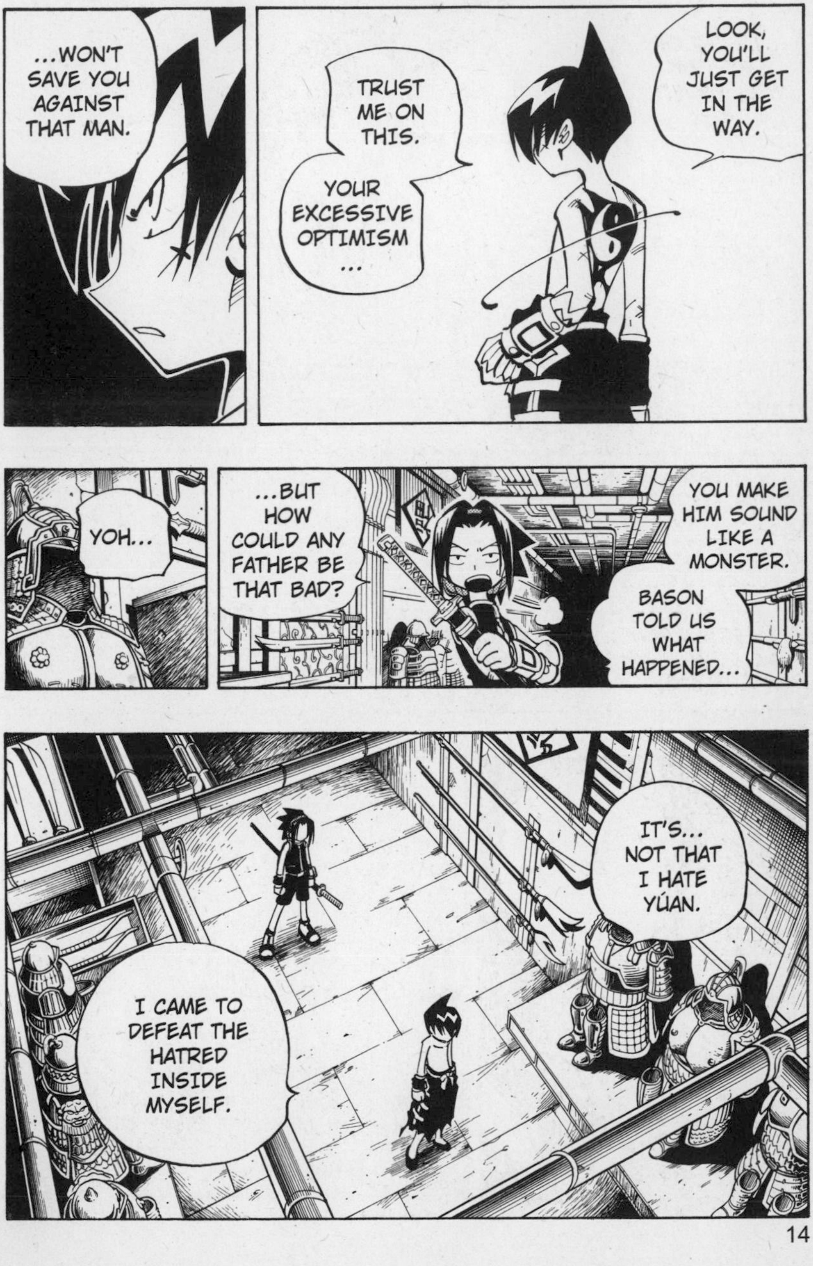
LOOK, YOU'LL JUST GET IN THE WAY.
TRUST ME ON THIS.
YOUR EXCESSIVE OPTIMISM ...
...WON'T SAVE YOU AGAINST THAT MAN.
YOU MAKE HIM SOUND LIKE A MONSTER.
BASON TOLD US WHAT HAPPENED...
...BUT HOW COULD ANY FATHER BE THAT BAD?
YOH...
IT'S... NOT THAT I HATE YÚAN.
I CAME TO DEFEAT THE HATRED INSIDE MYSELF.

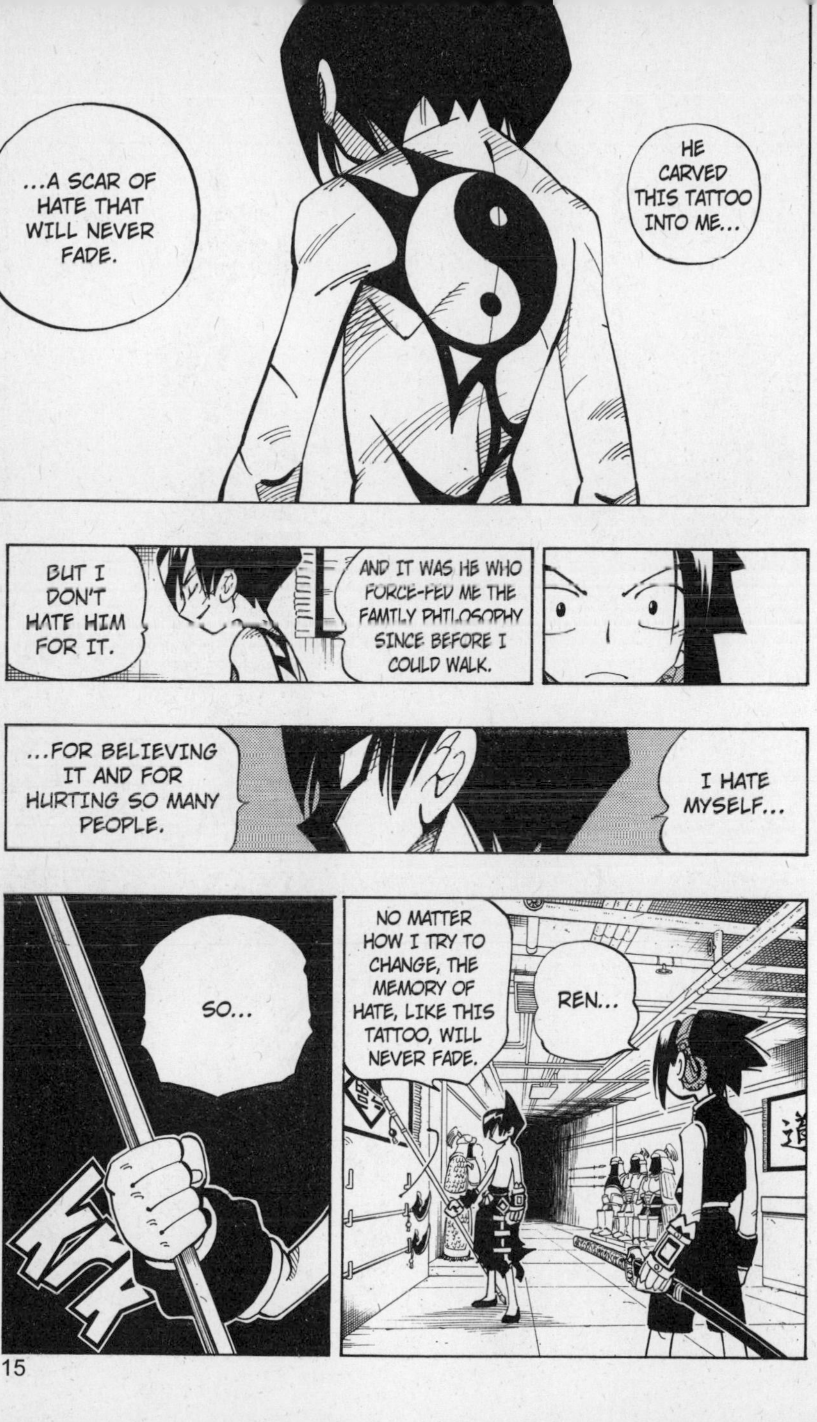
HE CARVED THIS TATTOO INTO ME...
...A SCAR OF HATE THAT WILL NEVER FADE.
AND IT WAS HE WHO FORCE-FED ME THE FAMILY PHILOSOPHY SINCE BEFORE I COULD WALK.
BUT I DON'T HATE HIM FOR IT.
I HATE MYSELF...
...FOR BELIEVING IT AND FOR HURTING SO MANY PEOPLE.
NO MATTER HOW I TRY TO CHANGE, THE MEMORY OF HATE, LIKE THIS TATTOO, WILL NEVER FADE.
REN...
SO...
KYK

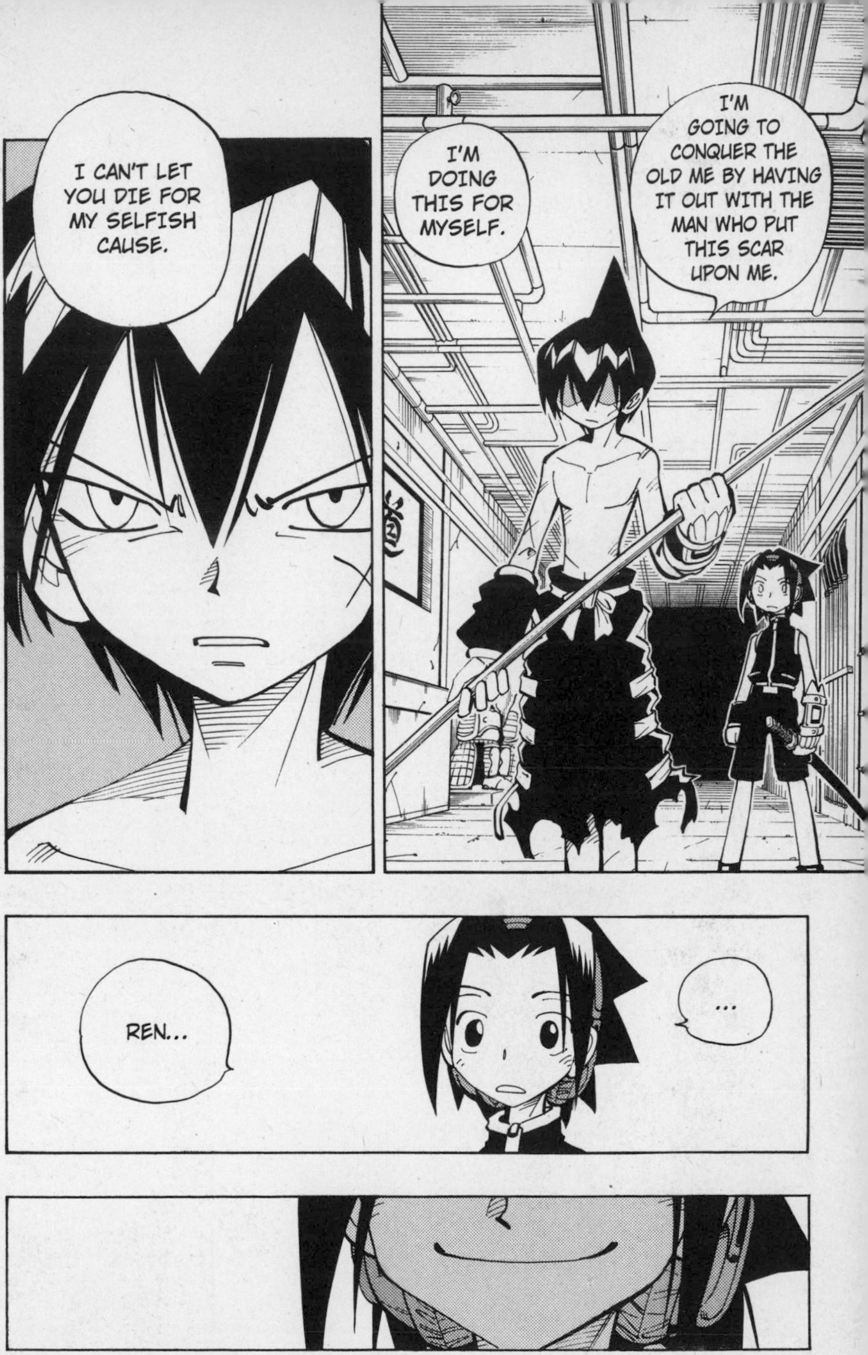
I'M GOING TO CONQUER THE OLD ME BY HAVING IT OUT WITH THE MAN WHO PUT THIS SCAR UPON ME.
I'M DOING THIS FOR MYSELF.
I CAN'T LET YOU DIE FOR MY SELFISH CAUSE.
...
REN...

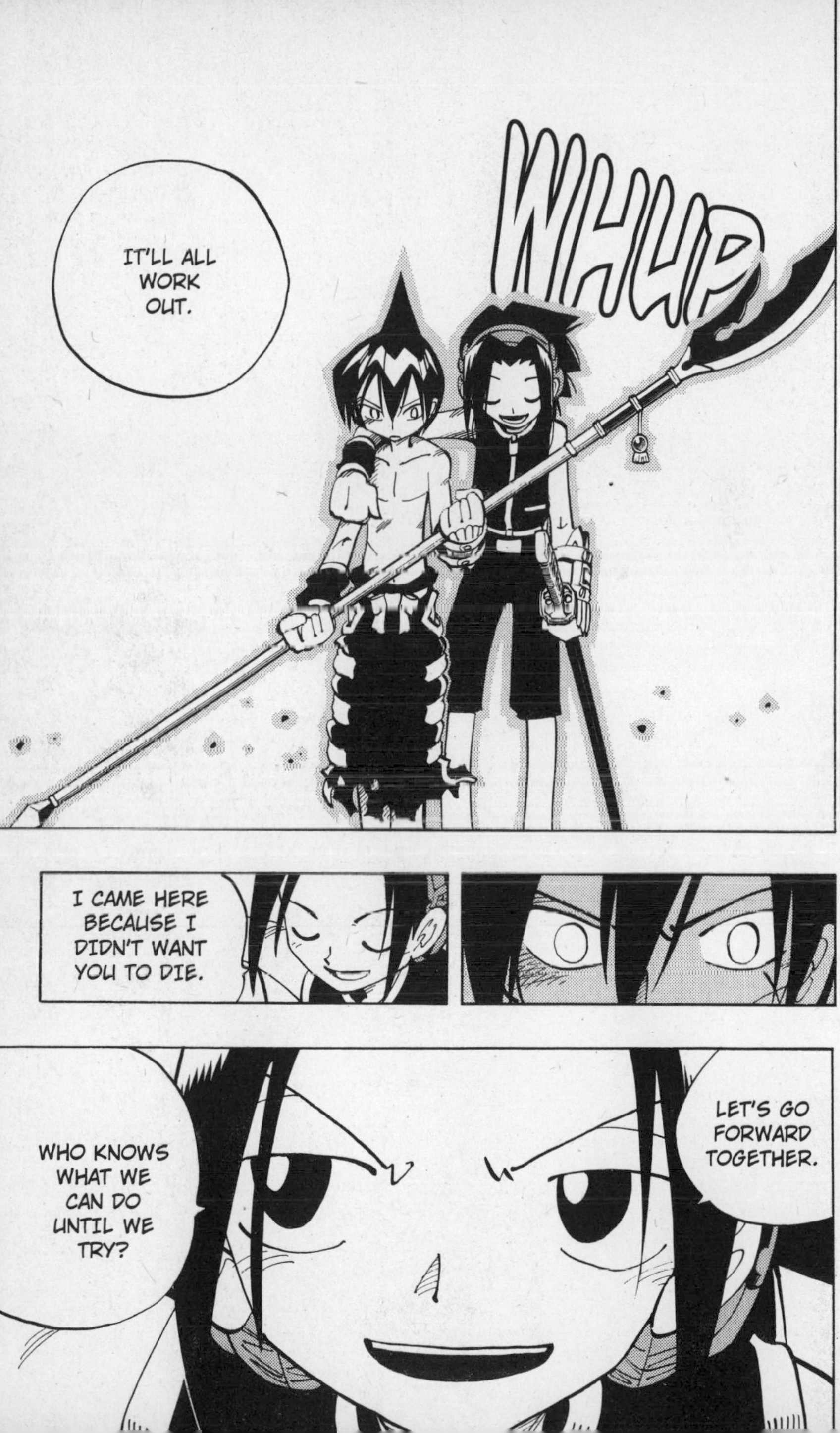
WHUP
IT'LL ALL WORK OUT.
I CAME HERE BECAUSE I DIDN'T WANT YOU TO DIE.
LET'S GO FORWARD TOGETHER.
WHO KNOWS WHAT WE CAN DO UNTIL WE TRY?

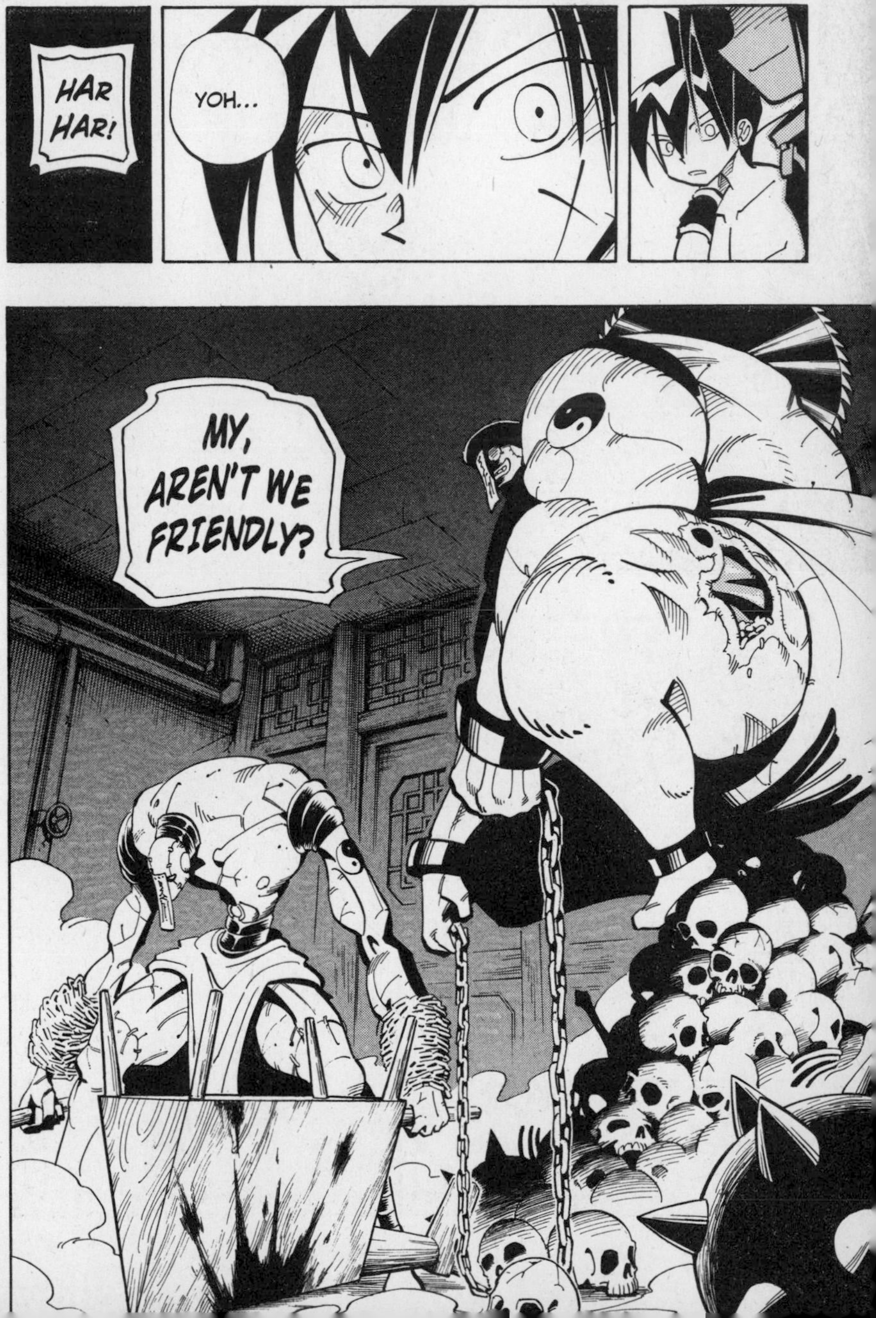
YOH...
HAR HAR!
MY, AREN'T WE FRIENDLY?

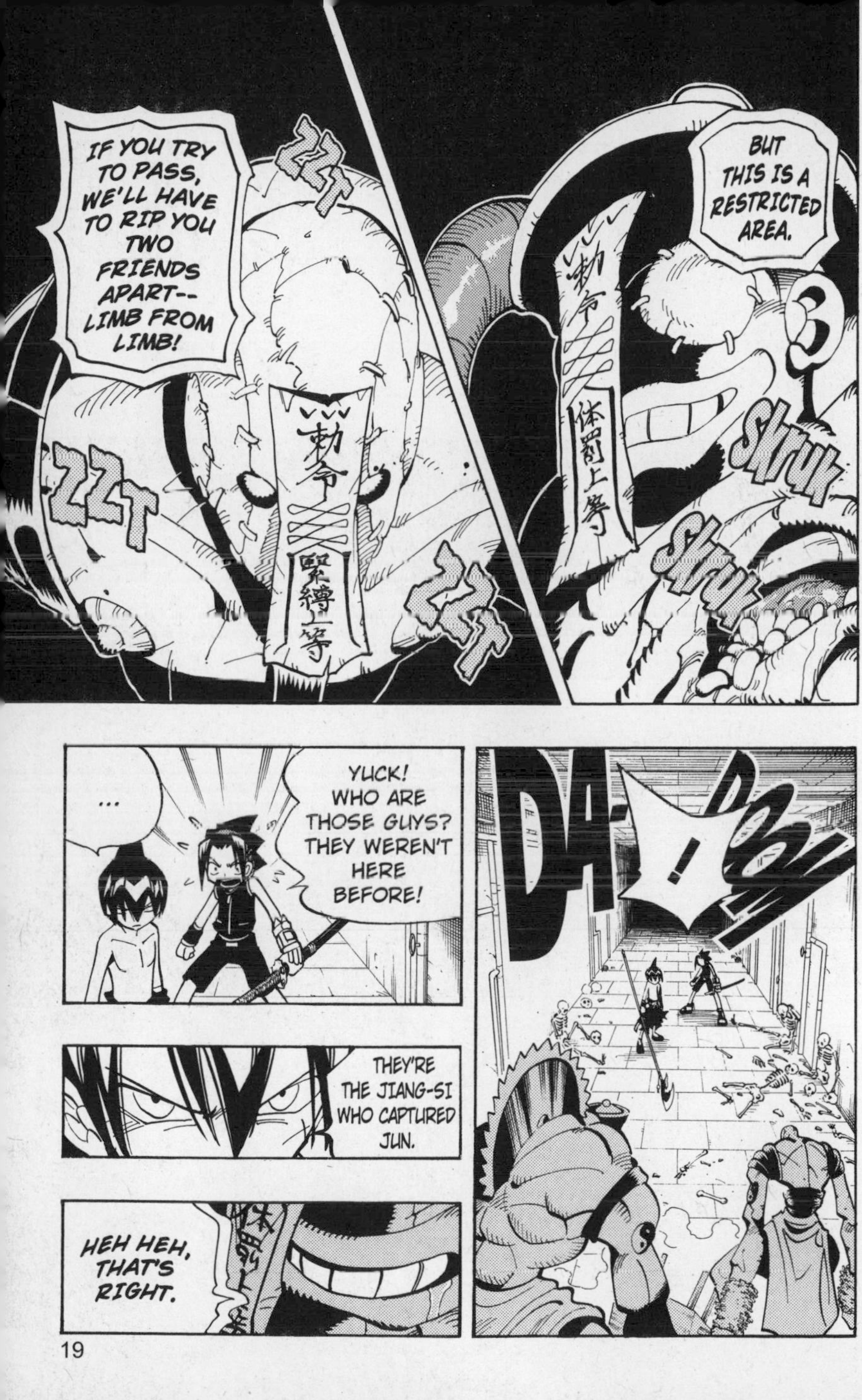
BUT THIS IS A RESTRICTED AREA.
勅令
体罰上等
SKRUK
SKRUK
IF YOU TRY TO PASS, WE'LL HAVE TO RIP YOU TWO FRIENDS APART-- LIMB FROM LIMB!
ZZT
ZZT
勅令
緊縛上等
ZZT
DA-DOM
!
YUCK! WHO ARE THOSE GUYS? THEY WEREN'T HERE BEFORE!
...
THEY'RE THE JIANG-SI WHO CAPTURED JUN.
HEH HEH, THAT'S RIGHT.

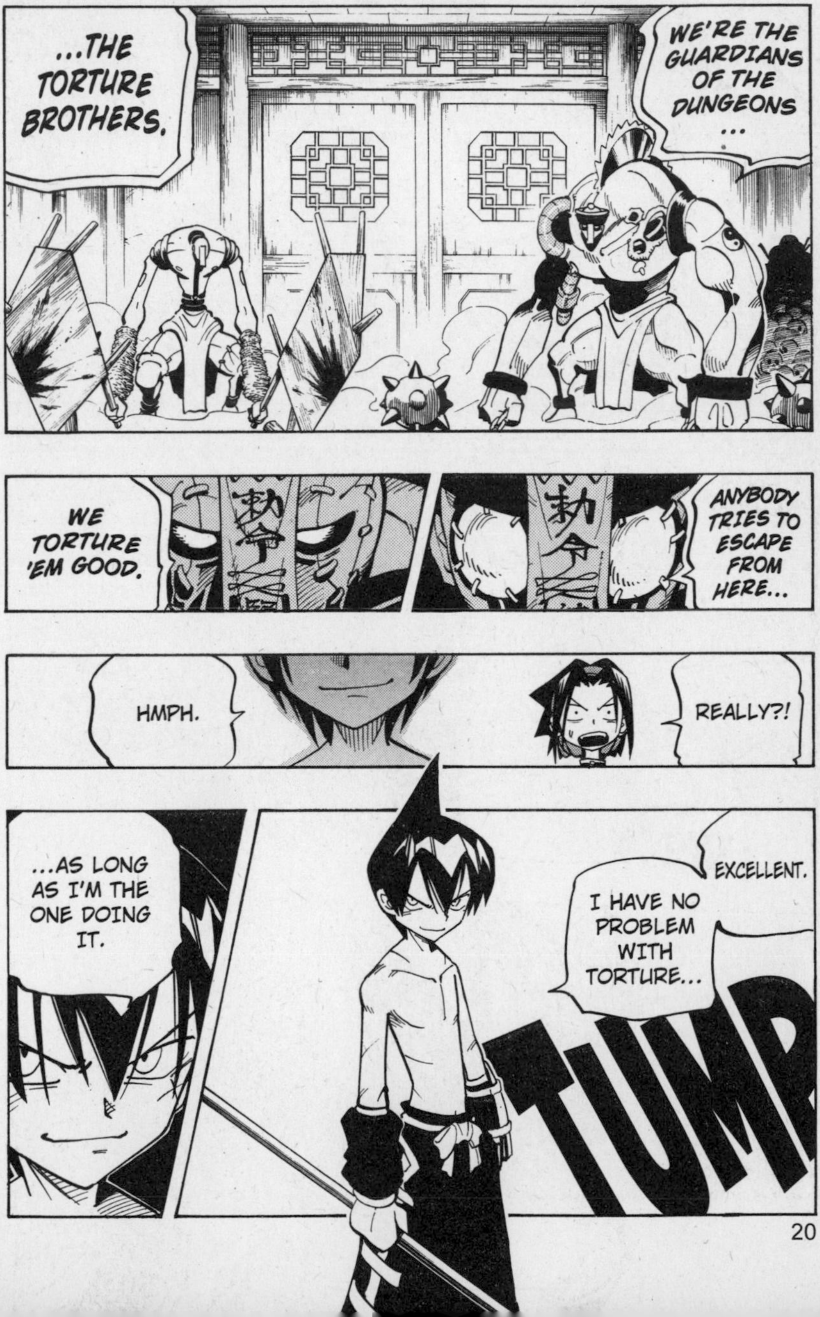
WE'RE THE GUARDIANS OF THE DUNGEONS ...
...THE TORTURE BROTHERS.
ANYBODY TRIES TO ESCAPE FROM HERE...
勅令
勅令
WE TORTURE 'EM GOOD.
REALLY?!
HMPH.
EXCELLENT.
I HAVE NO PROBLEM WITH TORTURE...
TUMP
...AS LONG AS I'M THE ONE DOING IT.

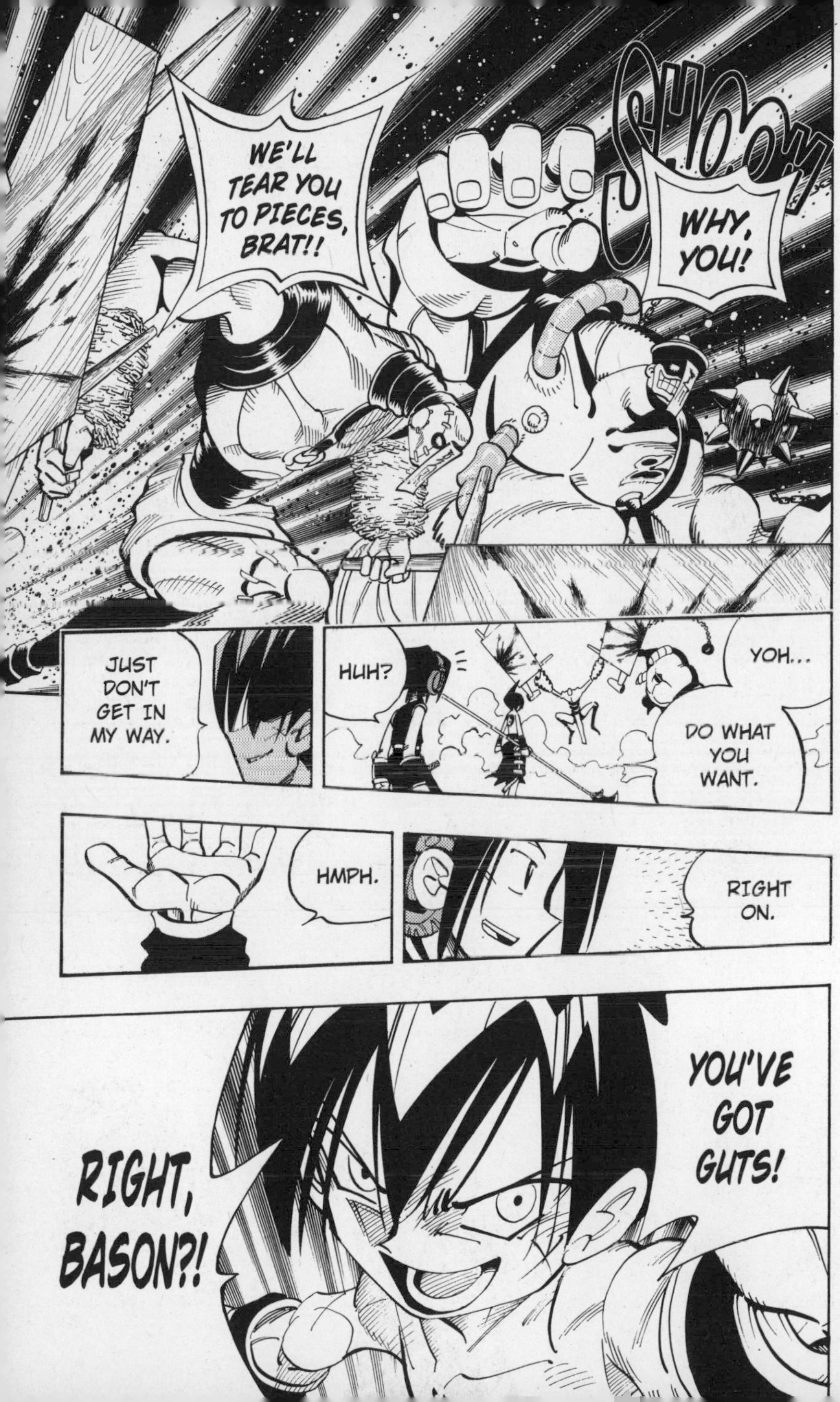
SHOOM
WHY, YOU!
WE'LL TEAR YOU TO PIECES, BRAT!!
YOH...
DO WHAT YOU WANT.
HUH?
JUST DON'T GET IN MY WAY.
RIGHT ON.
HMPH.
YOU'VE GOT GUTS!
RIGHT, BASON?!

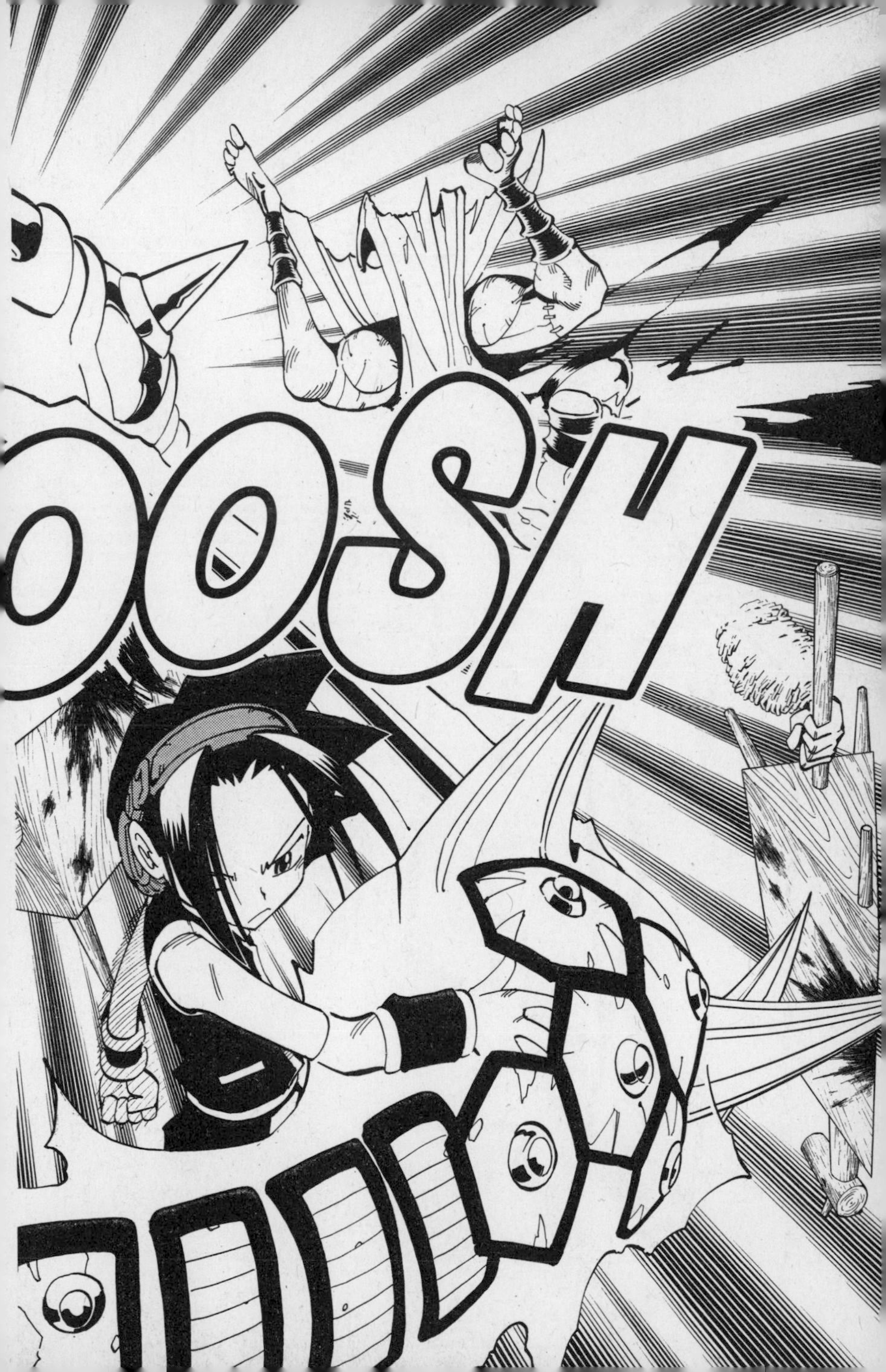
OOSH

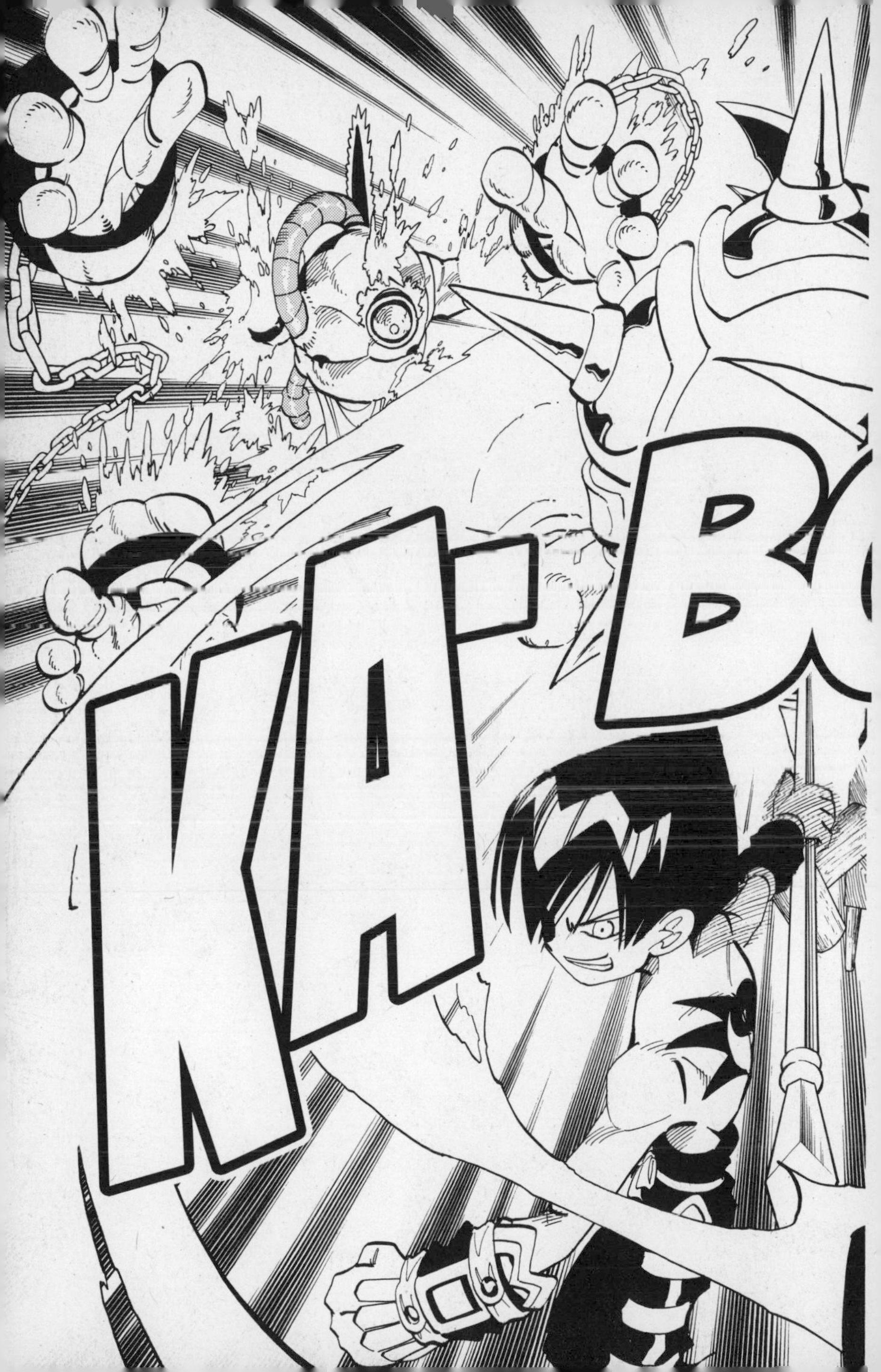
KA-BO

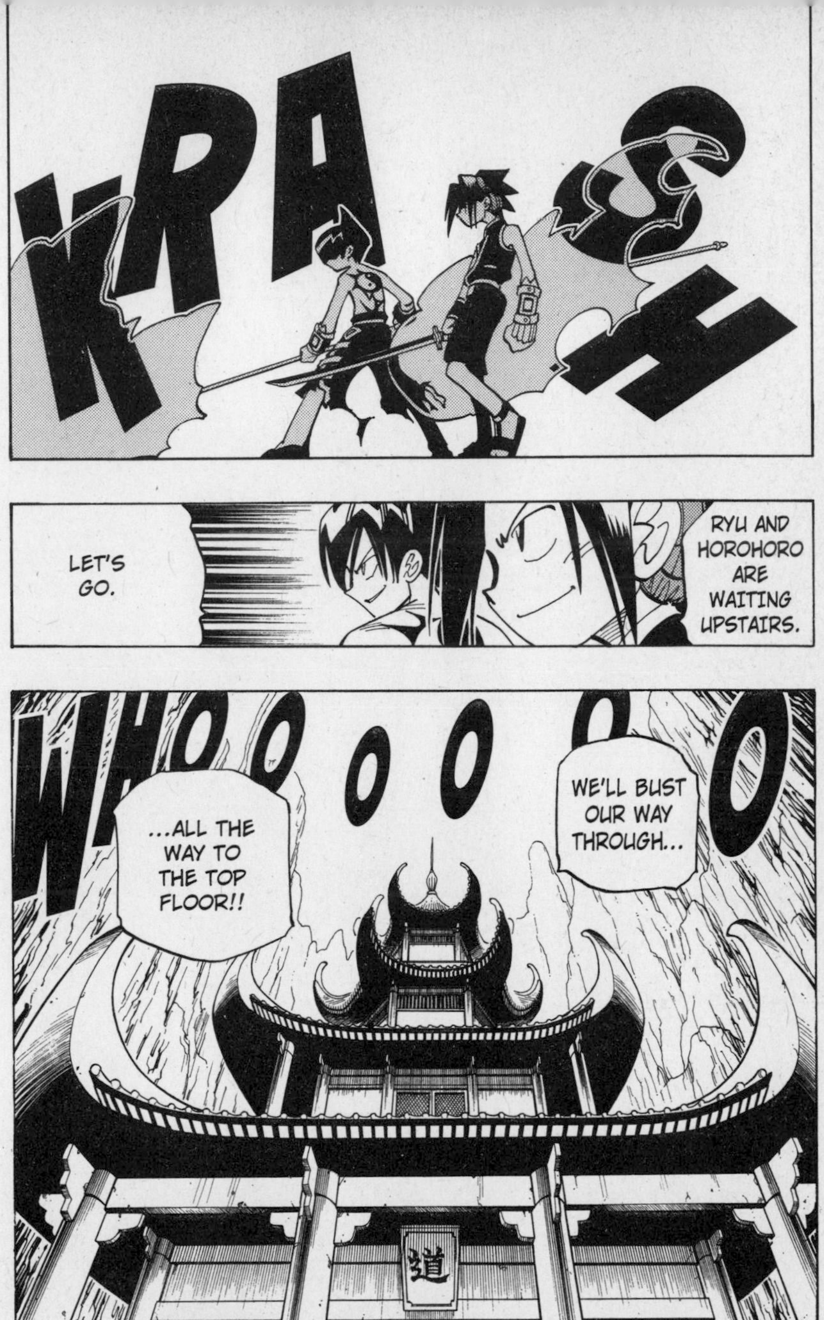
KRASH
RYU AND HOROHORO ARE WAITING UPSTAIRS.
LET'S GO.
WHOOOOOO
WE'LL BUST OUR WAY THROUGH...
...ALL THE WAY TO THE TOP FLOOR!!
道

# Reincarnation 73: Wrath of the Dao-shi Maiden

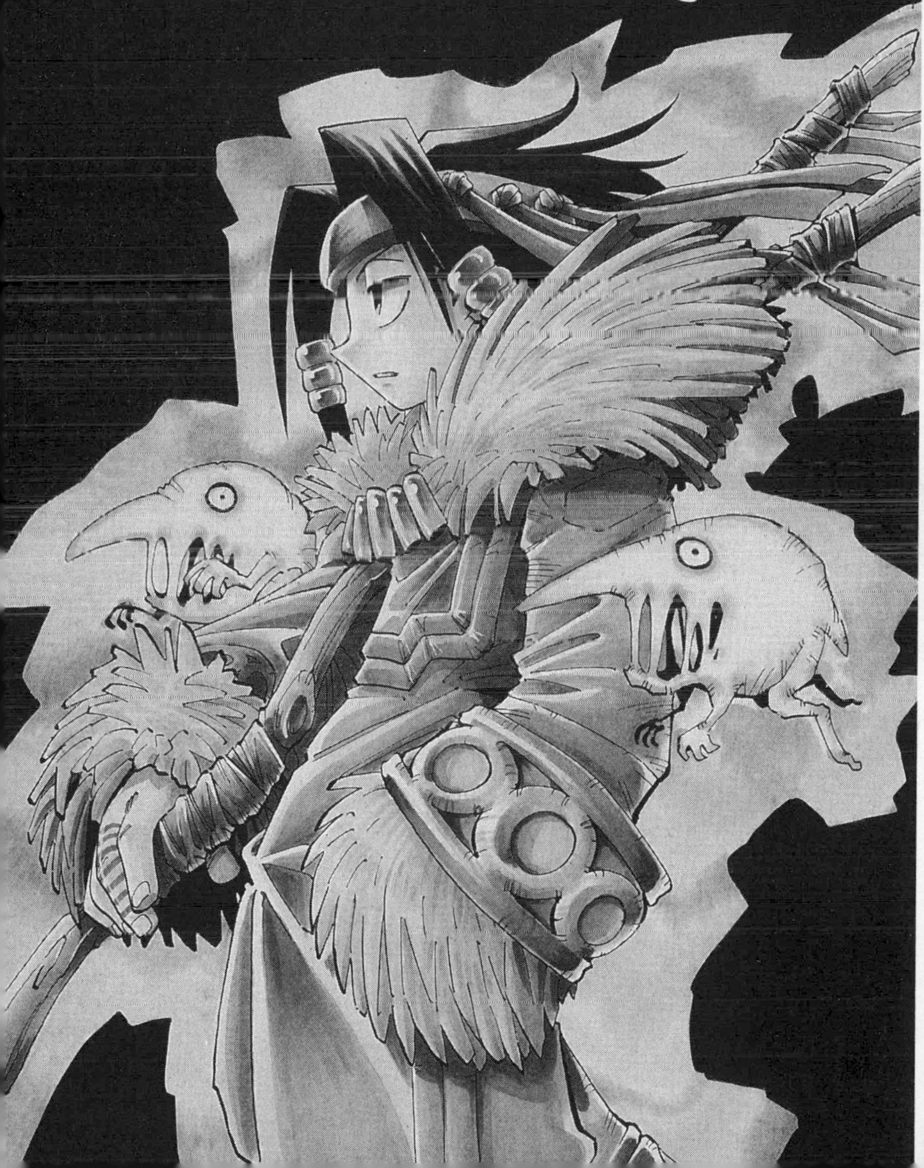

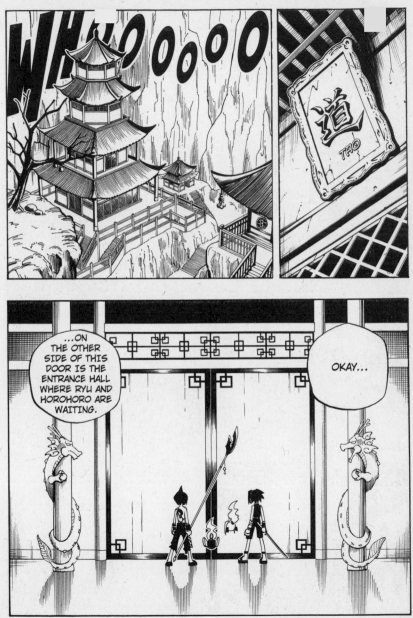

WHOOOOOO

...ON THE OTHER SIDE OF THIS DOOR IS THE ENTRANCE HALL WHERE RYU AND HOROHORO ARE WAITING.

OKAY...

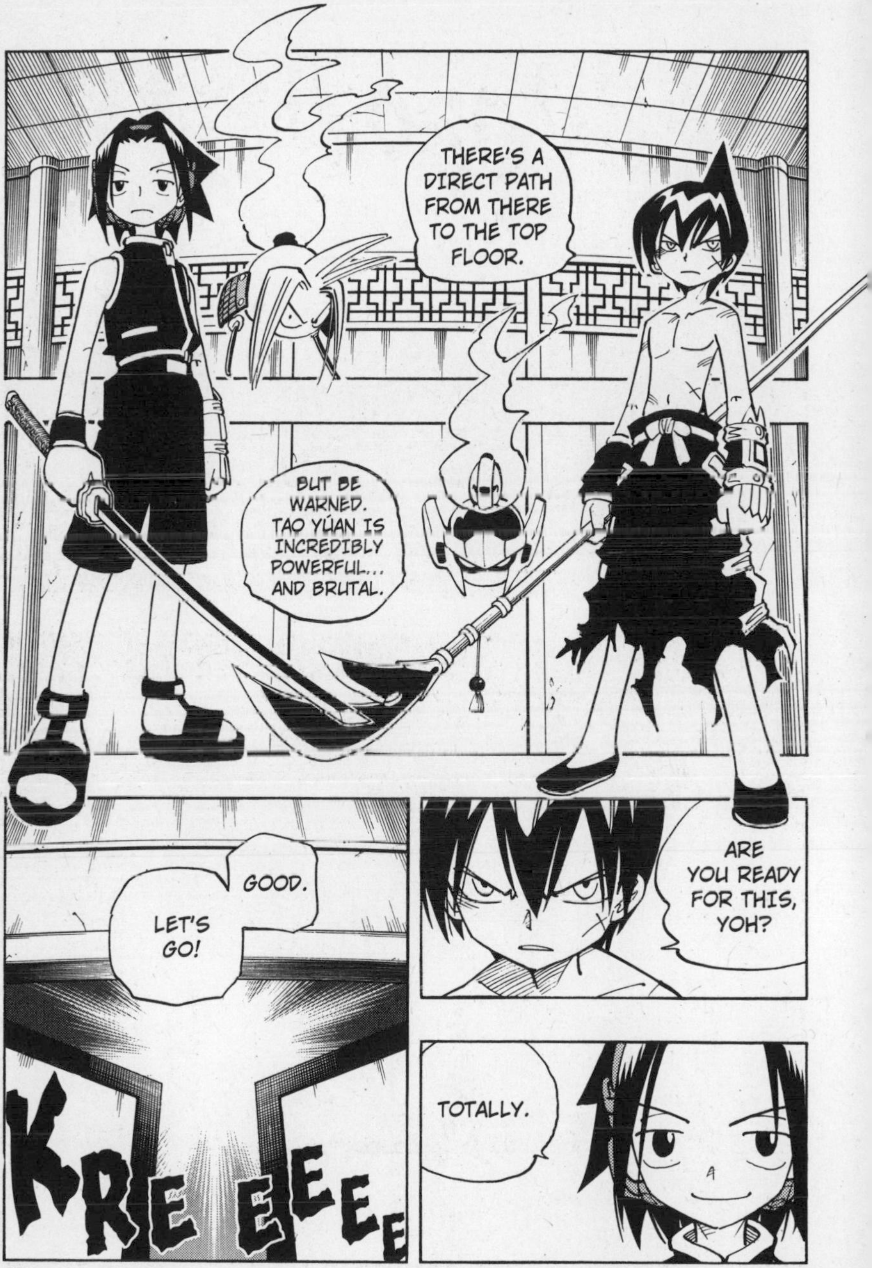
THERE'S A DIRECT PATH FROM THERE TO THE TOP FLOOR.
BUT BE WARNED. TAO YÚAN IS INCREDIBLY POWERFUL... AND BRUTAL.
ARE YOU READY FOR THIS, YOH?
TOTALLY.
GOOD.
LET'S GO!
KREEEEEE

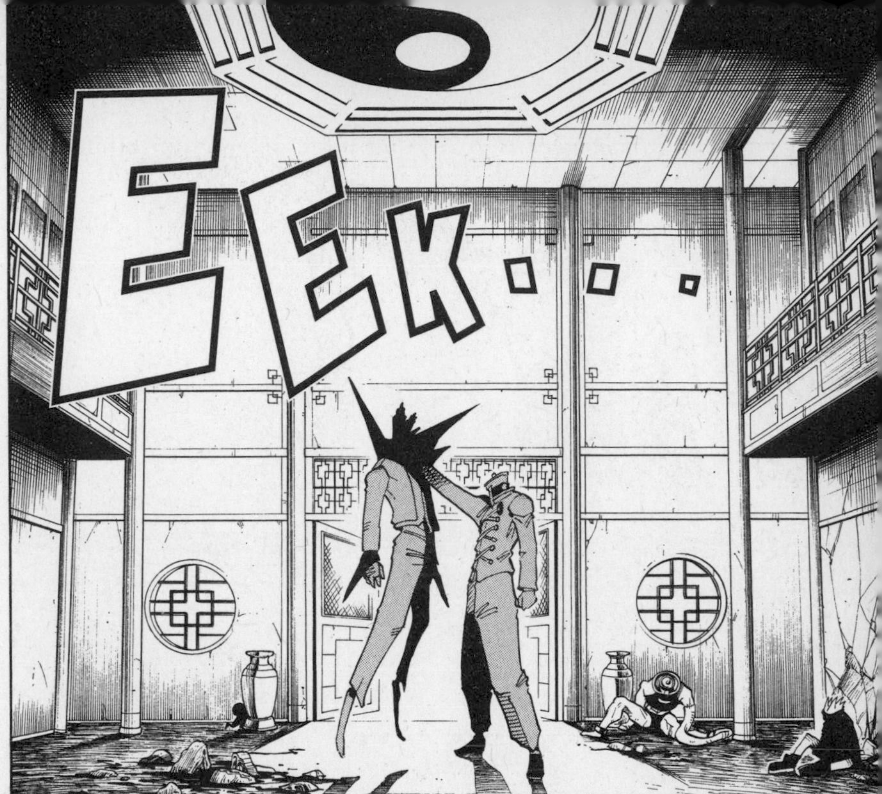
EEK...

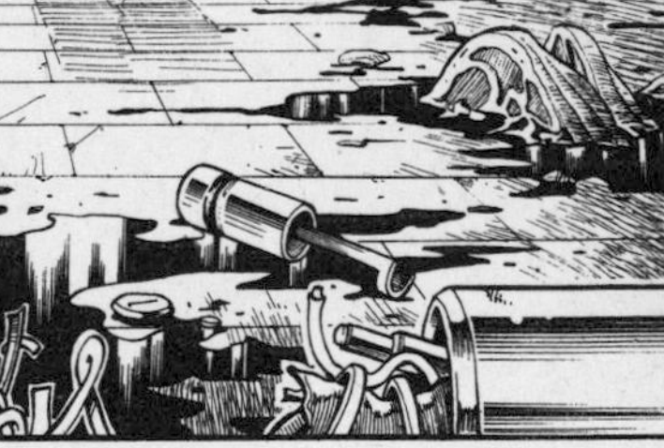
YOU'RE NOT GOING ...
...ANY-WHERE.

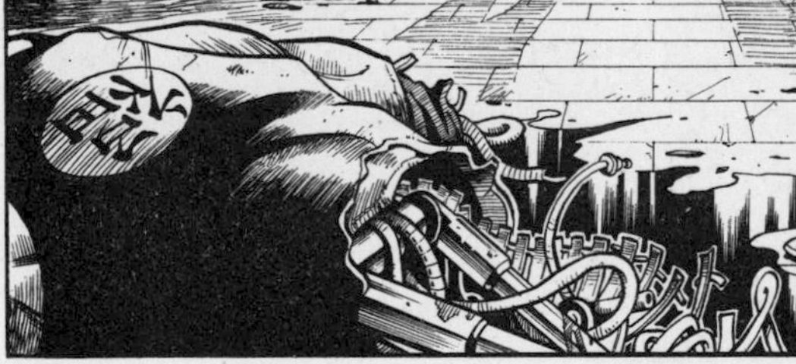
BECAUSE I...
...WILL REDUCE ALL OF YOU...

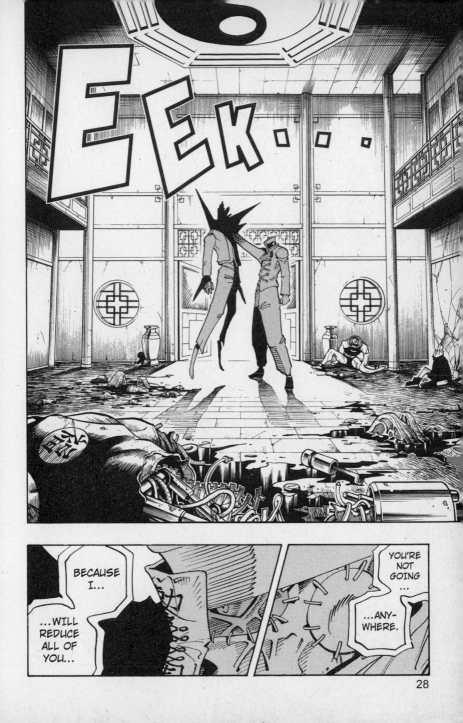

READ THIS WAY

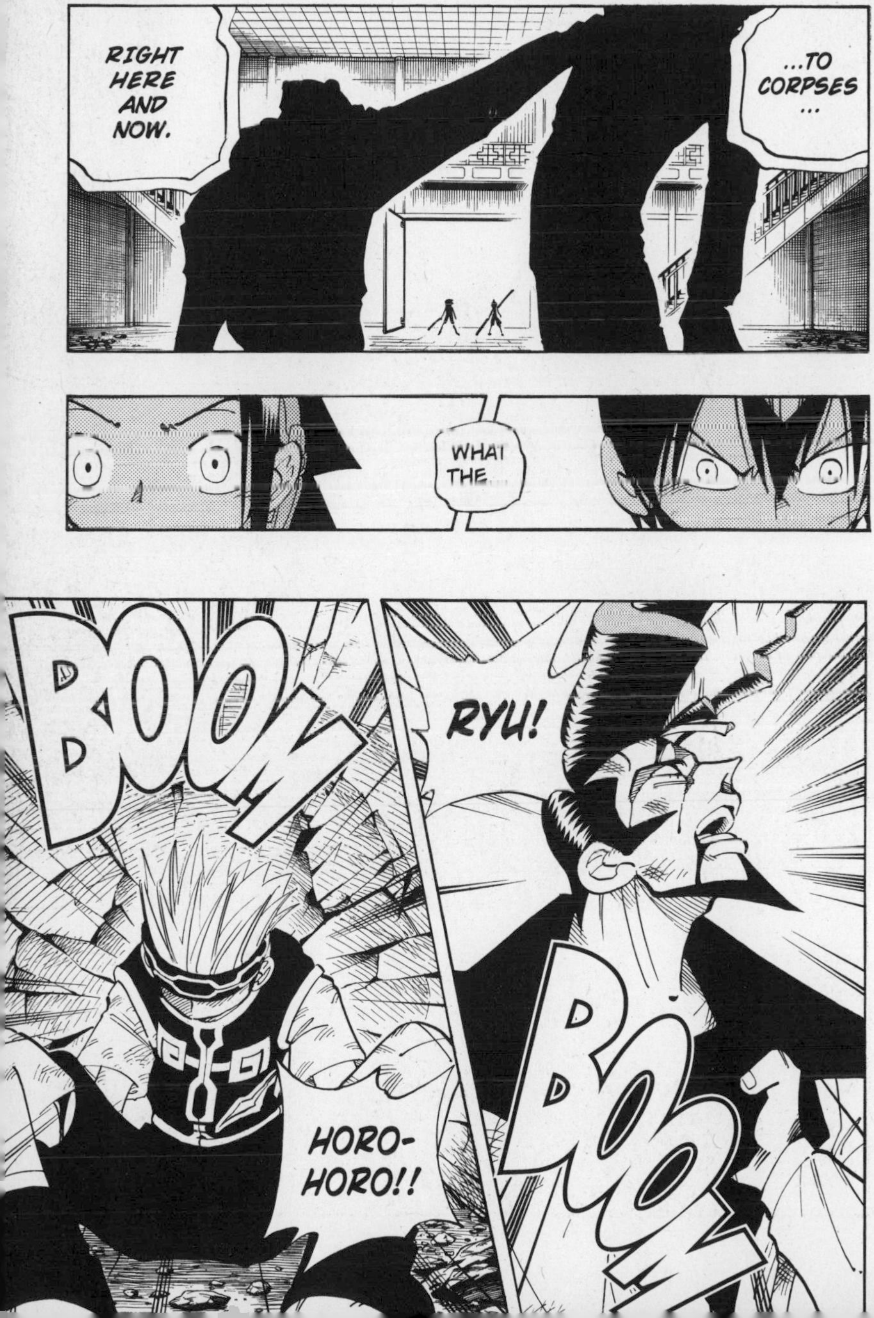
...TO CORPSES ...
RIGHT HERE AND NOW.
WHAT THE...
RYU!
BOOM
BOOM
HORO-HORO!!

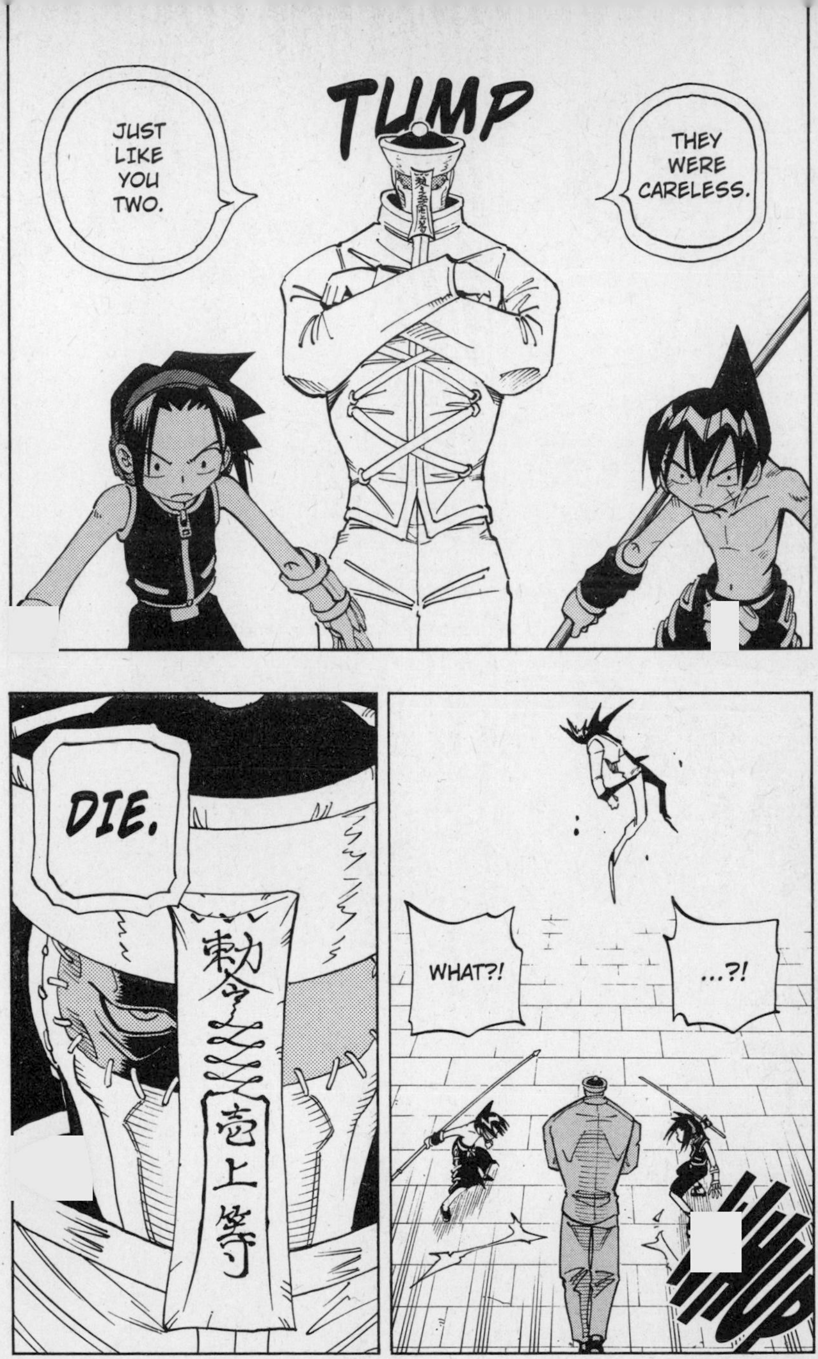
THEY WERE CARELESS.
TUMP
JUST LIKE YOU TWO.
...?!
WHAT?!
WHUP
DIE.

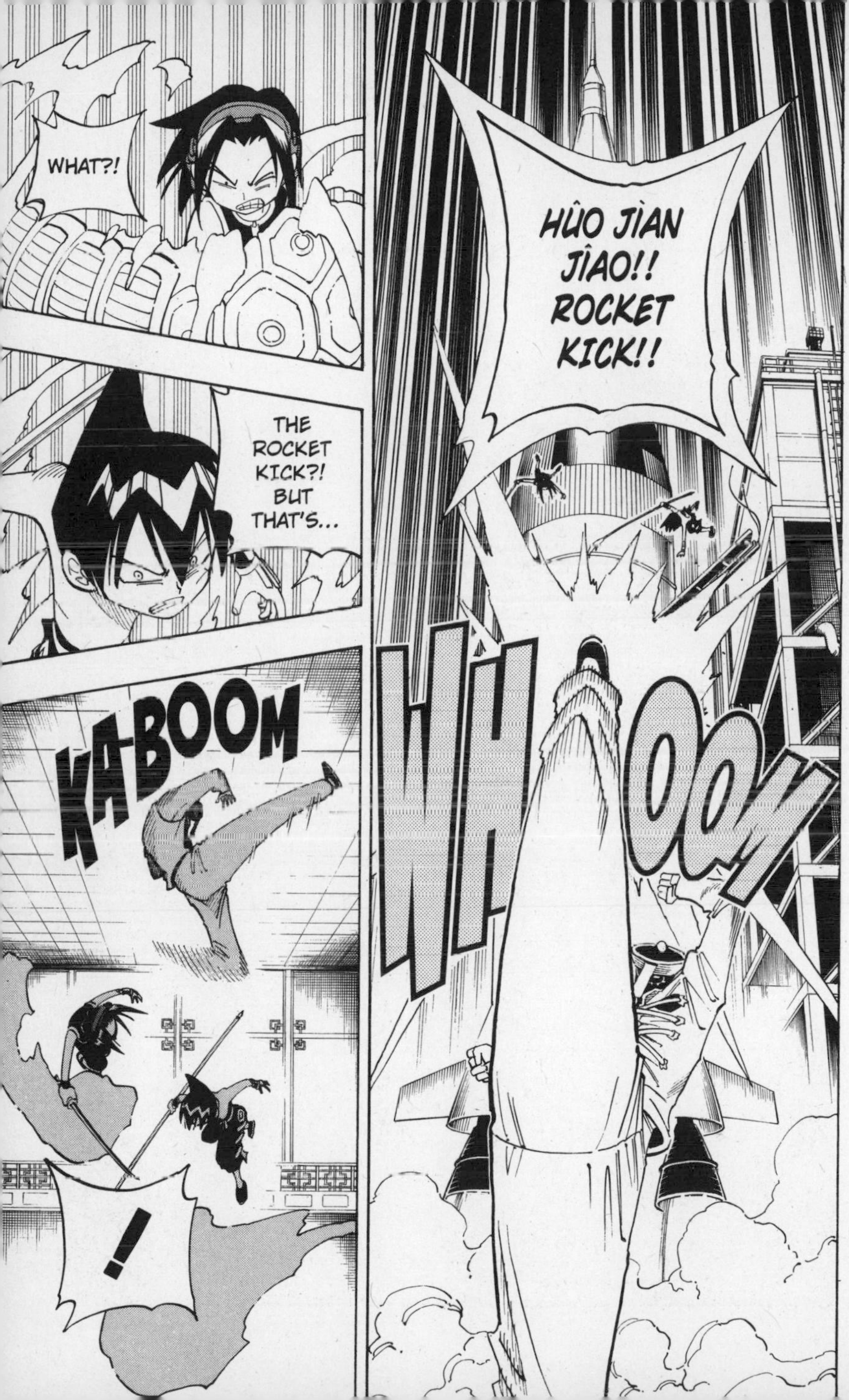
HÛO JÌAN JÎAO!! ROCKET KICK!!
WHOOM
WHAT?!
THE ROCKET KICK?! BUT THAT'S...
KABOOM
!

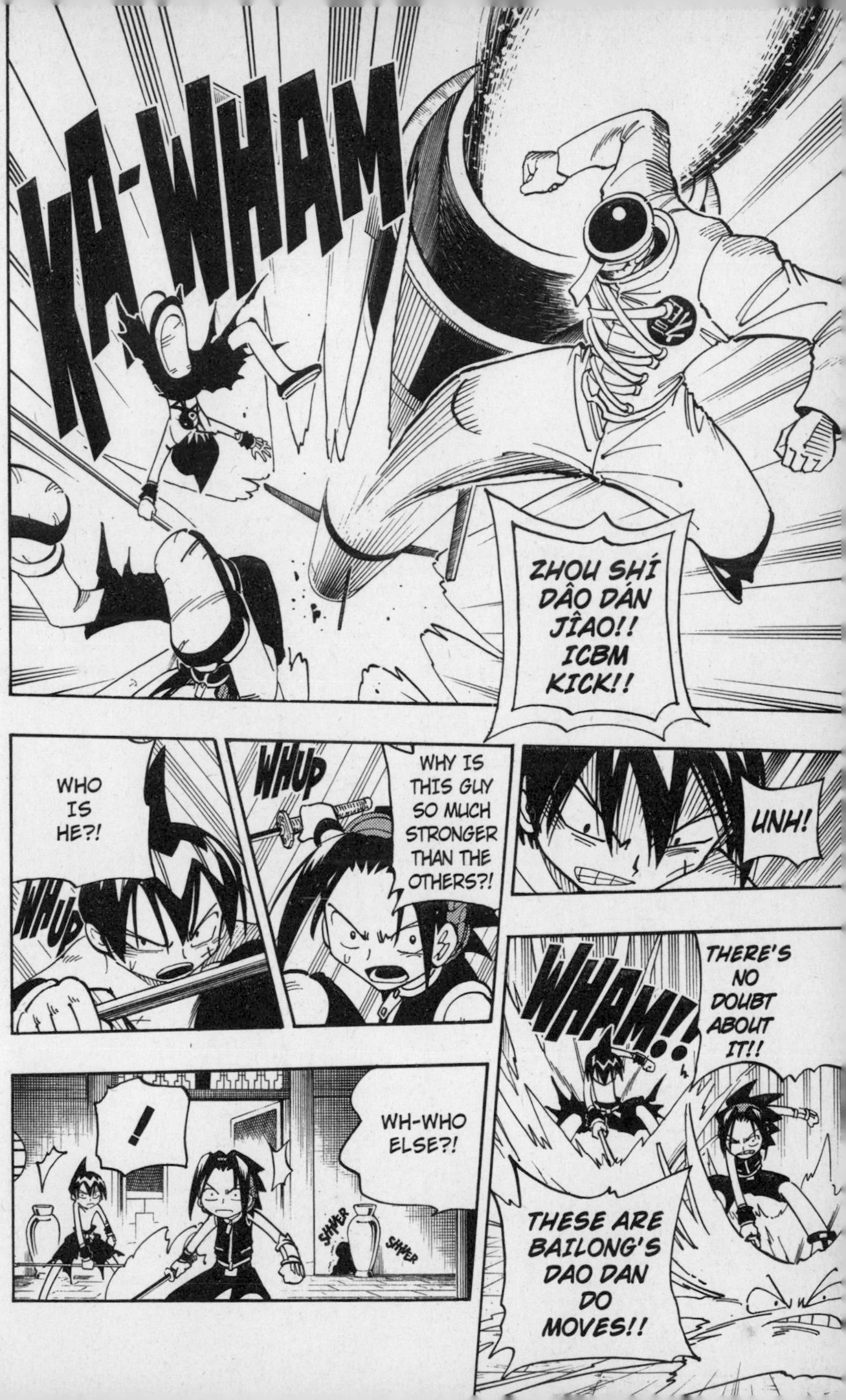
KA-WHAM
ZHOU SHÍ DÂO DÁN JÎAO!! ICBM KICK!!
UNH!
WHUP
WHY IS THIS GUY SO MUCH STRONGER THAN THE OTHERS?!
WHO IS HE?!
WHUP
WHAM!!
THERE'S NO DOUBT ABOUT IT!!
THESE ARE BAILONG'S DAO DAN DO MOVES!!
!
WH-WHO ELSE?!
SHIVER
SHIVER

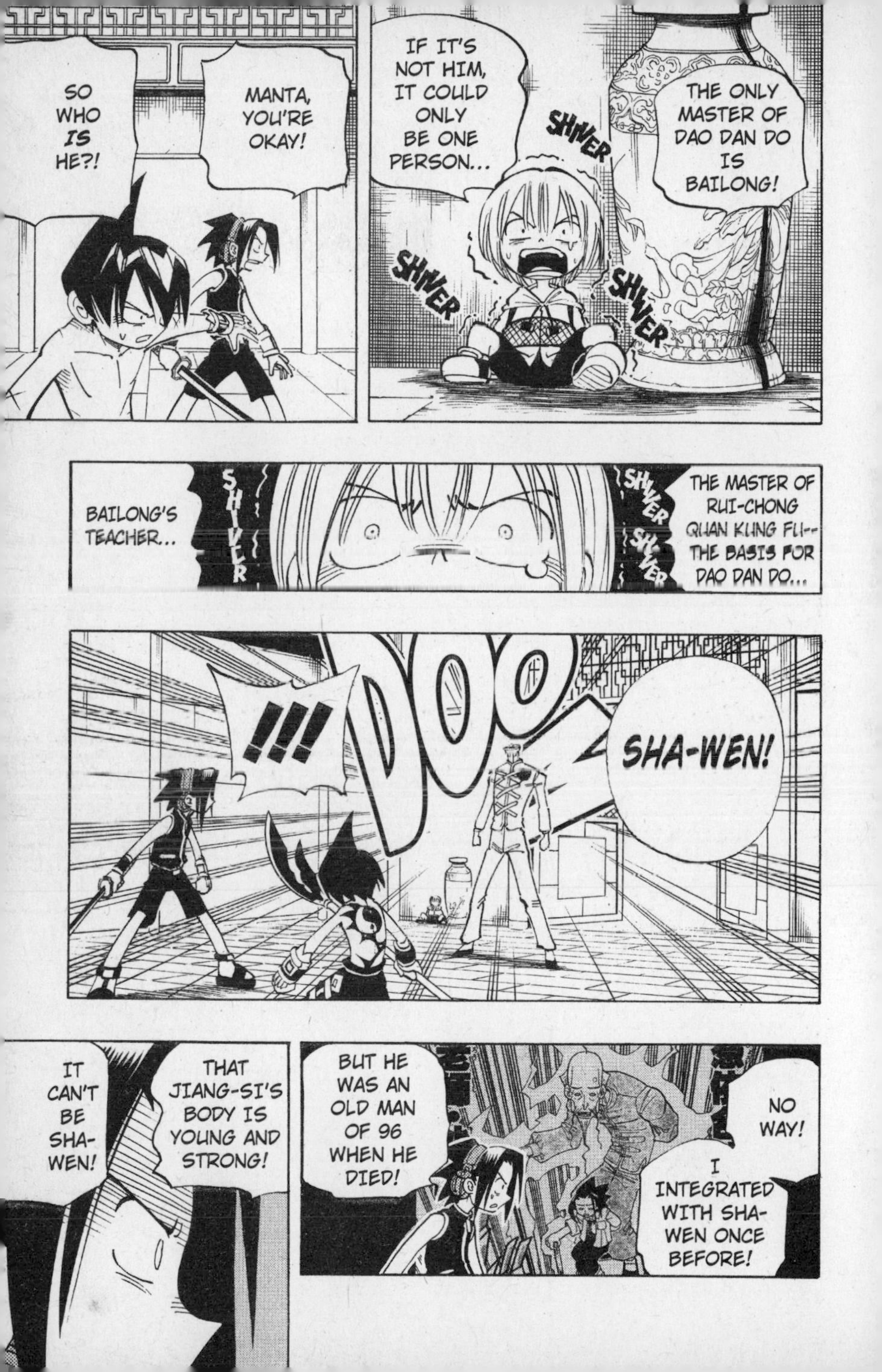
THE ONLY MASTER OF DAO DAN DO IS BAILONG!
IF IT'S NOT HIM, IT COULD ONLY BE ONE PERSON...
SHIVER
SHIVER
SHIVER
MANTA, YOU'RE OKAY!
SO WHO *IS* HE?!
THE MASTER OF RUI-CHONG QUAN KUNG FU-- THE BASIS FOR DAO DAN DO...
SHIVER
SHIVER
SHIVER
BAILONG'S TEACHER...
SHA-WEN!
DOOO
!!!
NO WAY!
I INTEGRATED WITH SHA-WEN ONCE BEFORE!
BUT HE WAS AN OLD MAN OF 96 WHEN HE DIED!
THAT JIANG-SI'S BODY IS YOUNG AND STRONG!
IT CAN'T BE SHA-WEN!

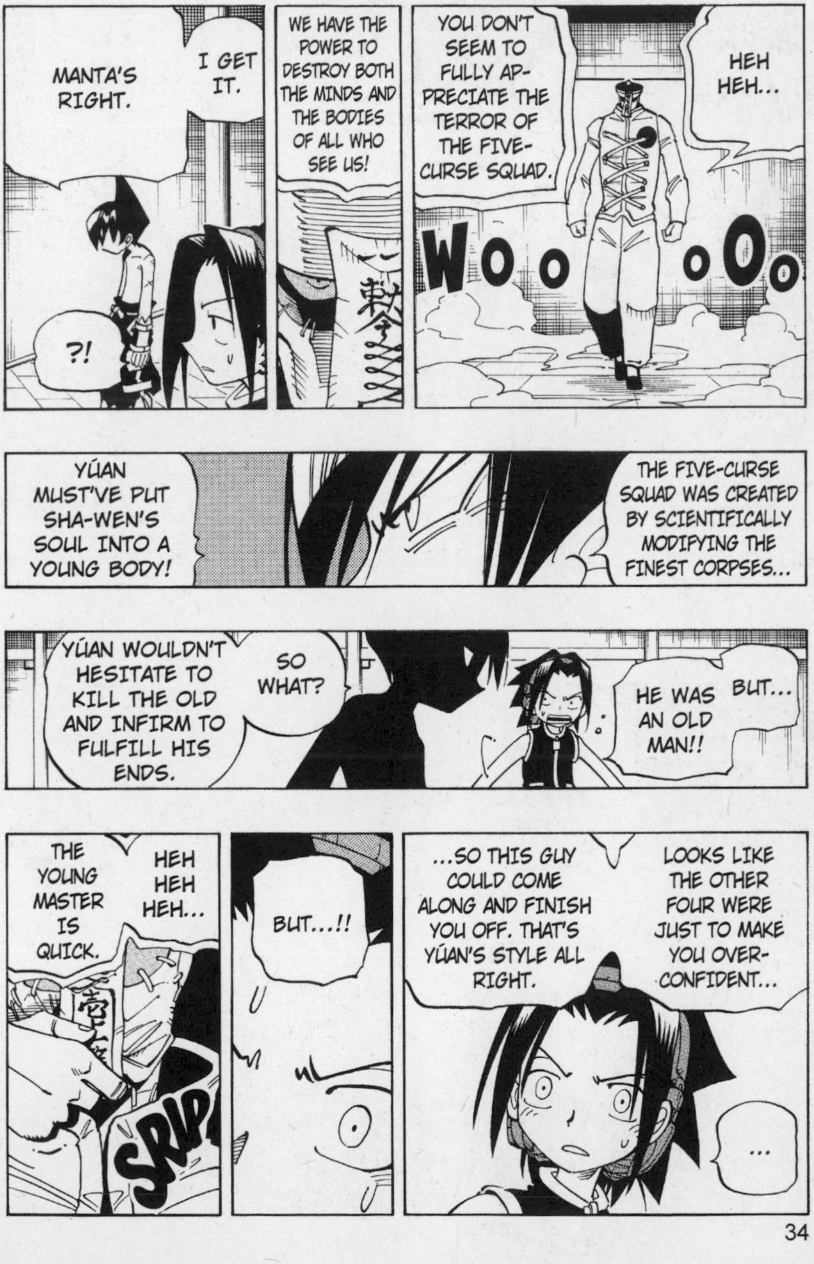
HEH HEH...
YOU DON'T SEEM TO FULLY APPRECIATE THE TERROR OF THE FIVE-CURSE SQUAD.
WOOOOO
WE HAVE THE POWER TO DESTROY BOTH THE MINDS AND THE BODIES OF ALL WHO SEE US!
I GET IT.
MANTA'S RIGHT.
?!
THE FIVE-CURSE SQUAD WAS CREATED BY SCIENTIFICALLY MODIFYING THE FINEST CORPSES...
YÚAN MUST'VE PUT SHA-WEN'S SOUL INTO A YOUNG BODY!
BUT...
HE WAS AN OLD MAN!!
SO WHAT?
YÚAN WOULDN'T HESITATE TO KILL THE OLD AND INFIRM TO FULFILL HIS ENDS.
LOOKS LIKE THE OTHER FOUR WERE JUST TO MAKE YOU OVER-CONFIDENT...
...SO THIS GUY COULD COME ALONG AND FINISH YOU OFF. THAT'S YÚAN'S STYLE ALL RIGHT.
...
BUT...!!
HEH HEH HEH...
THE YOUNG MASTER IS QUICK.
SRIP

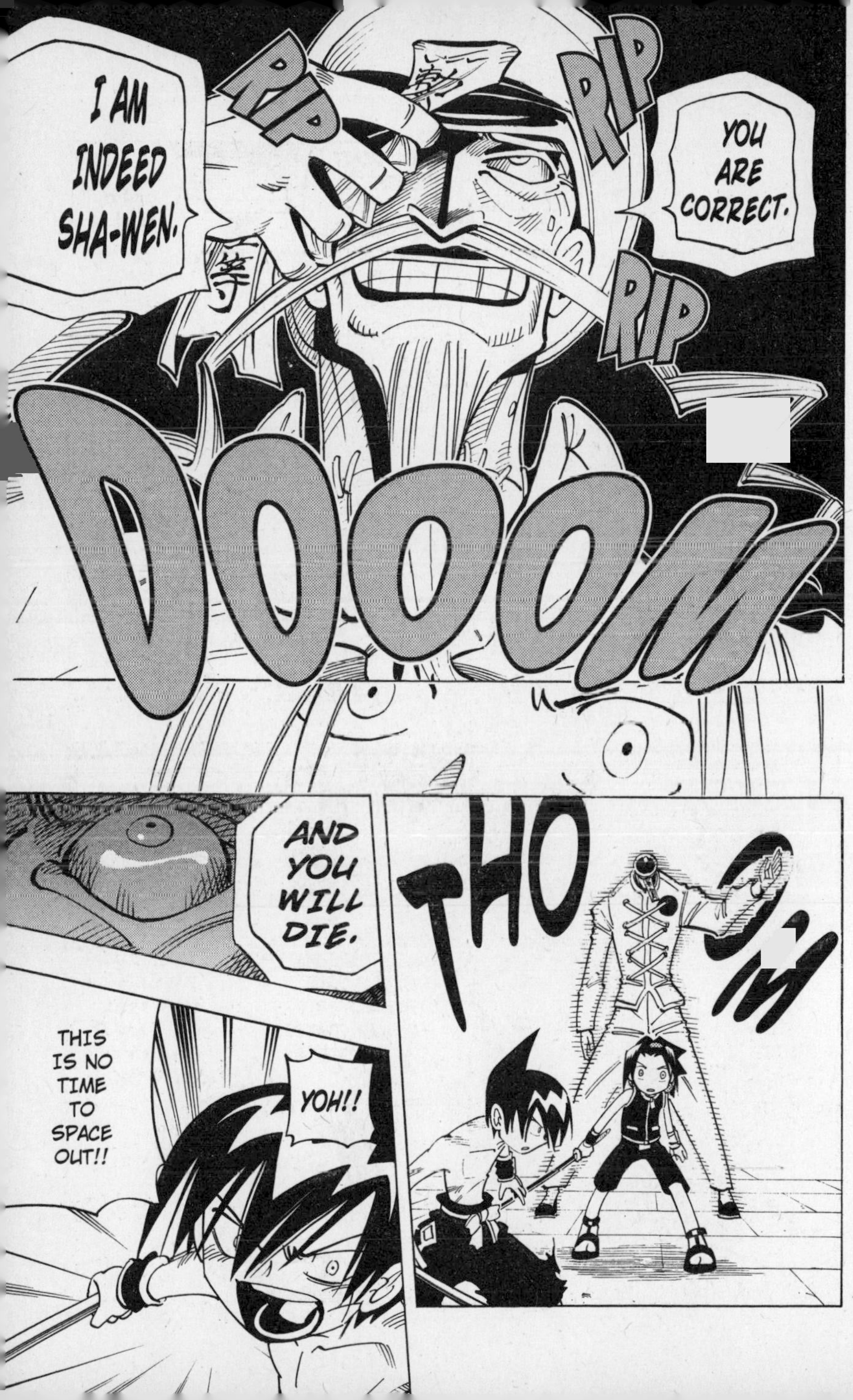
RIP
YOU ARE CORRECT.
RIP
I AM INDEED SHA-WEN.
RIP
DOOOM
THOOM
AND YOU WILL DIE.
YOH!!
THIS IS NO TIME TO SPACE OUT!!

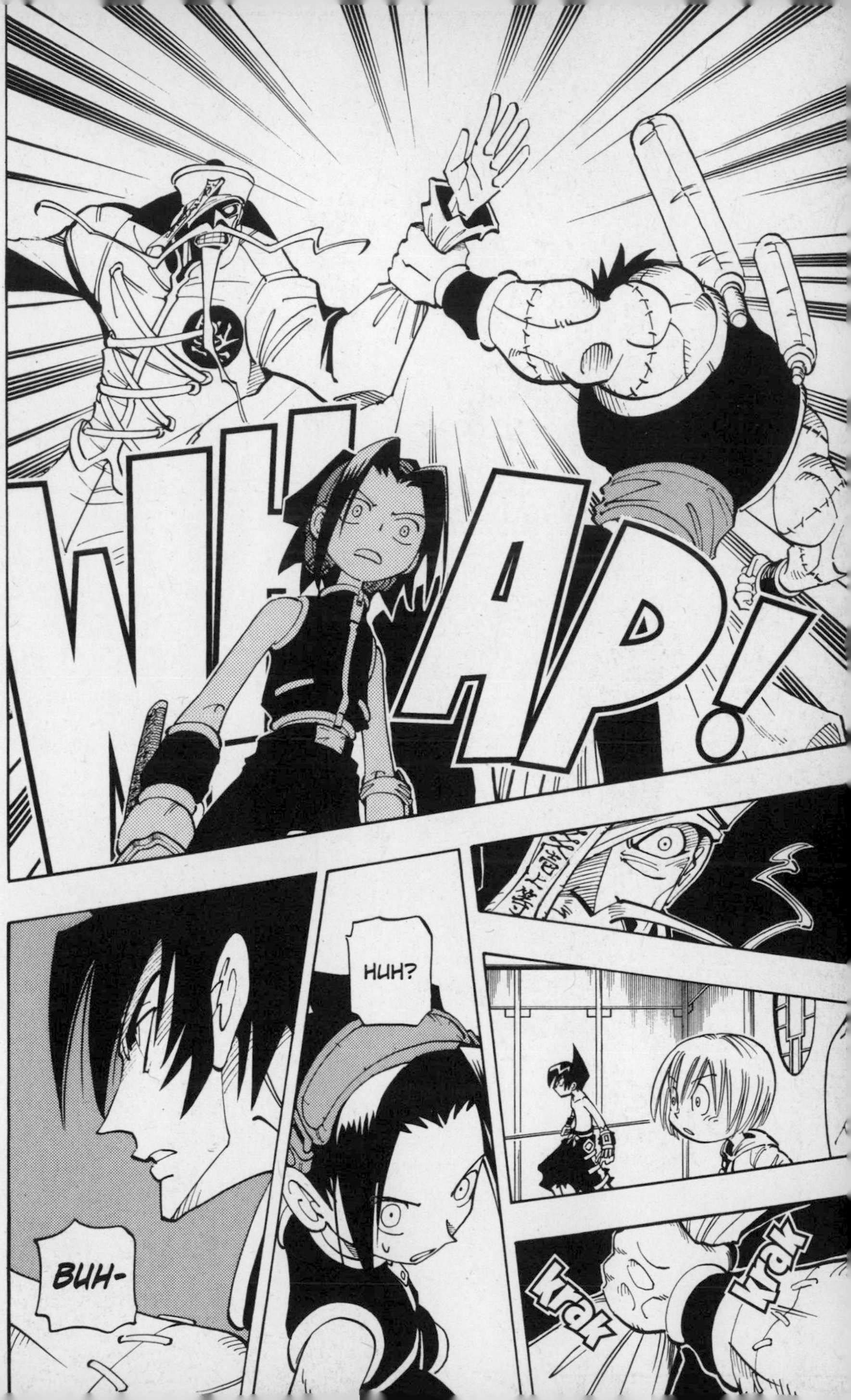
WHAP!
krak
krak
HUH?
BUH-

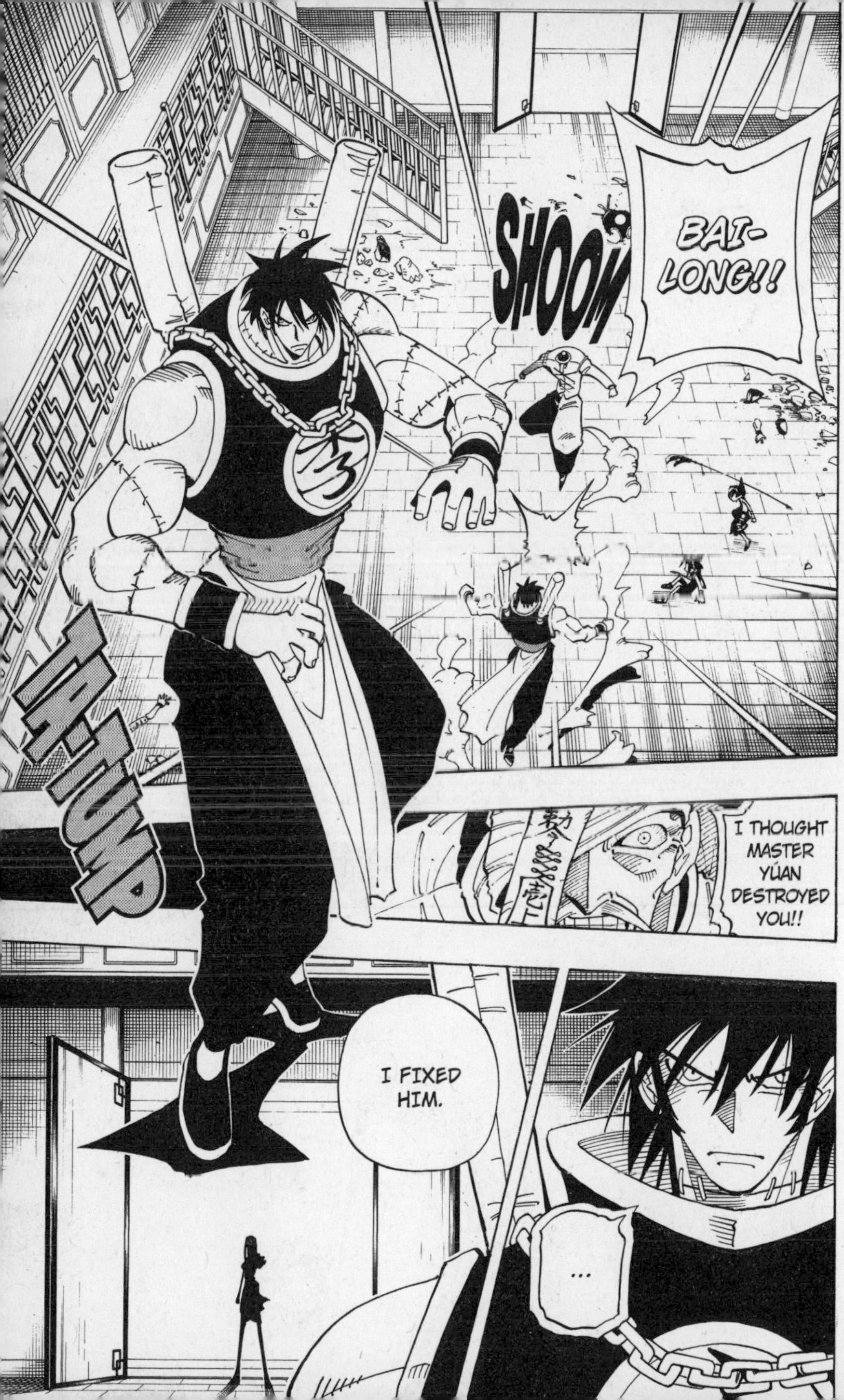
BAI-LONG!!
SHOOM
THA-THUMP
I THOUGHT MASTER YÚAN DESTROYED YOU!!
...
I FIXED HIM.

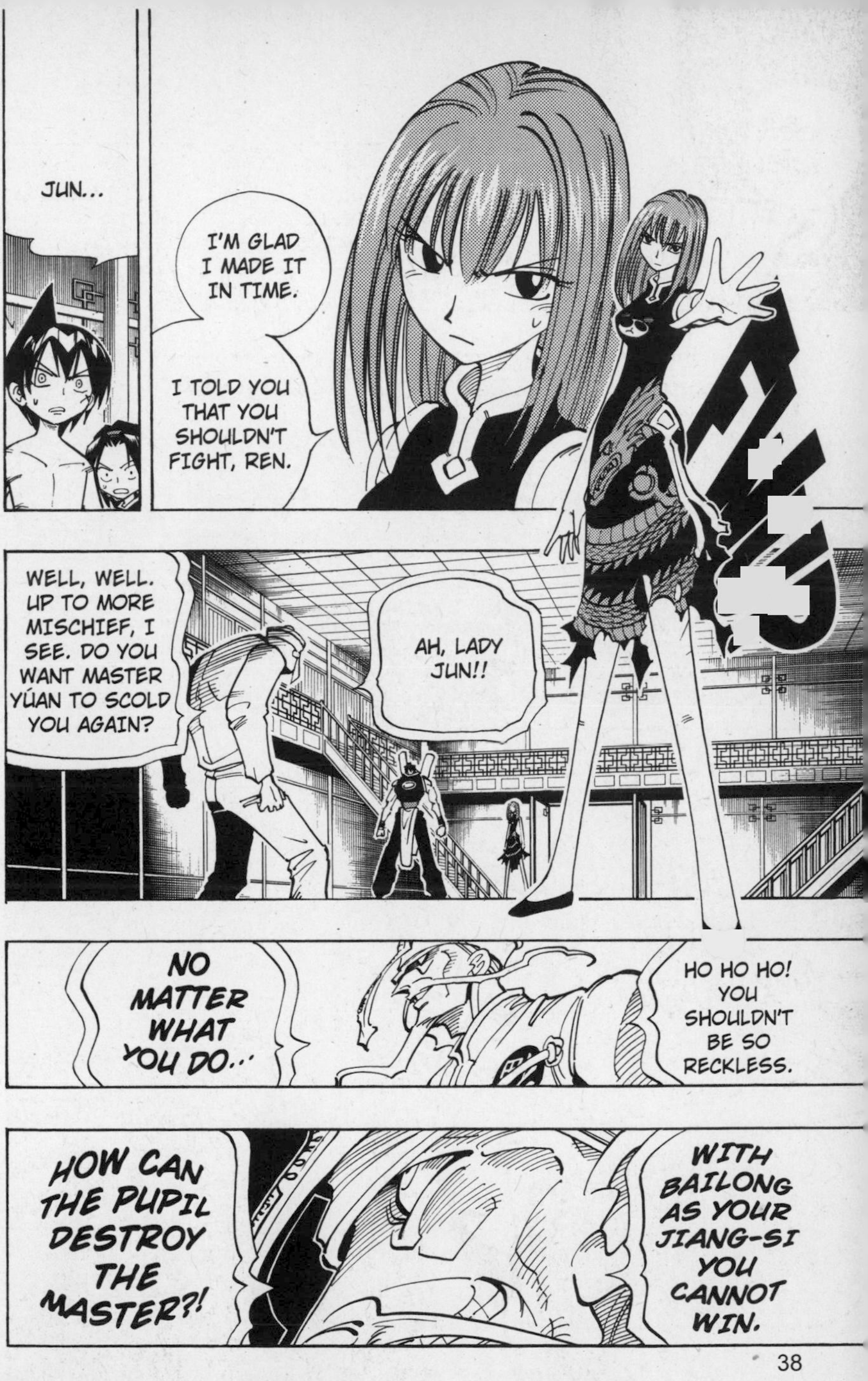
I'M GLAD I MADE IT IN TIME.
I TOLD YOU THAT YOU SHOULDN'T FIGHT, REN.
JUN...
AH, LADY JUN!!
WELL, WELL. UP TO MORE MISCHIEF, I SEE. DO YOU WANT MASTER YÚAN TO SCOLD YOU AGAIN?
HO HO HO! YOU SHOULDN'T BE SO RECKLESS.
NO MATTER WHAT YOU DO...
WITH BAILONG AS YOUR JIANG-SI YOU CANNOT WIN.
HOW CAN THE PUPIL DESTROY THE MASTER?!

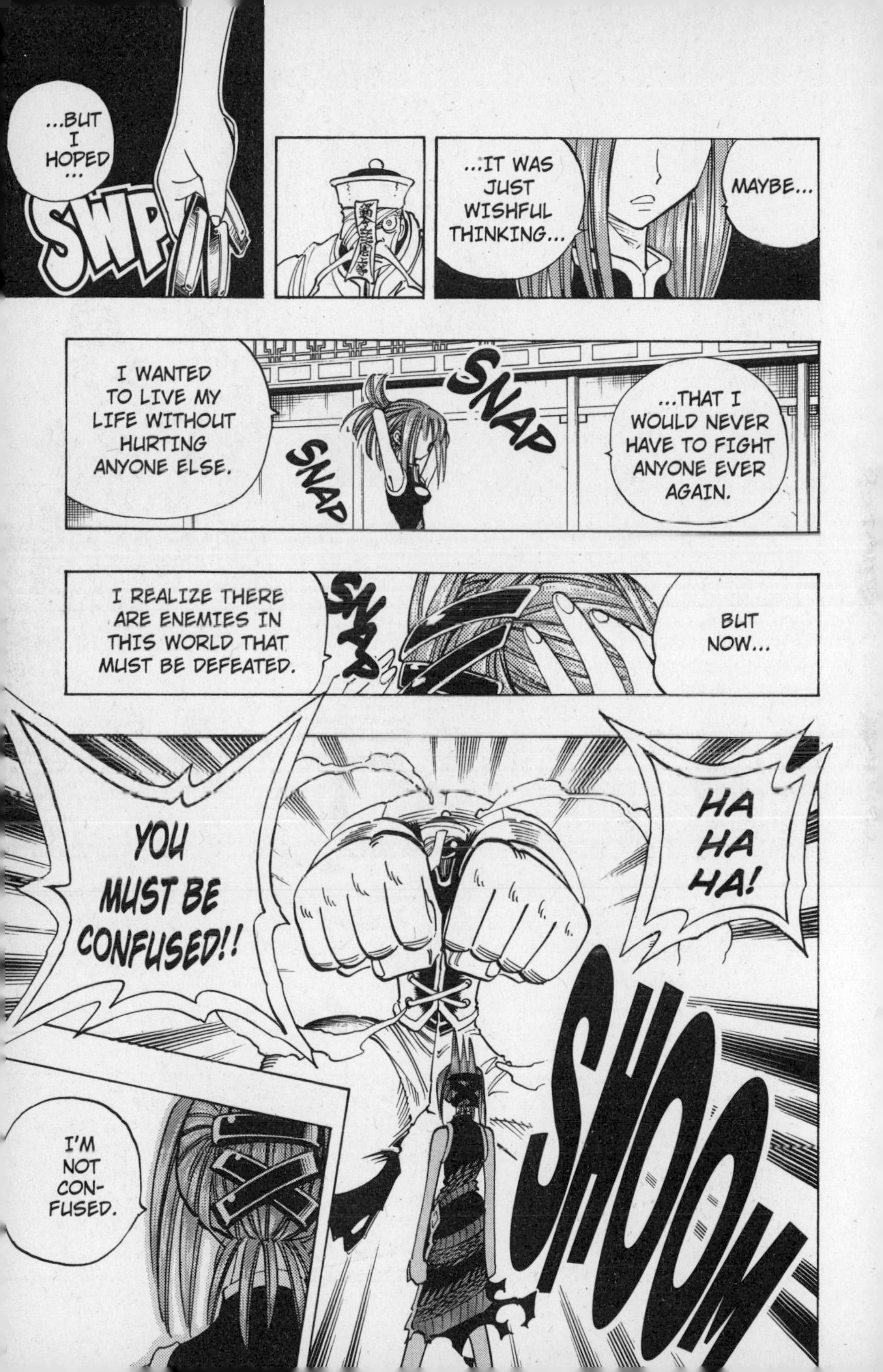
MAYBE...
...IT WAS JUST WISHFUL THINKING...
...BUT I HOPED ...
SNIP
...THAT I WOULD NEVER HAVE TO FIGHT ANYONE EVER AGAIN.
SNAP
SNAP
I WANTED TO LIVE MY LIFE WITHOUT HURTING ANYONE ELSE.
BUT NOW...
SNAP
I REALIZE THERE ARE ENEMIES IN THIS WORLD THAT MUST BE DEFEATED.
HA HA HA!
YOU MUST BE CONFUSED!!
SHOOM
I'M NOT CON-FUSED.

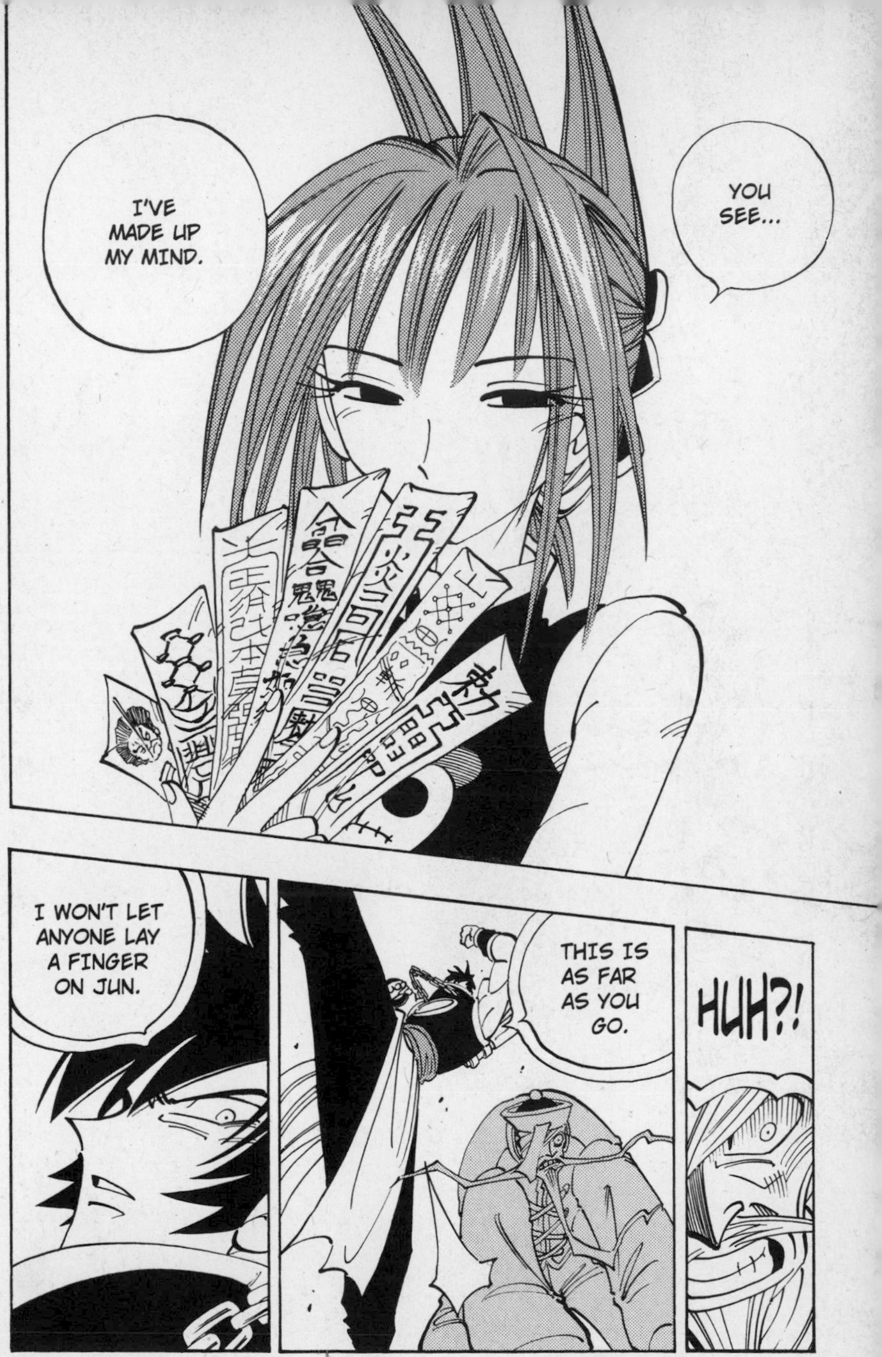
YOU SEE...
I'VE MADE UP MY MIND.
HUH?!
THIS IS AS FAR AS YOU GO.
I WON'T LET ANYONE LAY A FINGER ON JUN.

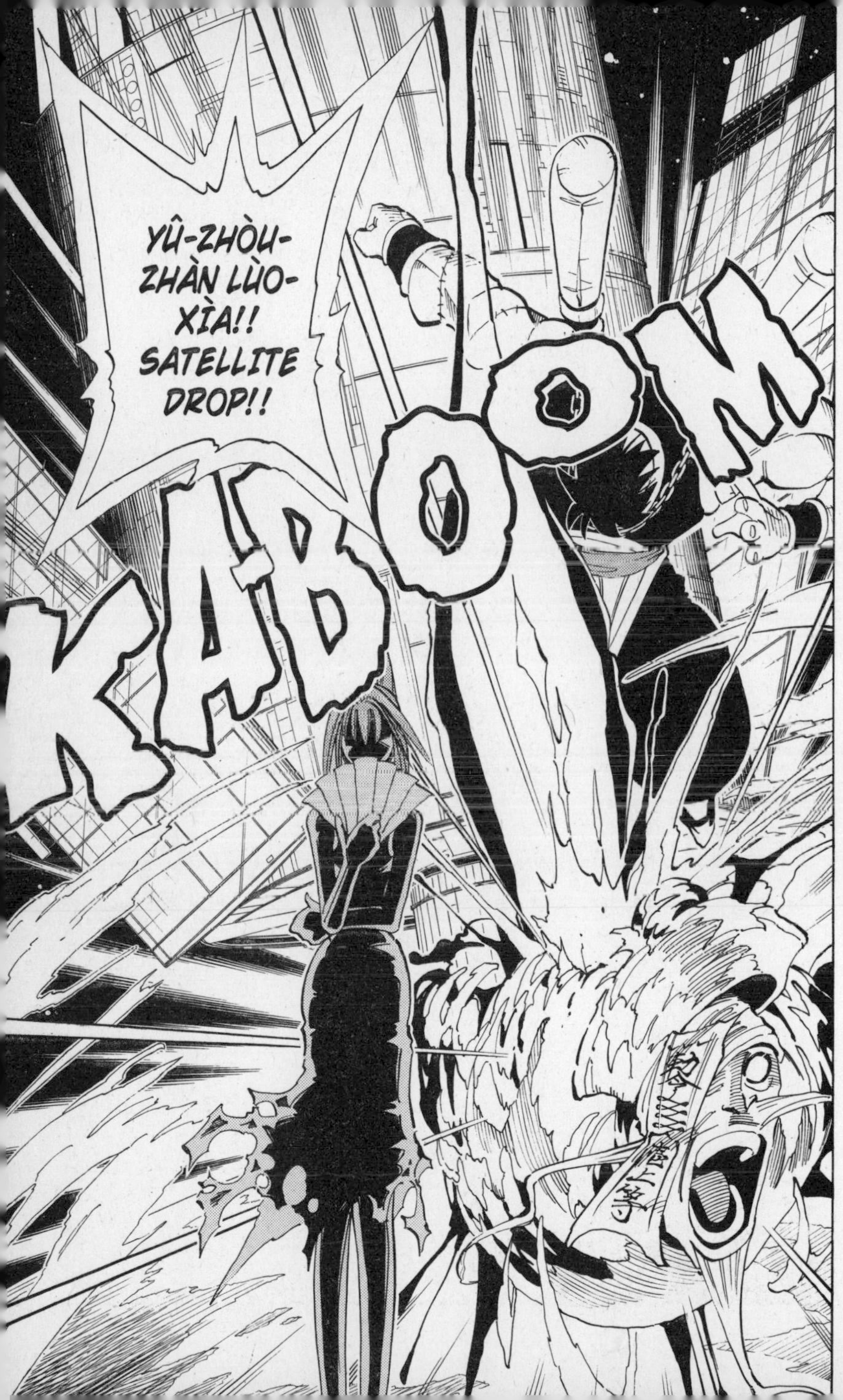
YÛ-ZHÒU-ZHÀN LÙO-XÌA!! SATELLITE DROP!!
KABOOM

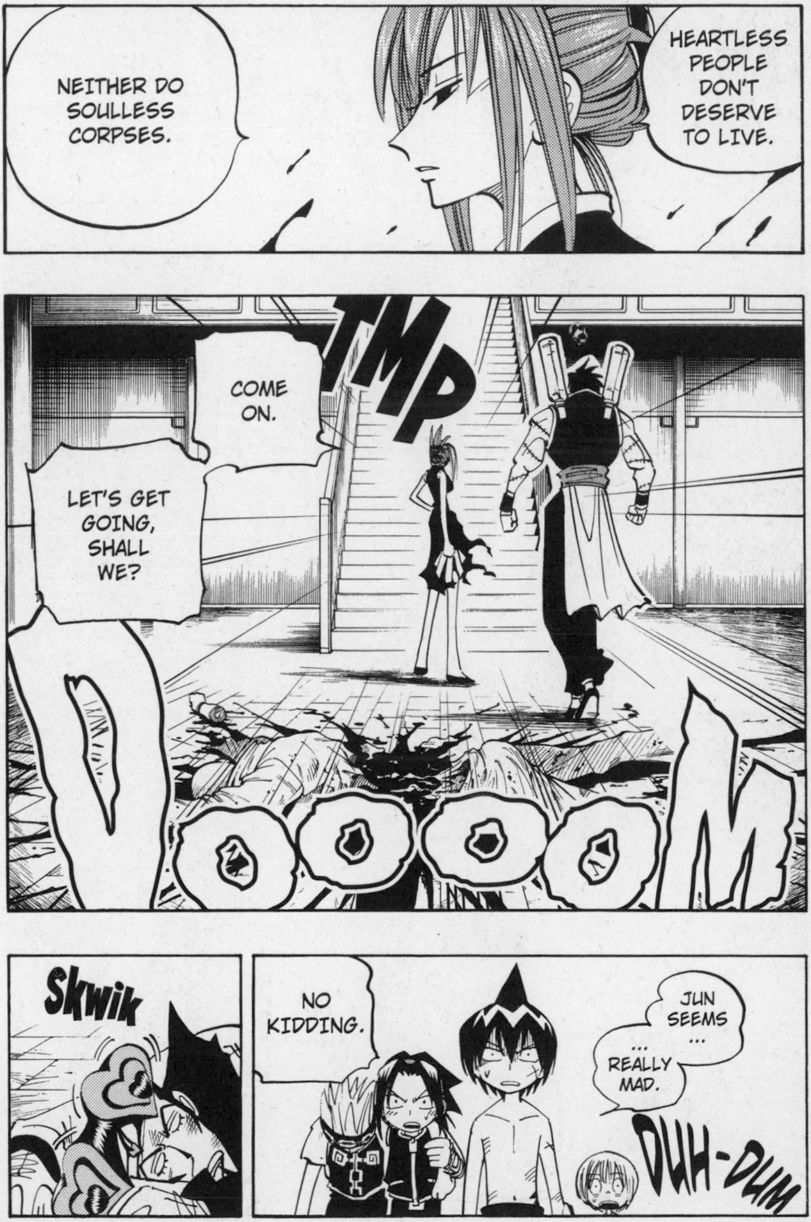
HEARTLESS PEOPLE DON'T DESERVE TO LIVE.
NEITHER DO SOULLESS CORPSES.
TMP
COME ON.
LET'S GET GOING, SHALL WE?
DOOOOOM
JUN SEEMS ... ... REALLY MAD.
NO KIDDING.
DUH-DUM
Skwik

READ THIS WAY

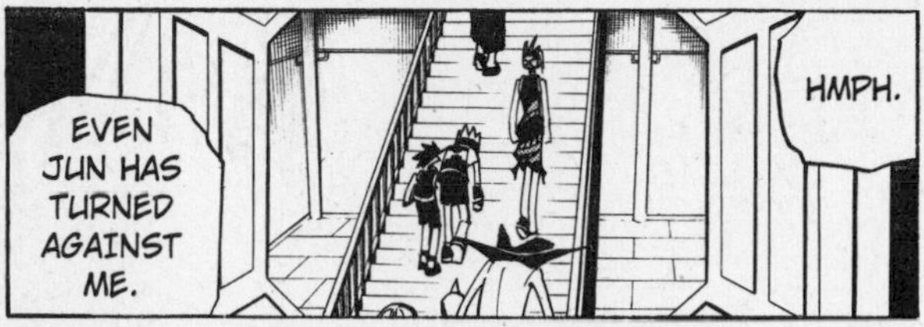
HMPH.
EVEN JUN HAS TURNED AGAINST ME.

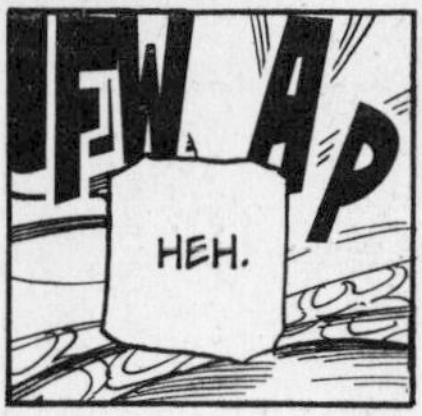
FWAP
HEH.

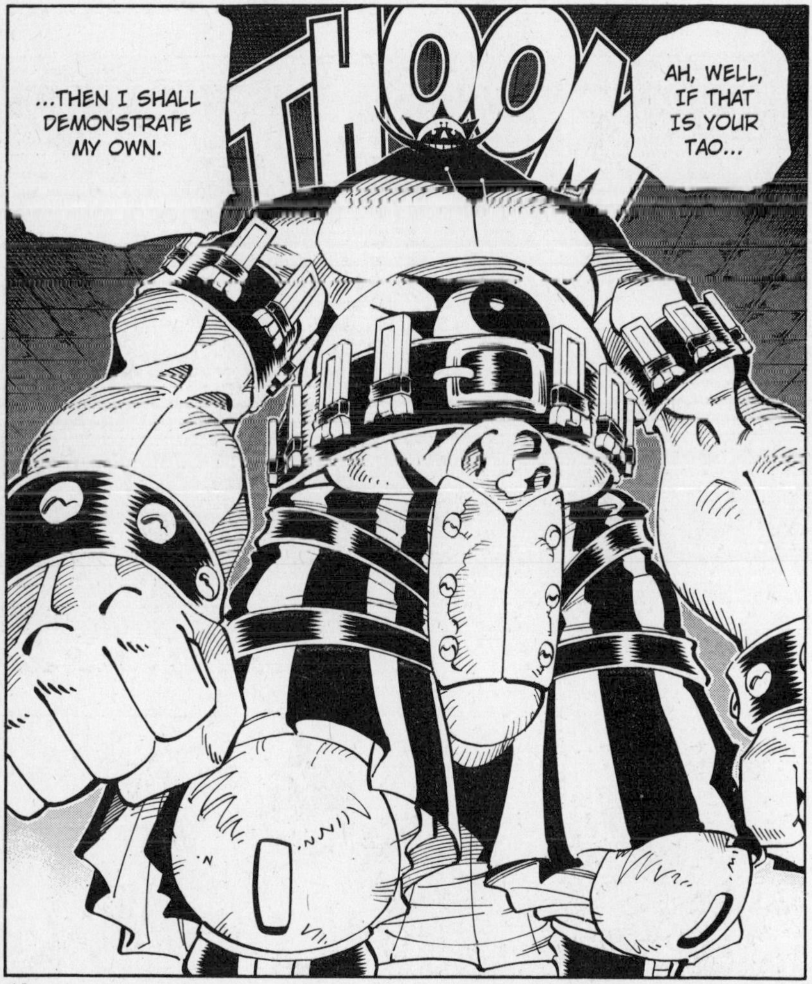
THOOM
AH, WELL, IF THAT IS YOUR TAO...
...THEN I SHALL DEMONSTRATE MY OWN.

## SHAMAN KING CHARACTER FILE No.40

# THE TORTURE BROTHERS

SHACKLER (YOUNGER)

FLOGGER (OLDER)

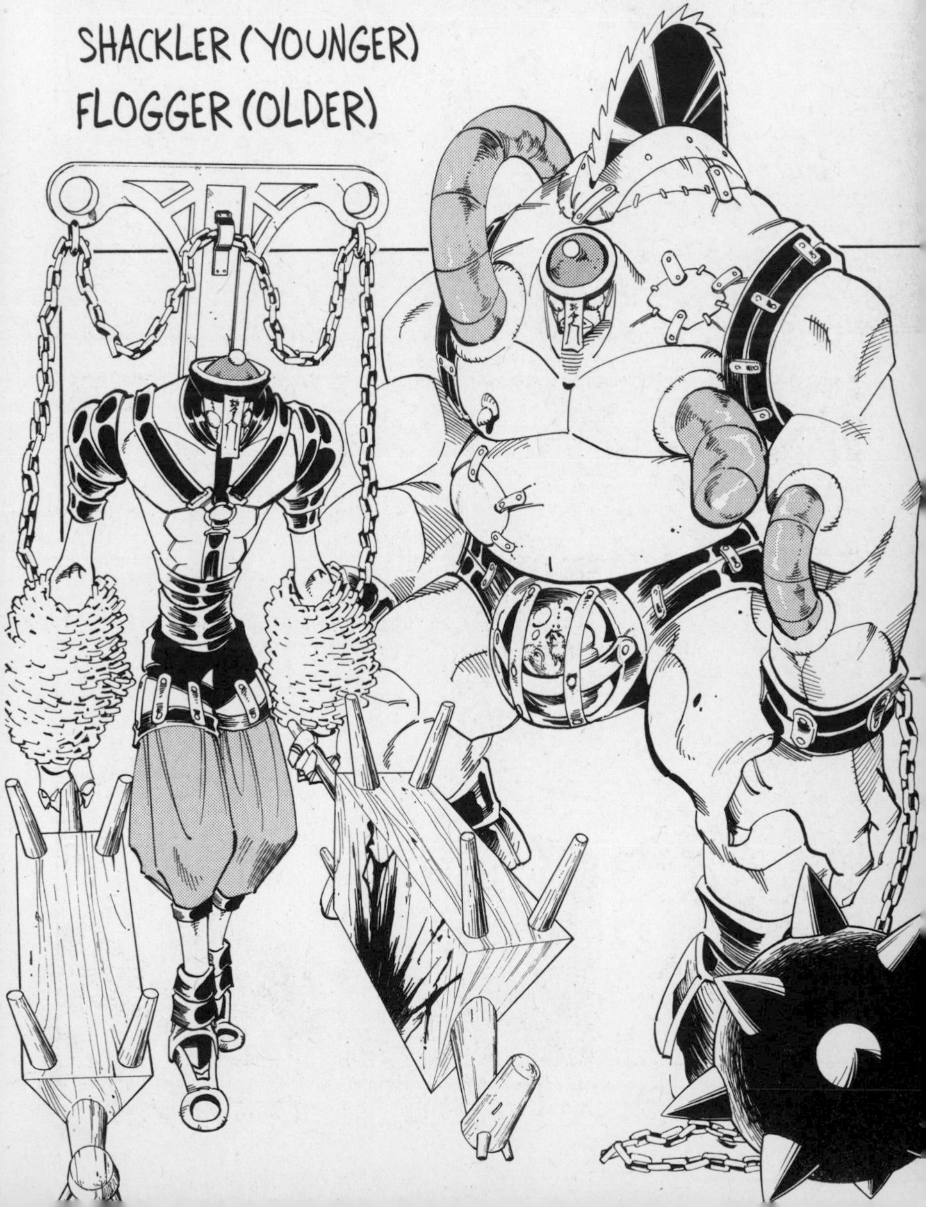

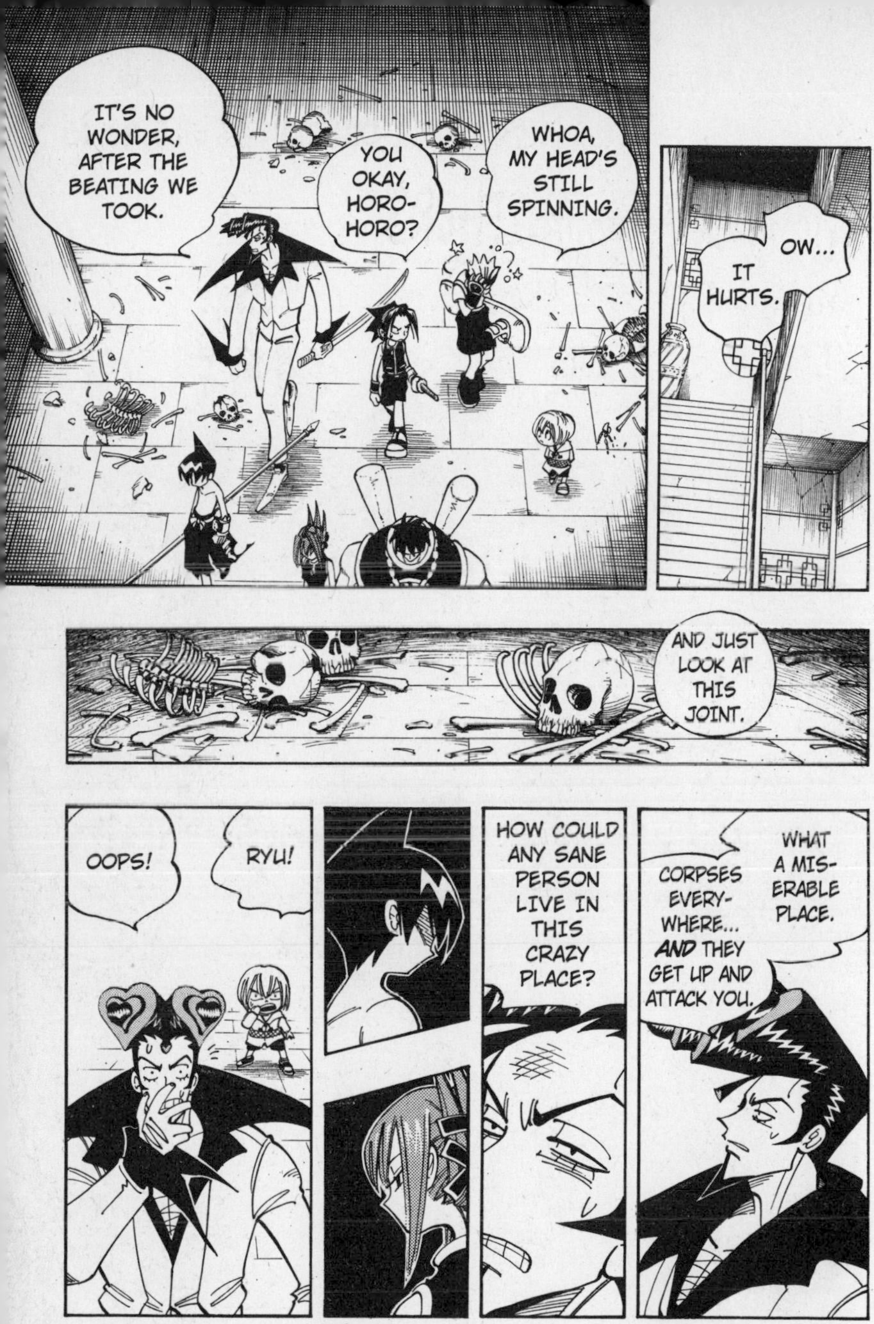
OW...
IT HURTS.
WHOA, MY HEAD'S STILL SPINNING.
YOU OKAY, HORO-HORO?
IT'S NO WONDER, AFTER THE BEATING WE TOOK.
AND JUST LOOK AT THIS JOINT.
WHAT A MIS-ERABLE PLACE.
CORPSES EVERY-WHERE... *AND* THEY GET UP AND ATTACK YOU.
HOW COULD ANY SANE PERSON LIVE IN THIS CRAZY PLACE?
RYU!
OOPS!

# Reincarnation 74: Tao Yuan: The Immortal Secret

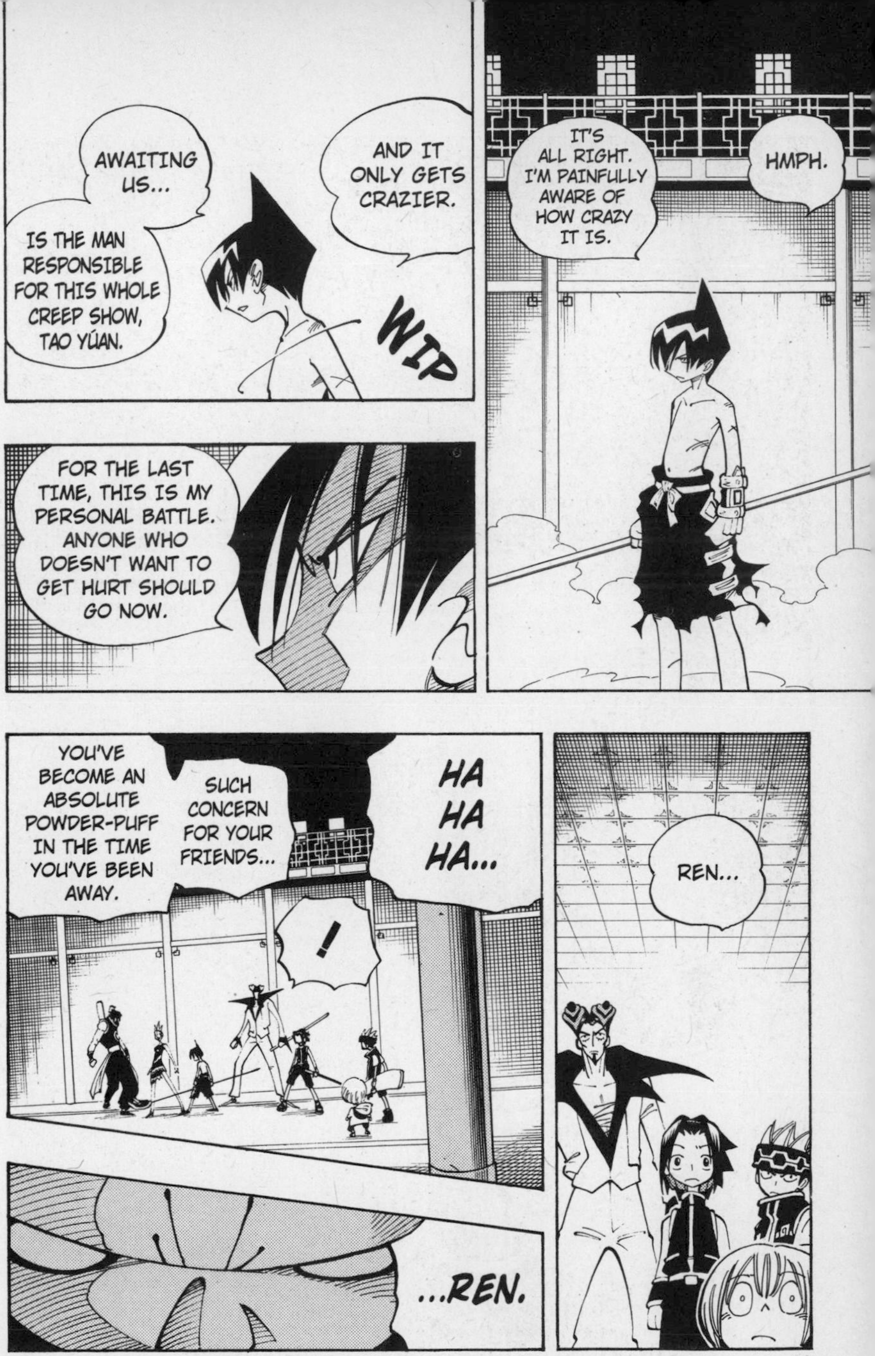
HMPH.
IT'S ALL RIGHT. I'M PAINFULLY AWARE OF HOW CRAZY IT IS.
AND IT ONLY GETS CRAZIER.
AWAITING US...
IS THE MAN RESPONSIBLE FOR THIS WHOLE CREEP SHOW, TAO YÚAN.
WIP
FOR THE LAST TIME, THIS IS MY PERSONAL BATTLE. ANYONE WHO DOESN'T WANT TO GET HURT SHOULD GO NOW.
REN...
HA HA HA...
SUCH CONCERN FOR YOUR FRIENDS...
YOU'VE BECOME AN ABSOLUTE POWDER-PUFF IN THE TIME YOU'VE BEEN AWAY.
!
...REN.

# Reincarnation 74:
# Tao Yúan: The Immortal Secret

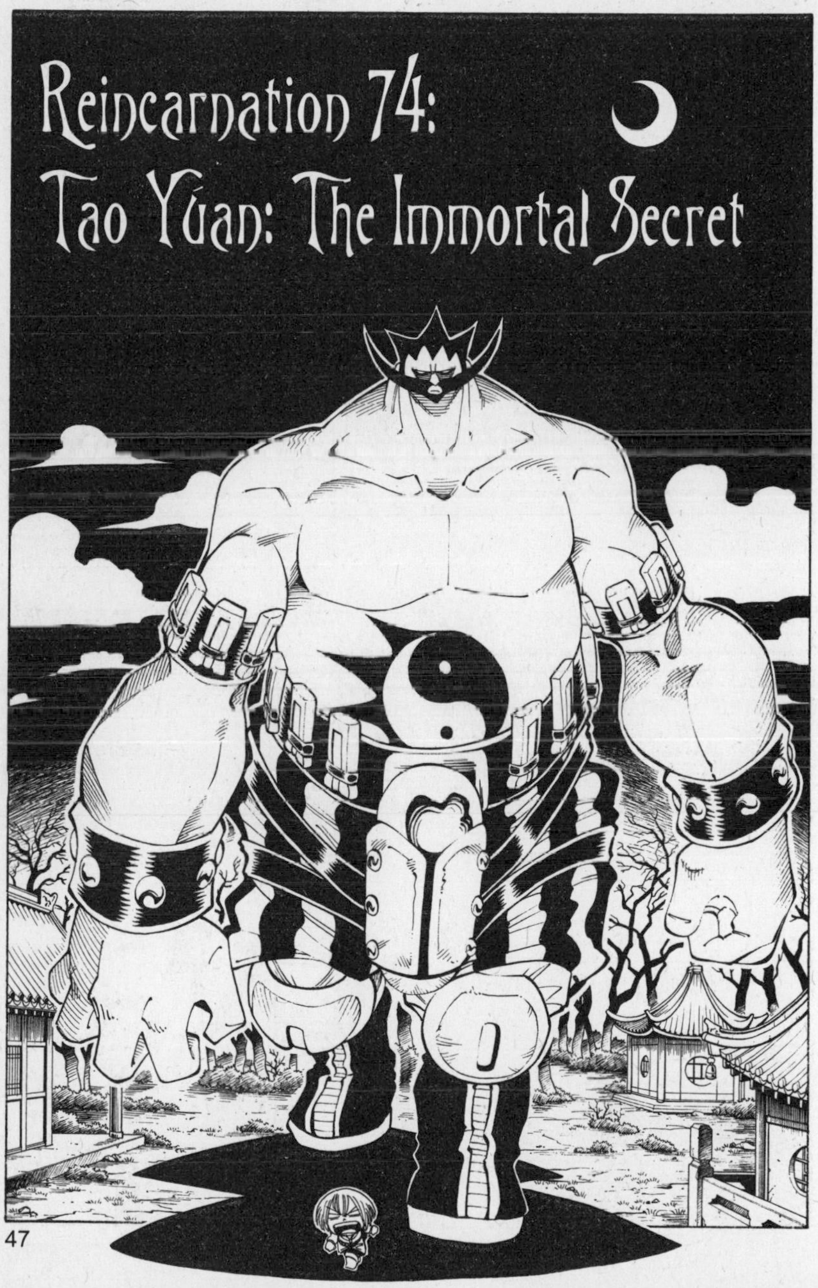

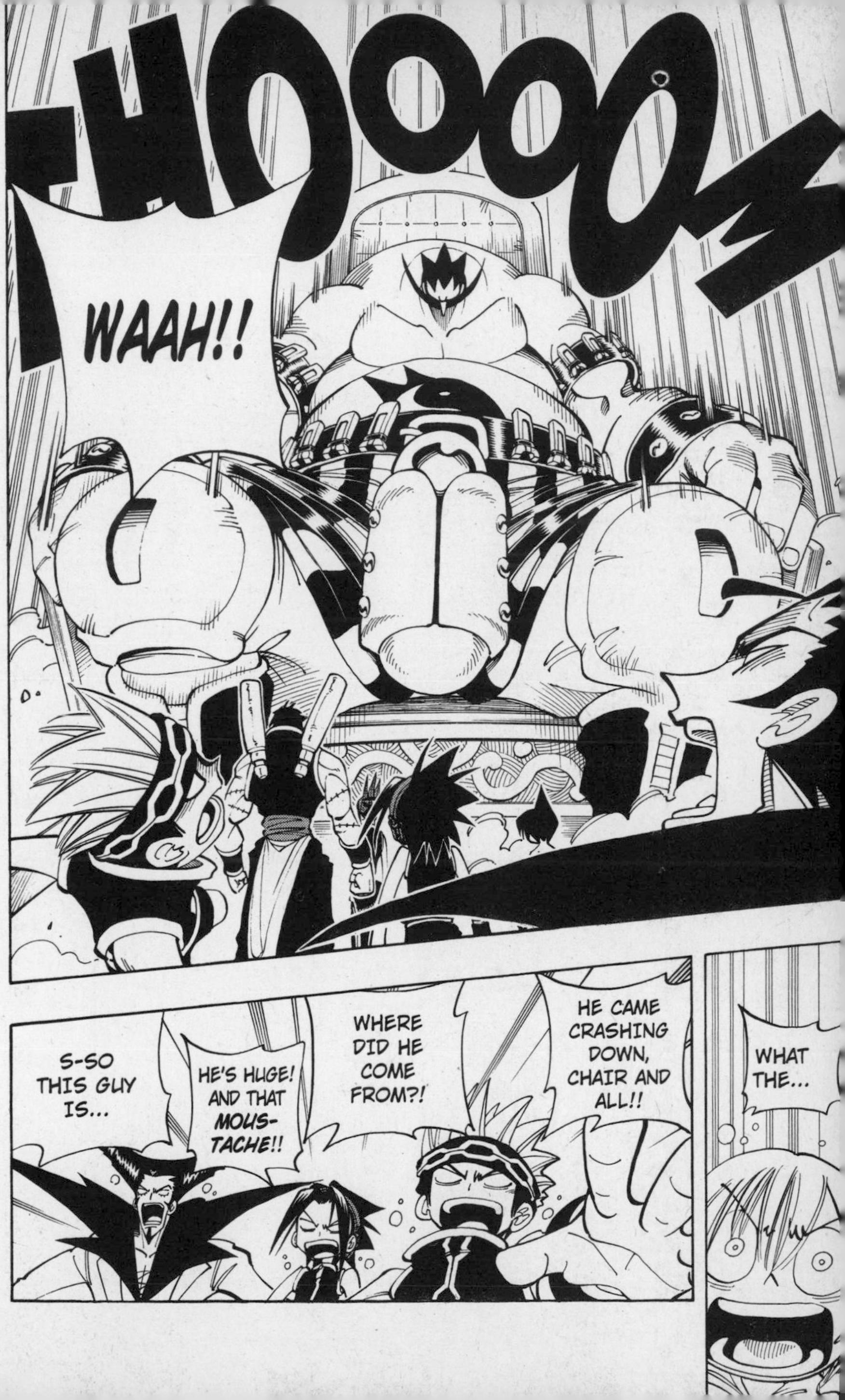
THOOOOM
WAAH!!
WHAT THE...
HE CAME CRASHING DOWN, CHAIR AND ALL!!
WHERE DID HE COME FROM?!
HE'S HUGE! AND THAT *MOUS-TACHE*!!
S-SO THIS GUY IS...

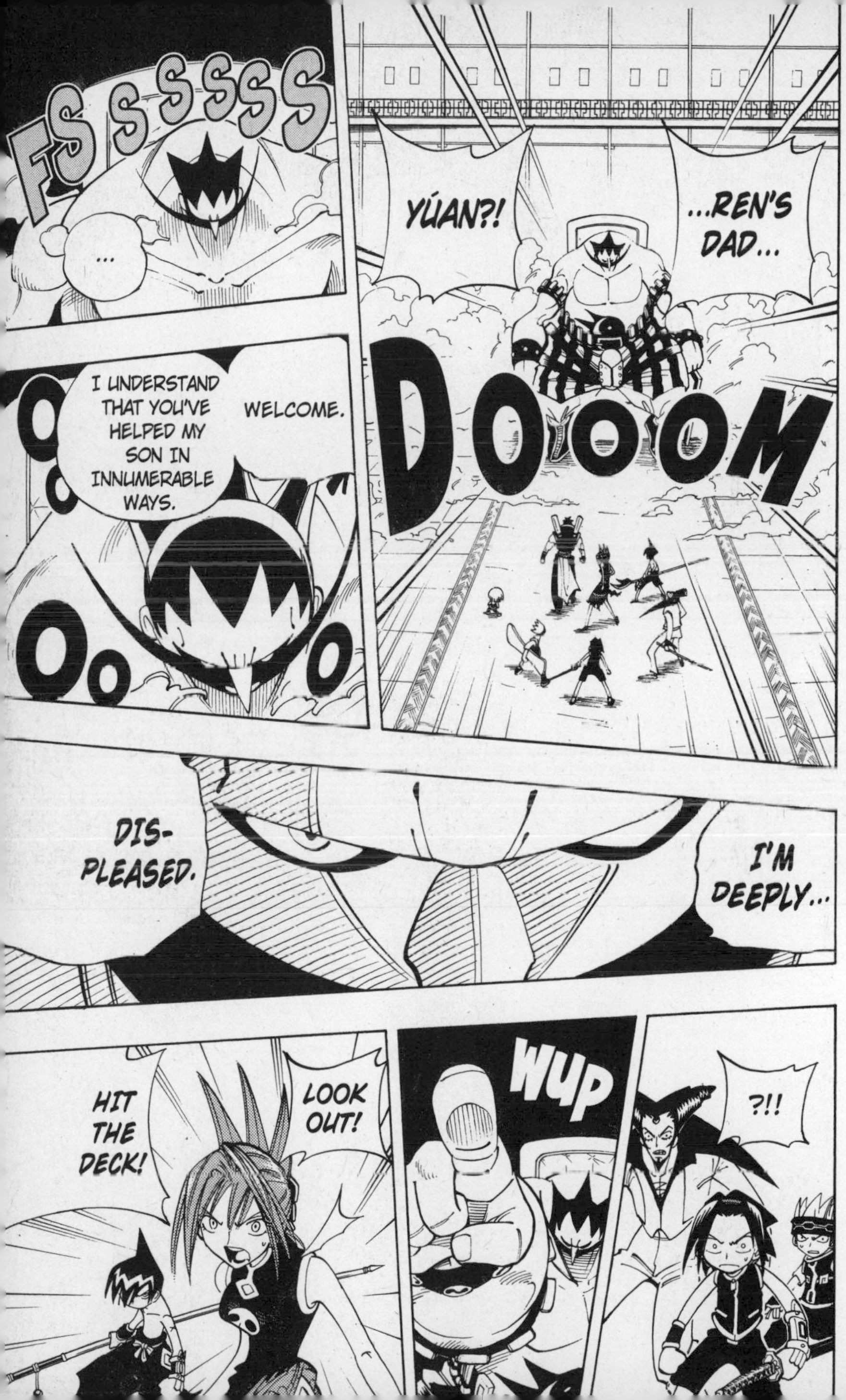
...REN'S DAD...
YÚAN?!
FSSSSSS
...
DOOOM
WELCOME.
I UNDERSTAND THAT YOU'VE HELPED MY SON IN INNUMERABLE WAYS.
I'M DEEPLY...
DIS-PLEASED.
?!!
WUP
LOOK OUT!
HIT THE DECK!

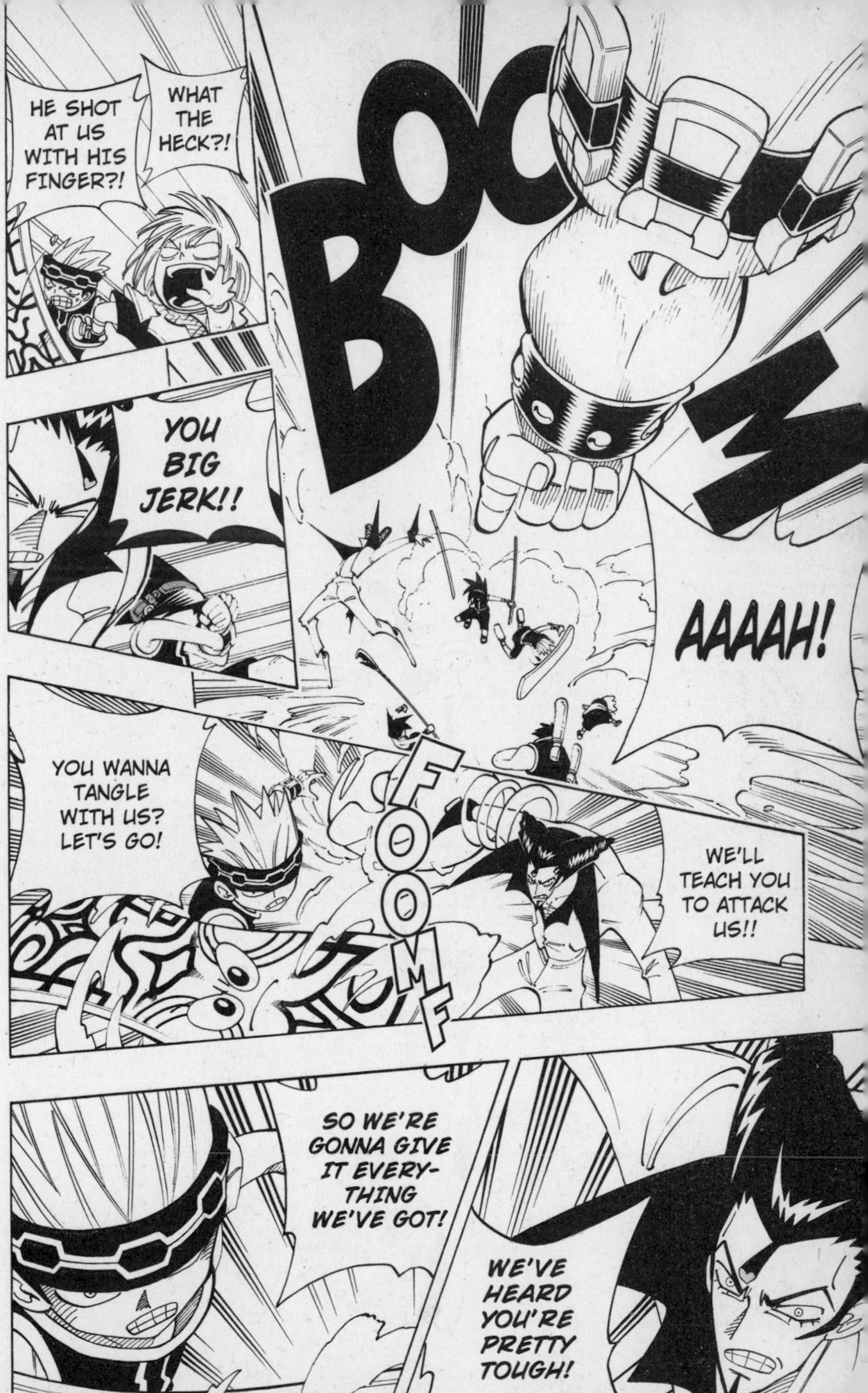
BOOM
AAAAH!
WHAT THE HECK?!
HE SHOT AT US WITH HIS FINGER?!
YOU BIG JERK!!
WE'LL TEACH YOU TO ATTACK US!!
FOOOMF
YOU WANNA TANGLE WITH US? LET'S GO!
WE'VE HEARD YOU'RE PRETTY TOUGH!
SO WE'RE GONNA GIVE IT EVERY-THING WE'VE GOT!

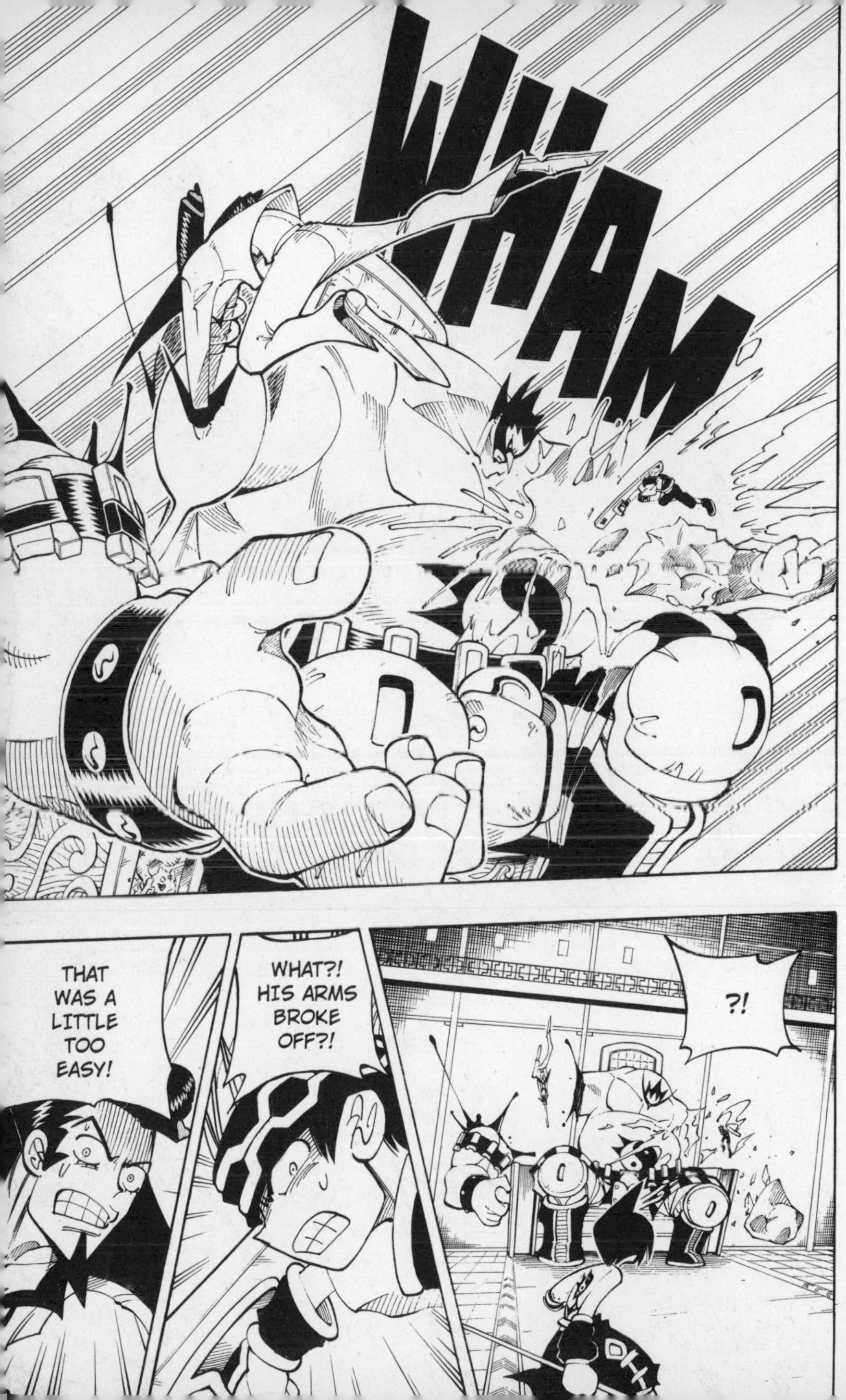
WHAM
?!
WHAT?! HIS ARMS BROKE OFF?!
THAT WAS A LITTLE TOO EASY!

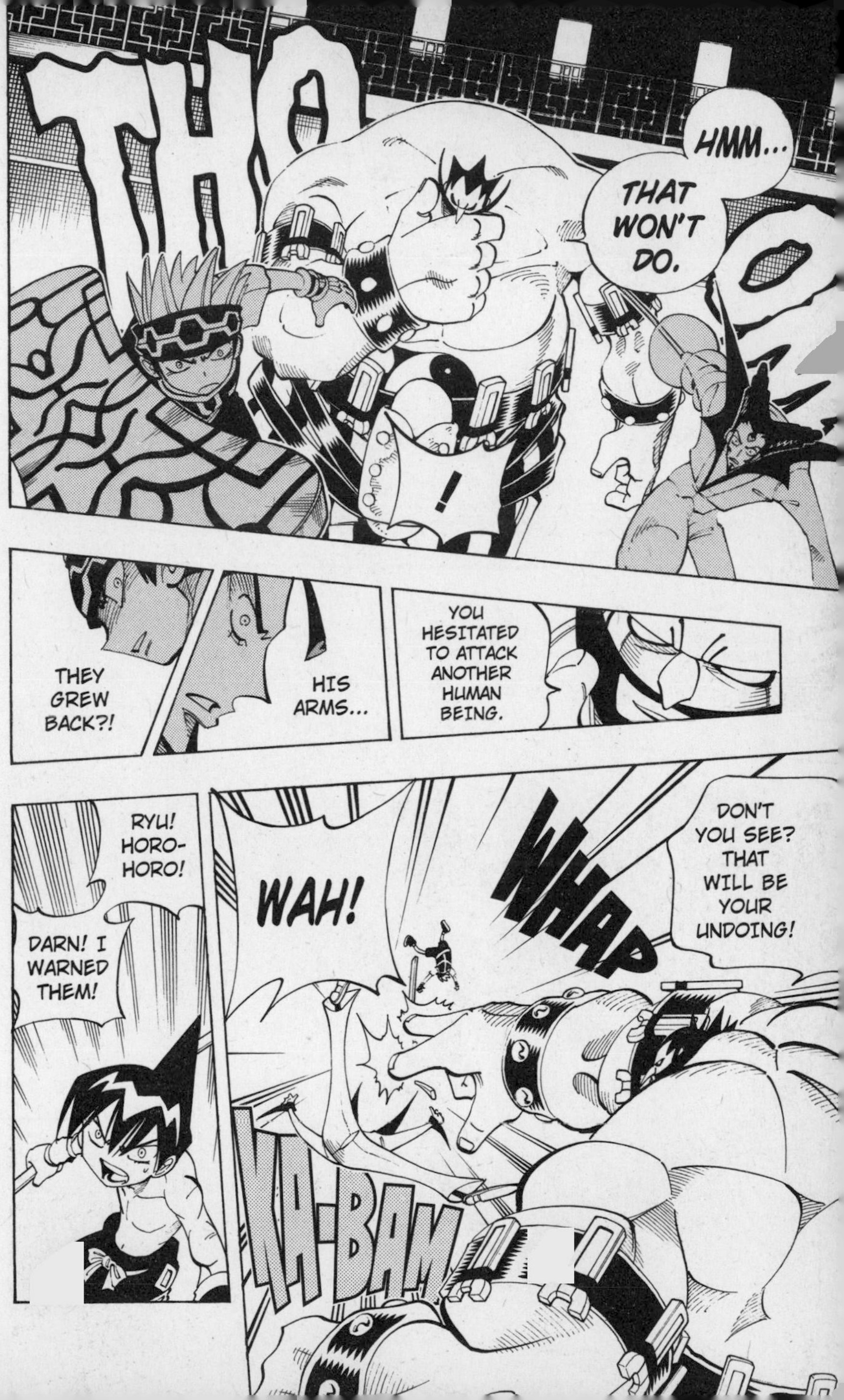
HMM...
THAT WON'T DO.
THO
!
YOU HESITATED TO ATTACK ANOTHER HUMAN BEING.
HIS ARMS...
THEY GREW BACK?!
DON'T YOU SEE? THAT WILL BE YOUR UNDOING!
WHAP
WAH!
KA-BAM
RYU! HORO-HORO!
DARN! I WARNED THEM!

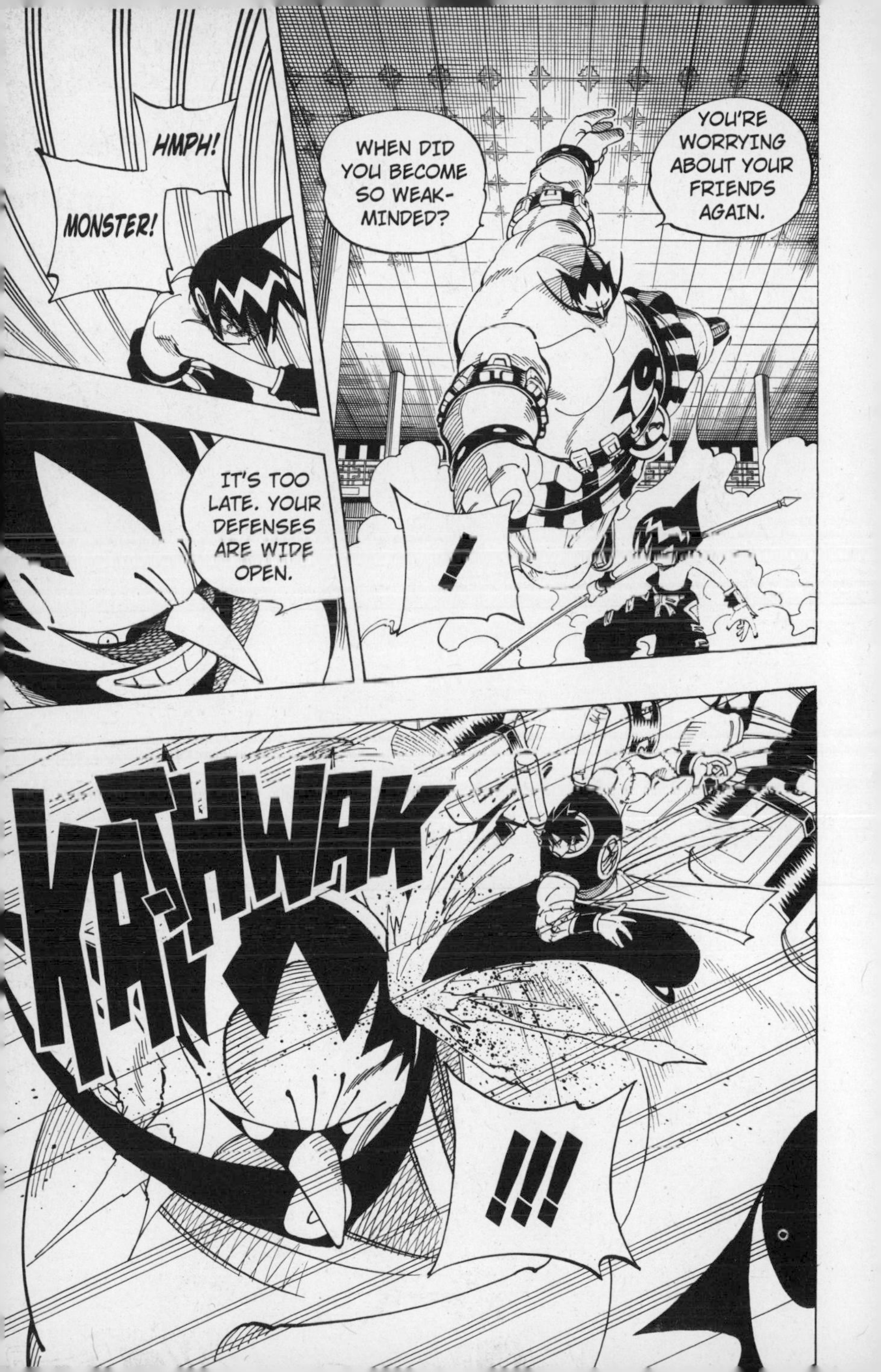
YOU'RE WORRYING ABOUT YOUR FRIENDS AGAIN.
WHEN DID YOU BECOME SO WEAK-MINDED?
!
HMPH!
MONSTER!
IT'S TOO LATE. YOUR DEFENSES ARE WIDE OPEN.
KA-HWAK
!!!

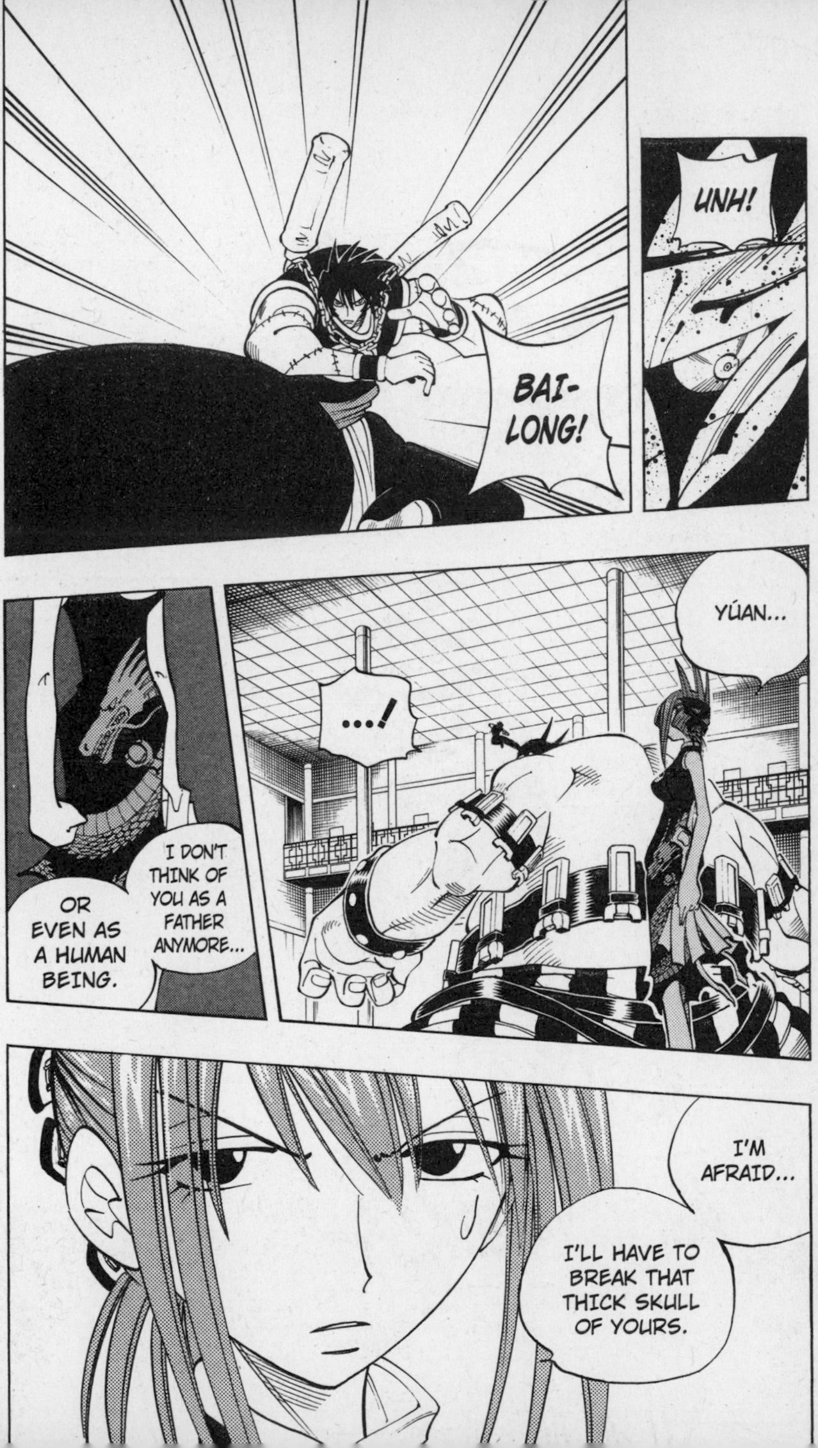
UNH!
BAI-LONG!
YÚAN...
...!
I DON'T THINK OF YOU AS A FATHER ANYMORE...
OR EVEN AS A HUMAN BEING.
I'M AFRAID...
I'LL HAVE TO BREAK THAT THICK SKULL OF YOURS.

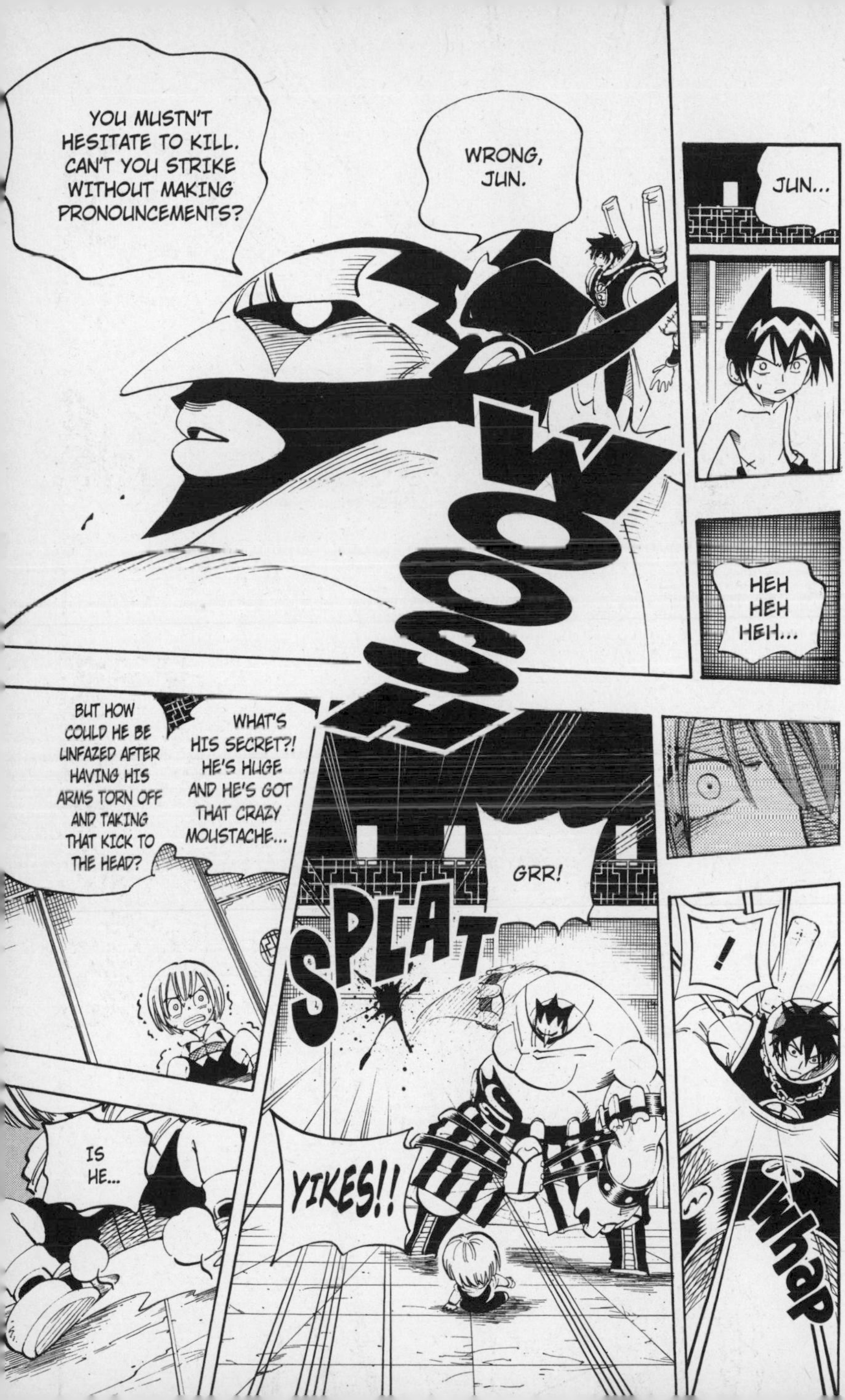
JUN...
HEH HEH HEH...
WRONG, JUN.
YOU MUSTN'T HESITATE TO KILL. CAN'T YOU STRIKE WITHOUT MAKING PRONOUNCEMENTS?
WHOOSH
!
WHAP
GRR!
SPLAT
WHAT'S HIS SECRET?! HE'S HUGE AND HE'S GOT THAT CRAZY MOUSTACHE...
BUT HOW COULD HE BE UNFAZED AFTER HAVING HIS ARMS TORN OFF AND TAKING THAT KICK TO THE HEAD?
YIKES!!
IS HE...

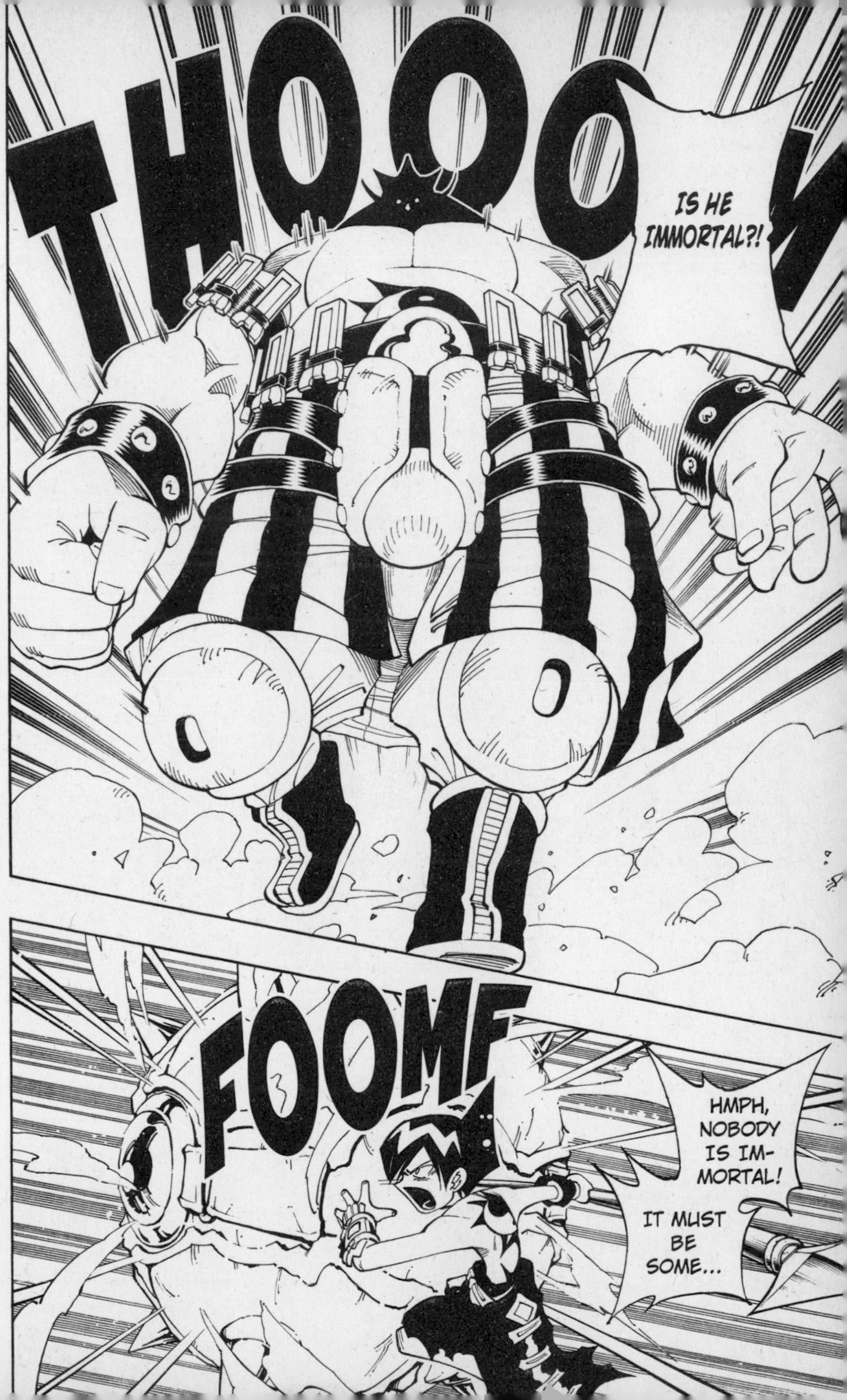
THOOOM
IS HE IMMORTAL?!
FOOMF
HMPH, NOBODY IS IM- MORTAL!
IT MUST BE SOME...

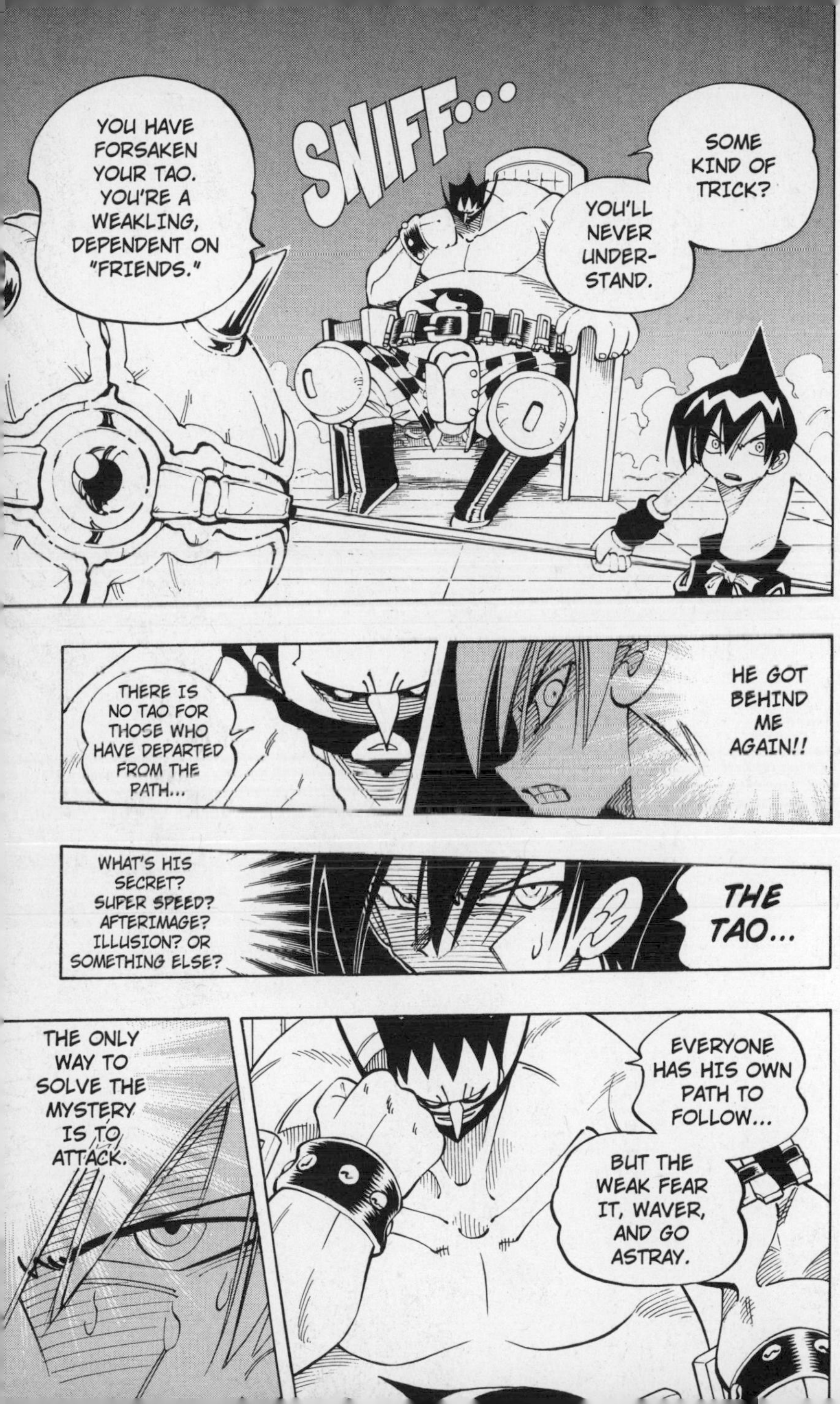
SOME KIND OF TRICK?
YOU'LL NEVER UNDER-STAND.
SNIFF...
YOU HAVE FORSAKEN YOUR TAO. YOU'RE A WEAKLING, DEPENDENT ON "FRIENDS."
HE GOT BEHIND ME AGAIN!!
THERE IS NO TAO FOR THOSE WHO HAVE DEPARTED FROM THE PATH...
THE TAO...
WHAT'S HIS SECRET? SUPER SPEED? AFTERIMAGE? ILLUSION? OR SOMETHING ELSE?
EVERYONE HAS HIS OWN PATH TO FOLLOW...
BUT THE WEAK FEAR IT, WAVER, AND GO ASTRAY.
THE ONLY WAY TO SOLVE THE MYSTERY IS TO ATTACK.

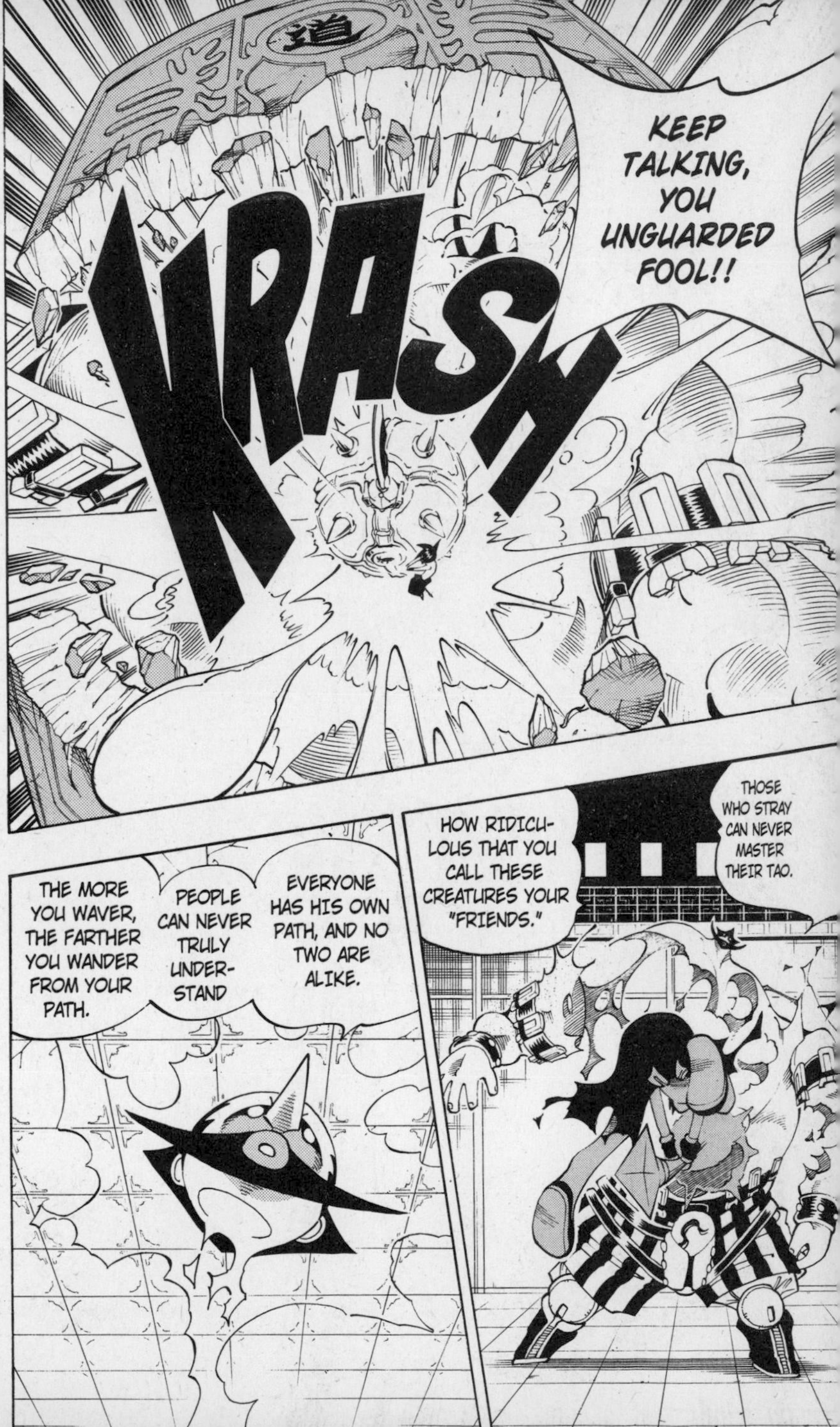
KEEP TALKING, YOU UNGUARDED FOOL!!
道
KRASH
THOSE WHO STRAY CAN NEVER MASTER THEIR TAO.
HOW RIDICU-LOUS THAT YOU CALL THESE CREATURES YOUR "FRIENDS."
EVERYONE HAS HIS OWN PATH, AND NO TWO ARE ALIKE.
PEOPLE CAN NEVER TRULY UNDER-STAND
THE MORE YOU WAVER, THE FARTHER YOU WANDER FROM YOUR PATH.

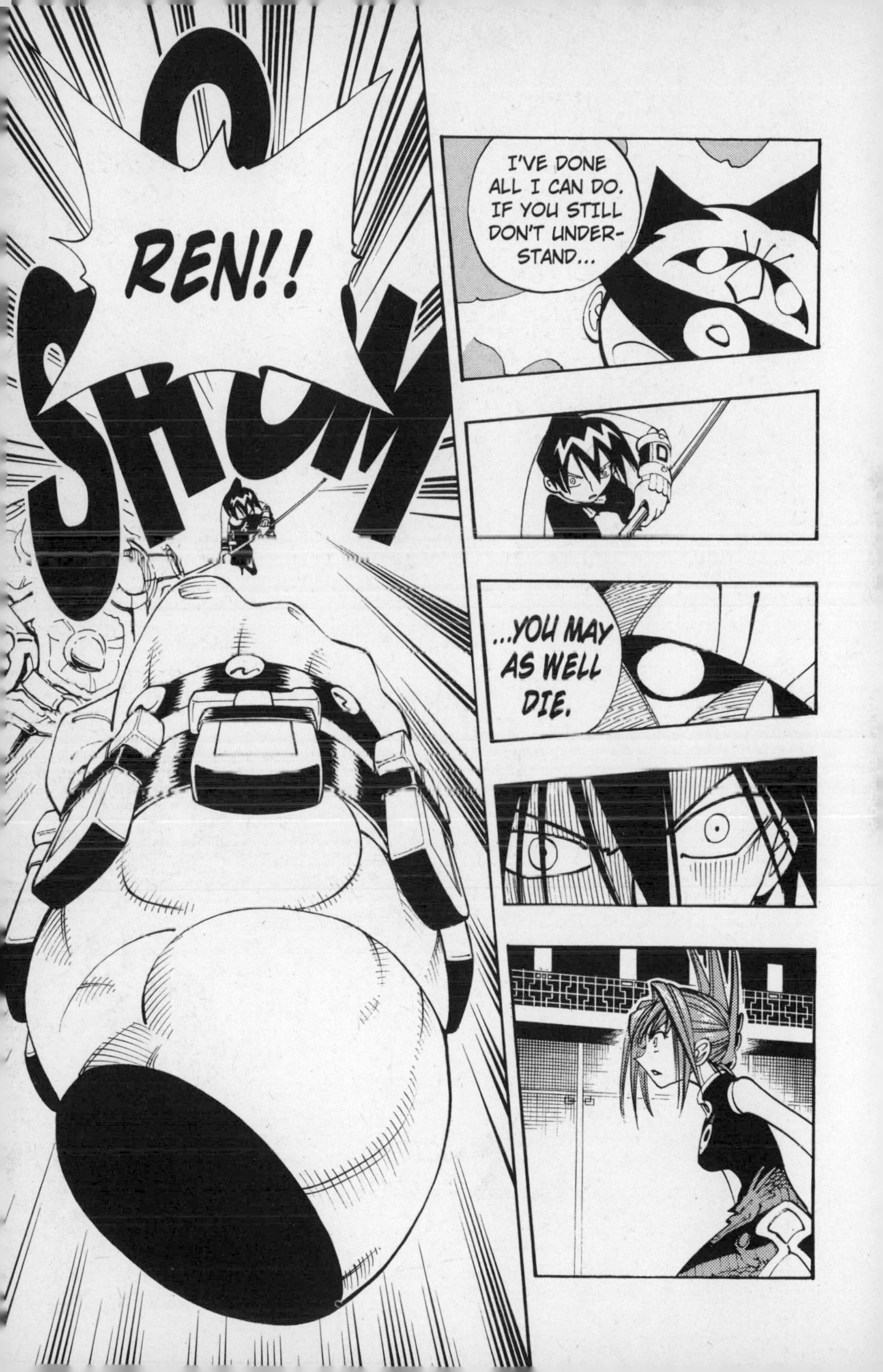
I'VE DONE ALL I CAN DO. IF YOU STILL DON'T UNDER-STAND...
...YOU MAY AS WELL DIE.
REN!!

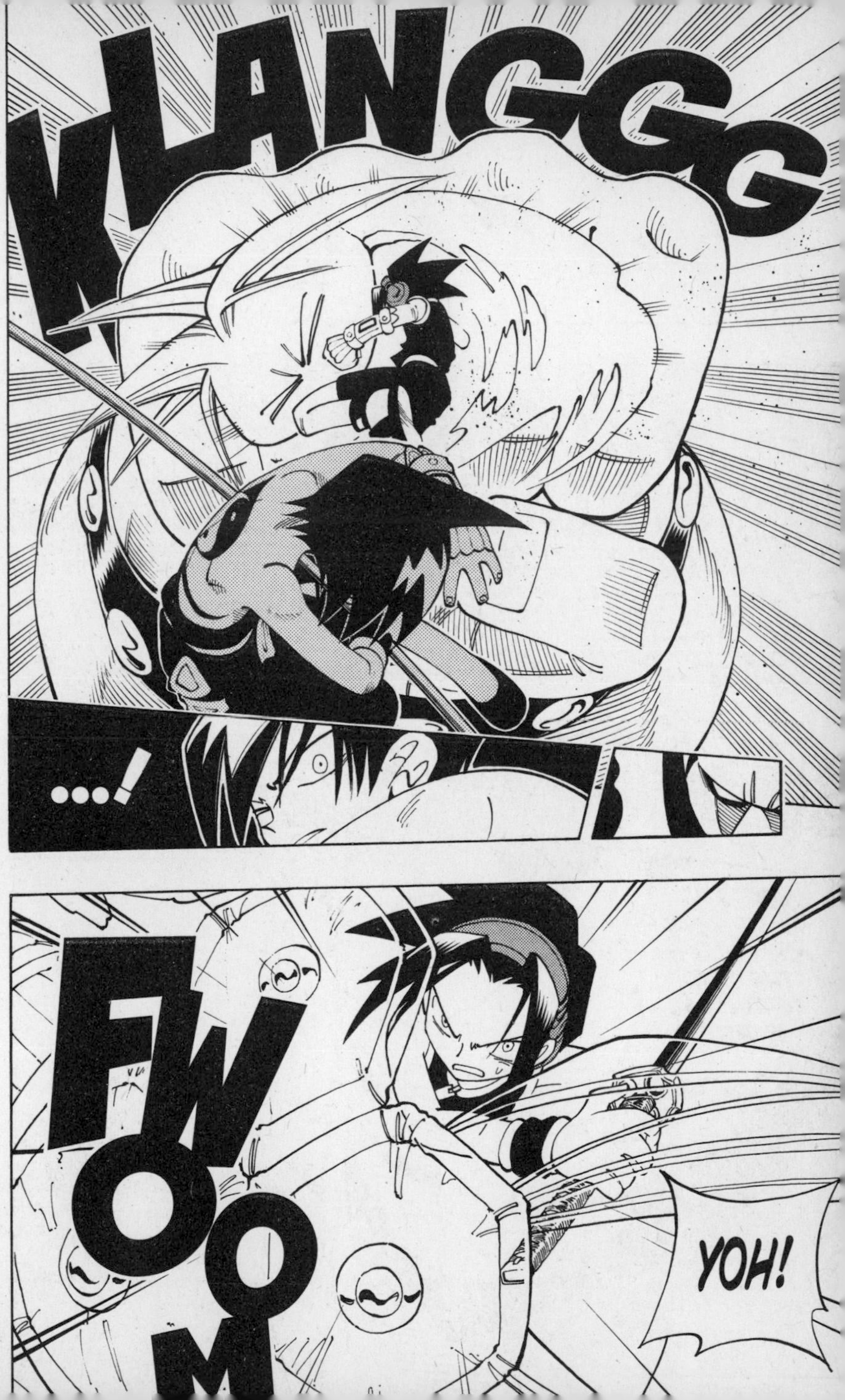
KLANGG
...!
YOH!
FWOOM

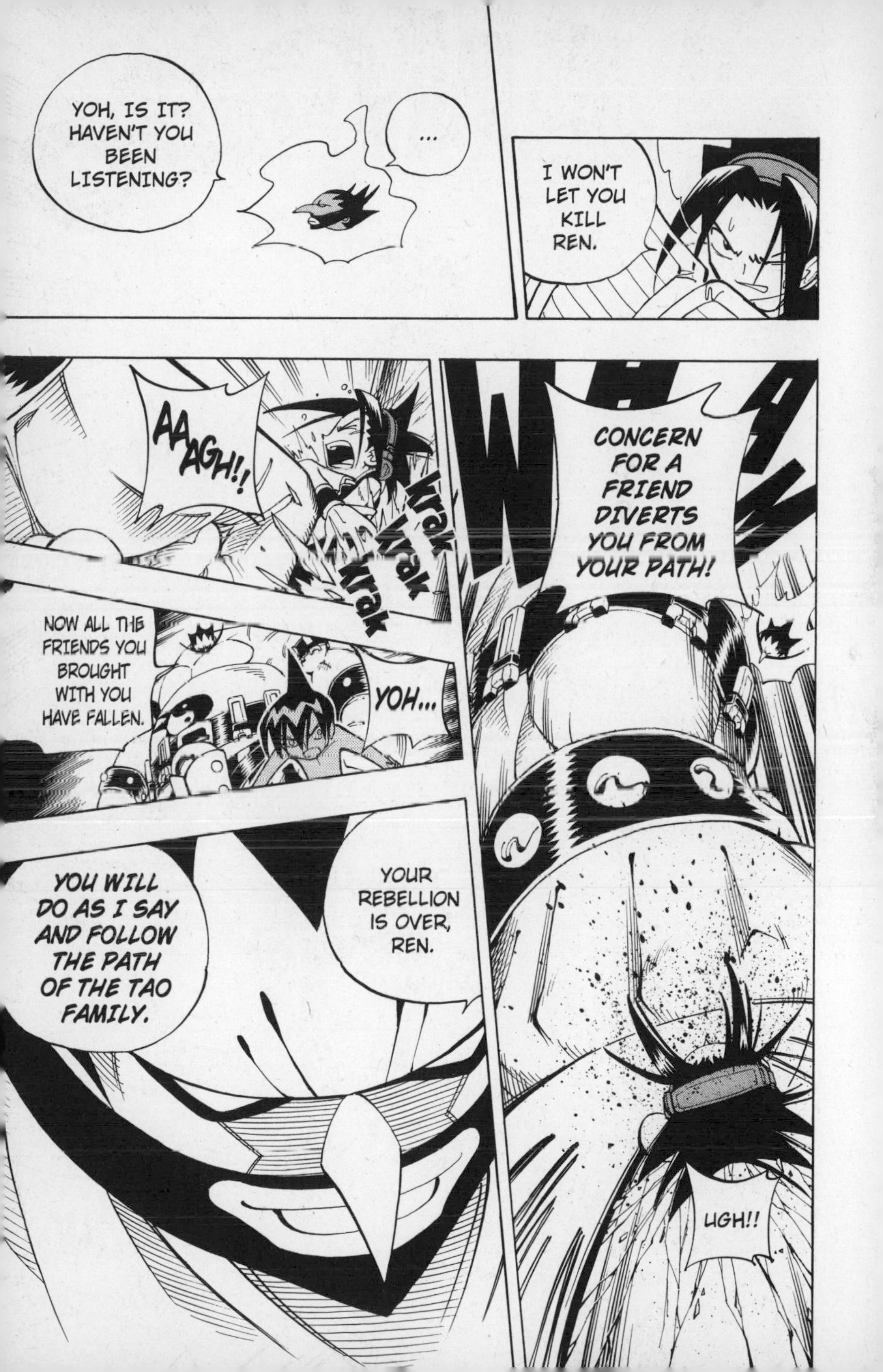
I WON'T LET YOU KILL REN.
...
YOH, IS IT? HAVEN'T YOU BEEN LISTENING?
CONCERN FOR A FRIEND DIVERTS YOU FROM YOUR PATH!
UGH!!
AAAGH!!
krak krak krak
NOW ALL THE FRIENDS YOU BROUGHT WITH YOU HAVE FALLEN.
YOH...
YOUR REBELLION IS OVER, REN.
YOU WILL DO AS I SAY AND FOLLOW THE PATH OF THE TAO FAMILY.

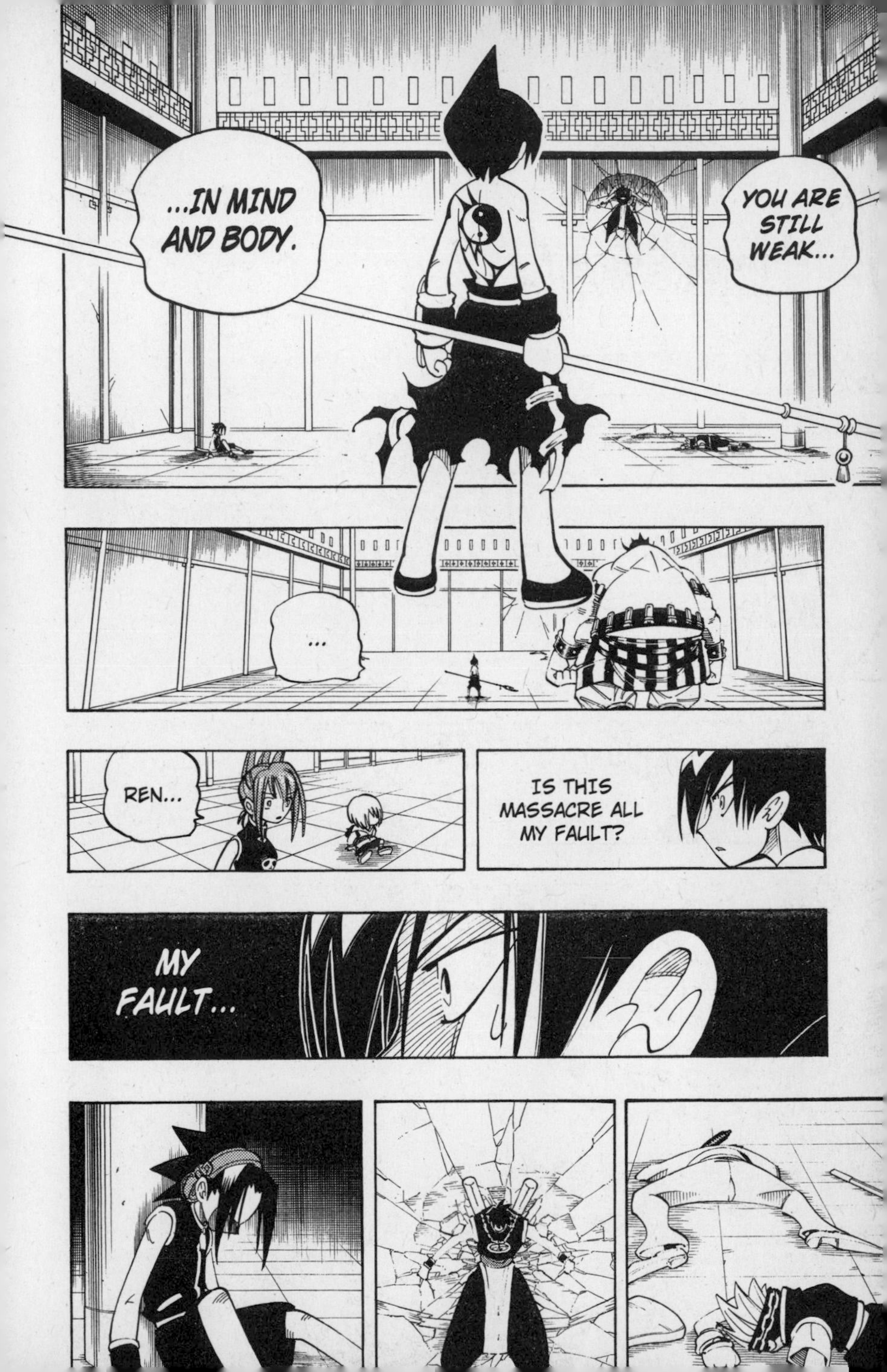
YOU ARE STILL WEAK...
...IN MIND AND BODY.
...
IS THIS MASSACRE ALL MY FAULT?
REN...
MY FAULT...

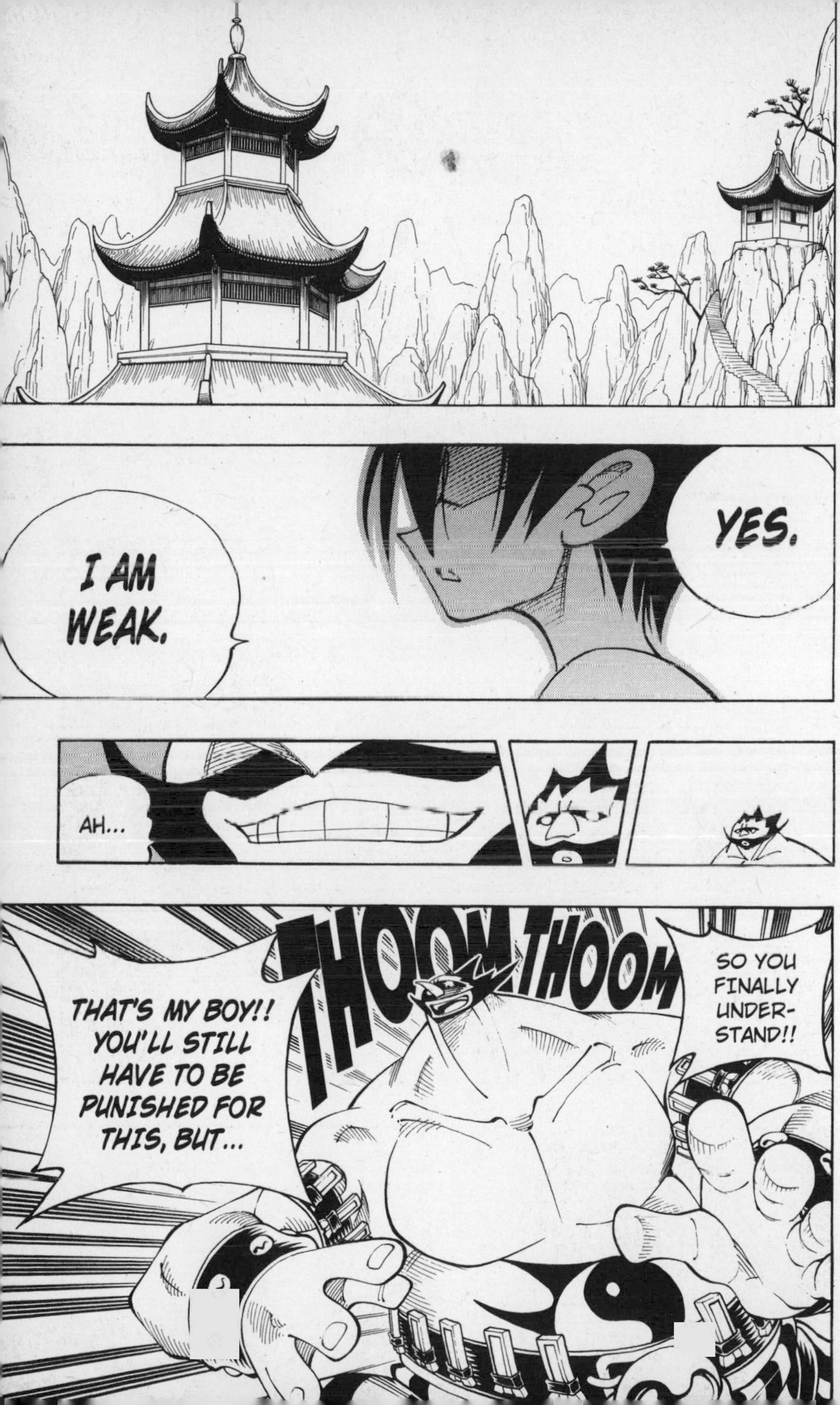
YES.
I AM WEAK.
AH...
SO YOU FINALLY UNDER-STAND!!
THOOM THOOM
THAT'S MY BOY!! YOU'LL STILL HAVE TO BE PUNISHED FOR THIS, BUT...

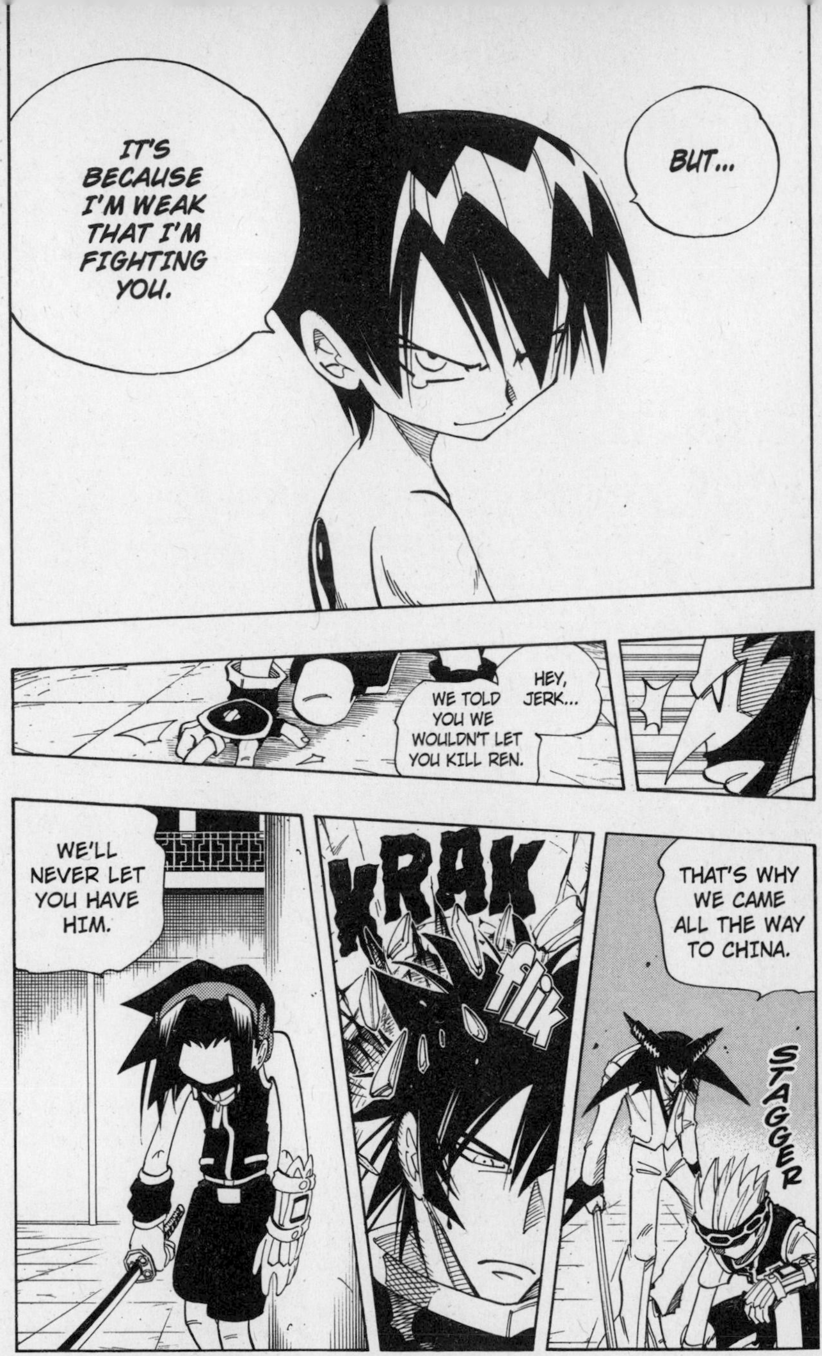
BUT...
IT'S BECAUSE I'M WEAK THAT I'M FIGHTING YOU.
HEY, JERK...
WE TOLD YOU WE WOULDN'T LET YOU KILL REN.
THAT'S WHY WE CAME ALL THE WAY TO CHINA.
STAGGER
KRAK
flik
WE'LL NEVER LET YOU HAVE HIM.

READ THIS WAY

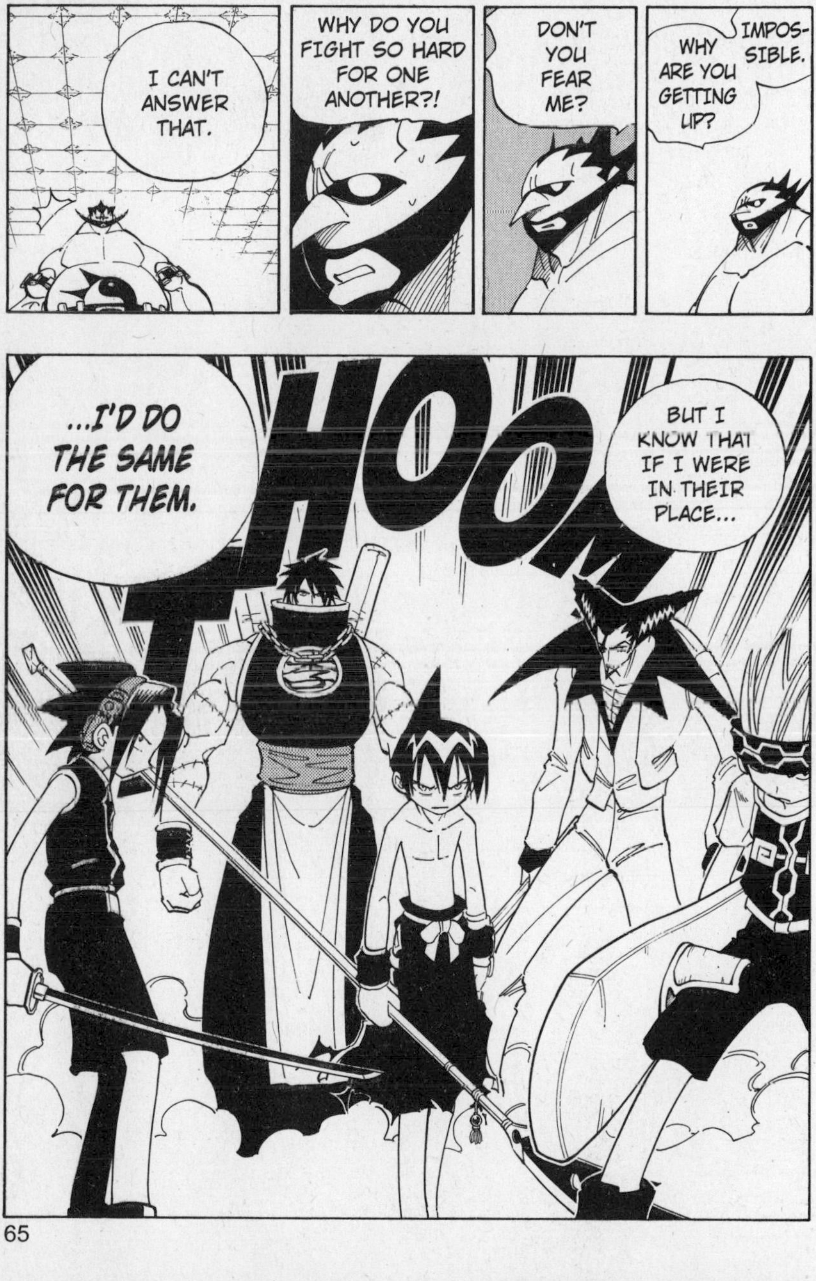
IMPOS-SIBLE.
WHY ARE YOU GETTING UP?
DON'T YOU FEAR ME?
WHY DO YOU FIGHT SO HARD FOR ONE ANOTHER?!
I CAN'T ANSWER THAT.
BUT I KNOW THAT IF I WERE IN THEIR PLACE...
THOOM
...I'D DO THE SAME FOR THEM.

SHAMAN
KING
**9**

TAO CASTLE

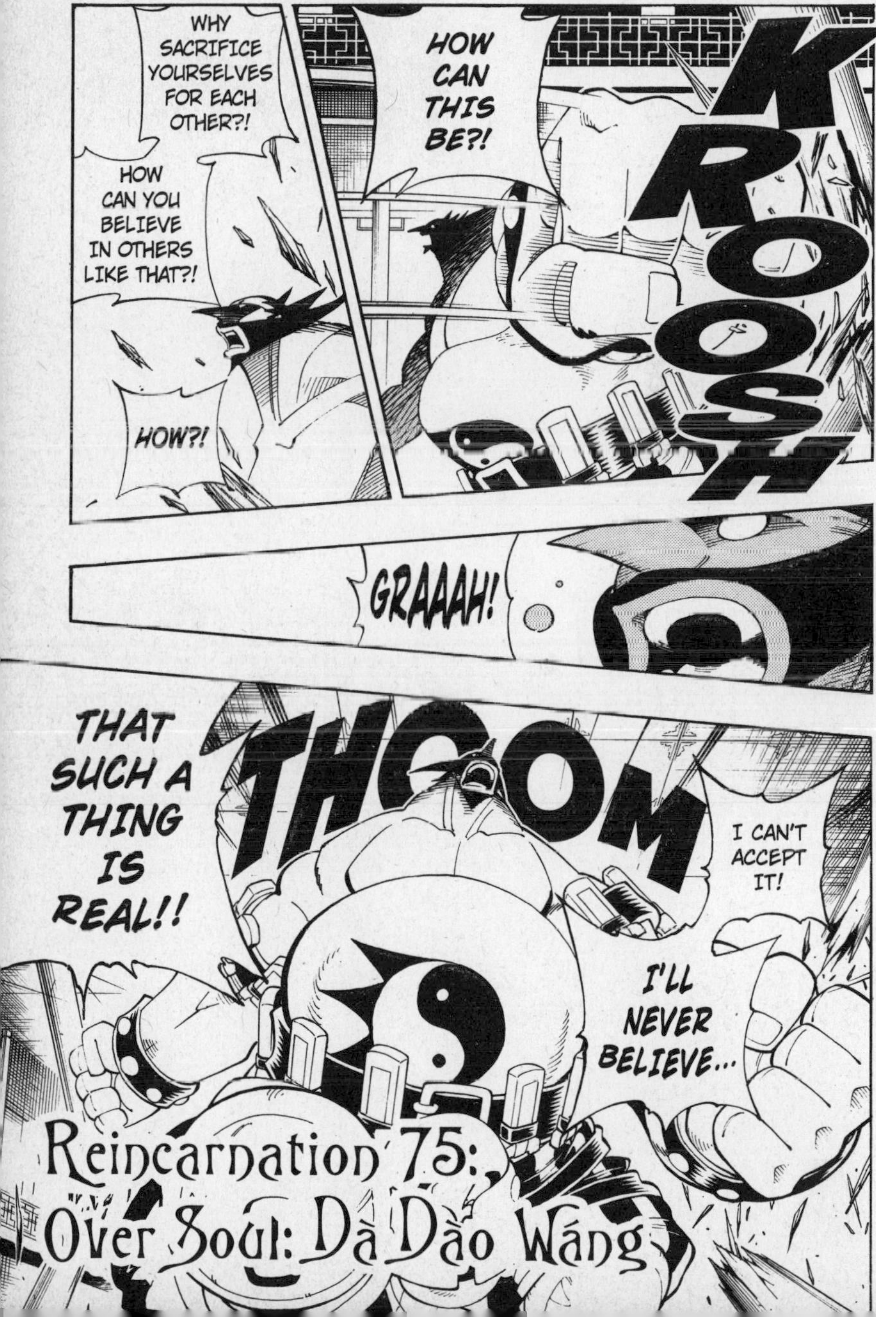
KROOSH
HOW CAN THIS BE?!
WHY SACRIFICE YOURSELVES FOR EACH OTHER?!
HOW CAN YOU BELIEVE IN OTHERS LIKE THAT?!
HOW?!
GRAAAH!
I CAN'T ACCEPT IT!
THOOM
I'LL NEVER BELIEVE...
THAT SUCH A THING IS REAL!!

# Reincarnation 75: Over Soul: Dà Dǎo Wáng

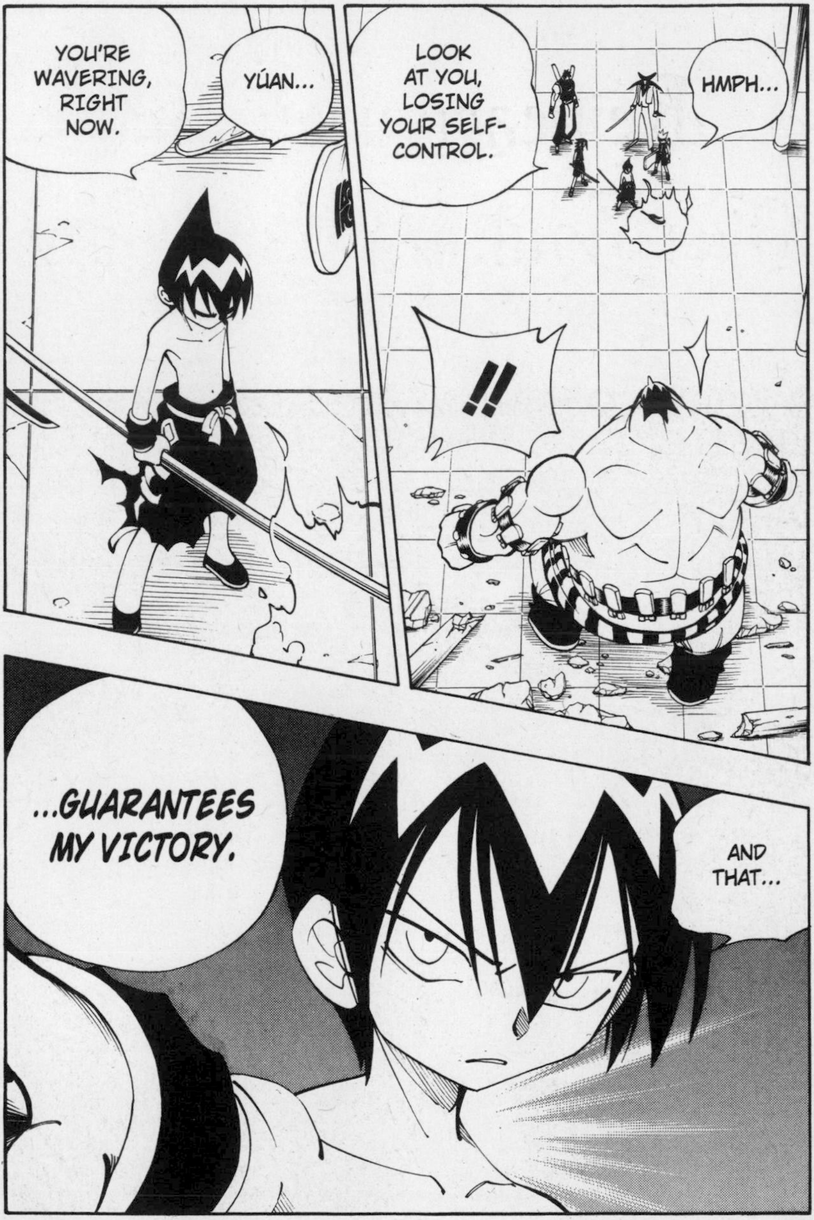
HMPH...
LOOK AT YOU, LOSING YOUR SELF-CONTROL.
!!
YÚAN...
YOU'RE WAVERING, RIGHT NOW.
AND THAT...
...GUARANTEES MY VICTORY.

# Reincarnation 75: Over Soul: Dà Dào Wáng

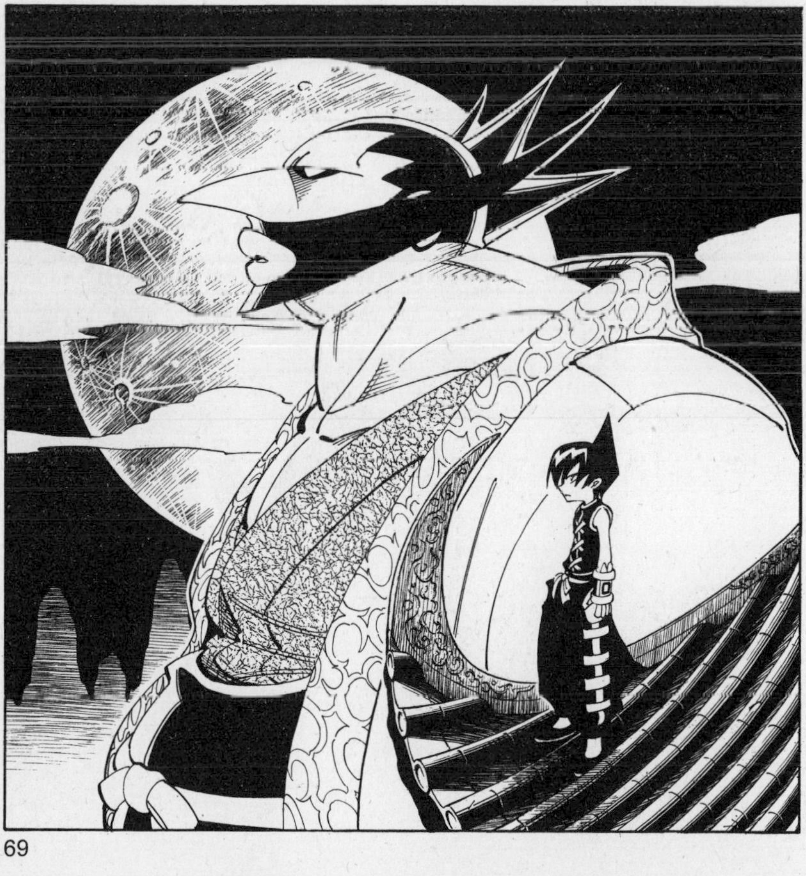

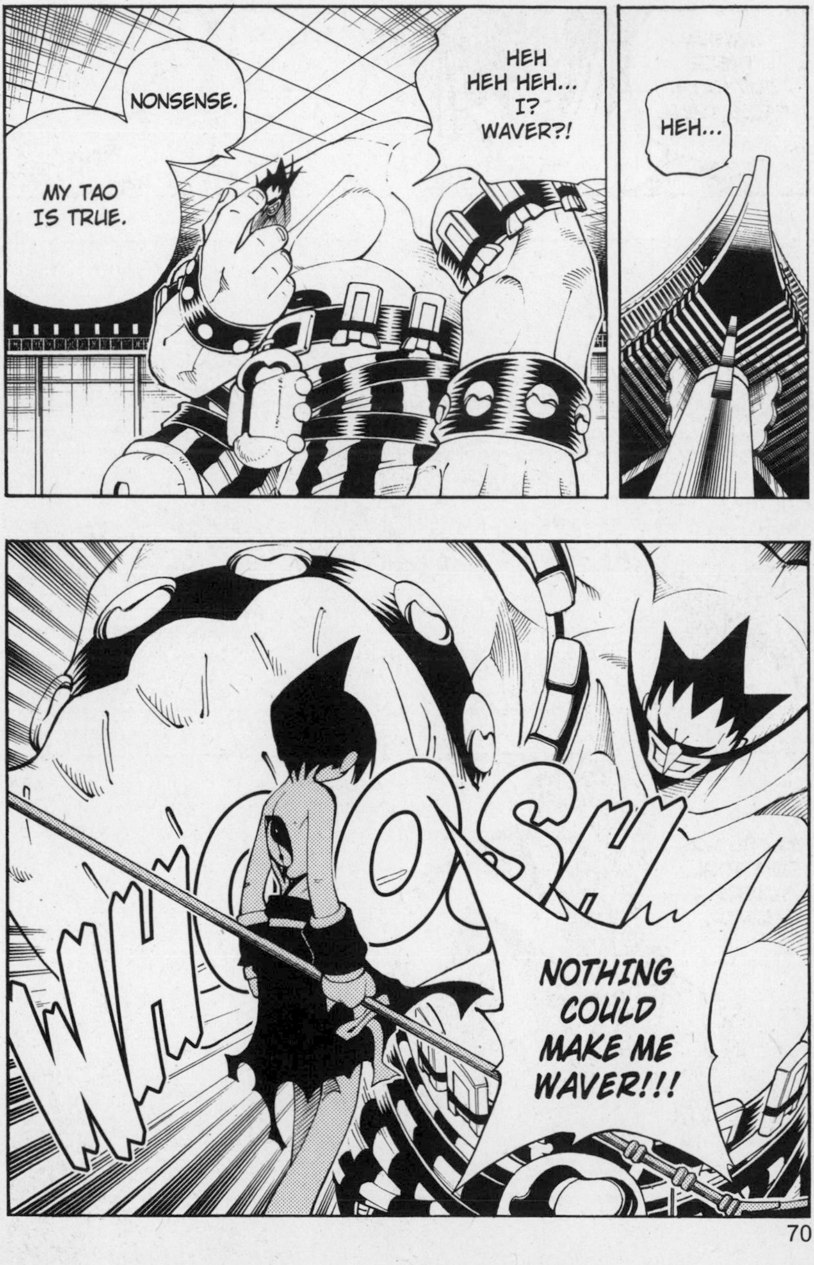
HEH...
HEH HEH HEH... I? WAVER?!
NONSENSE.
MY TAO IS TRUE.
WHOOSH
NOTHING COULD MAKE ME WAVER!!!

READ THIS WAY

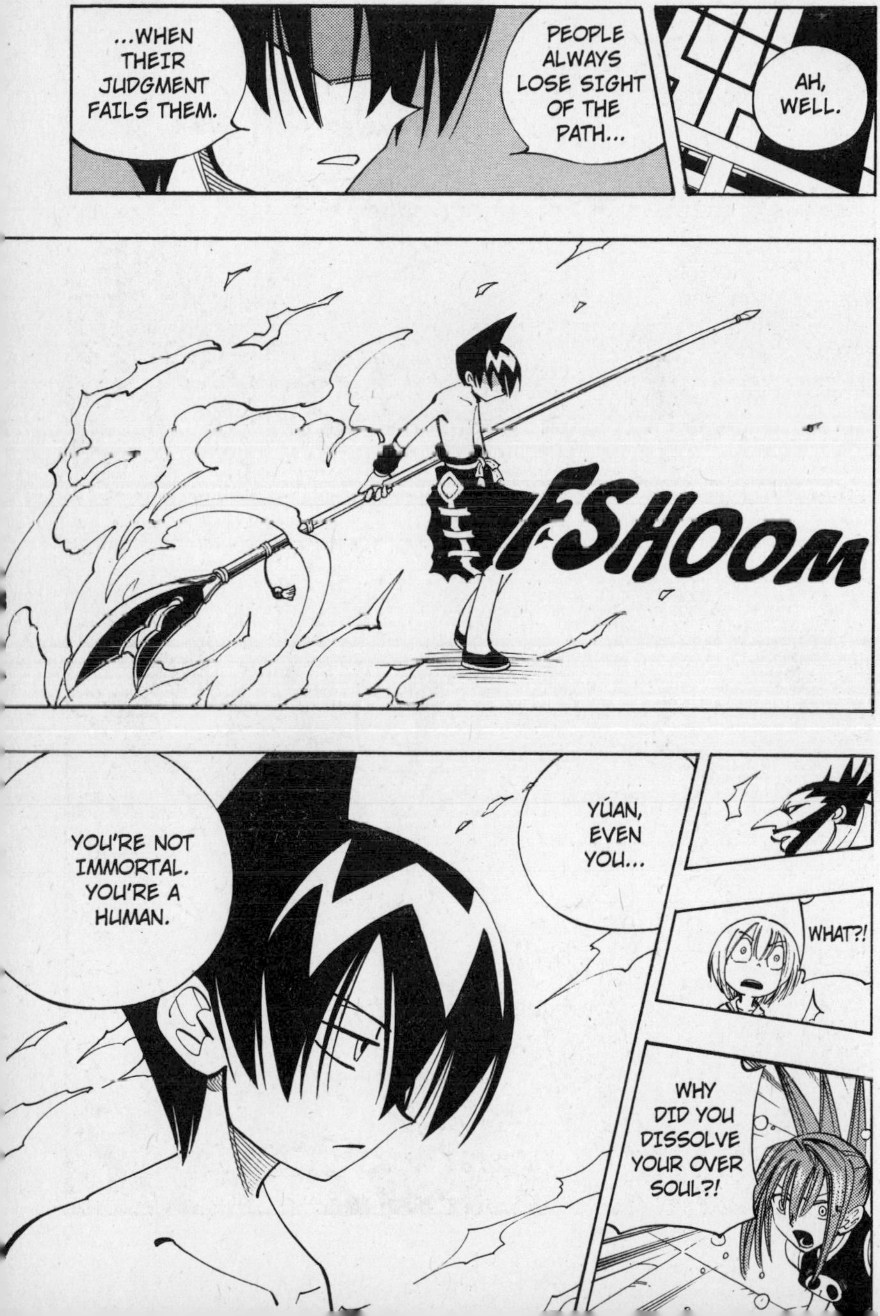
AH, WELL.
PEOPLE ALWAYS LOSE SIGHT OF THE PATH...
...WHEN THEIR JUDGMENT FAILS THEM.
FSHOOM
WHAT?!
WHY DID YOU DISSOLVE YOUR OVER SOUL?!
YÚAN, EVEN YOU...
YOU'RE NOT IMMORTAL. YOU'RE A HUMAN.

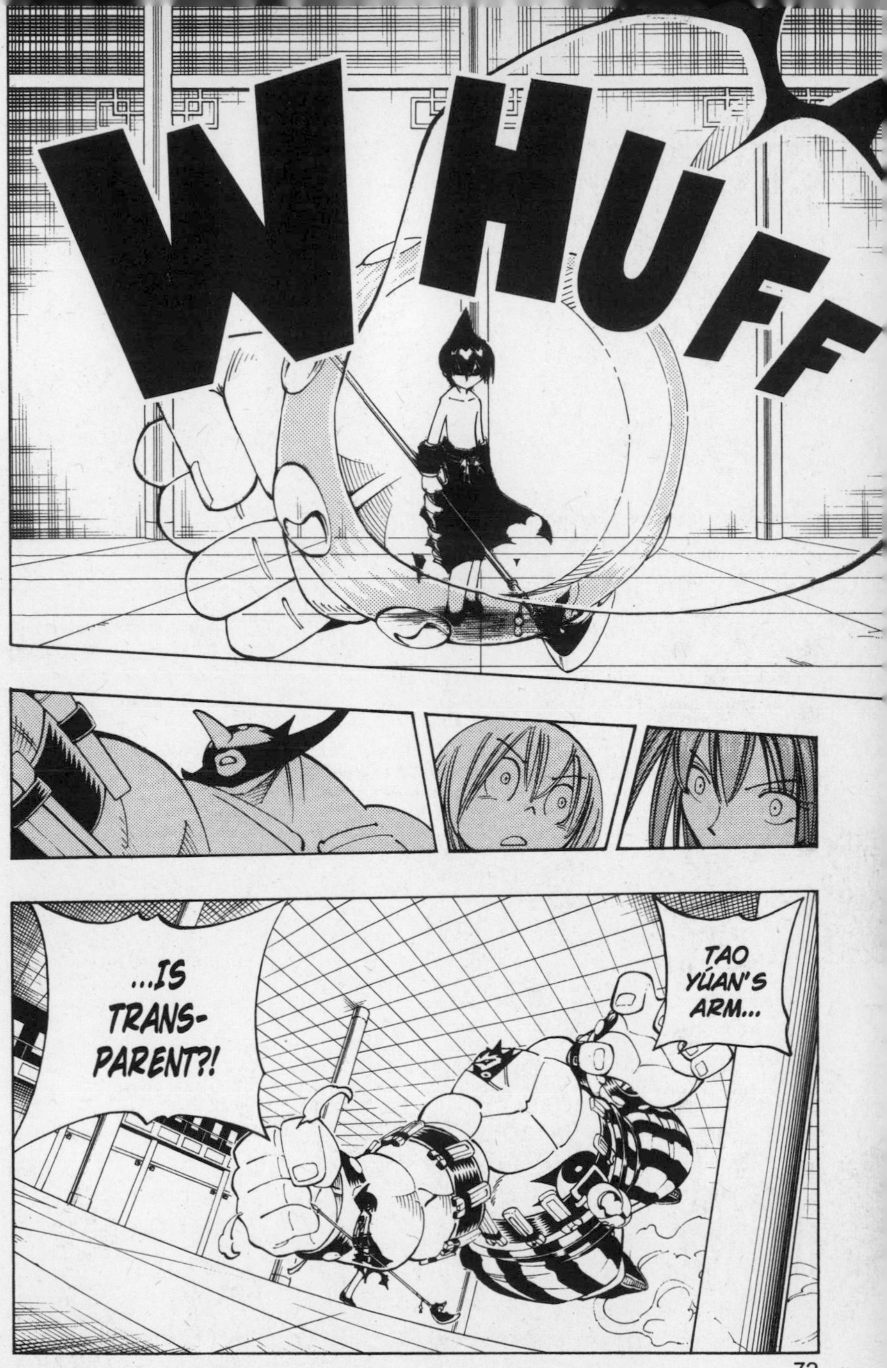
WHUFF
TAO YÚAN'S ARM...
...IS TRANS-PARENT?!

READ THIS WAY

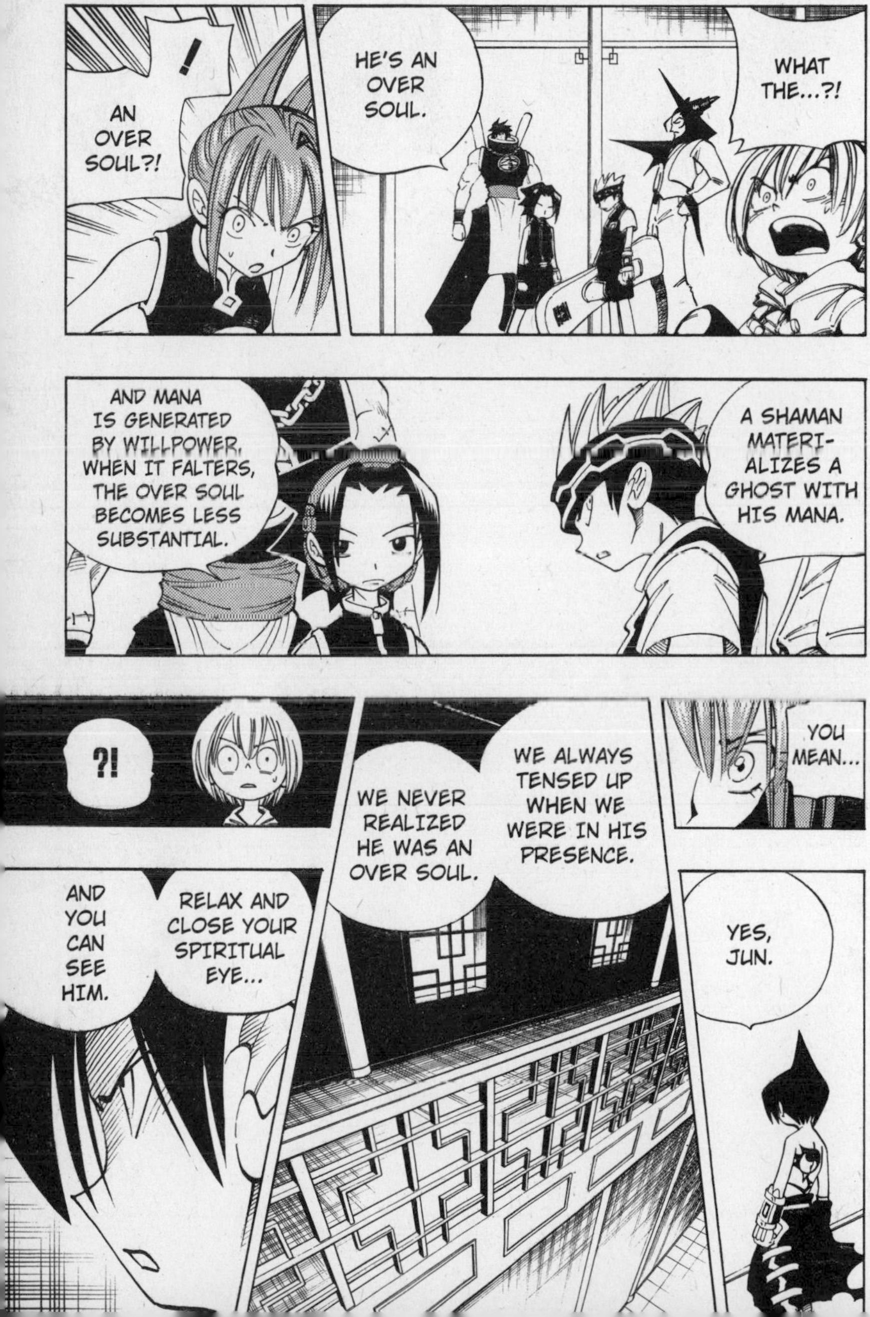
WHAT THE...?!
HE'S AN OVER SOUL.
!
AN OVER SOUL?!
A SHAMAN MATERIALIZES A GHOST WITH HIS MANA.
AND MANA IS GENERATED BY WILLPOWER. WHEN IT FALTERS, THE OVER SOUL BECOMES LESS SUBSTANTIAL.
YOU MEAN...
YES, JUN.
WE ALWAYS TENSED UP WHEN WE WERE IN HIS PRESENCE.
WE NEVER REALIZED HE WAS AN OVER SOUL.
?!
RELAX AND CLOSE YOUR SPIRITUAL EYE...
AND YOU CAN SEE HIM.

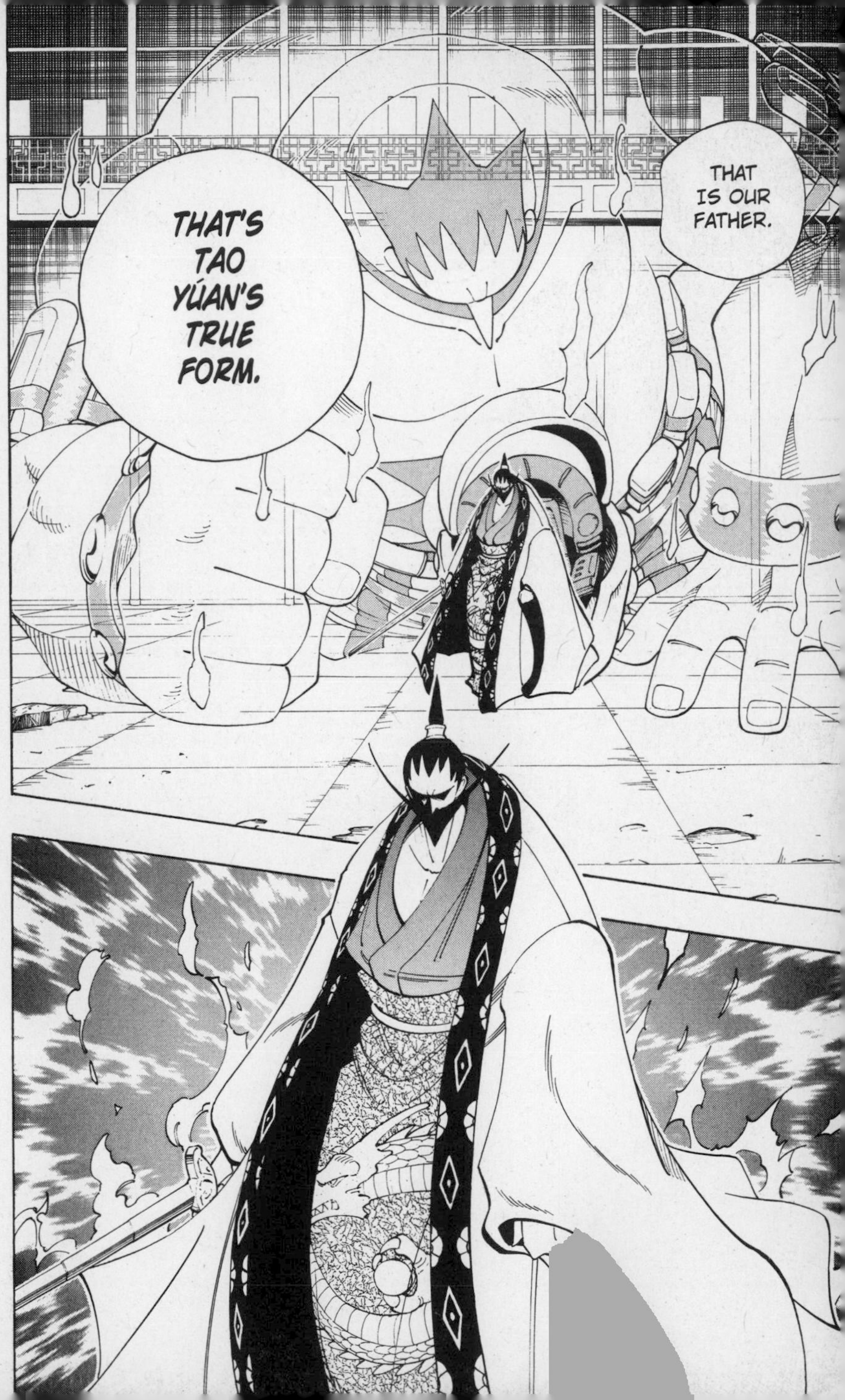
THAT IS OUR FATHER.
THAT'S TAO YÚAN'S TRUE FORM.

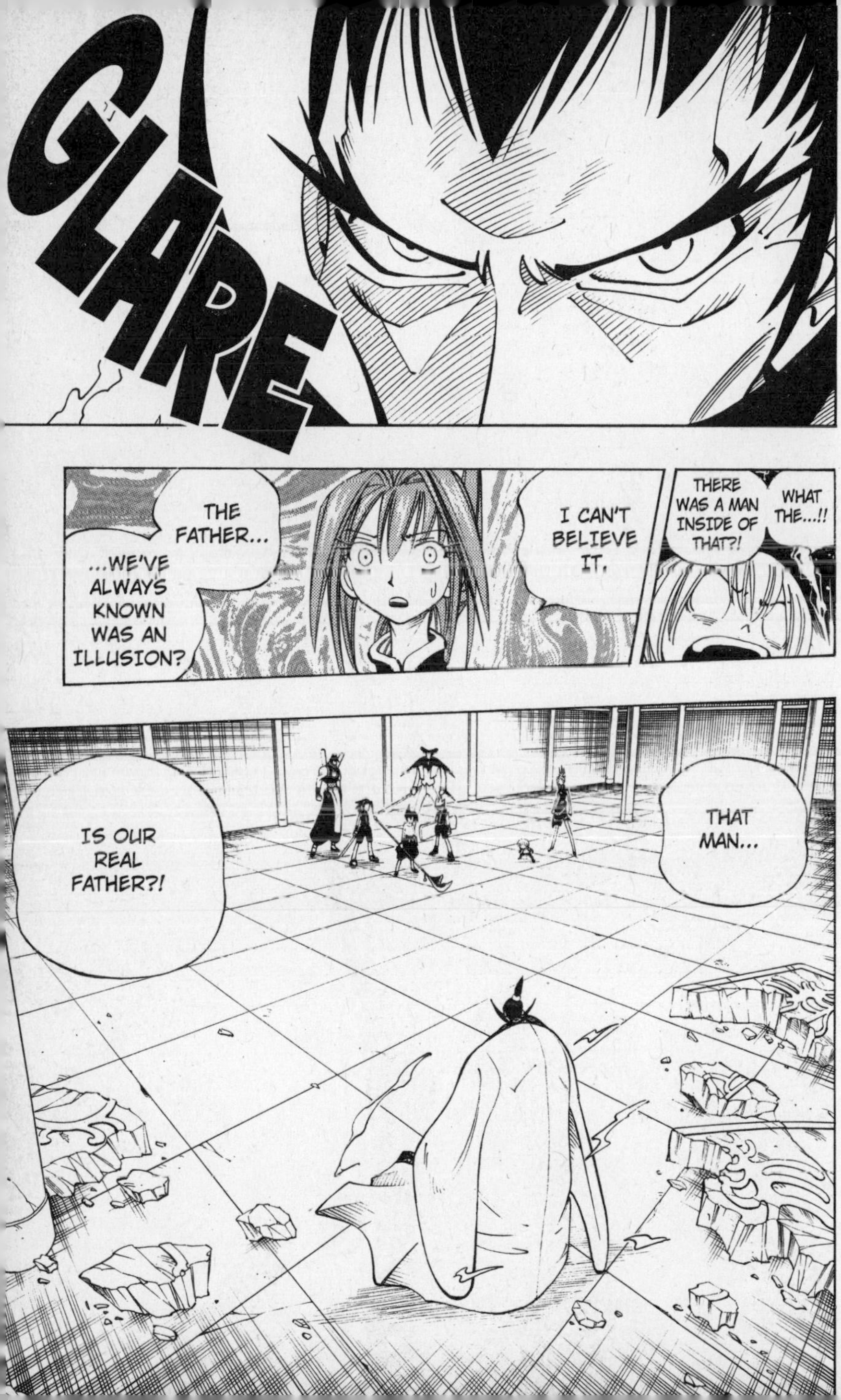
GLARE
WHAT THE...!!
THERE WAS A MAN INSIDE OF THAT?!
I CAN'T BELIEVE IT.
THE FATHER...
...WE'VE ALWAYS KNOWN WAS AN ILLUSION?
THAT MAN...
IS OUR REAL FATHER?!

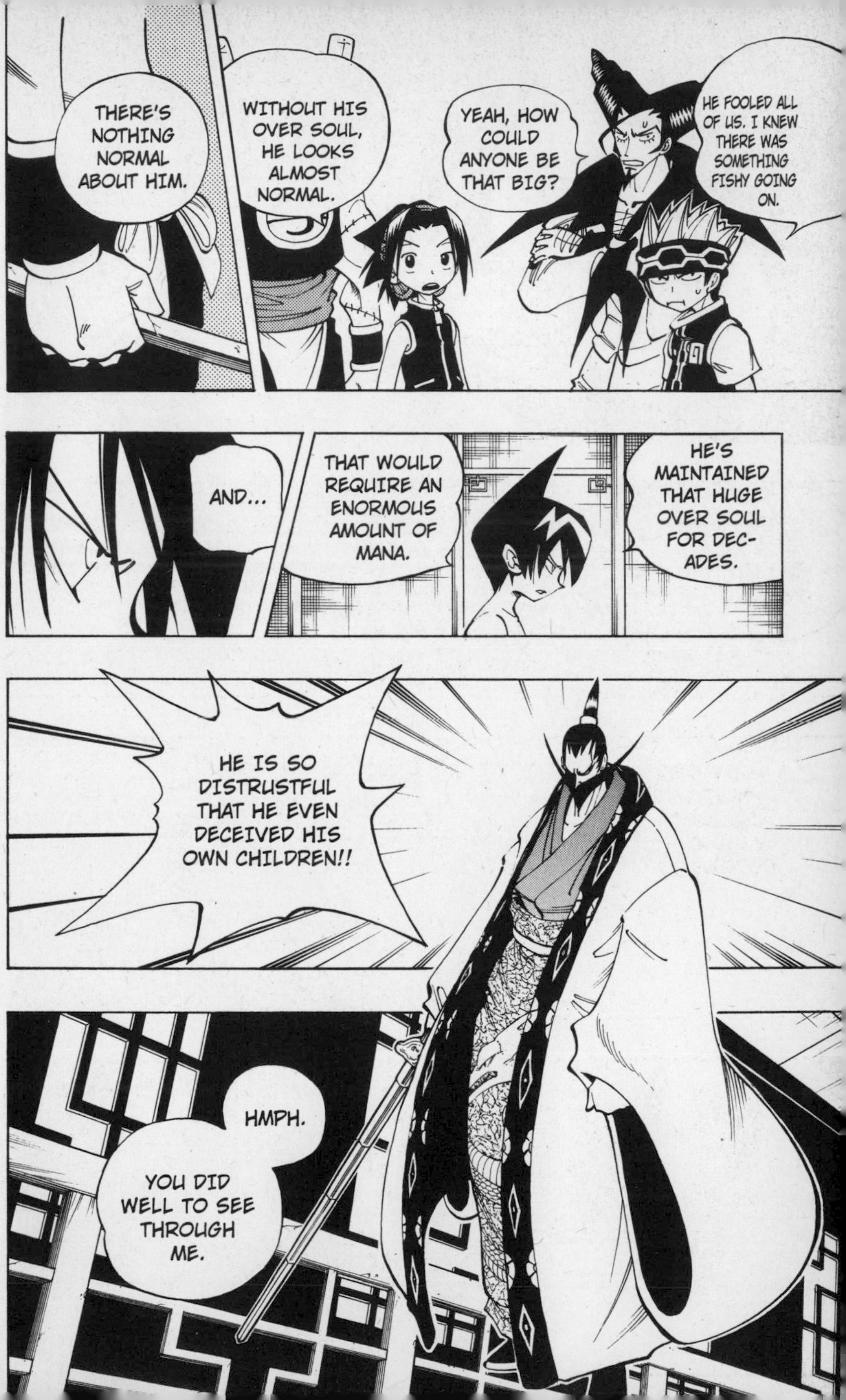
HE FOOLED ALL OF US. I KNEW THERE WAS SOMETHING FISHY GOING ON.
YEAH, HOW COULD ANYONE BE THAT BIG?
WITHOUT HIS OVER SOUL, HE LOOKS ALMOST NORMAL.
THERE'S NOTHING NORMAL ABOUT HIM.
HE'S MAINTAINED THAT HUGE OVER SOUL FOR DEC-ADES.
THAT WOULD REQUIRE AN ENORMOUS AMOUNT OF MANA.
AND...
HE IS SO DISTRUSTFUL THAT HE EVEN DECEIVED HIS OWN CHILDREN!!
HMPH.
YOU DID WELL TO SEE THROUGH ME.

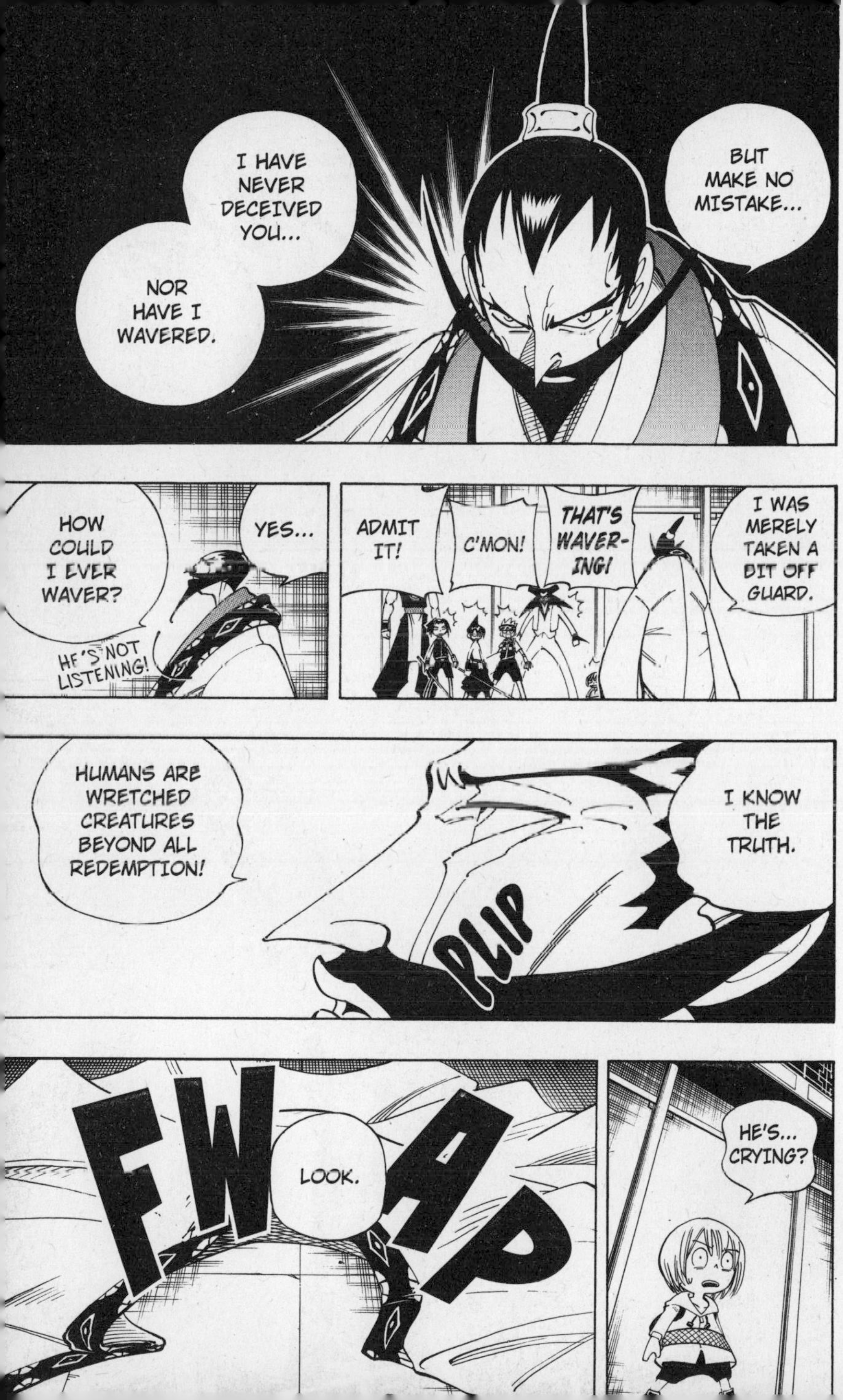
BUT MAKE NO MISTAKE...
I HAVE NEVER DECEIVED YOU...
NOR HAVE I WAVERED.
I WAS MERELY TAKEN A BIT OFF GUARD.
THAT'S WAVERING!
C'MON!
ADMIT IT!
YES...
HOW COULD I EVER WAVER?
HE'S NOT LISTENING!
I KNOW THE TRUTH.
HUMANS ARE WRETCHED CREATURES BEYOND ALL REDEMPTION!
PLIP
HE'S... CRYING?
FWAP
LOOK.

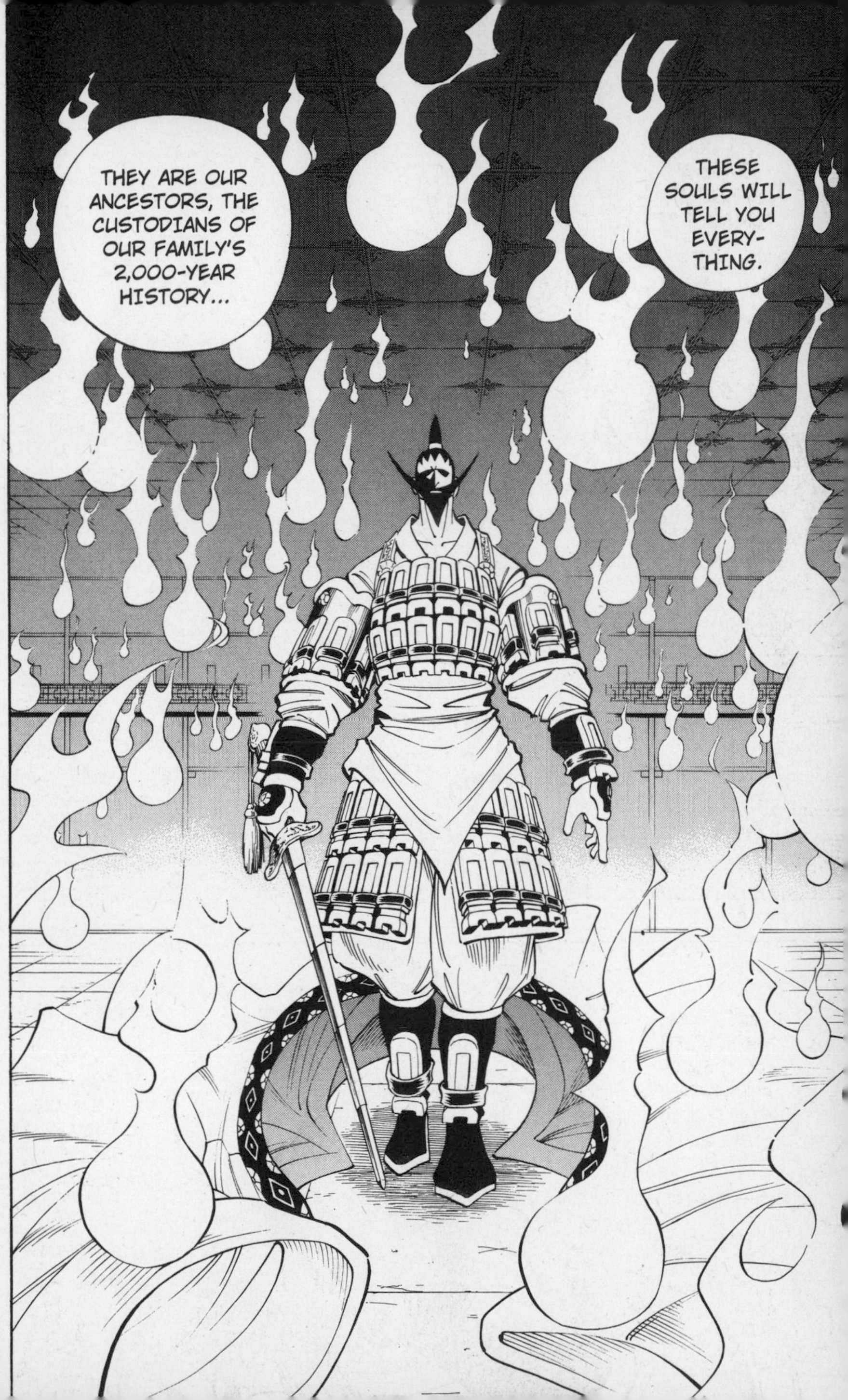
THESE SOULS WILL TELL YOU EVERY-THING.
THEY ARE OUR ANCESTORS, THE CUSTODIANS OF OUR FAMILY'S 2,000-YEAR HISTORY...

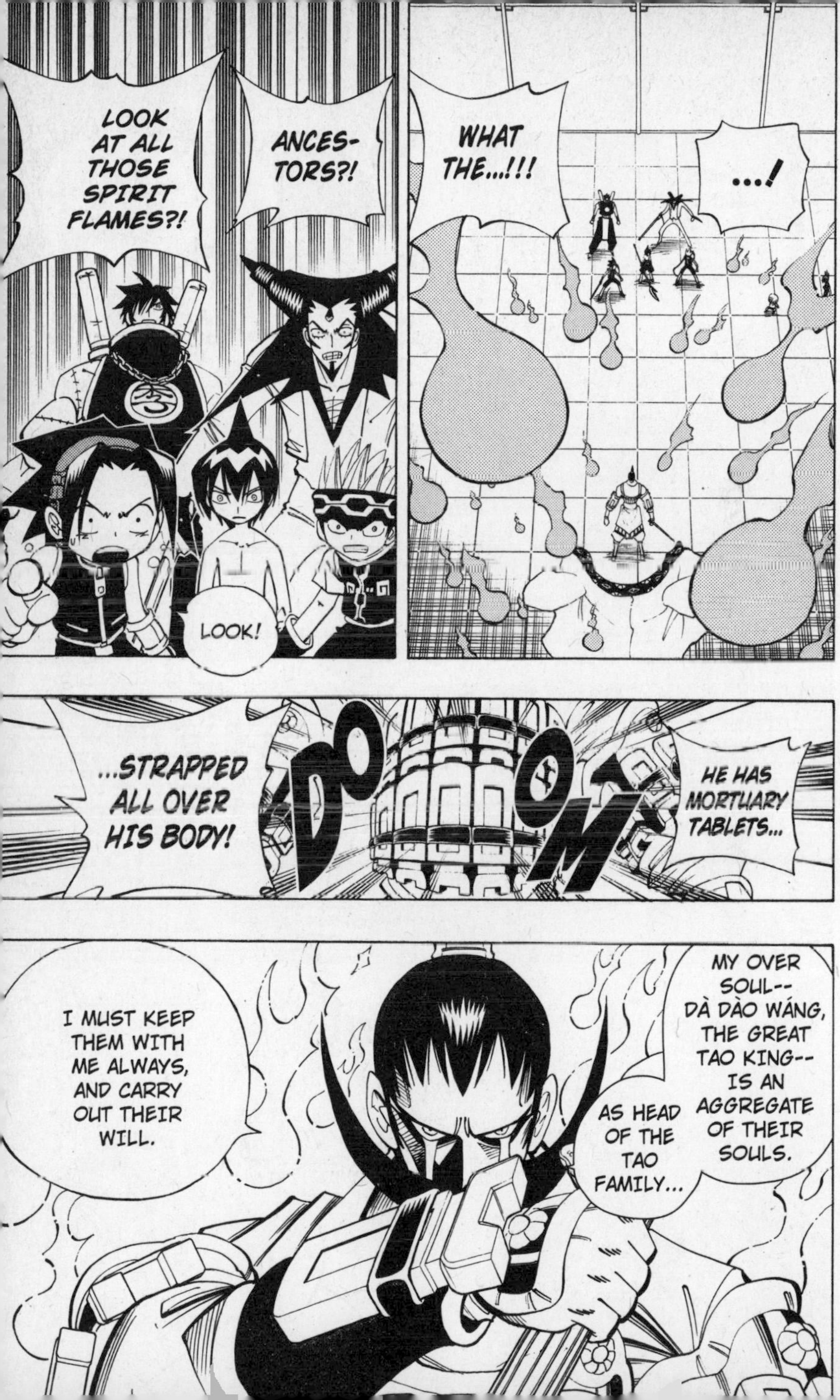
...!
WHAT THE...!!!
ANCES-TORS?!
LOOK AT ALL THOSE SPIRIT FLAMES?!
LOOK!
HE HAS MORTUARY TABLETS...
DOOOM
...STRAPPED ALL OVER HIS BODY!
MY OVER SOUL-- DÀ DÀO WÁNG, THE GREAT TAO KING-- IS AN AGGREGATE OF THEIR SOULS.
AS HEAD OF THE TAO FAMILY...
I MUST KEEP THEM WITH ME ALWAYS, AND CARRY OUT THEIR WILL.

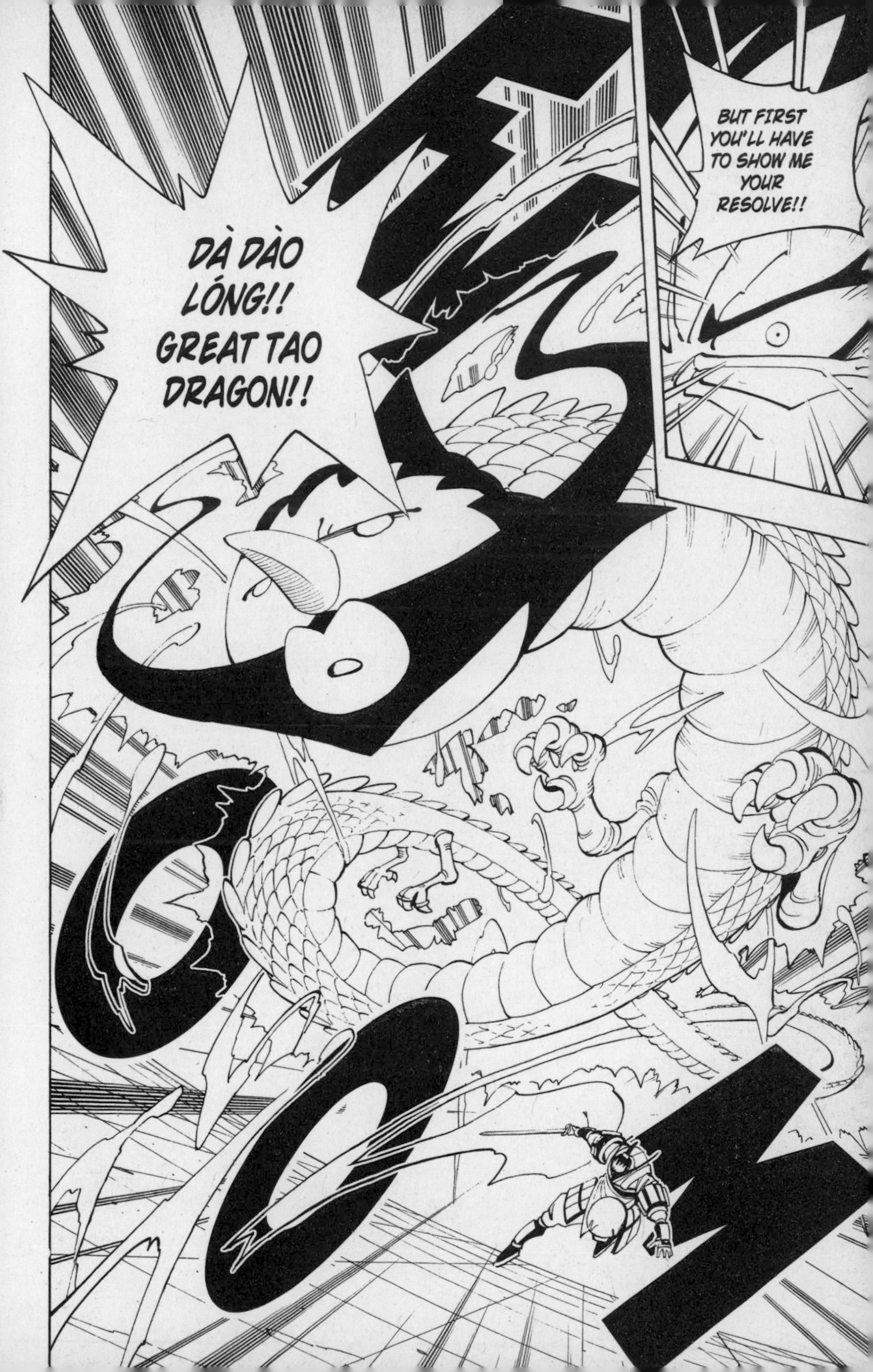
BUT FIRST YOU'LL HAVE TO SHOW ME YOUR RESOLVE!!
DÀ DÀO LÓNG!! GREAT TAO DRAGON!!

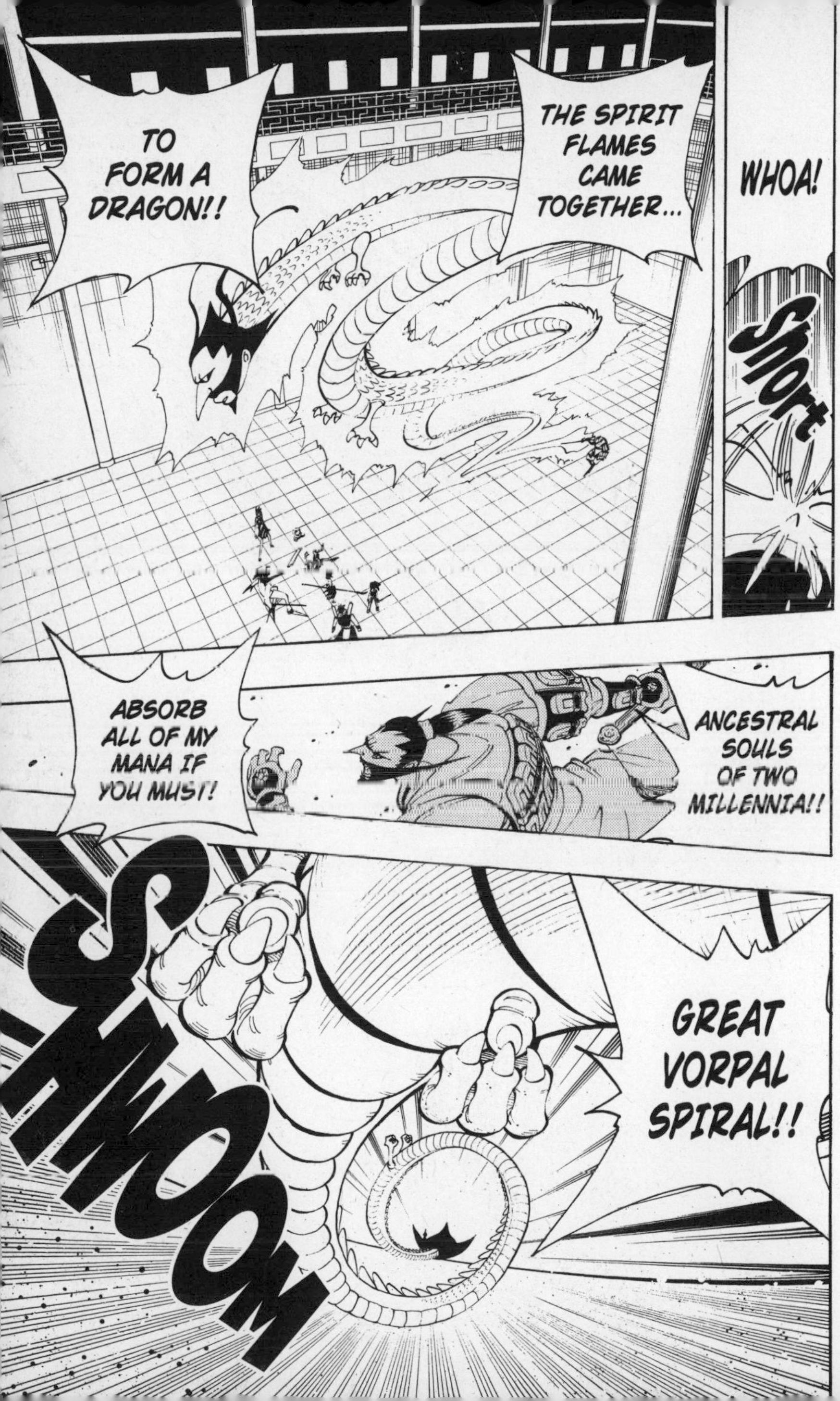
WHOA!
Short
THE SPIRIT FLAMES CAME TOGETHER...
TO FORM A DRAGON!!
ANCESTRAL SOULS OF TWO MILLENNIA!!
ABSORB ALL OF MY MANA IF YOU MUST!
GREAT VORPAL SPIRAL!!
SHWOOM

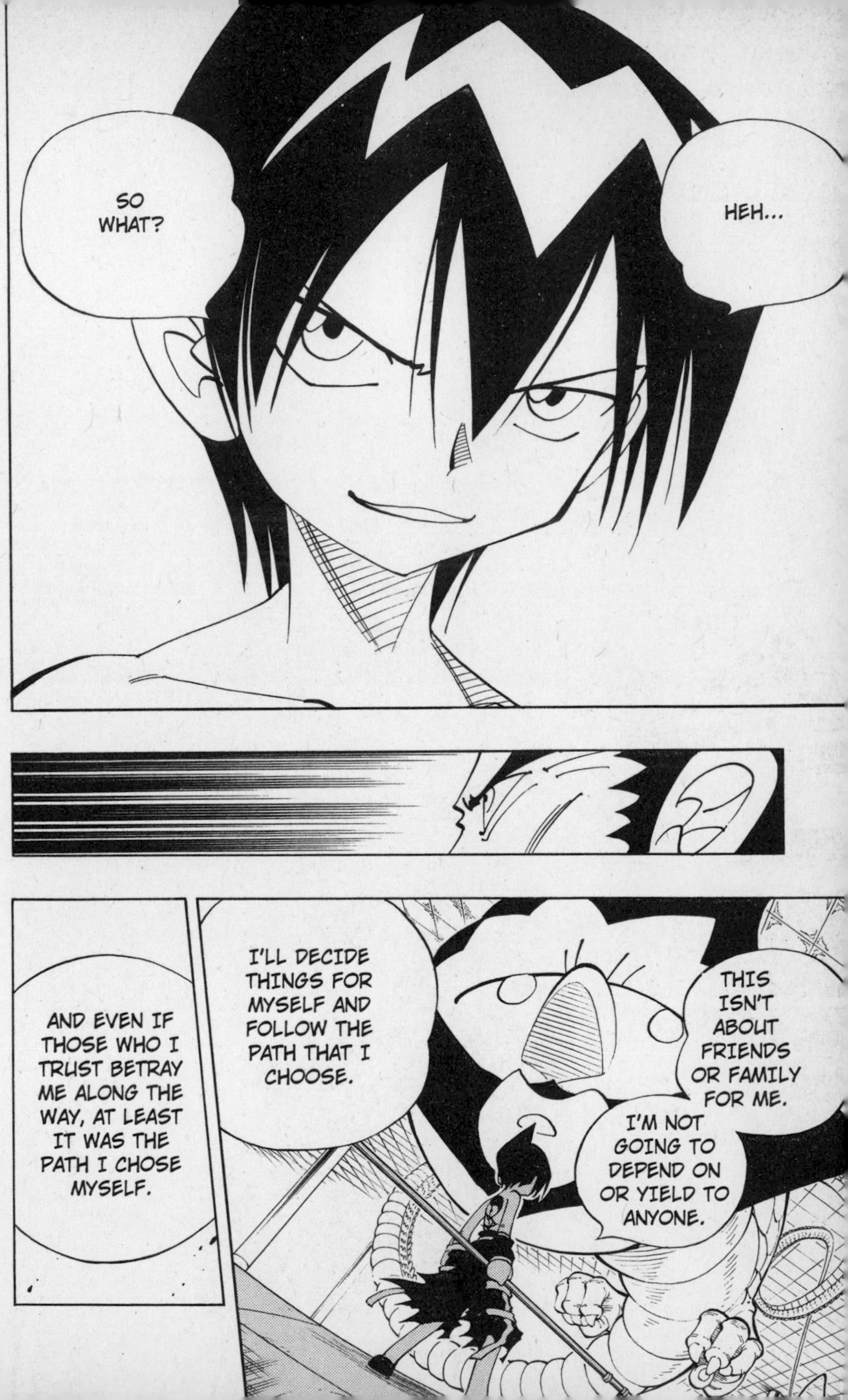
HEH...
SO WHAT?
THIS ISN'T ABOUT FRIENDS OR FAMILY FOR ME.
I'M NOT GOING TO DEPEND ON OR YIELD TO ANYONE.
I'LL DECIDE THINGS FOR MYSELF AND FOLLOW THE PATH THAT I CHOOSE.
AND EVEN IF THOSE WHO I TRUST BETRAY ME ALONG THE WAY, AT LEAST IT WAS THE PATH I CHOSE MYSELF.

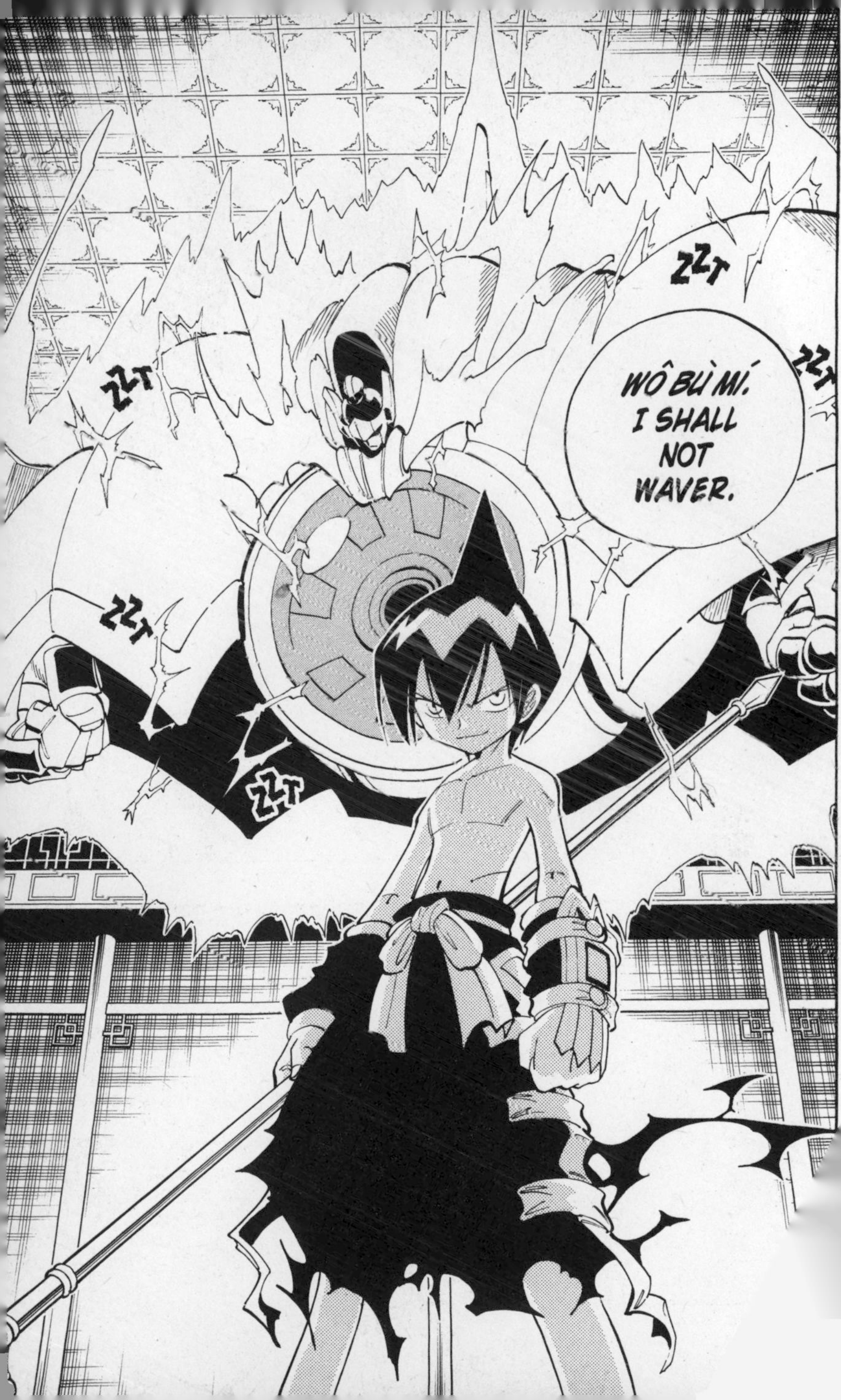
ZZT
ZZT
WÔ BÙ MÍ. I SHALL NOT WAVER.
ZZT
ZZT
ZZT

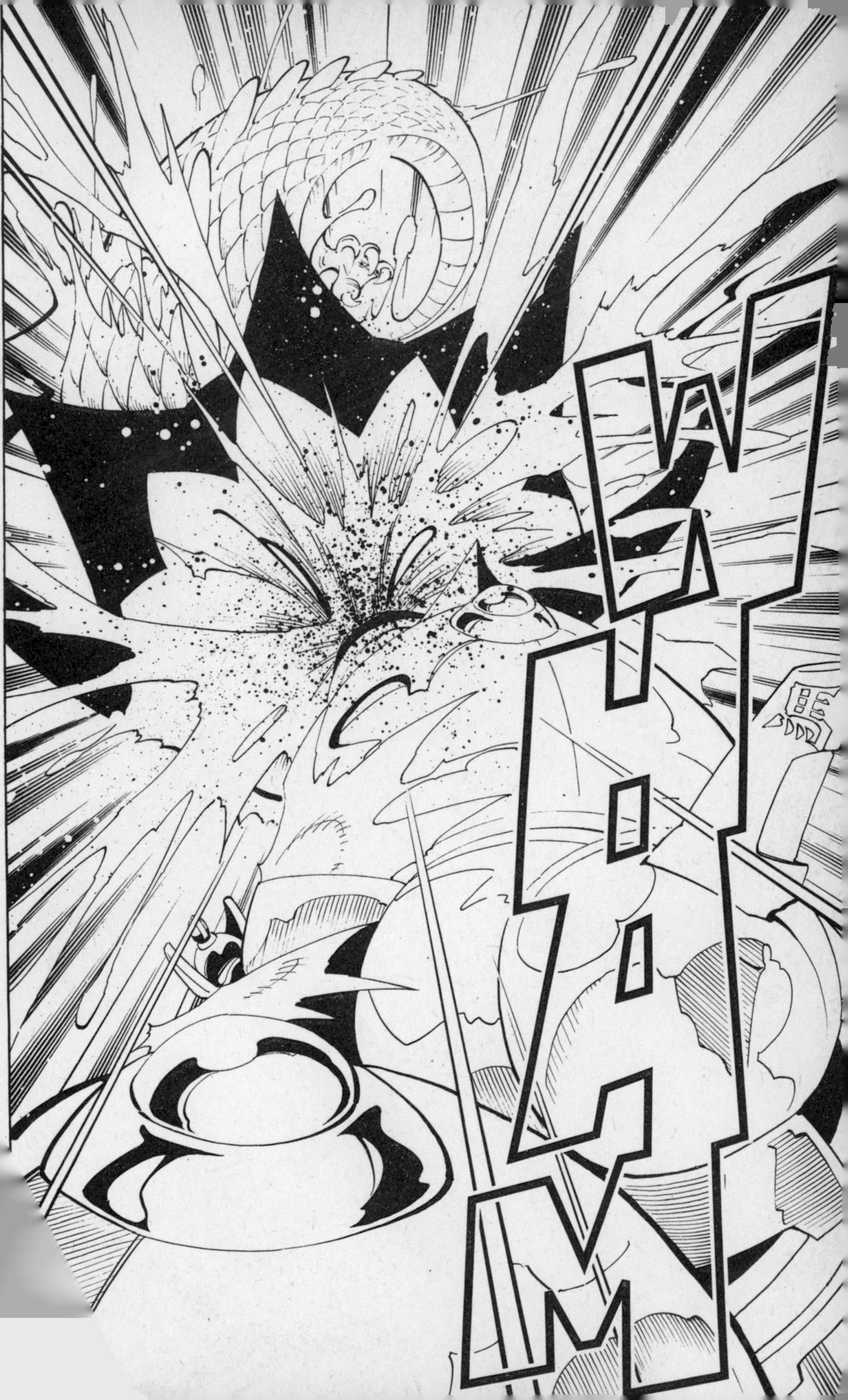
WHAM

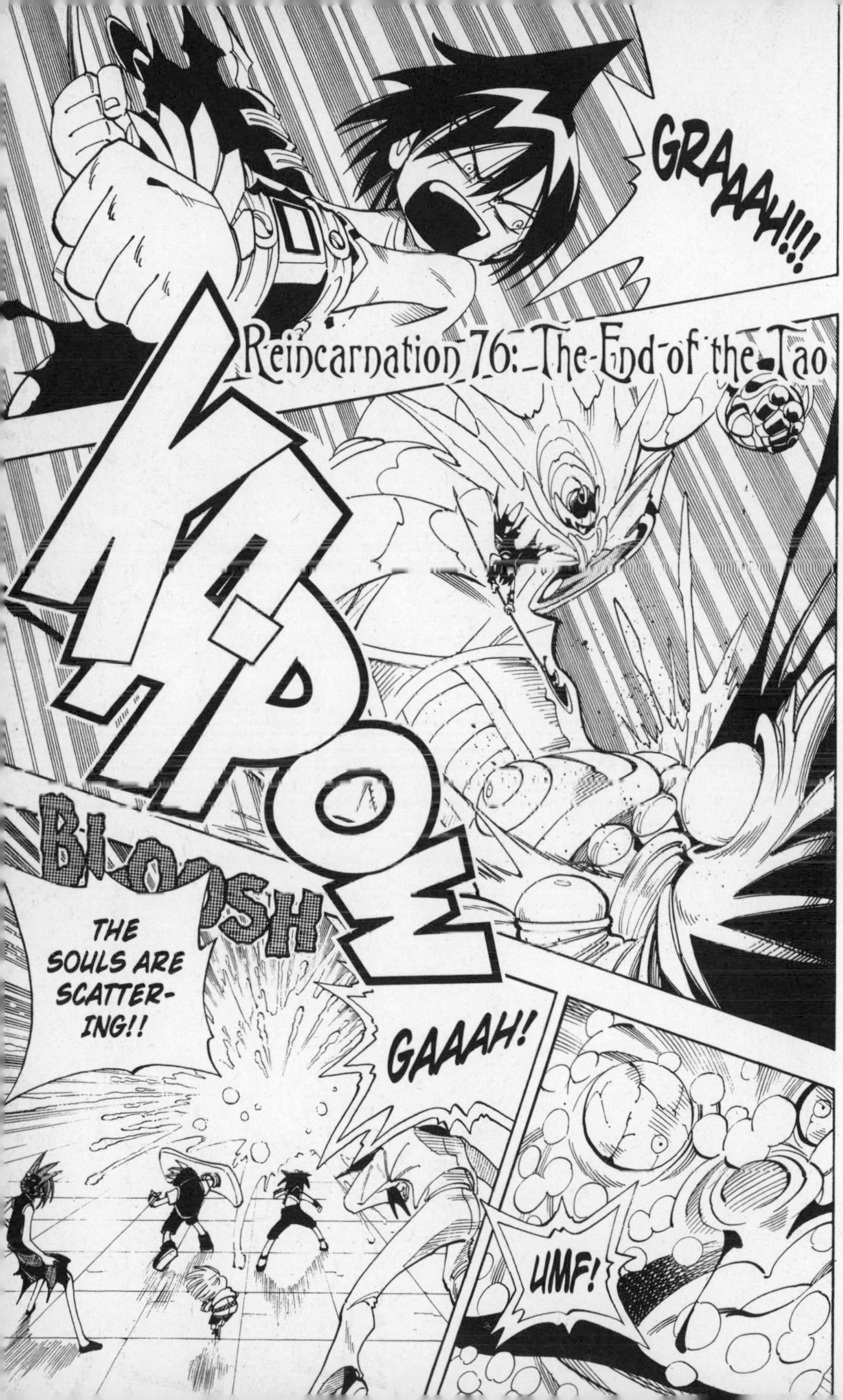
GRAAAH!!!
Reincarnation 76: The End of the Tao
UMF!
GAAAH!
THE SOULS ARE SCATTER-ING!!

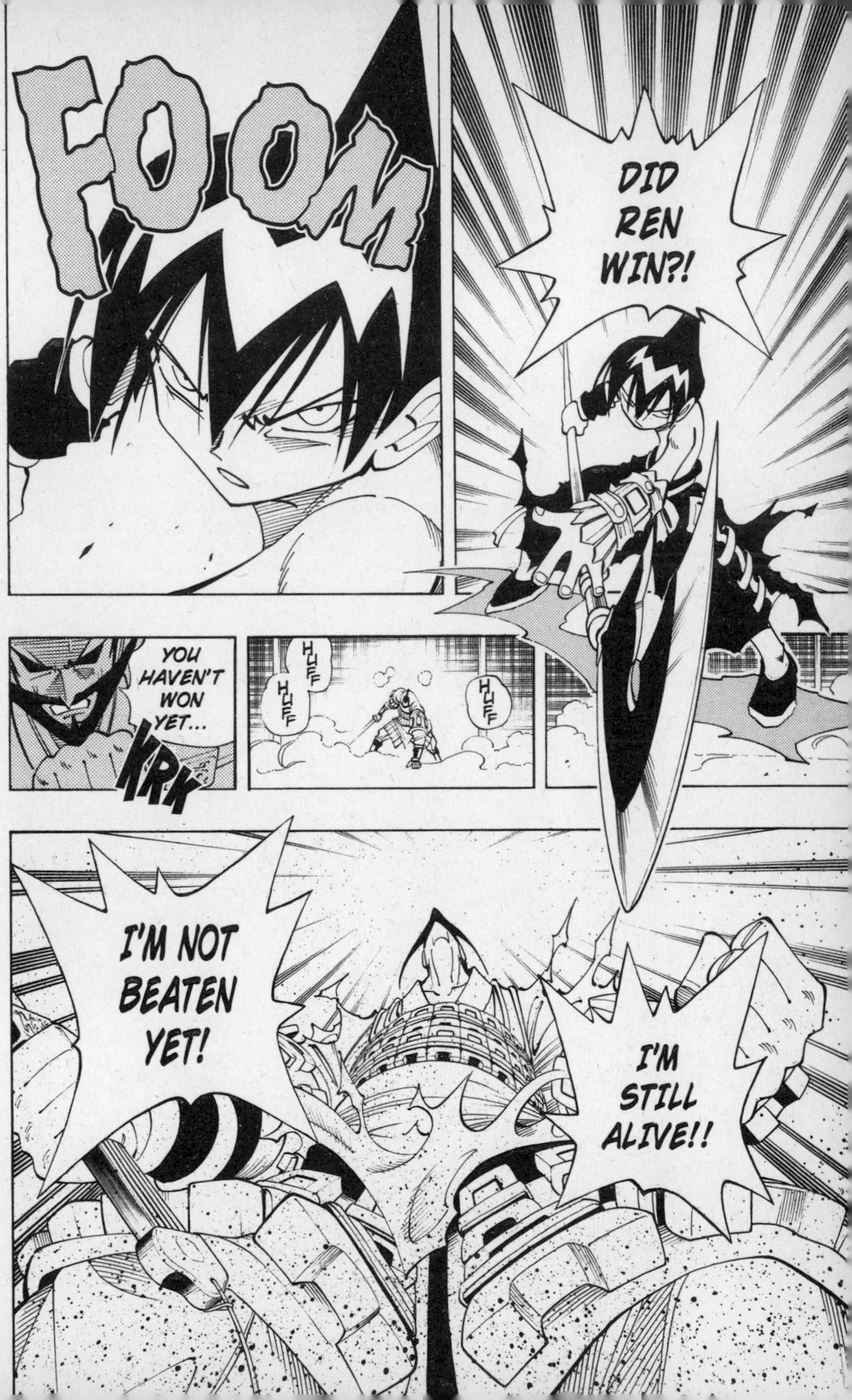
DID REN WIN?!
FOOM
HUFF
HUFF
HUFF
YOU HAVEN'T WON YET...
KRK
I'M NOT BEATEN YET!
I'M STILL ALIVE!!

# Reincarnation 76:
# The End of the Tao

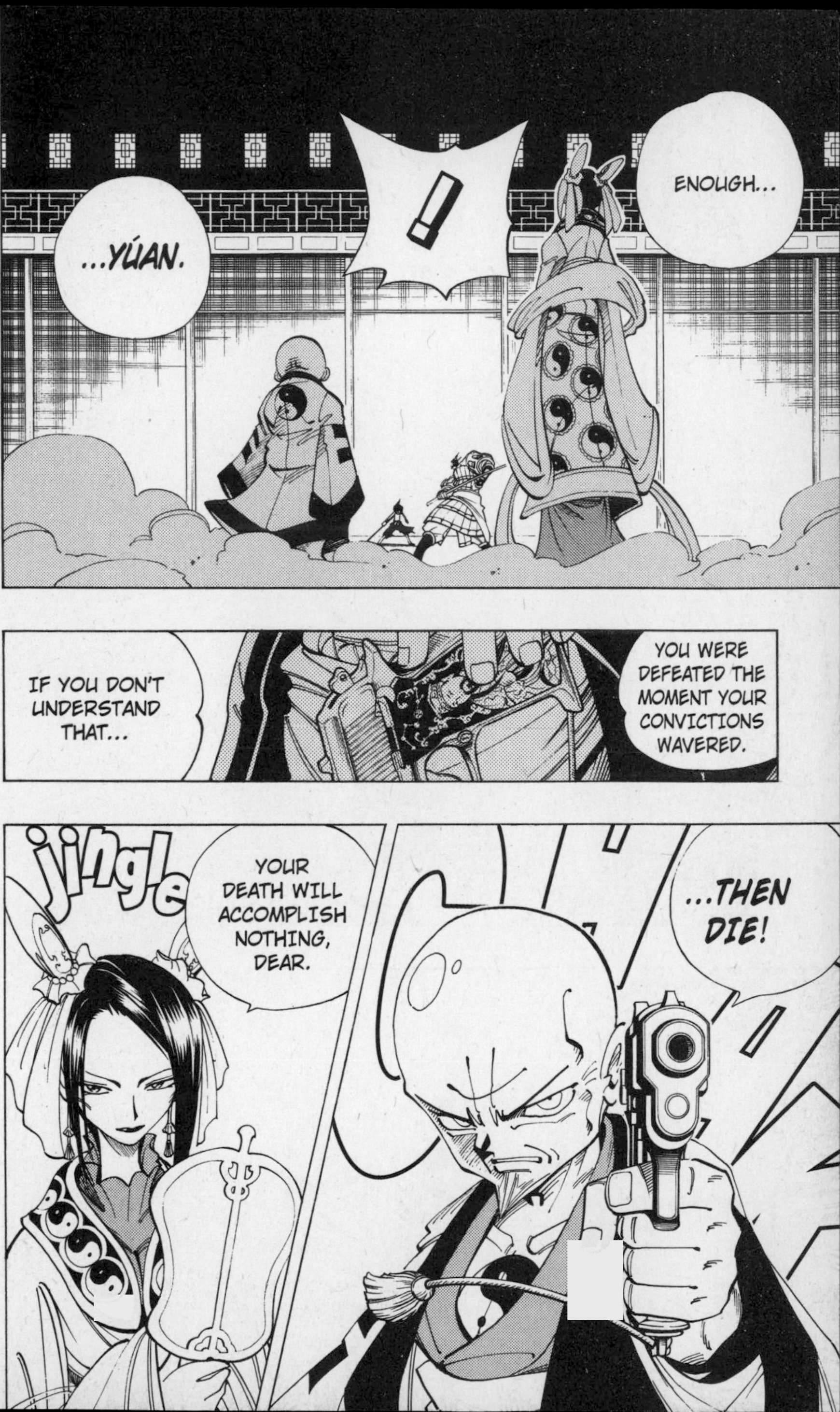
ENOUGH...
!
...YÚAN.
YOU WERE DEFEATED THE MOMENT YOUR CONVICTIONS WAVERED.
IF YOU DON'T UNDERSTAND THAT...
...THEN DIE!
jingle
YOUR DEATH WILL ACCOMPLISH NOTHING, DEAR.

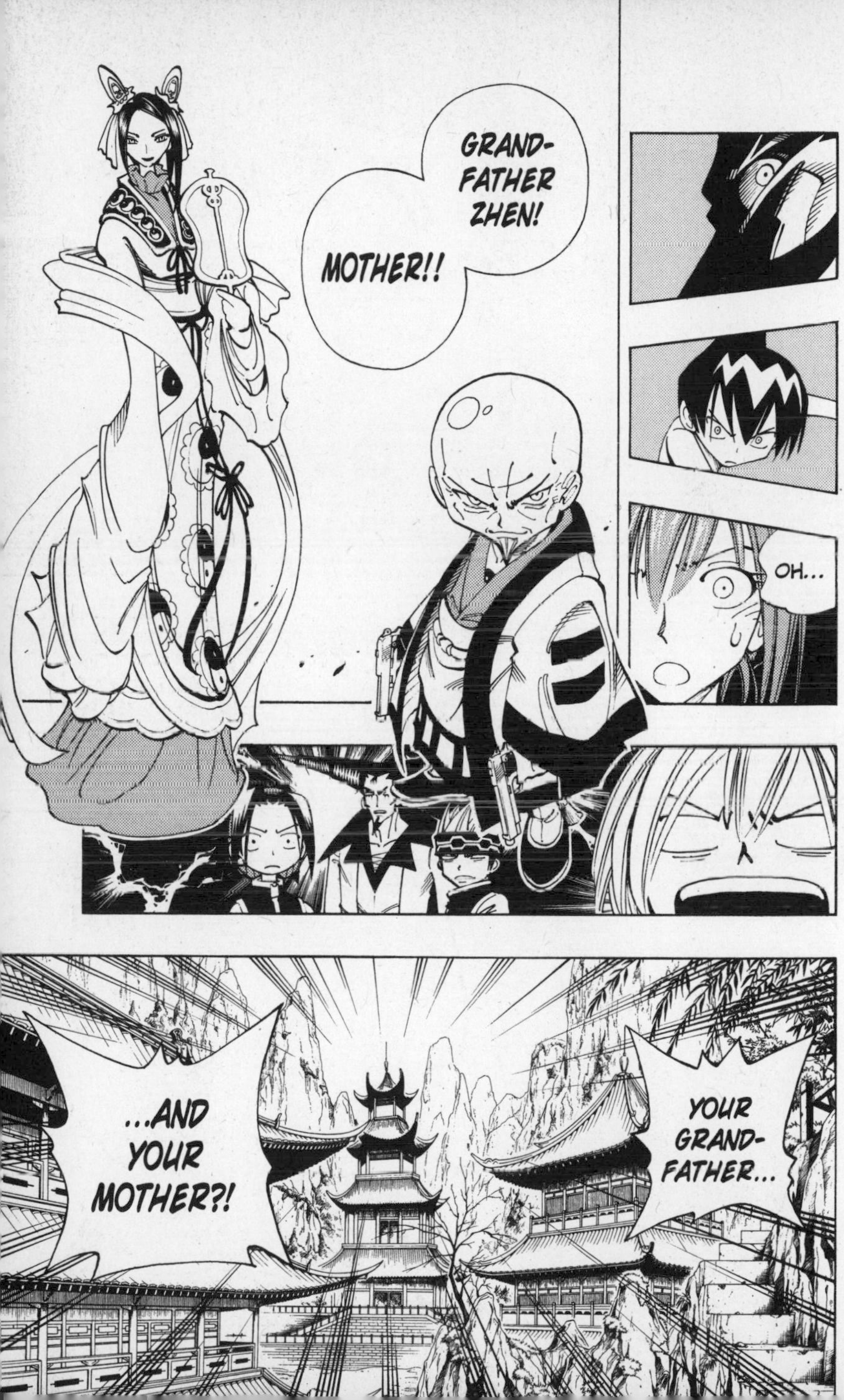
OH...
GRAND-FATHER ZHEN!
MOTHER!!
YOUR GRAND-FATHER...
...AND YOUR MOTHER?!

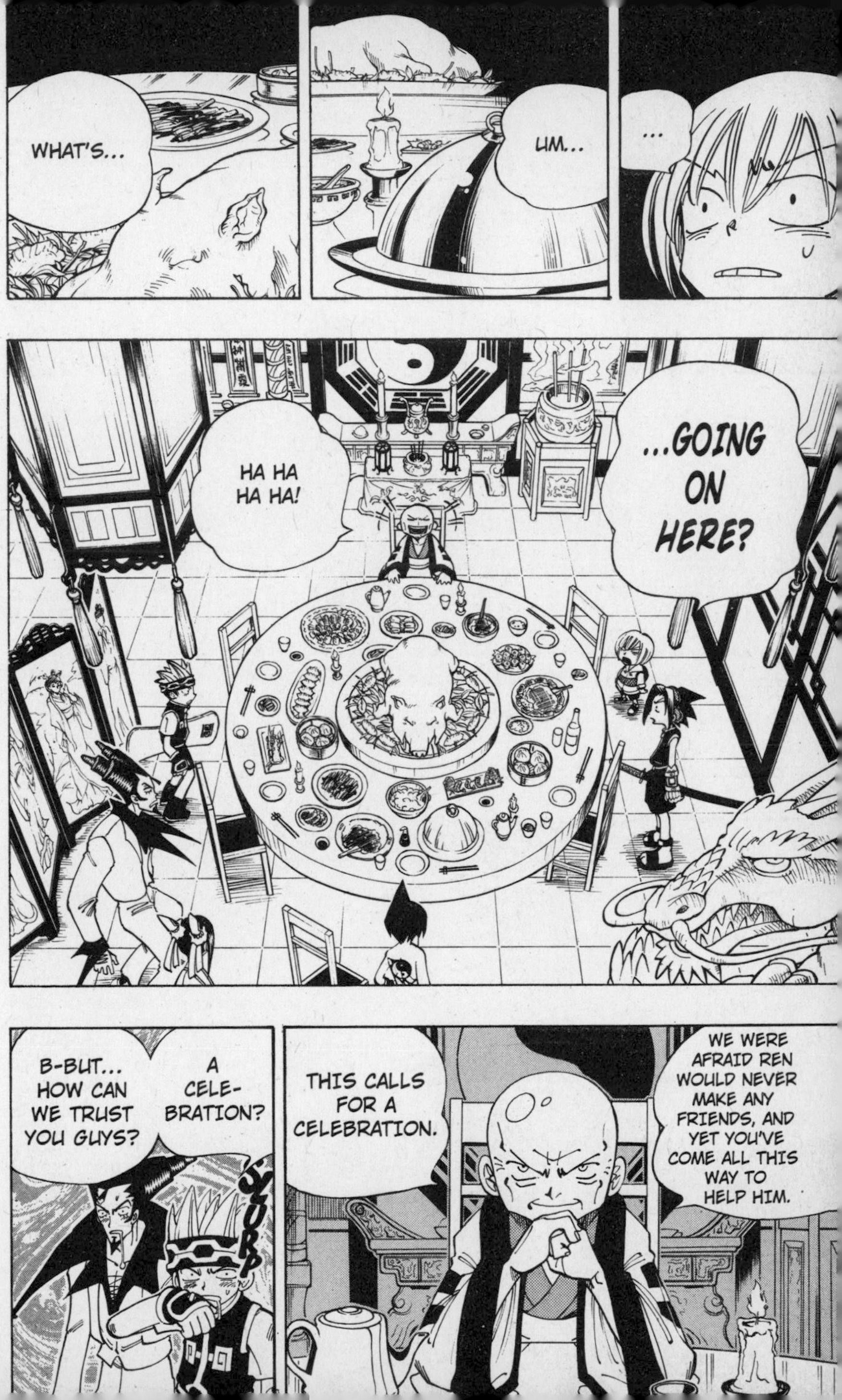
...
UM...
WHAT'S...
...GOING ON HERE?
HA HA HA HA!
WE WERE AFRAID REN WOULD NEVER MAKE ANY FRIENDS, AND YET YOU'VE COME ALL THIS WAY TO HELP HIM.
THIS CALLS FOR A CELEBRATION.
A CELE-BRATION?
B-BUT... HOW CAN WE TRUST YOU GUYS?
SLURP

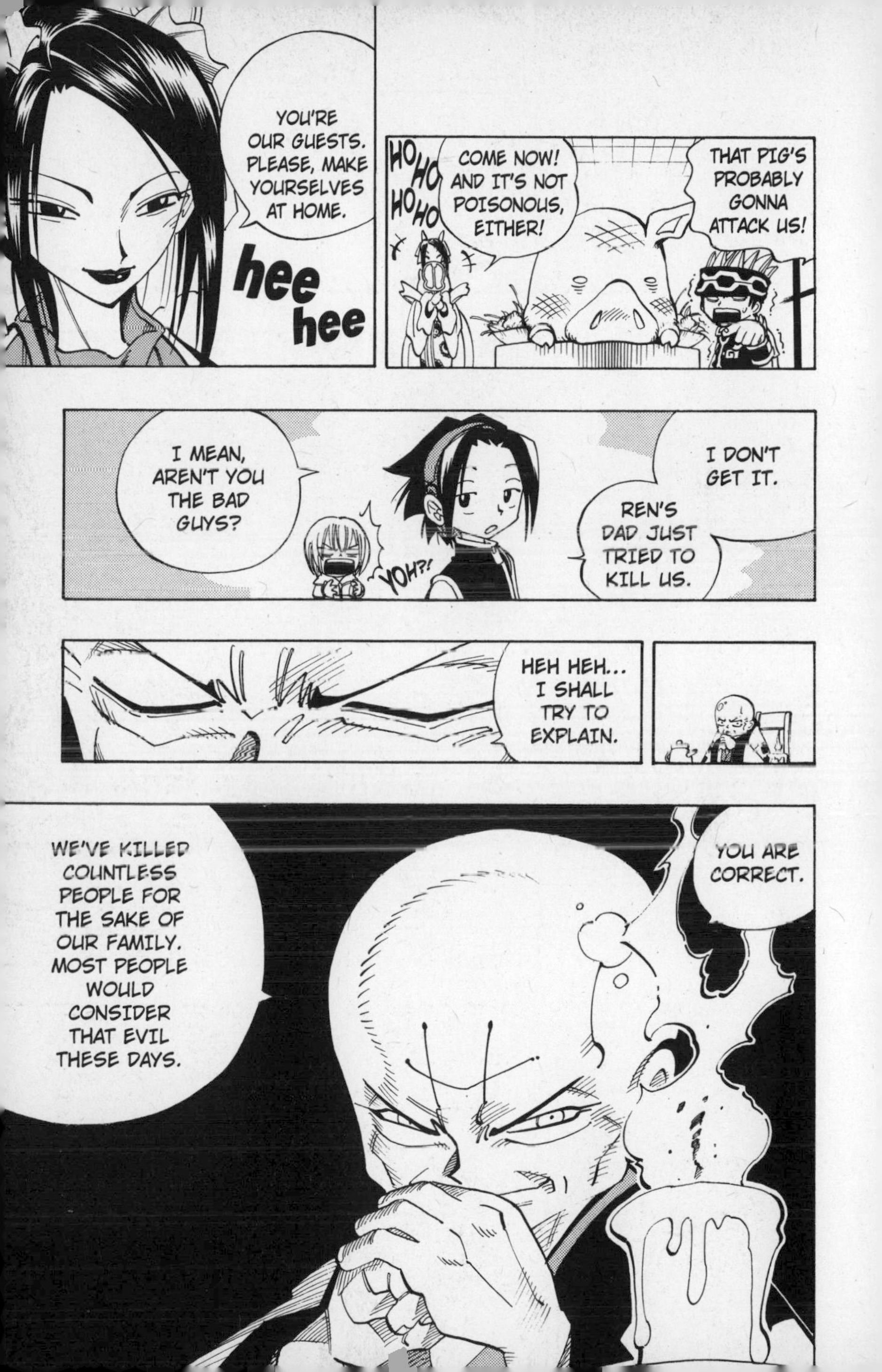
THAT PIG'S PROBABLY GONNA ATTACK US!
COME NOW! AND IT'S NOT POISONOUS, EITHER!
HO HO HO HO
YOU'RE OUR GUESTS. PLEASE, MAKE YOURSELVES AT HOME.
hee hee
I DON'T GET IT.
REN'S DAD JUST TRIED TO KILL US.
YOH?!
I MEAN, AREN'T YOU THE BAD GUYS?
HEH HEH... I SHALL TRY TO EXPLAIN.
YOU ARE CORRECT.
WE'VE KILLED COUNTLESS PEOPLE FOR THE SAKE OF OUR FAMILY. MOST PEOPLE WOULD CONSIDER THAT EVIL THESE DAYS.

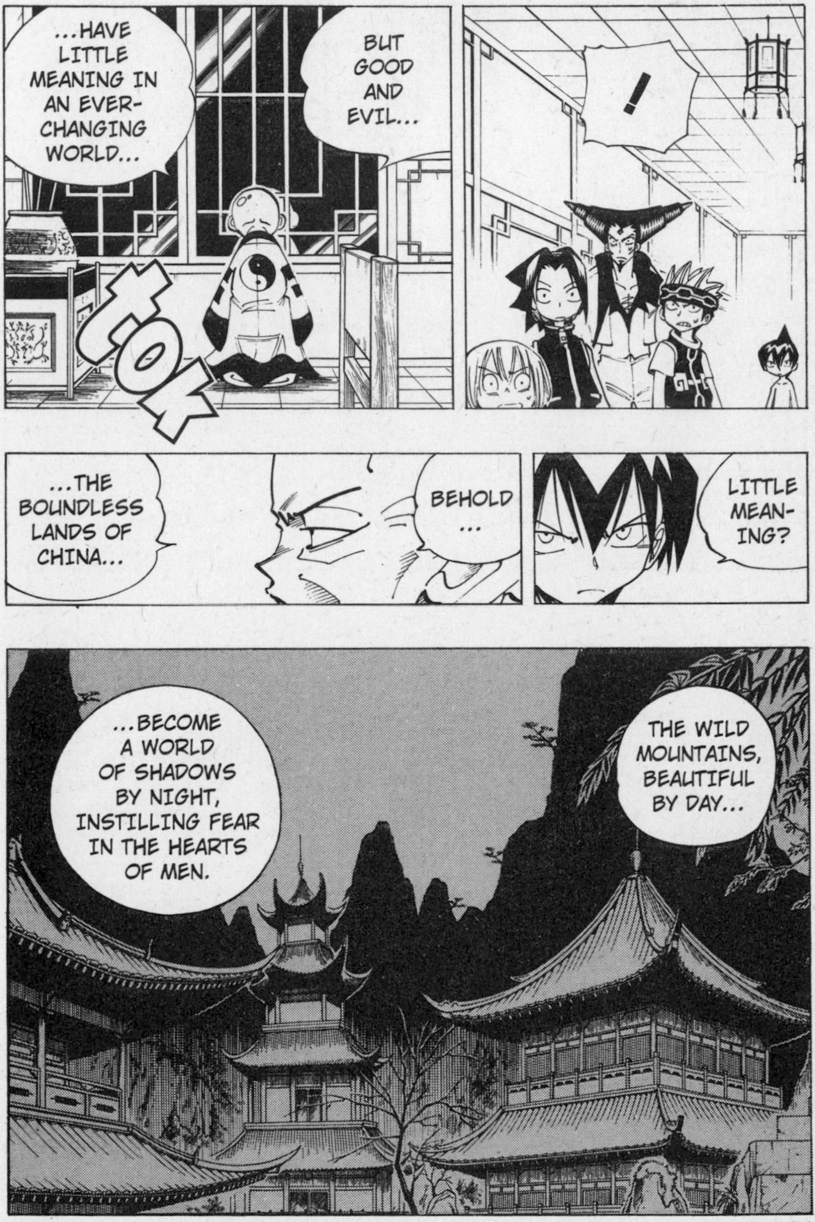
!
BUT GOOD AND EVIL...
...HAVE LITTLE MEANING IN AN EVER-CHANGING WORLD...
TOK
LITTLE MEANING?
BEHOLD...
...THE BOUNDLESS LANDS OF CHINA...
THE WILD MOUNTAINS, BEAUTIFUL BY DAY...
...BECOME A WORLD OF SHADOWS BY NIGHT, INSTILLING FEAR IN THE HEARTS OF MEN.

READ THIS WAY

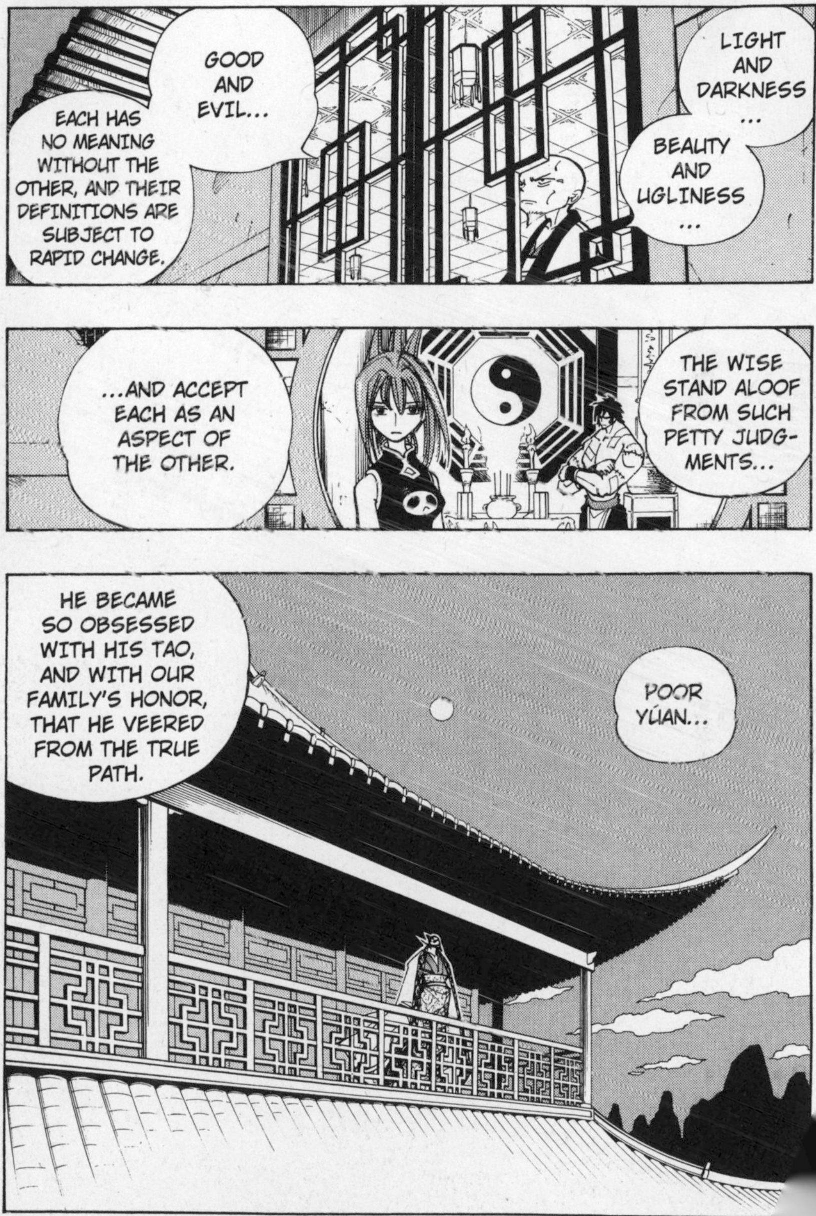
LIGHT AND DARKNESS...
BEAUTY AND UGLINESS...
GOOD AND EVIL...
EACH HAS NO MEANING WITHOUT THE OTHER, AND THEIR DEFINITIONS ARE SUBJECT TO RAPID CHANGE.
THE WISE STAND ALOOF FROM SUCH PETTY JUDG-MENTS...
...AND ACCEPT EACH AS AN ASPECT OF THE OTHER.
POOR YÚAN...
HE BECAME SO OBSESSED WITH HIS TAO, AND WITH OUR FAMILY'S HONOR, THAT HE VEERED FROM THE TRUE PATH.

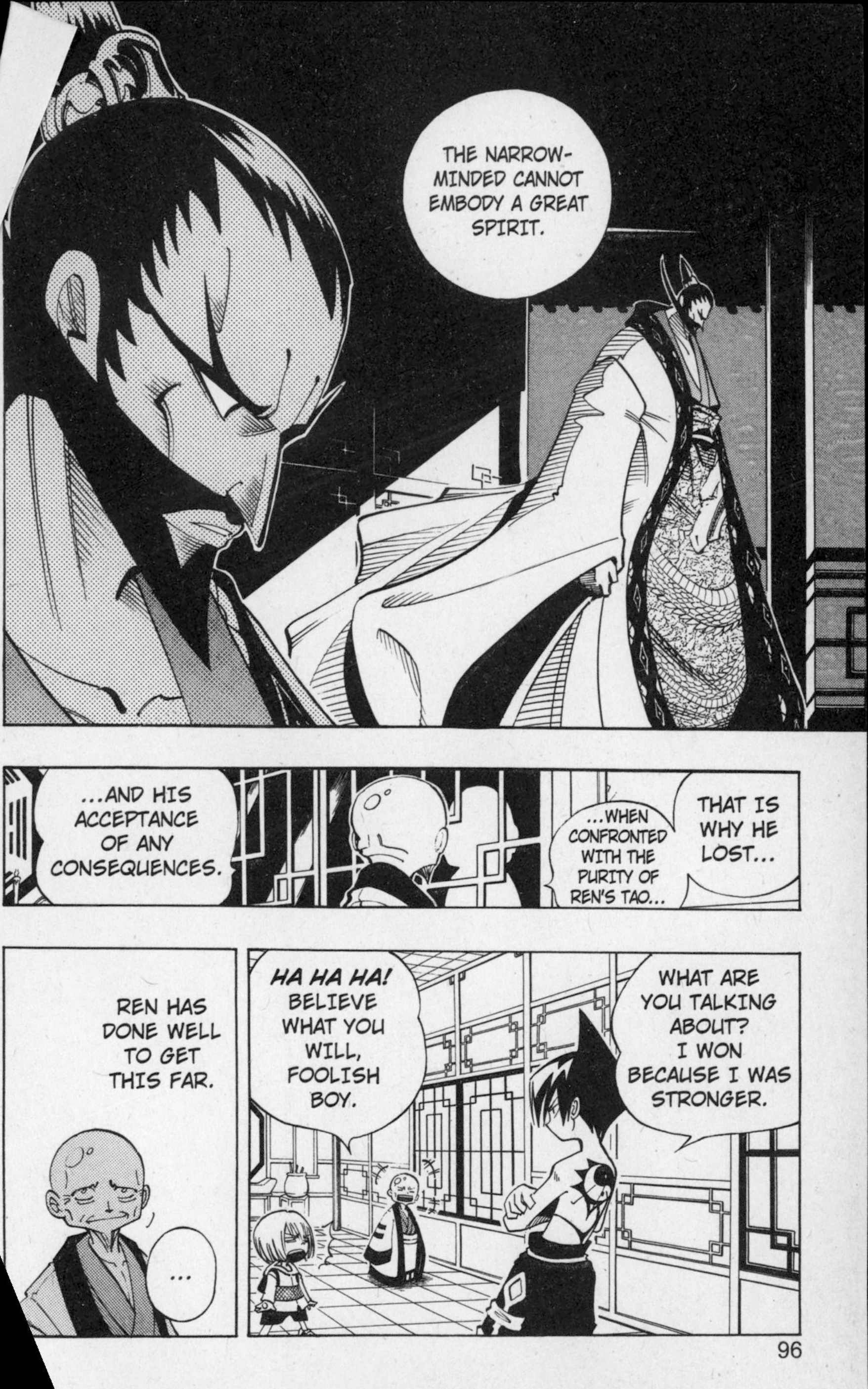
THE NARROW-MINDED CANNOT EMBODY A GREAT SPIRIT.
THAT IS WHY HE LOST...
...WHEN CONFRONTED WITH THE PURITY OF REN'S TAO...
...AND HIS ACCEPTANCE OF ANY CONSEQUENCES.
WHAT ARE YOU TALKING ABOUT? I WON BECAUSE I WAS STRONGER.
*HA HA HA!* BELIEVE WHAT YOU WILL, FOOLISH BOY.
REN HAS DONE WELL TO GET THIS FAR.
...

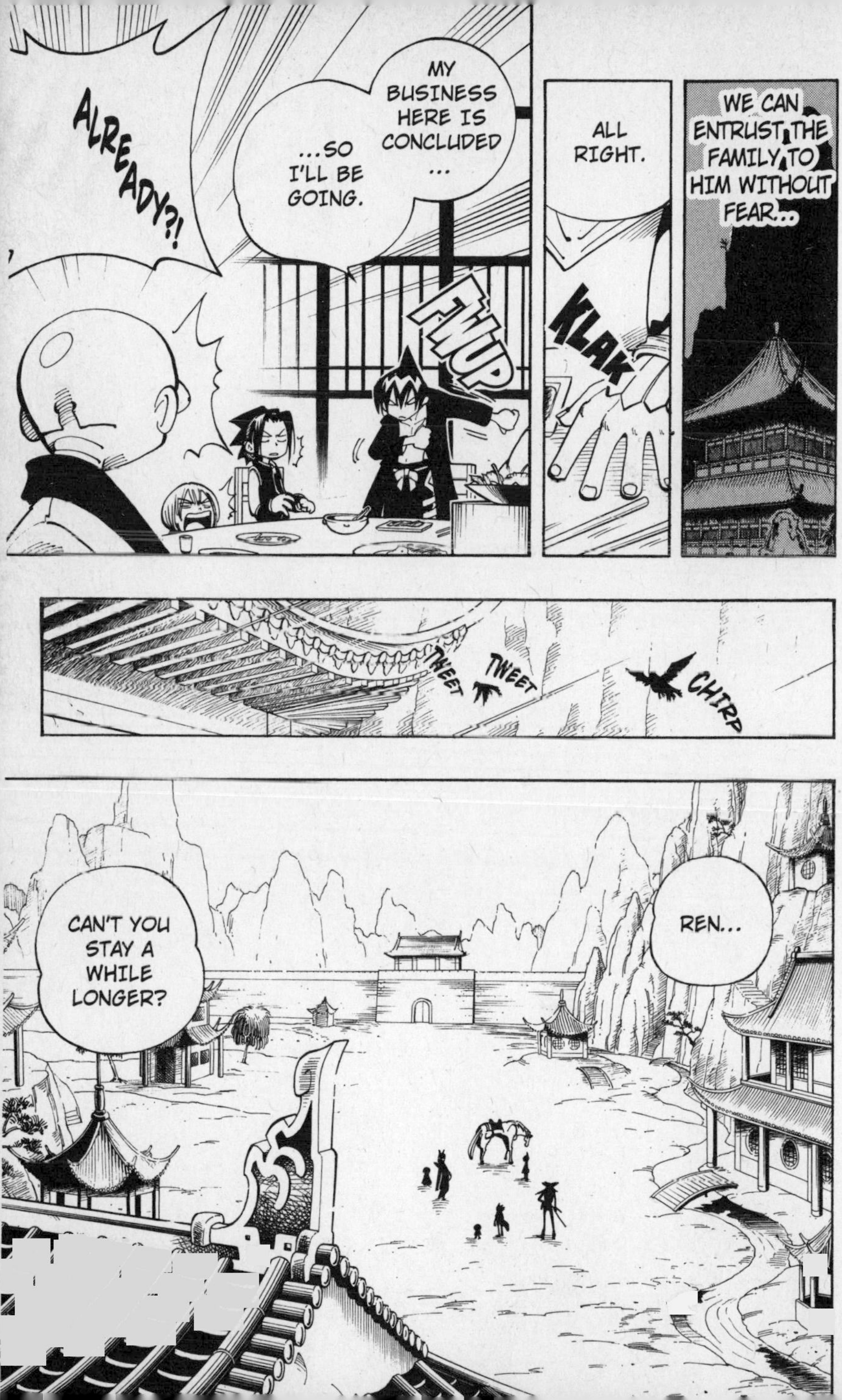
WE CAN ENTRUST THE FAMILY TO HIM WITHOUT FEAR...
ALL RIGHT.
KLAK
MY BUSINESS HERE IS CONCLUDED...
...SO I'LL BE GOING.
FWUP
ALREADY?!
CHIRP
TWEET
TWEET
REN...
CAN'T YOU STAY A WHILE LONGER?

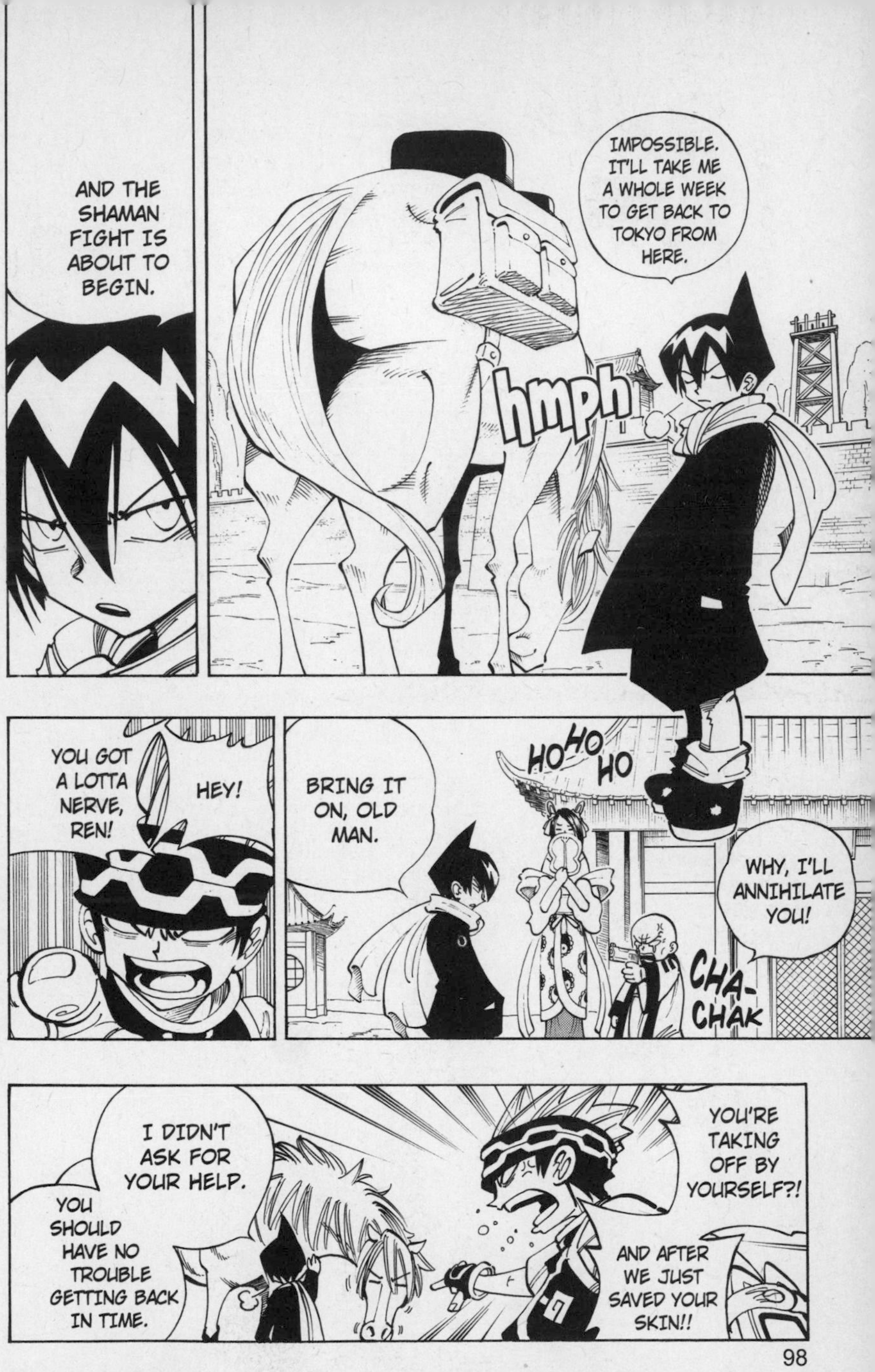
IMPOSSIBLE. IT'LL TAKE ME A WHOLE WEEK TO GET BACK TO TOKYO FROM HERE.
hmph
AND THE SHAMAN FIGHT IS ABOUT TO BEGIN.
HO HO HO
BRING IT ON, OLD MAN.
WHY, I'LL ANNIHILATE YOU!
CHA-CHAK
HEY!
YOU GOT A LOTTA NERVE, REN!
YOU'RE TAKING OFF BY YOURSELF?!
AND AFTER WE JUST SAVED YOUR SKIN!!
I DIDN'T ASK FOR YOUR HELP.
YOU SHOULD HAVE NO TROUBLE GETTING BACK IN TIME.

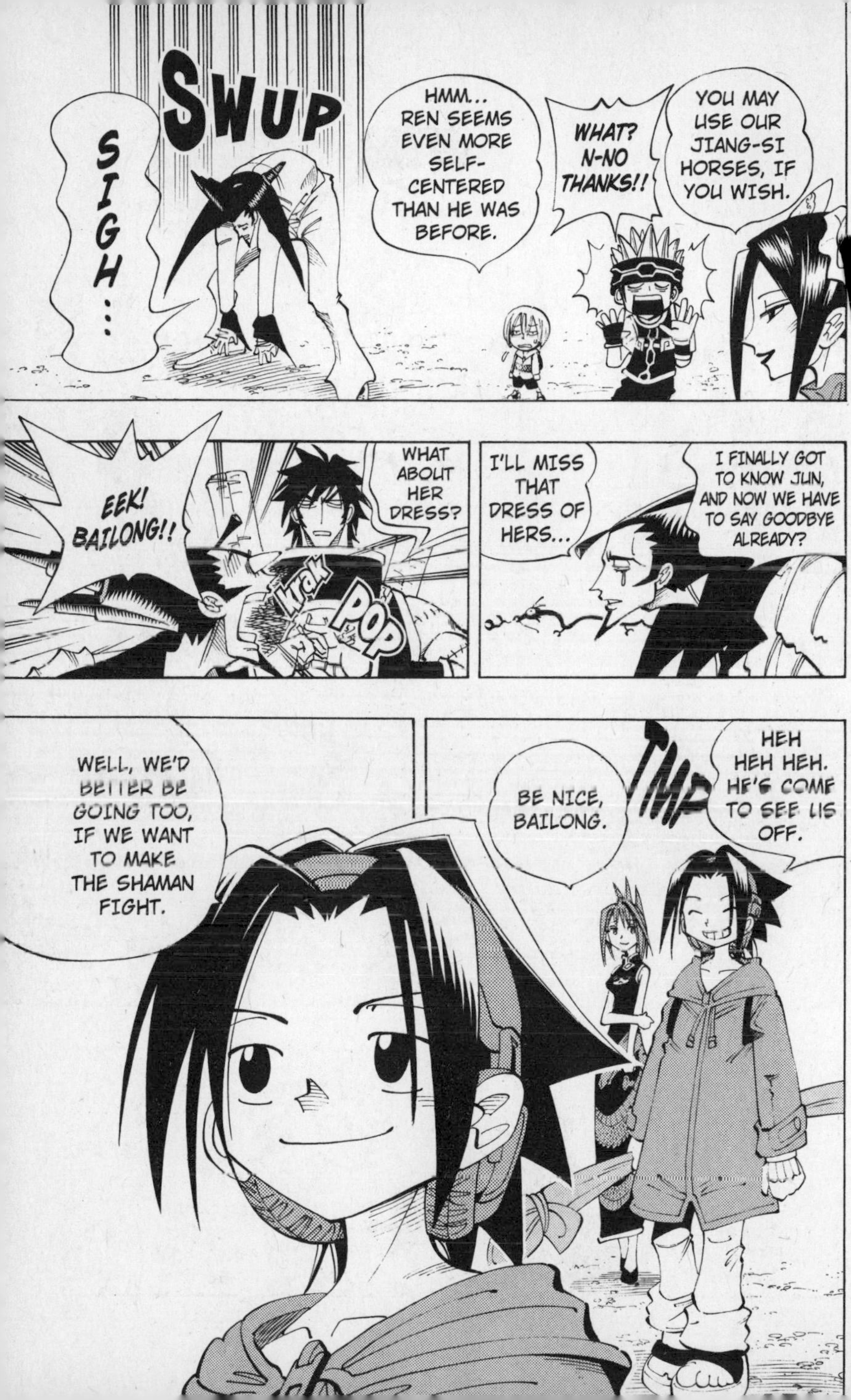
YOU MAY USE OUR JIANG-SI HORSES, IF YOU WISH.
WHAT? N-NO THANKS!!
HMM... REN SEEMS EVEN MORE SELF-CENTERED THAN HE WAS BEFORE.
SWUP
SIGH...
I FINALLY GOT TO KNOW JUN, AND NOW WE HAVE TO SAY GOODBYE ALREADY?
I'LL MISS THAT DRESS OF HERS...
WHAT ABOUT HER DRESS?
KRAK
POP
EEK! BAILONG!!
HEH HEH HEH. HE'S COME TO SEE US OFF.
TMP
BE NICE, BAILONG.
WELL, WE'D BETTER BE GOING TOO, IF WE WANT TO MAKE THE SHAMAN FIGHT.

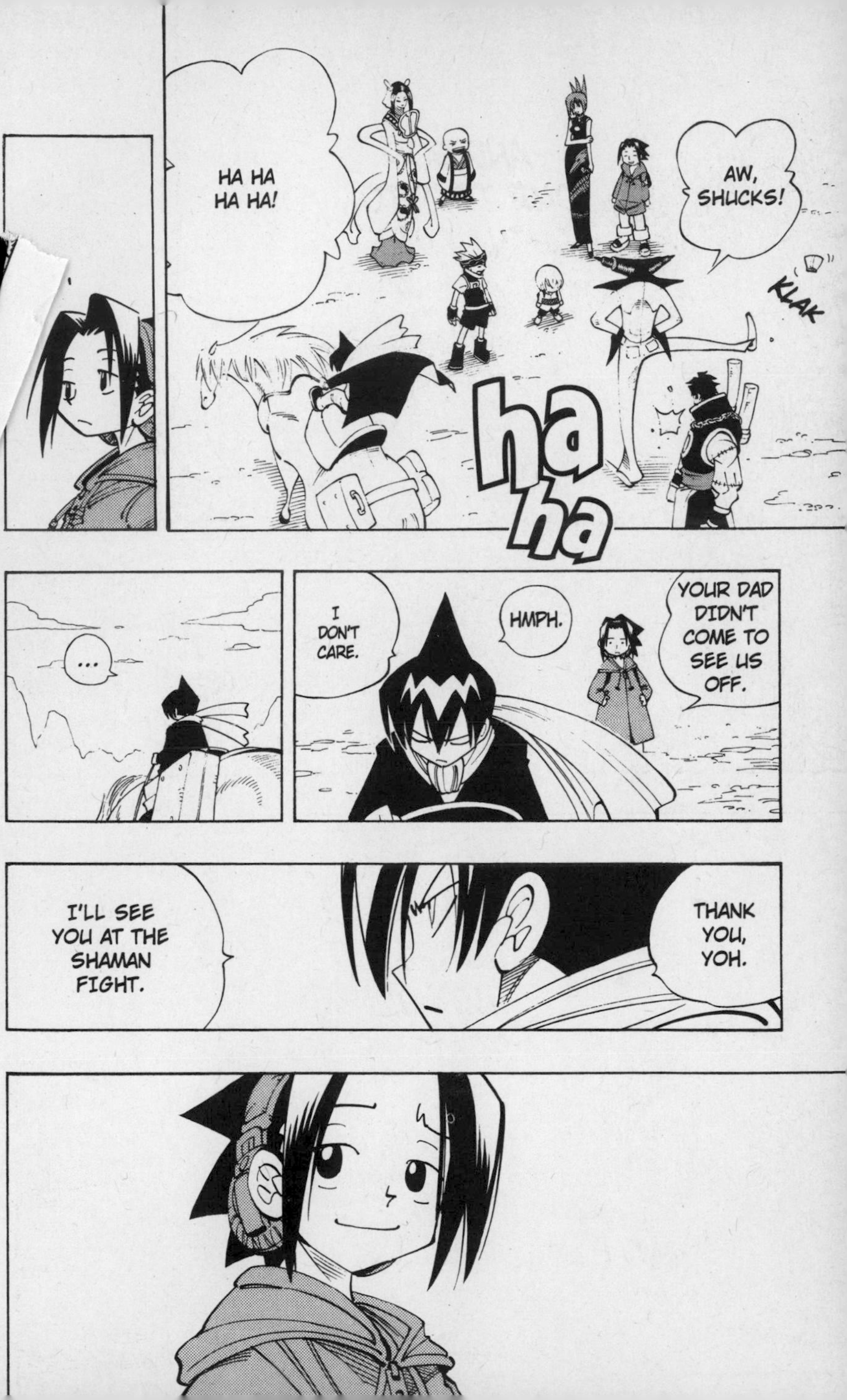
AW, SHUCKS!
KLAK
HA HA HA HA!
ha ha
YOUR DAD DIDN'T COME TO SEE US OFF.
HMPH.
I DON'T CARE.
...
THANK YOU, YOH.
I'LL SEE YOU AT THE SHAMAN FIGHT.

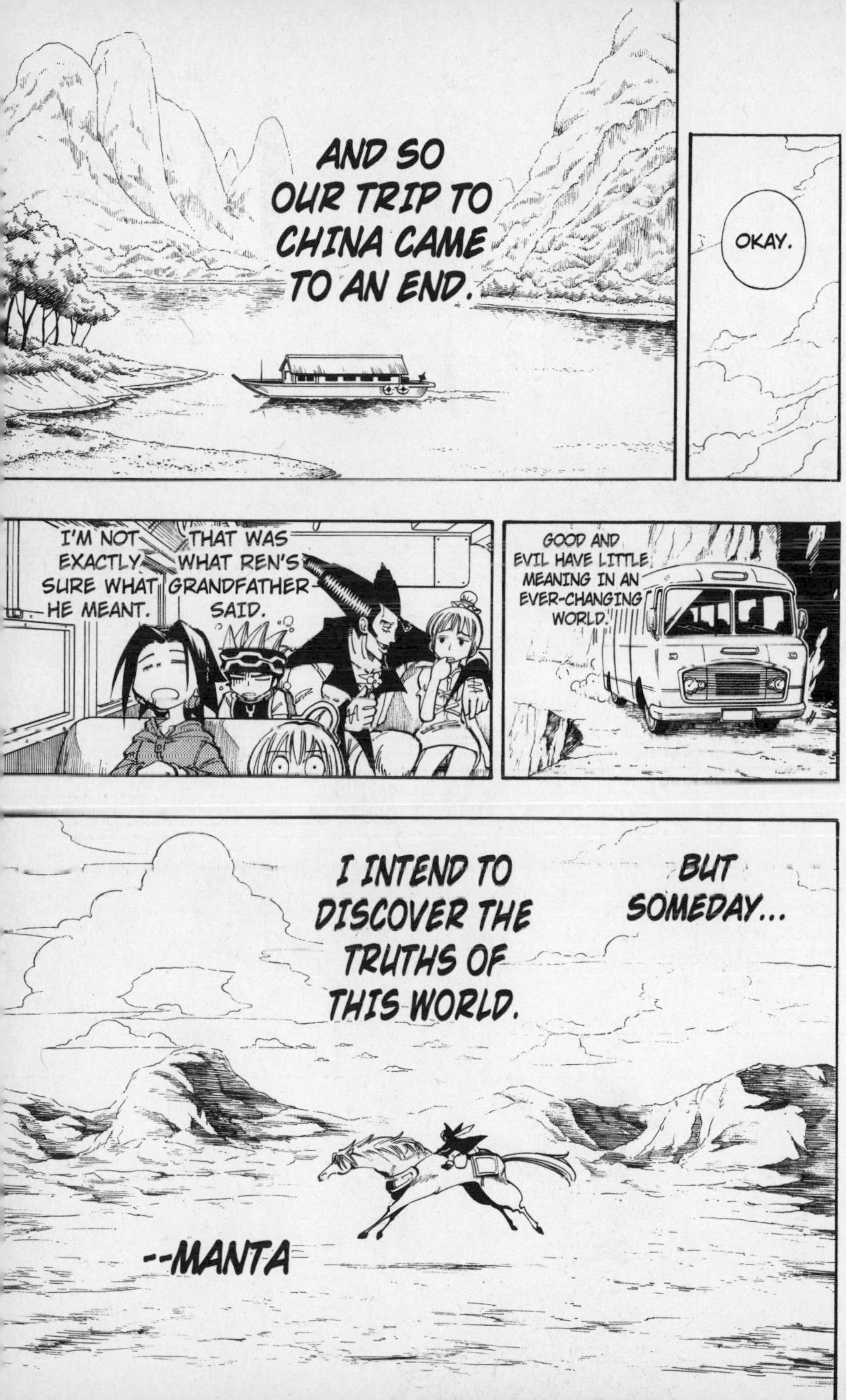
OKAY.
AND SO OUR TRIP TO CHINA CAME TO AN END.
GOOD AND EVIL HAVE LITTLE MEANING IN AN EVER-CHANGING WORLD.
THAT WAS WHAT REN'S GRANDFATHER SAID.
I'M NOT EXACTLY SURE WHAT HE MEANT.
BUT SOMEDAY...
I INTEND TO DISCOVER THE TRUTHS OF THIS WORLD.
--MANTA

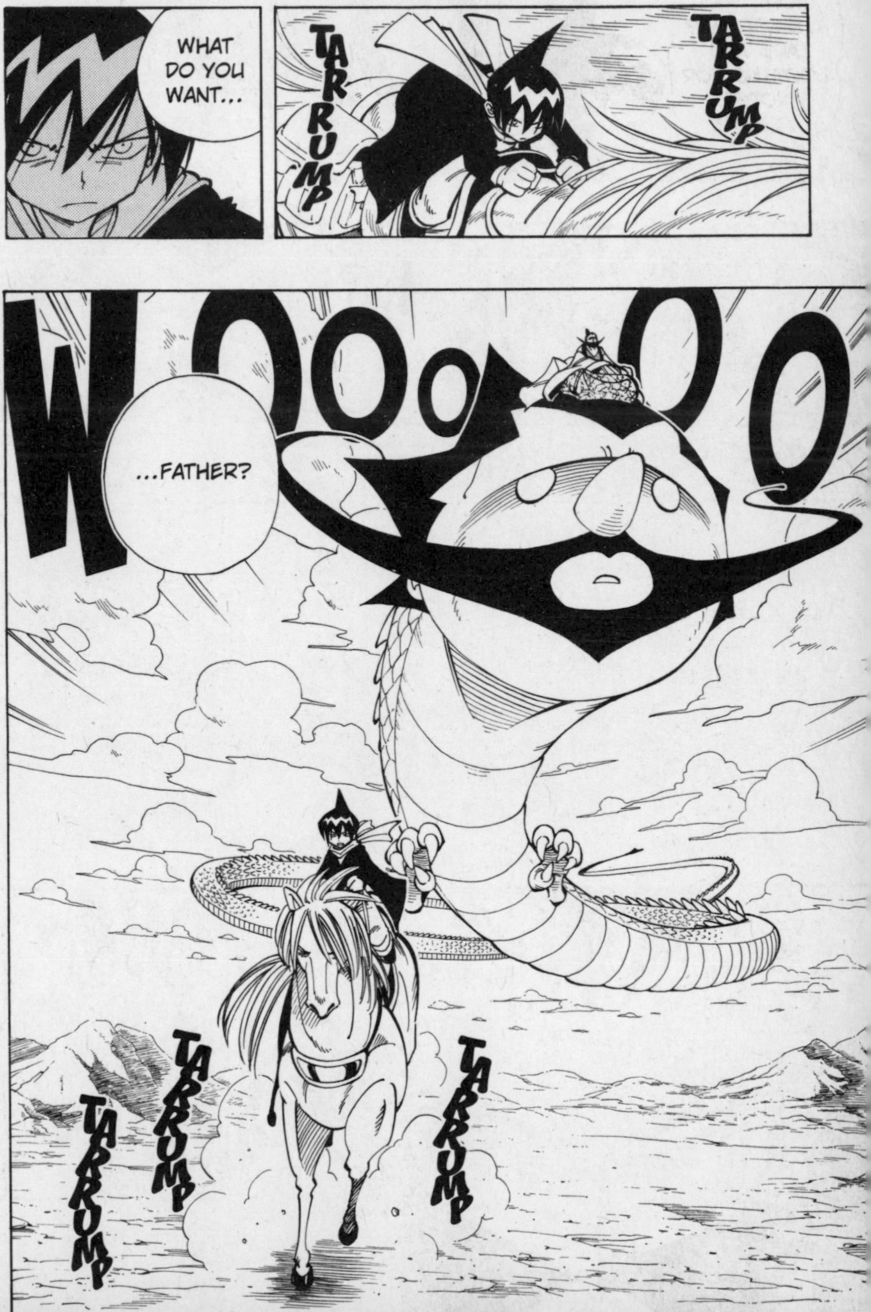
TARRUMP
TARRUMP
WHAT DO YOU WANT...
WOOOOOO
...FATHER?
TARRUMP
TARRUMP
TARRUMP

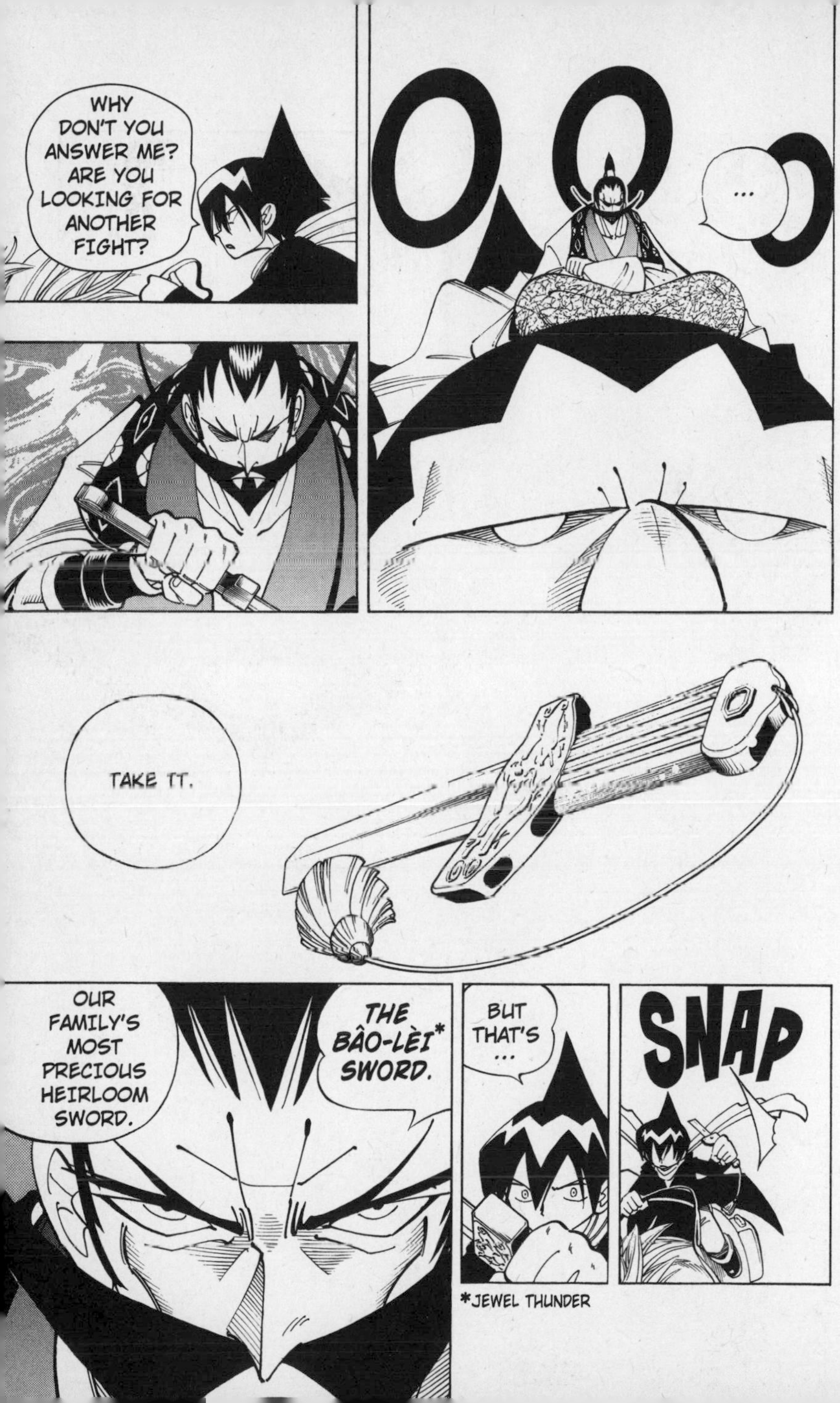
…
WHY DON'T YOU ANSWER ME? ARE YOU LOOKING FOR ANOTHER FIGHT?
TAKE IT.
SNAP
BUT THAT'S …
THE BÂO-LÈI* SWORD.
OUR FAMILY'S MOST PRECIOUS HEIRLOOM SWORD.

*JEWEL THUNDER

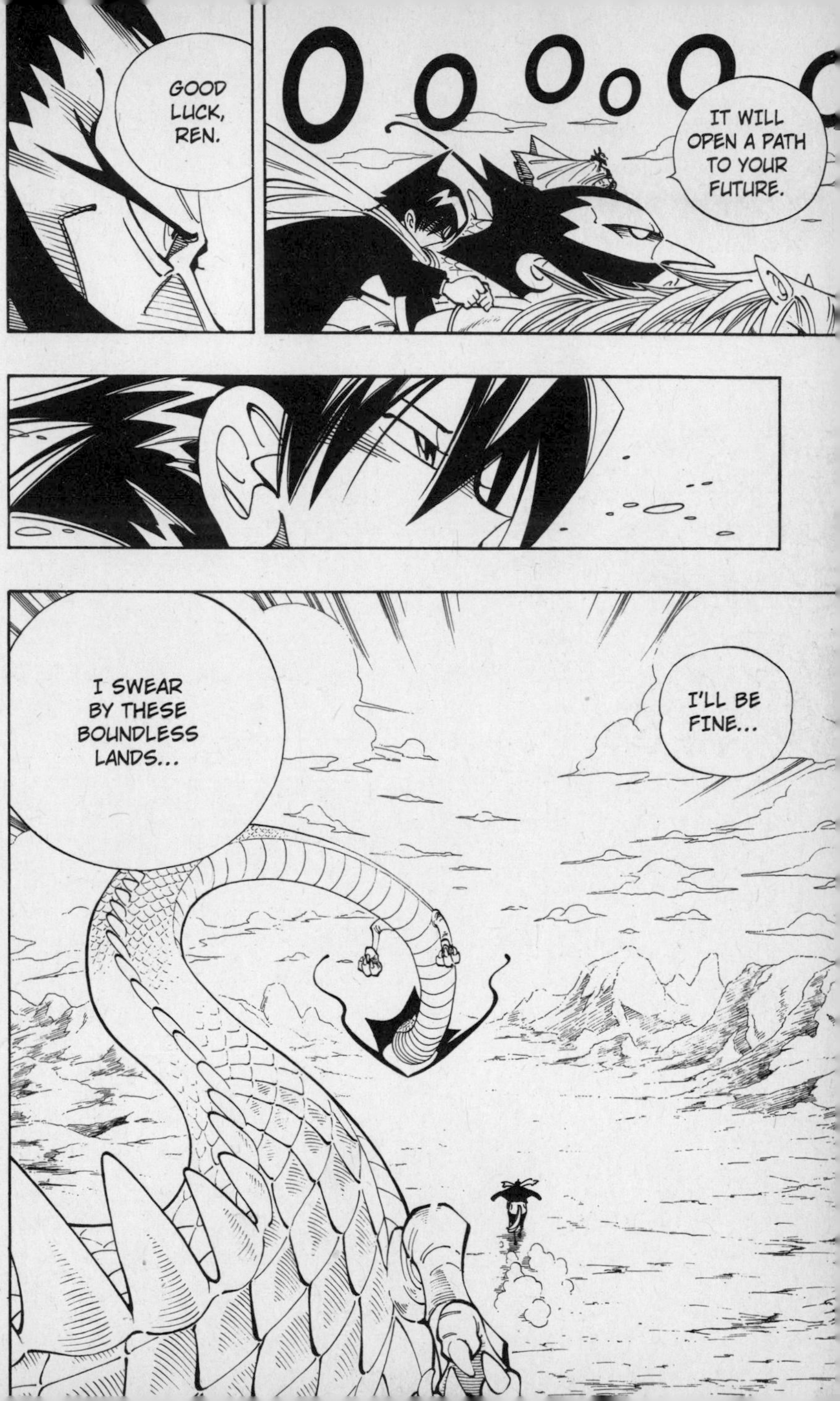

OOOOOO
IT WILL OPEN A PATH TO YOUR FUTURE.
GOOD LUCK, REN.
I'LL BE FINE...
I SWEAR BY THESE BOUNDLESS LANDS...

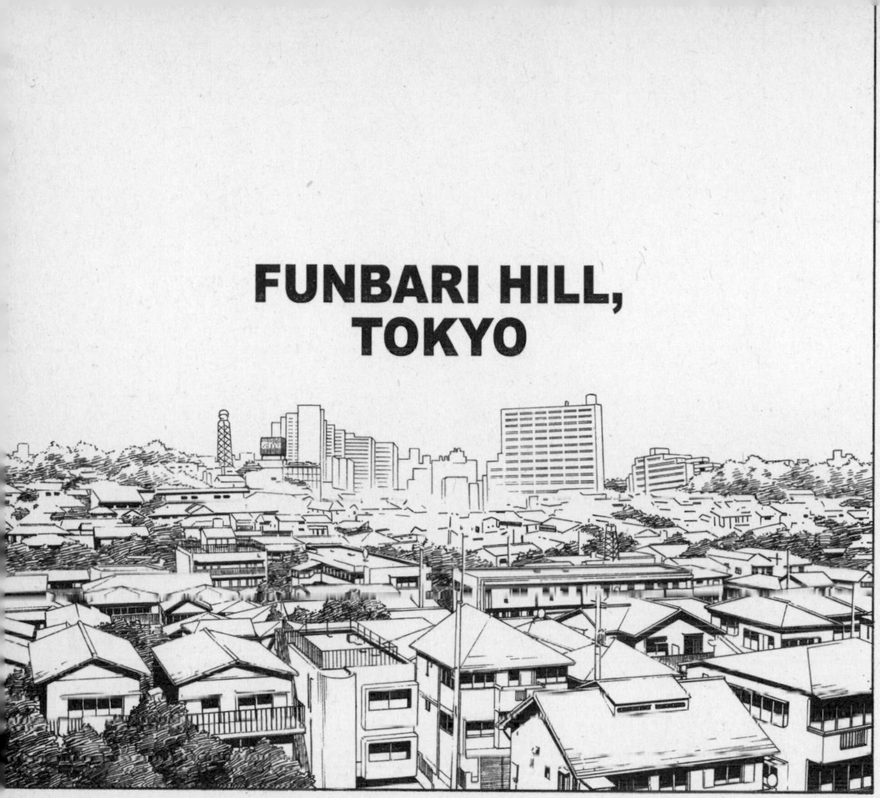
FUNBARI HILL,
TOKYO
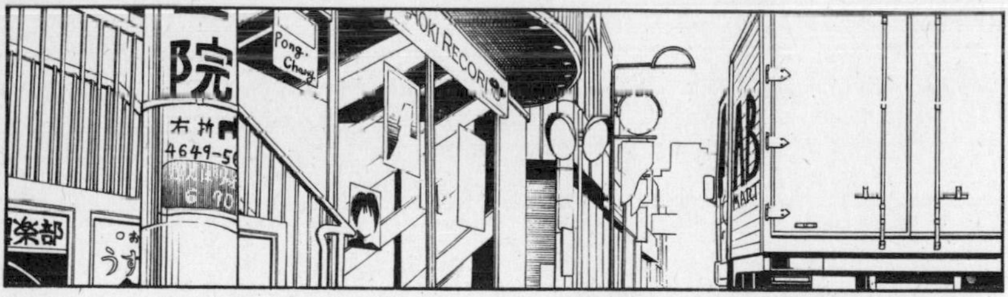
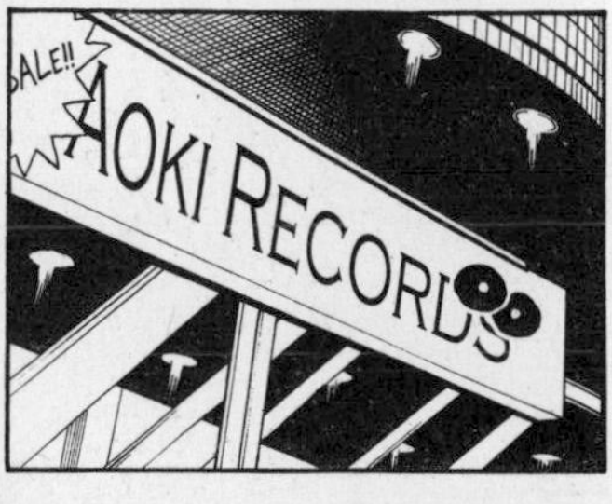
SALE!!
AOKI RECORDS
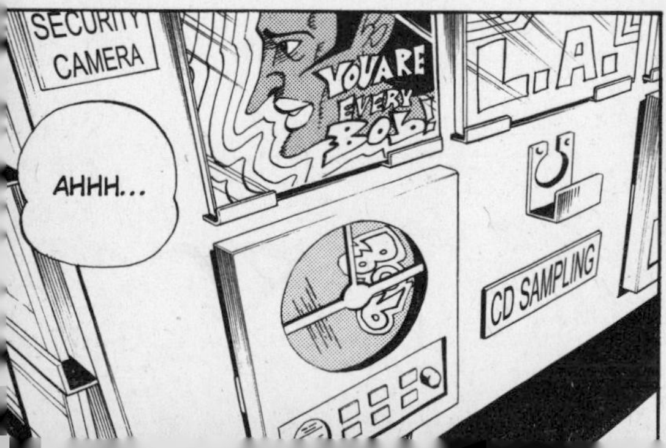
SECURITY
CAMERA
AHHH...
L.A.
CD SAMPLING

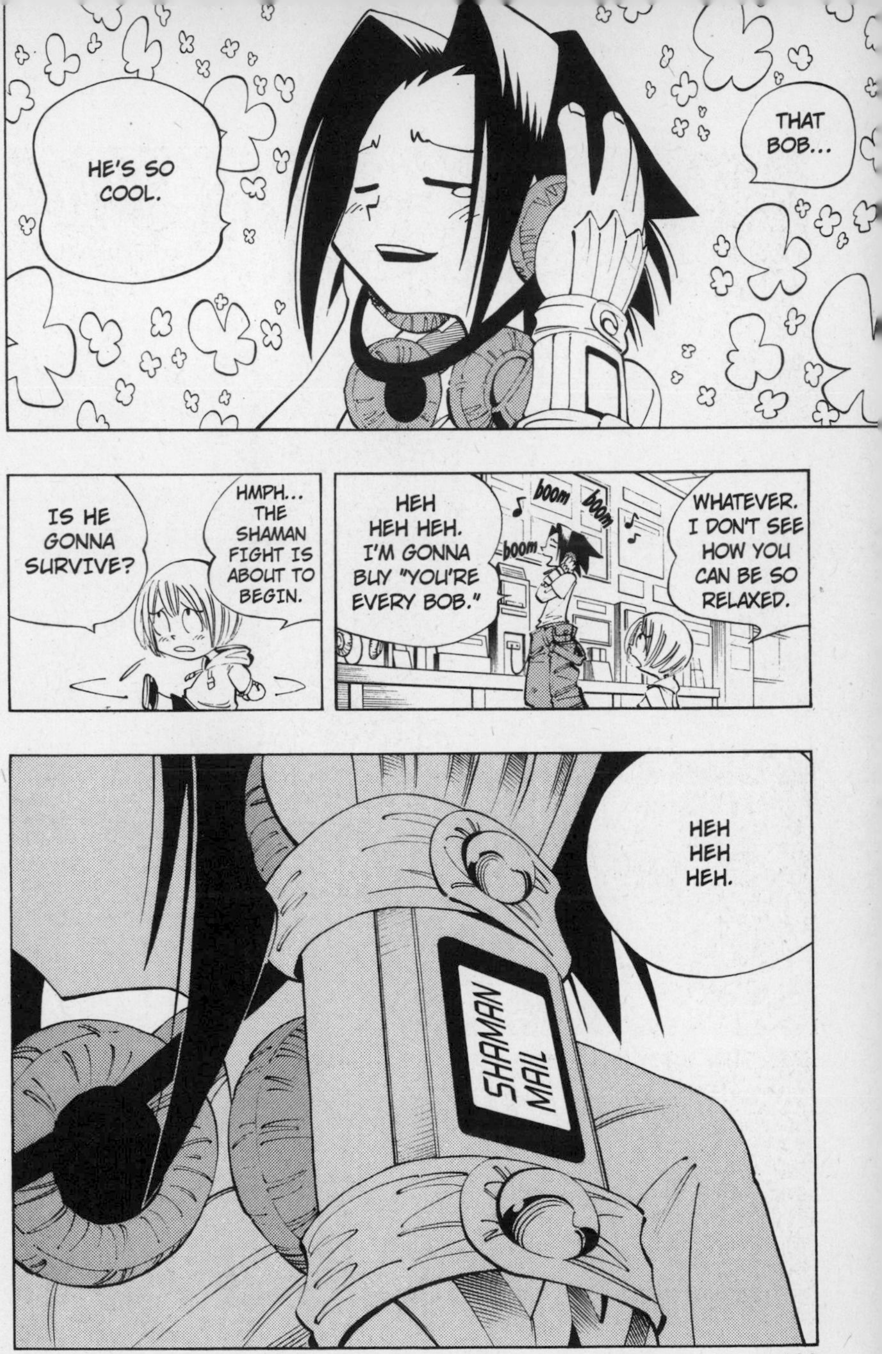
THAT BOB...
HE'S SO COOL.
WHATEVER. I DON'T SEE HOW YOU CAN BE SO RELAXED.
boom boom boom
HEH HEH HEH. I'M GONNA BUY "YOU'RE EVERY BOB."
HMPH... THE SHAMAN FIGHT IS ABOUT TO BEGIN.
IS HE GONNA SURVIVE?
HEH HEH HEH.
SHAMAN MAIL

# Reincarnation 77: Voyage of the Shaman

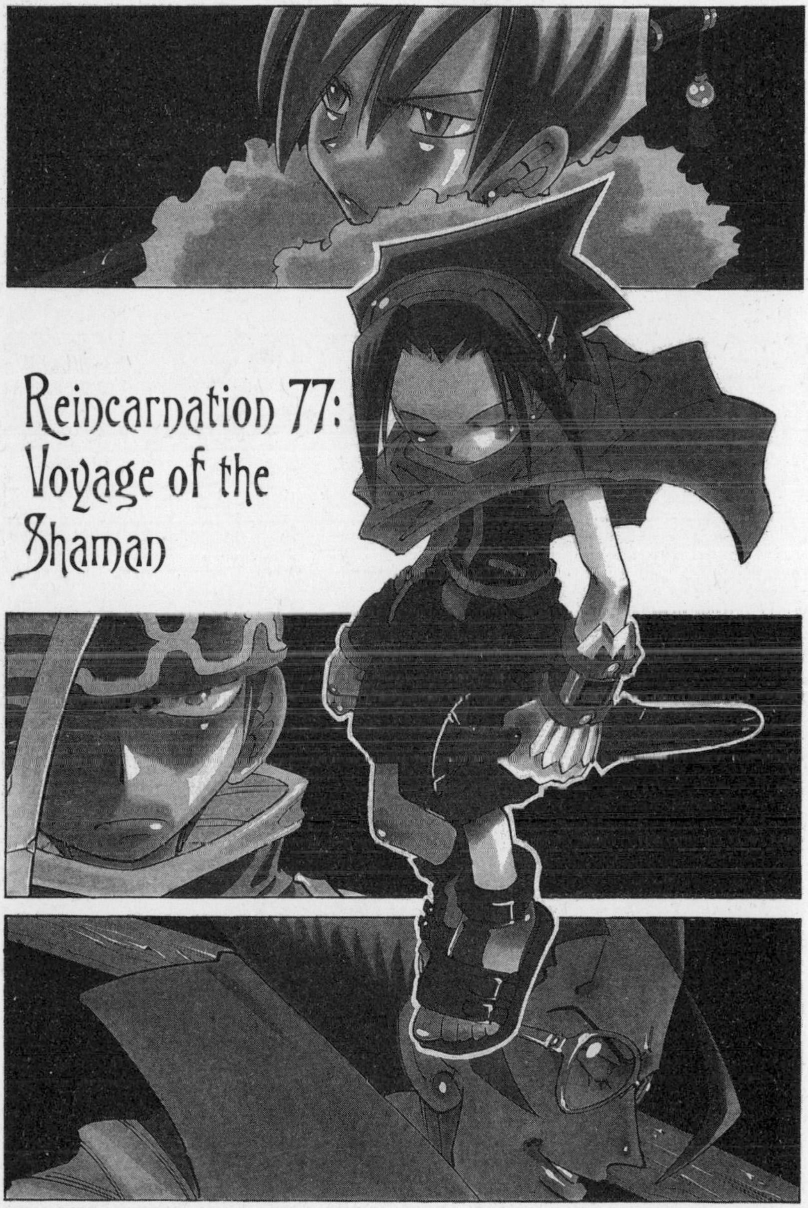

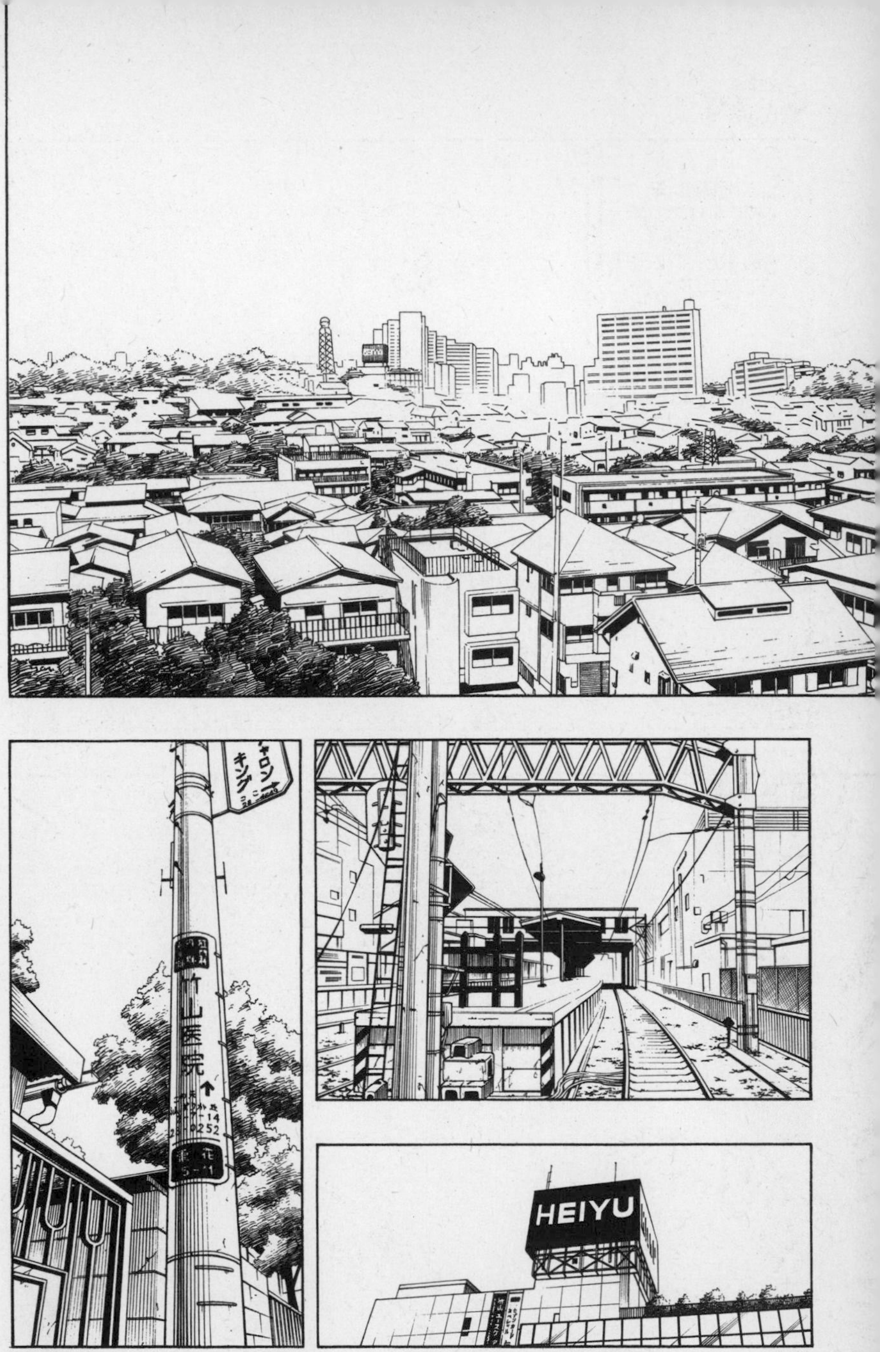
HEIYU
キング
竹山医院
5-11

READ THIS WAY

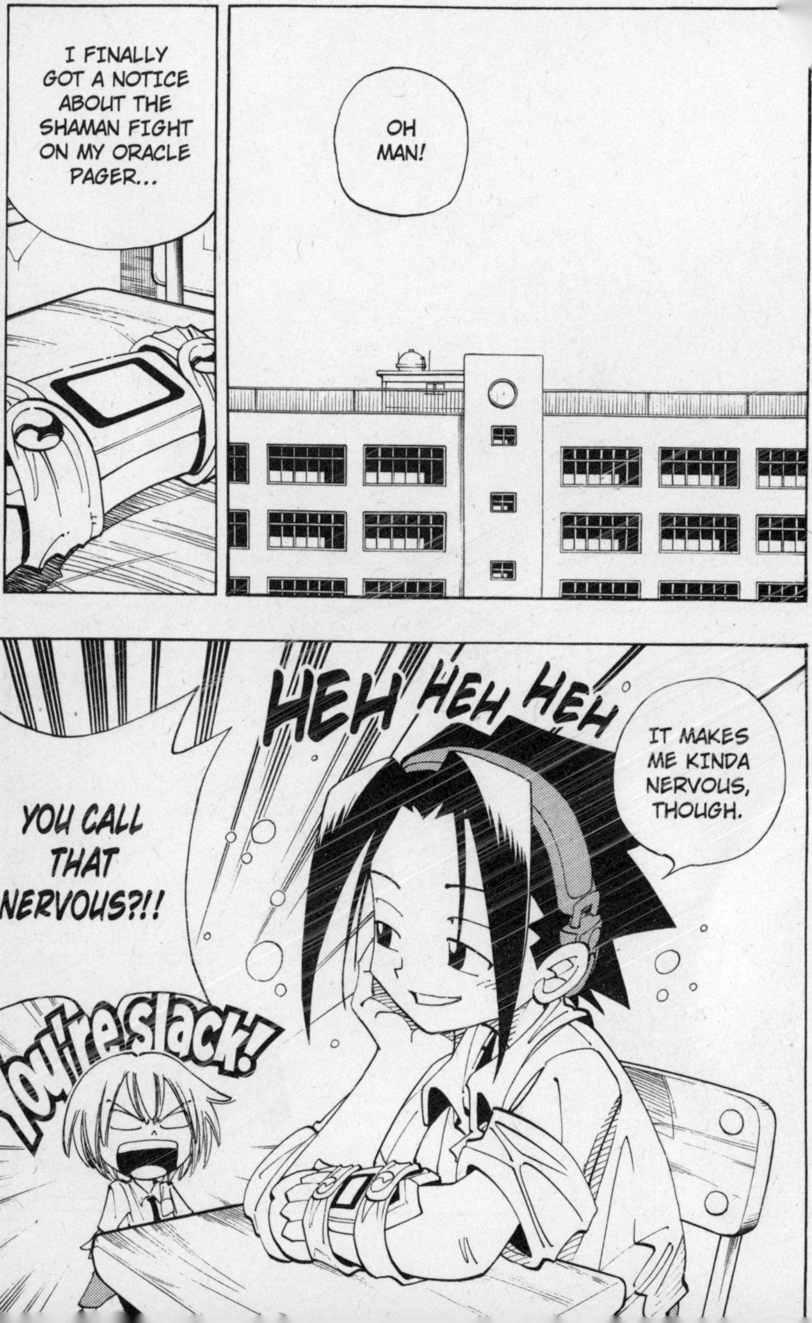
OH MAN!
I FINALLY GOT A NOTICE ABOUT THE SHAMAN FIGHT ON MY ORACLE PAGER...
IT MAKES ME KINDA NERVOUS, THOUGH.
HEH HEH HEH
YOU CALL THAT NERVOUS?!!
You're slack!

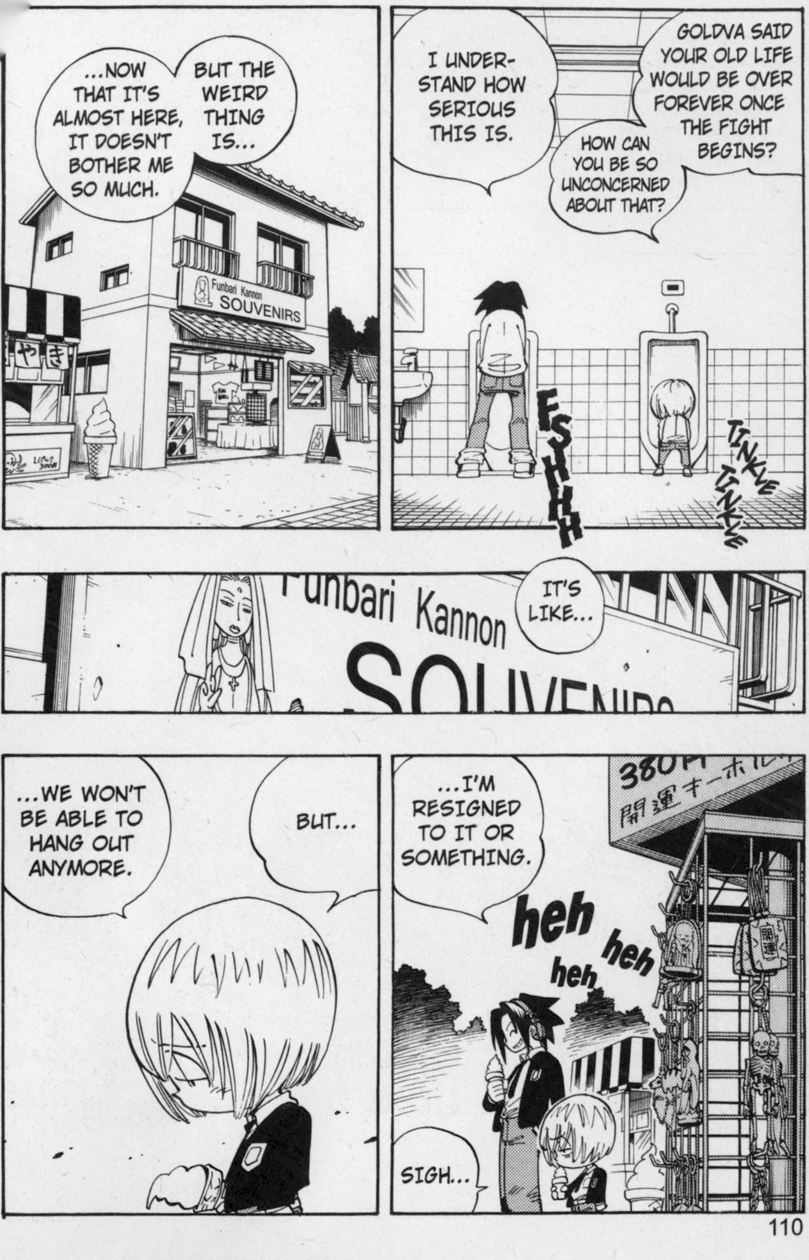
GOLDVA SAID YOUR OLD LIFE WOULD BE OVER FOREVER ONCE THE FIGHT BEGINS?
HOW CAN YOU BE SO UNCONCERNED ABOUT THAT?
I UNDERSTAND HOW SERIOUS THIS IS.
TINKLE TINKLE
FSHHHH
Funbari Kannon SOUVENIRS
BUT THE WEIRD THING IS...
...NOW THAT IT'S ALMOST HERE, IT DOESN'T BOTHER ME SO MUCH.
IT'S LIKE...
Funbari Kannon
...I'M RESIGNED TO IT OR SOMETHING.
heh heh heh
SIGH...
BUT...
...WE WON'T BE ABLE TO HANG OUT ANYMORE.

READ THIS WAY

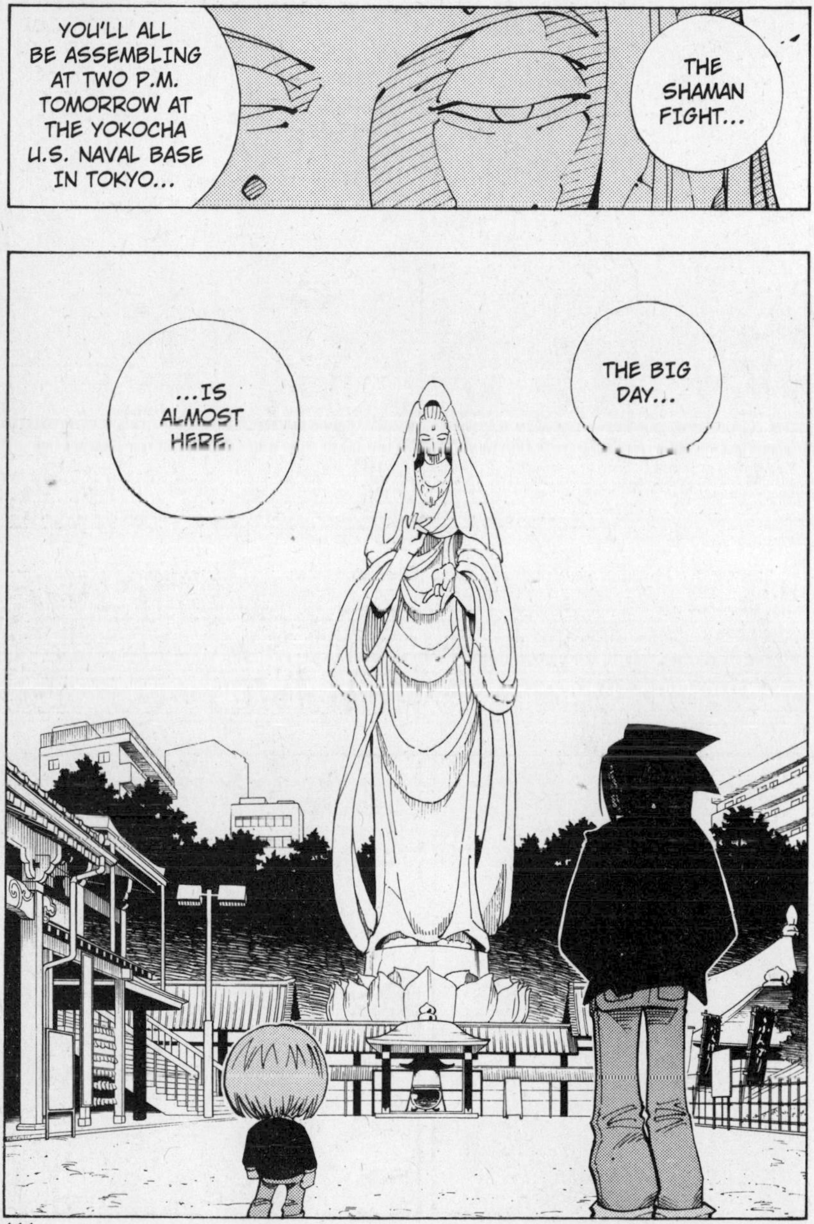
THE SHAMAN FIGHT...
YOU'LL ALL BE ASSEMBLING AT TWO P.M. TOMORROW AT THE YOKOCHA U.S. NAVAL BASE IN TOKYO...
THE BIG DAY...
...IS ALMOST HERE.

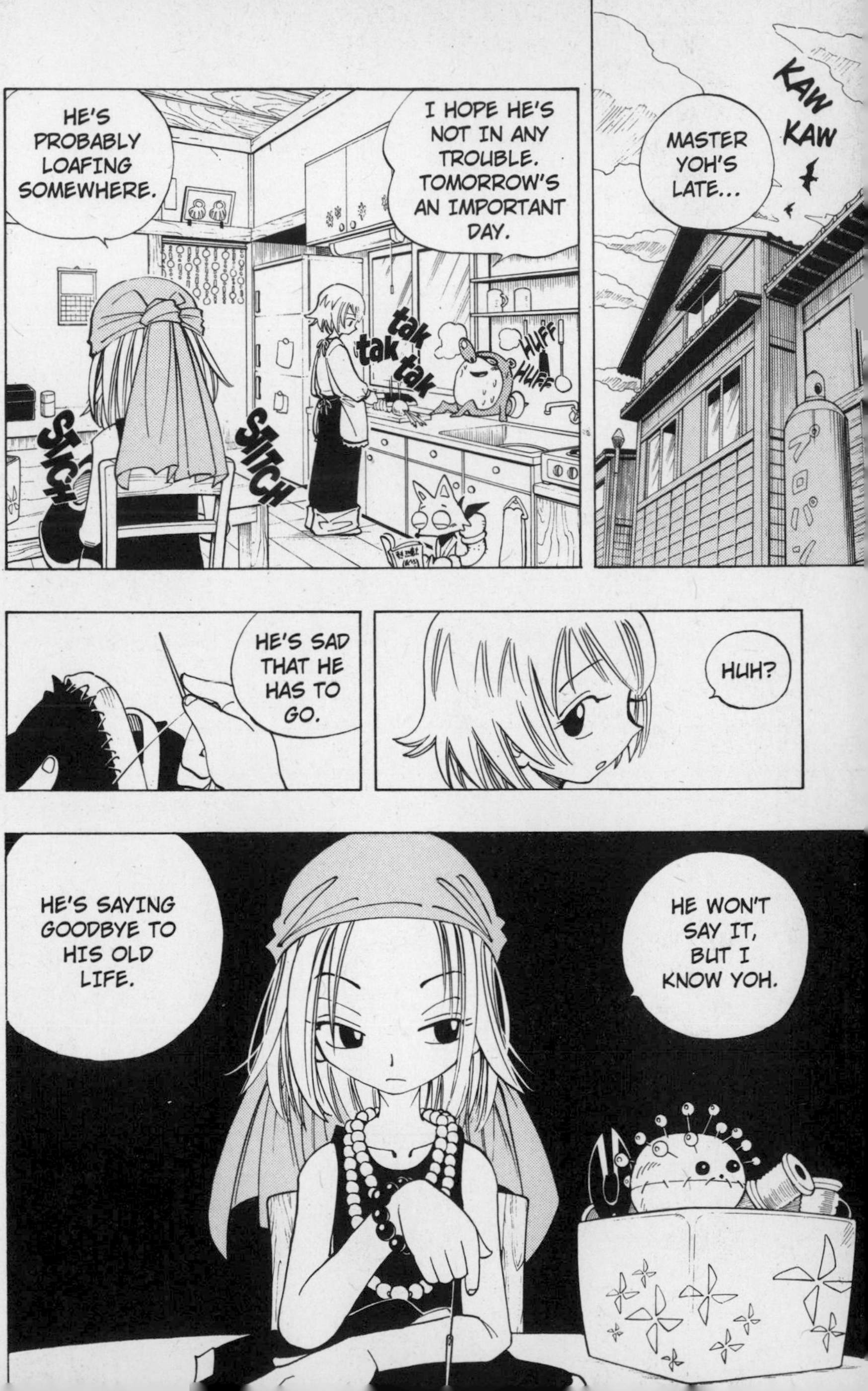
KAW KAW
MASTER YOH'S LATE...
I HOPE HE'S NOT IN ANY TROUBLE. TOMORROW'S AN IMPORTANT DAY.
HE'S PROBABLY LOAFING SOMEWHERE.
HUFF HUFF
tak tak tak
STITCH
STITCH
HUH?
HE'S SAD THAT HE HAS TO GO.
HE WON'T SAY IT, BUT I KNOW YOH.
HE'S SAYING GOODBYE TO HIS OLD LIFE.

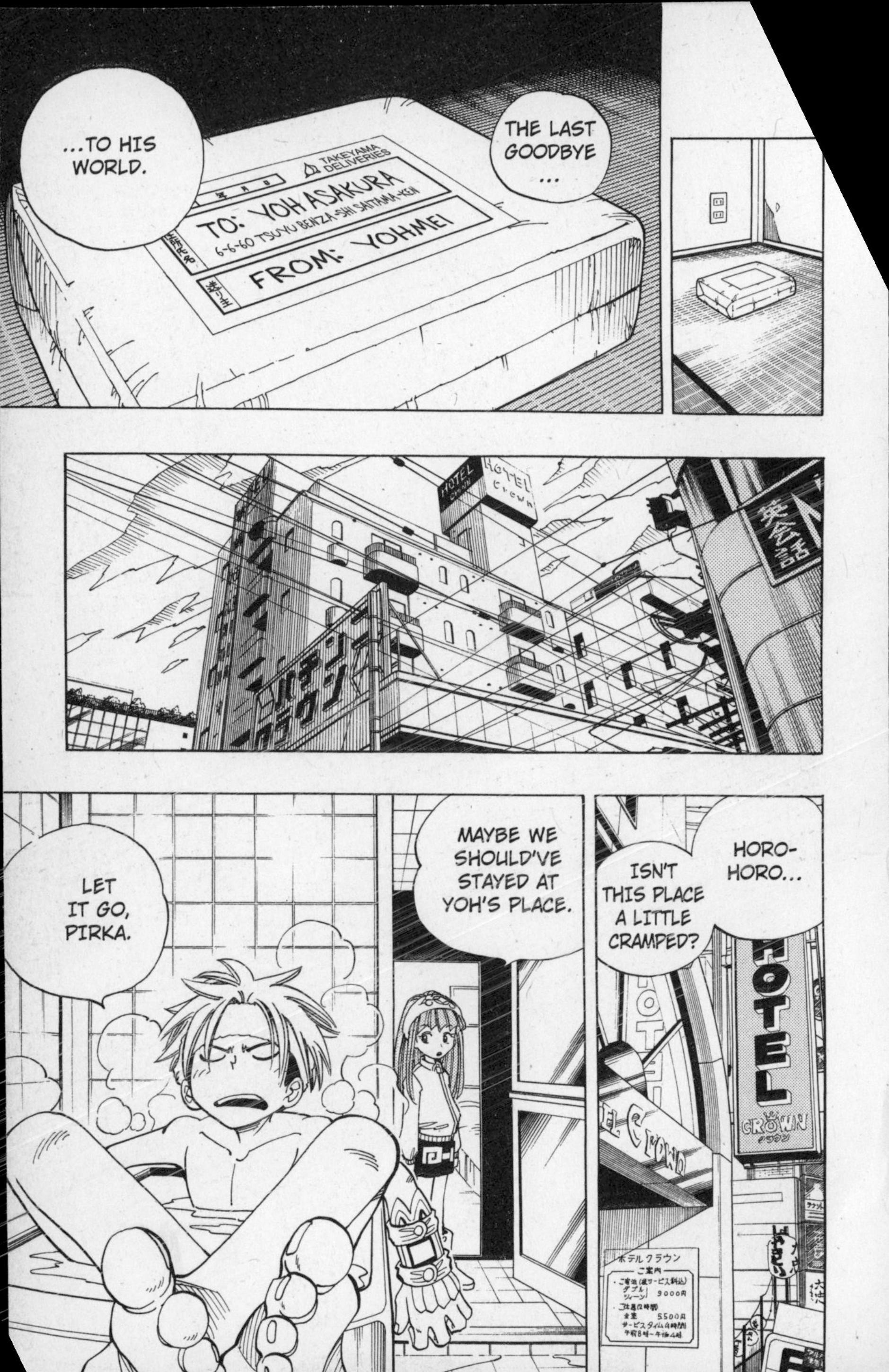
THE LAST GOODBYE...
...TO HIS WORLD.
TAKEYAMA DELIVERIES
TO: YOH ASAKURA
6-6-60 TSUYU BENZA-SHI SAITAMA-KEN
FROM: YOHMEI
HOTEL
HOTEL CROWN
英会話
HORO-HORO...
ISN'T THIS PLACE A LITTLE CRAMPED?
HOTEL
CROWN
ホテルクラウン
ご案内
MAYBE WE SHOULD'VE STAYED AT YOH'S PLACE.
LET IT GO, PIRKA.

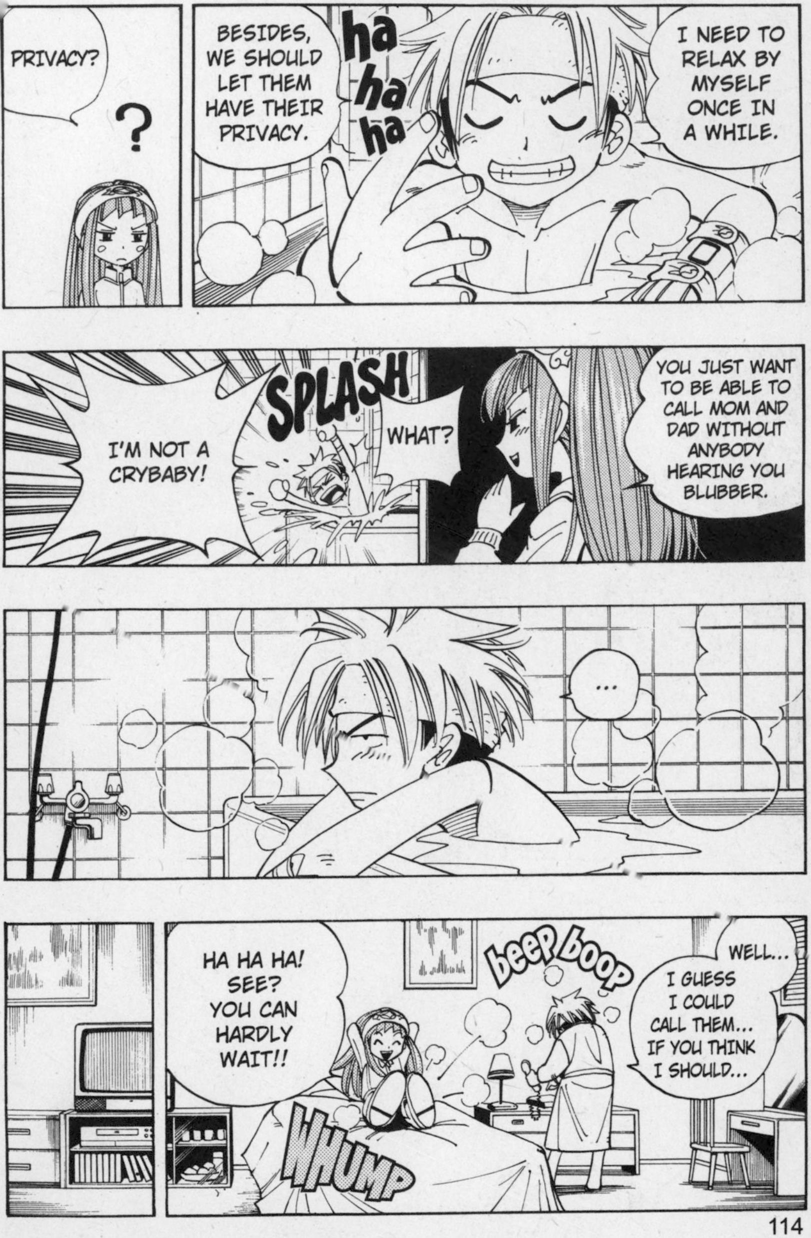
I NEED TO RELAX BY MYSELF ONCE IN A WHILE.
ha ha ha
BESIDES, WE SHOULD LET THEM HAVE THEIR PRIVACY.
PRIVACY?
?
YOU JUST WANT TO BE ABLE TO CALL MOM AND DAD WITHOUT ANYBODY HEARING YOU BLUBBER.
WHAT?
SPLASH
I'M NOT A CRYBABY!
...
WELL... I GUESS I COULD CALL THEM... IF YOU THINK I SHOULD...
beep boop
HA HA HA! SEE? YOU CAN HARDLY WAIT!!
WHUMP

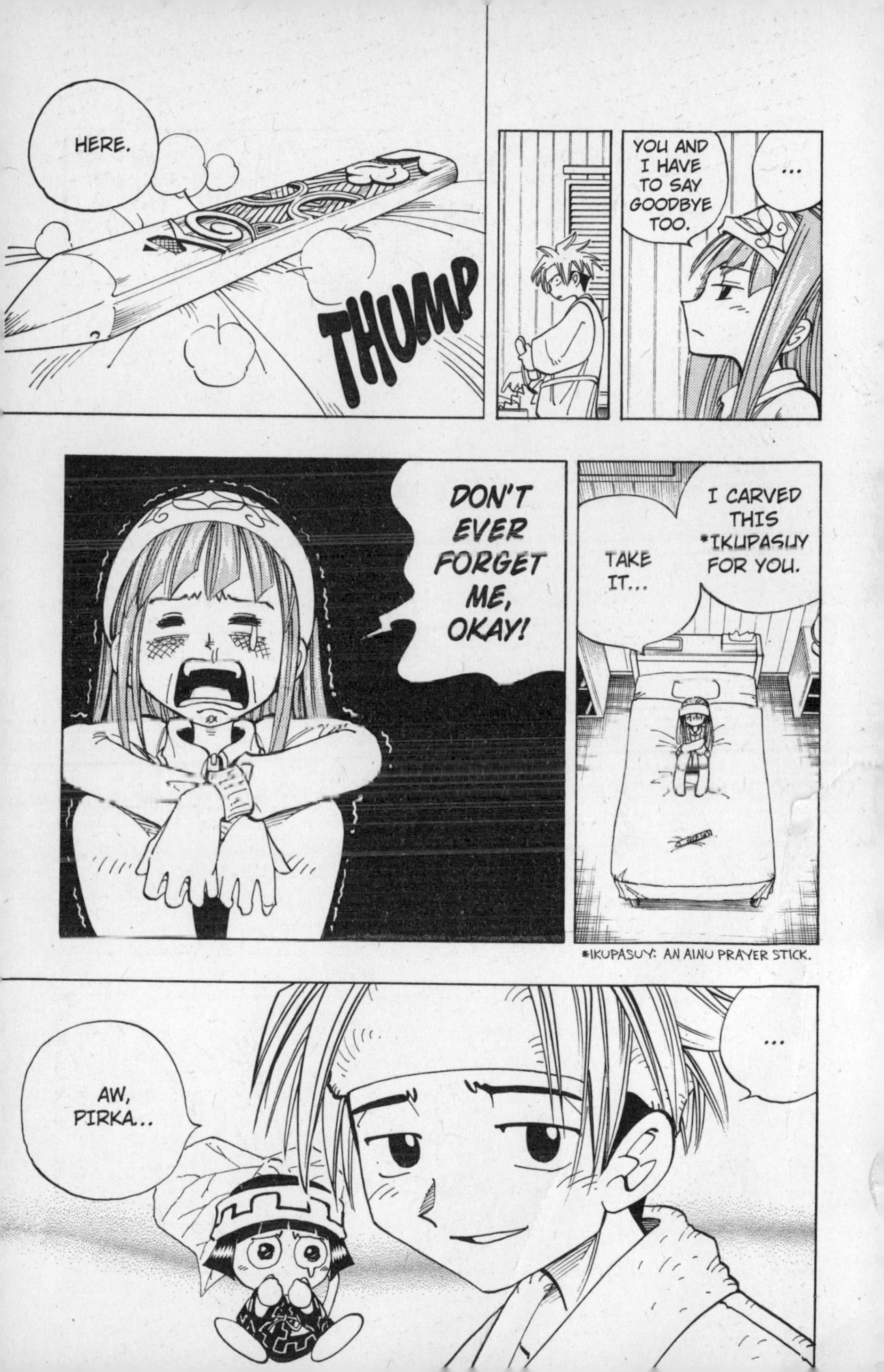
...
YOU AND I HAVE TO SAY GOODBYE TOO.
HERE.
THUMP
I CARVED THIS *IKUPASUY FOR YOU.
TAKE IT...
DON'T EVER FORGET ME, OKAY!
*IKUPASUY: AN AINU PRAYER STICK.
...
AW, PIRKA...

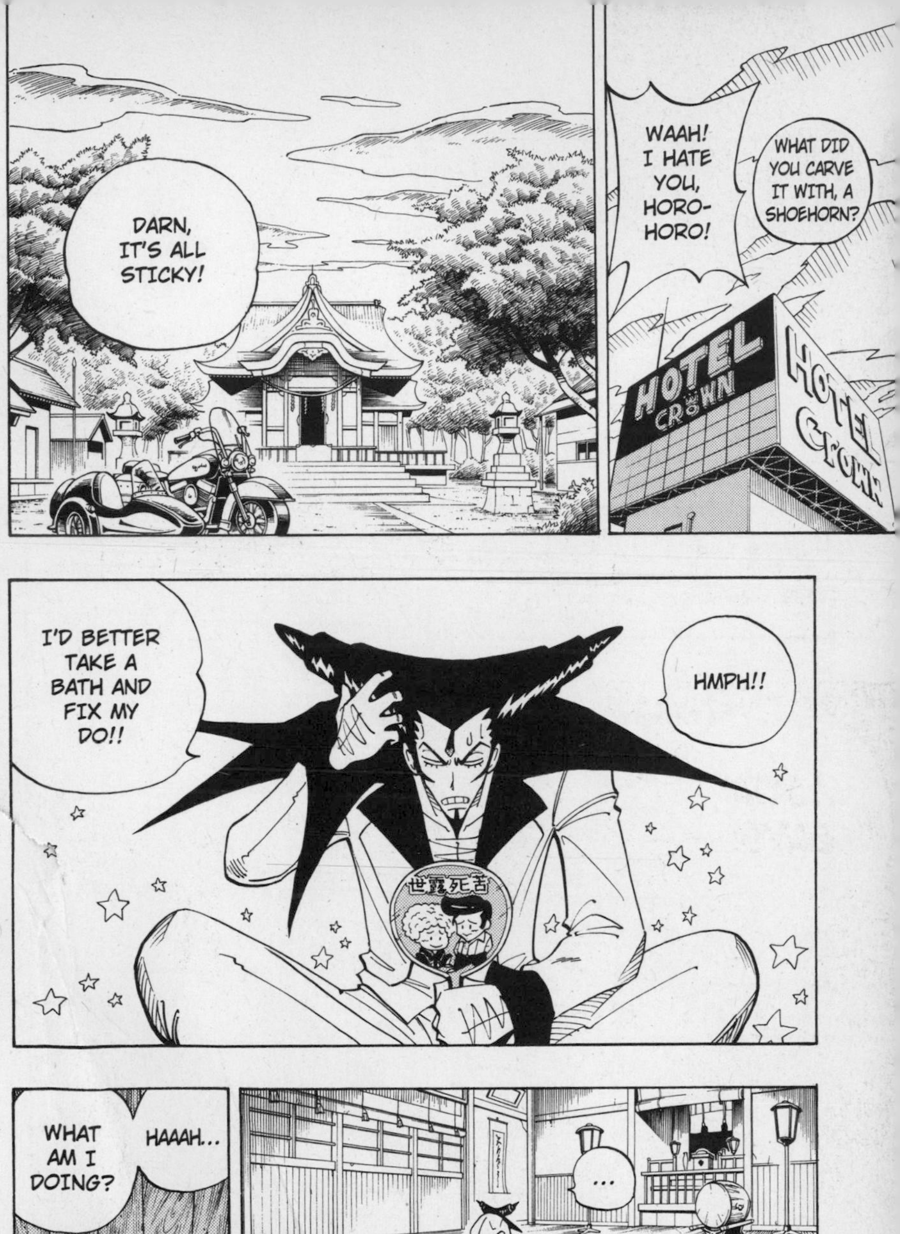
WHAT DID YOU CARVE IT WITH, A SHOEHORN?
WAAH! I HATE YOU, HORO-HORO!
HOTEL CROWN
DARN, IT'S ALL STICKY!
HMPH!!
世露死苦
I'D BETTER TAKE A BATH AND FIX MY DO!!
...
HAAAH...
WHAT AM I DOING?

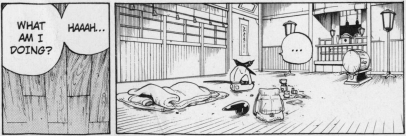

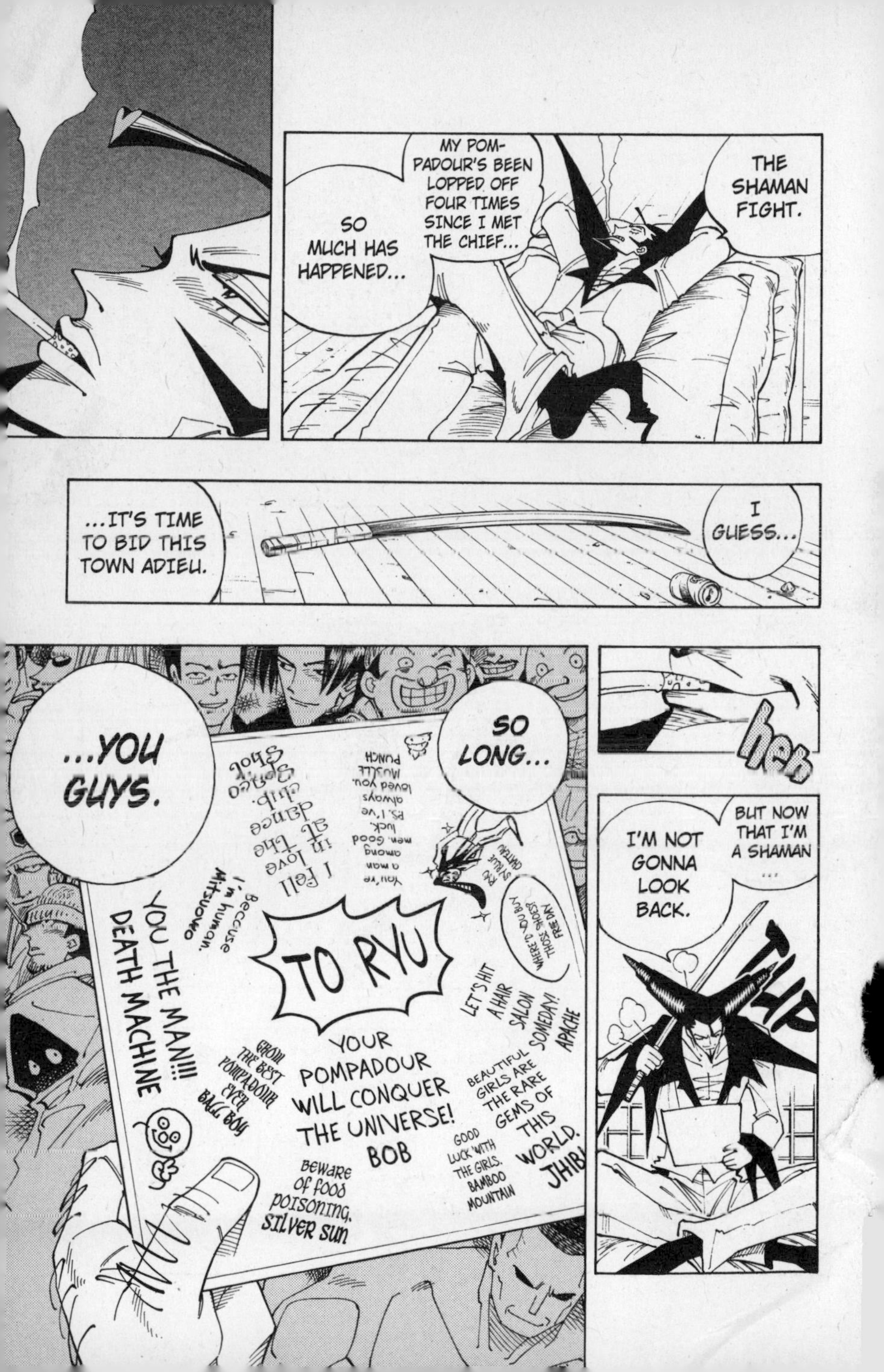
THE SHAMAN FIGHT.
MY POMPADOUR'S BEEN LOPPED OFF FOUR TIMES SINCE I MET THE CHIEF...
SO MUCH HAS HAPPENED...
I GUESS...
...IT'S TIME TO BID THIS TOWN ADIEU.
heh
BUT NOW THAT I'M A SHAMAN ...
I'M NOT GONNA LOOK BACK.
THIP
SO LONG...
...YOU GUYS.
TO RYU
You're a man among men. Good luck. P.S. I've always loved you. MUSCLE PUNCH
I Fell in love at the dance club. Shoko
Because I'm human. Mitsuowo
WHERE'D YOU BUY THOSE SHOES? FREE DAY
LET'S HIT A HAIR SALON SOMEDAY! APACHE
YOU THE MAN!!! DEATH MACHINE
GROW THE BEST POMPADOUR EVER BALL BOY
YOUR POMPADOUR WILL CONQUER THE UNIVERSE! BOB
BEAUTIFUL GIRLS ARE THE RARE GEMS OF THIS WORLD. JHIBI
GOOD LUCK WITH THE GIRLS. BAMBOO MOUNTAIN
Beware of food poisoning. SILVER SUN

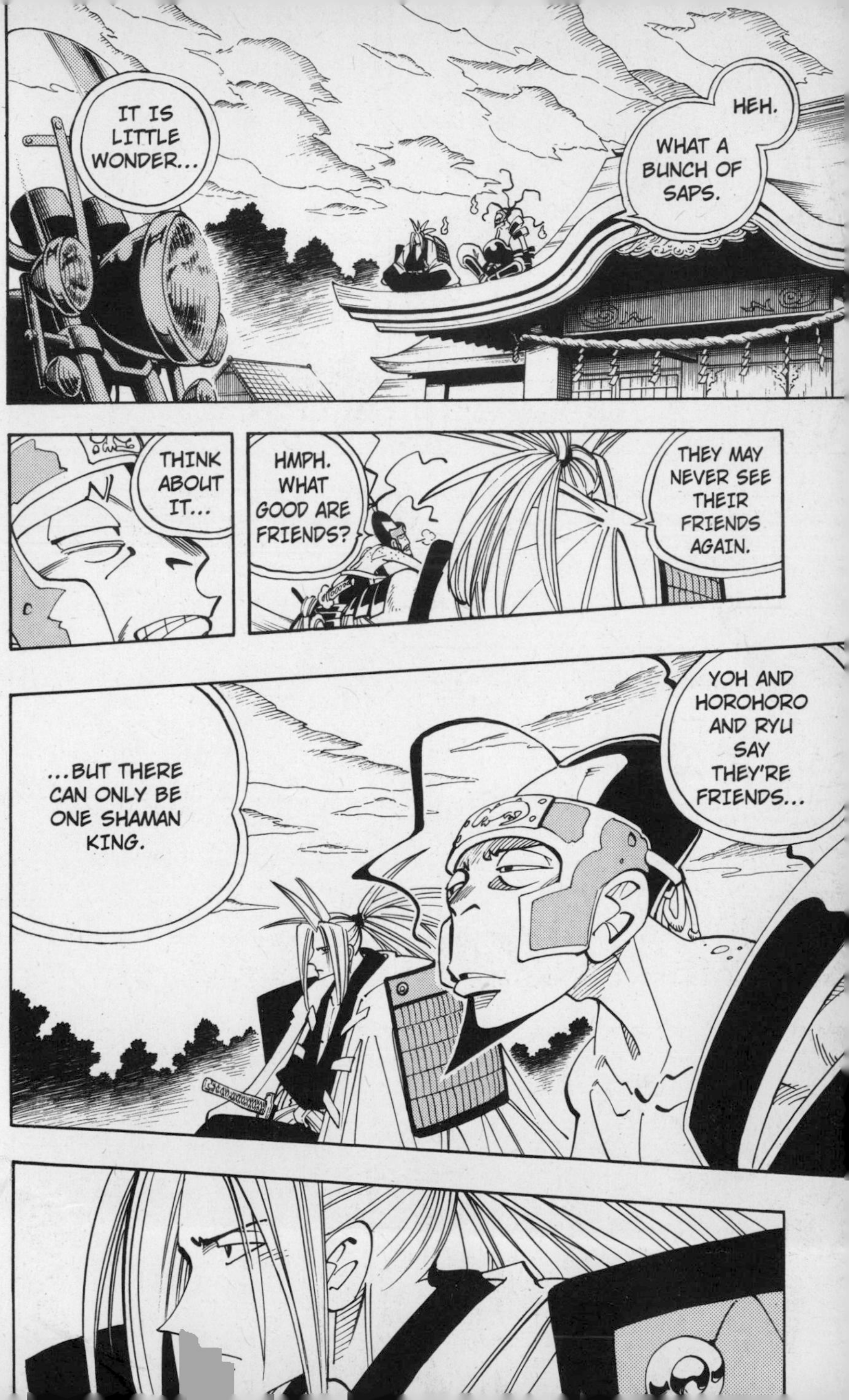
HEH. WHAT A BUNCH OF SAPS.
IT IS LITTLE WONDER...
THEY MAY NEVER SEE THEIR FRIENDS AGAIN.
HMPH. WHAT GOOD ARE FRIENDS?
THINK ABOUT IT...
YOH AND HOROHORO AND RYU SAY THEY'RE FRIENDS...
...BUT THERE CAN ONLY BE ONE SHAMAN KING.

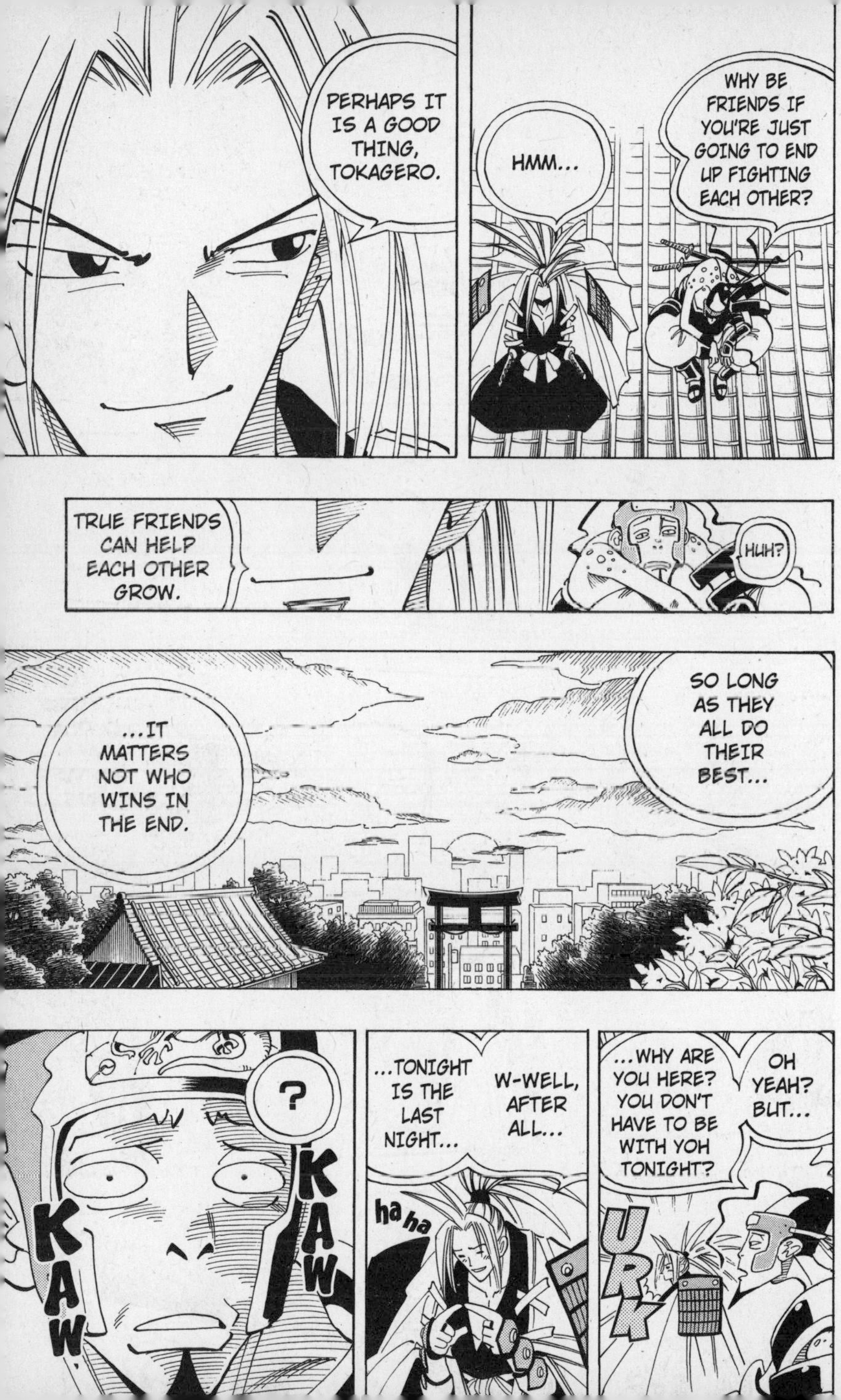
WHY BE FRIENDS IF YOU'RE JUST GOING TO END UP FIGHTING EACH OTHER?
HMM...
PERHAPS IT IS A GOOD THING, TOKAGERO.
TRUE FRIENDS CAN HELP EACH OTHER GROW.
HUH?
SO LONG AS THEY ALL DO THEIR BEST...
...IT MATTERS NOT WHO WINS IN THE END.
OH YEAH? BUT...
...WHY ARE YOU HERE? YOU DON'T HAVE TO BE WITH YOH TONIGHT?
URK
W-WELL, AFTER ALL...
...TONIGHT IS THE LAST NIGHT...
ha ha
?
KAW
KAW
KAW
KAW

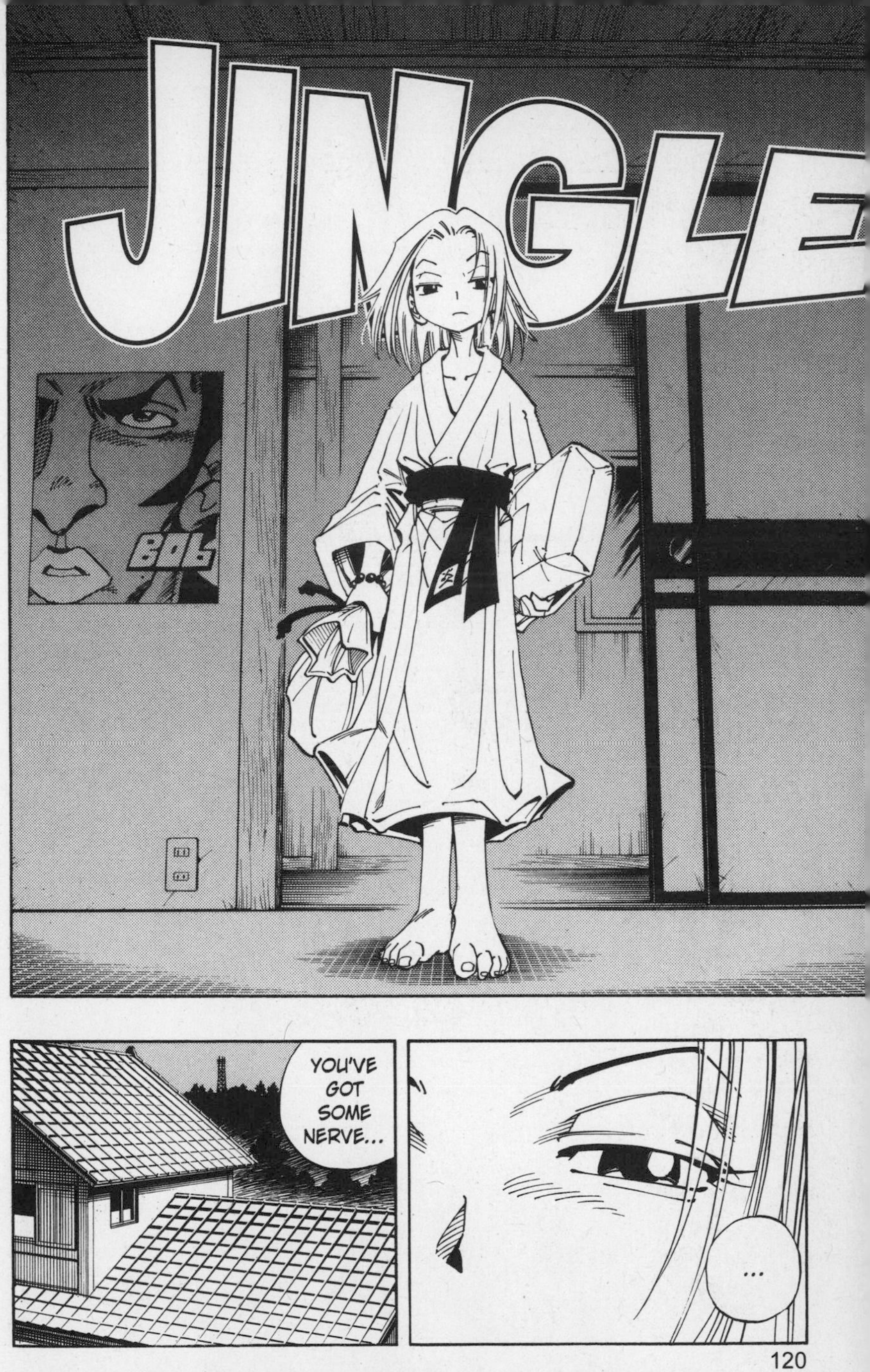
JINGLE
BOB
...
YOU'VE GOT SOME NERVE...

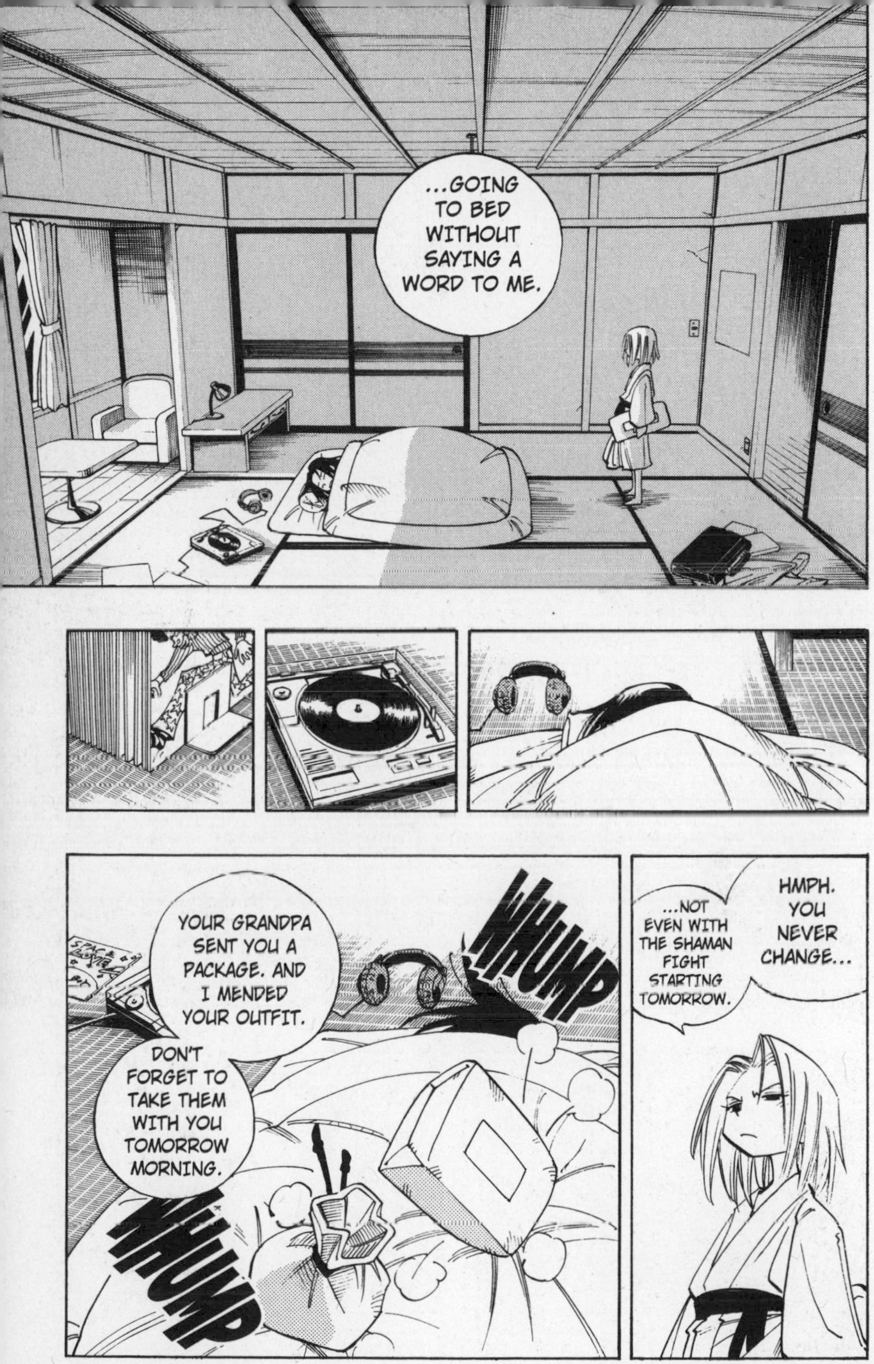
...GOING TO BED WITHOUT SAYING A WORD TO ME.
HMPH. YOU NEVER CHANGE...
...NOT EVEN WITH THE SHAMAN FIGHT STARTING TOMORROW.
WHUMP
YOUR GRANDPA SENT YOU A PACKAGE. AND I MENDED YOUR OUTFIT.
DON'T FORGET TO TAKE THEM WITH YOU TOMORROW MORNING.
WHUMP

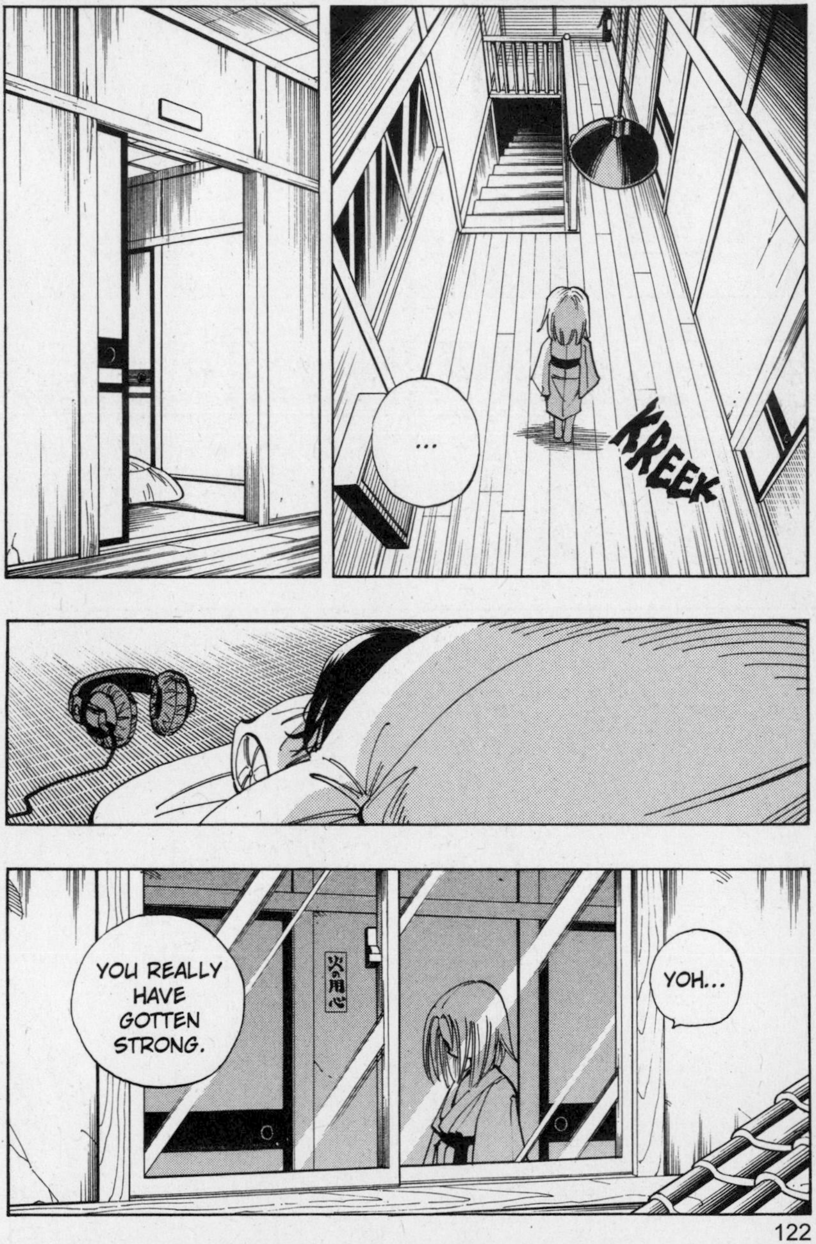
...
KREEK
YOH...
火の用心
YOU REALLY HAVE GOTTEN STRONG.

READ THIS WAY

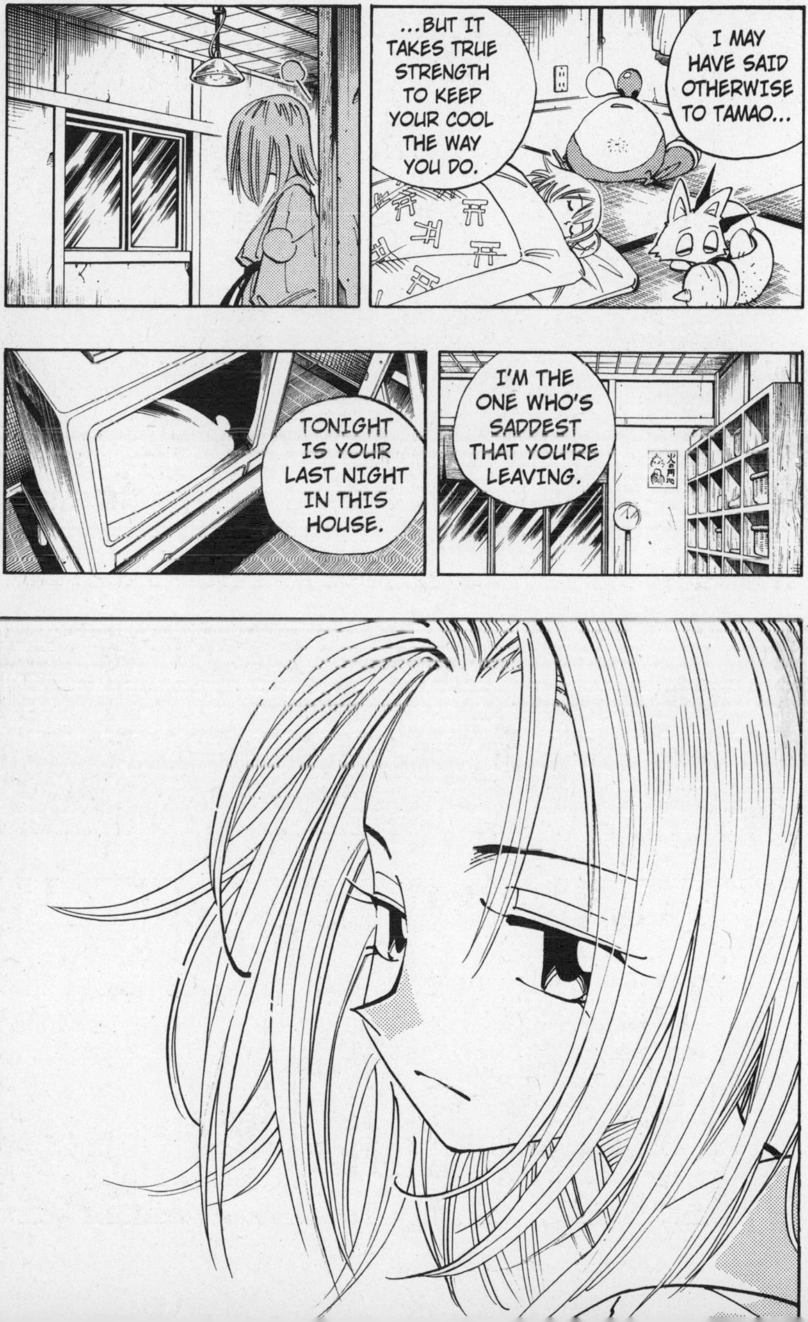
I MAY HAVE SAID OTHERWISE TO TAMAO...
...BUT IT TAKES TRUE STRENGTH TO KEEP YOUR COOL THE WAY YOU DO.
I'M THE ONE WHO'S SADDEST THAT YOU'RE LEAVING.
TONIGHT IS YOUR LAST NIGHT IN THIS HOUSE.

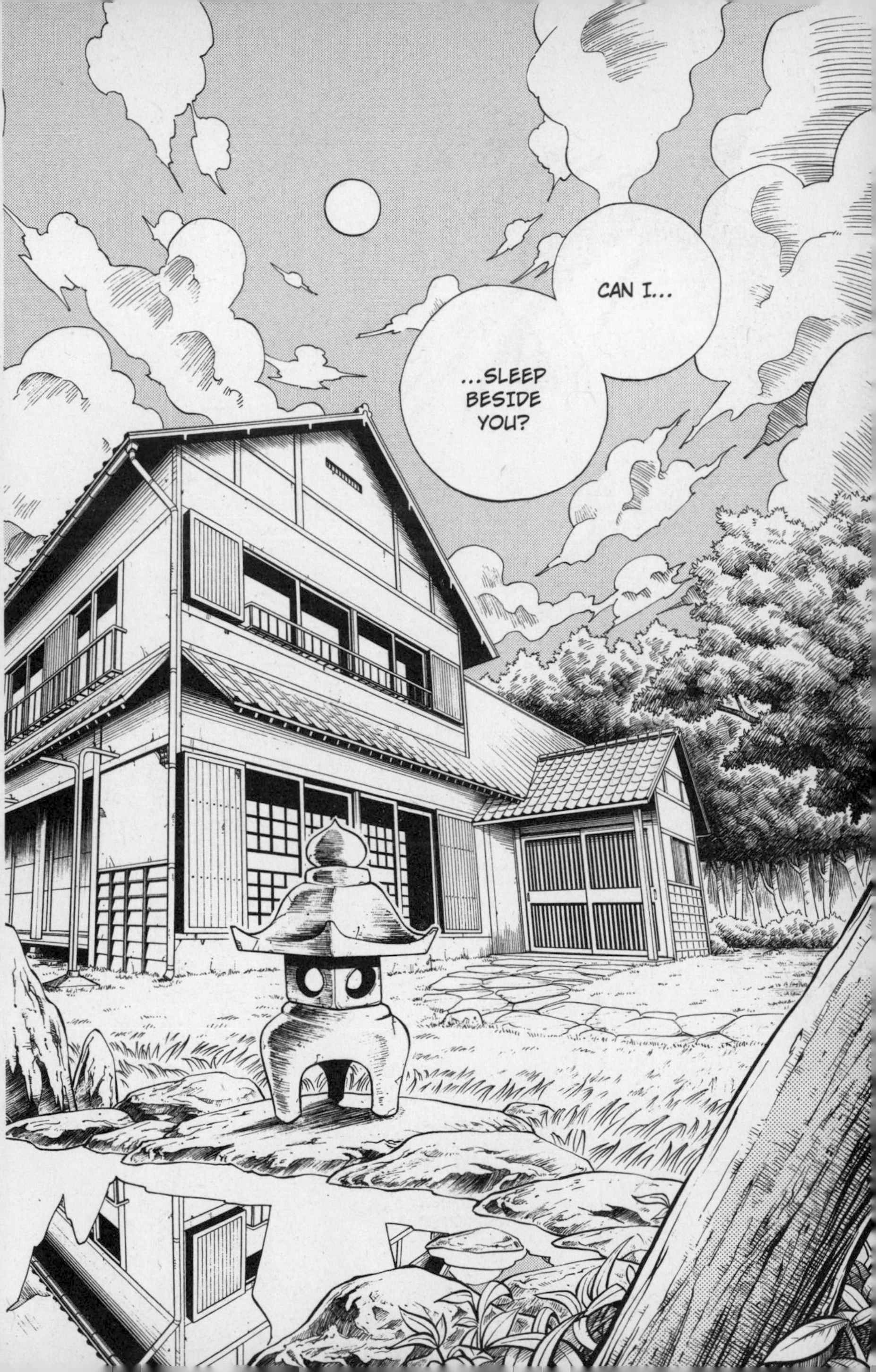
CAN I...
...SLEEP BESIDE YOU?

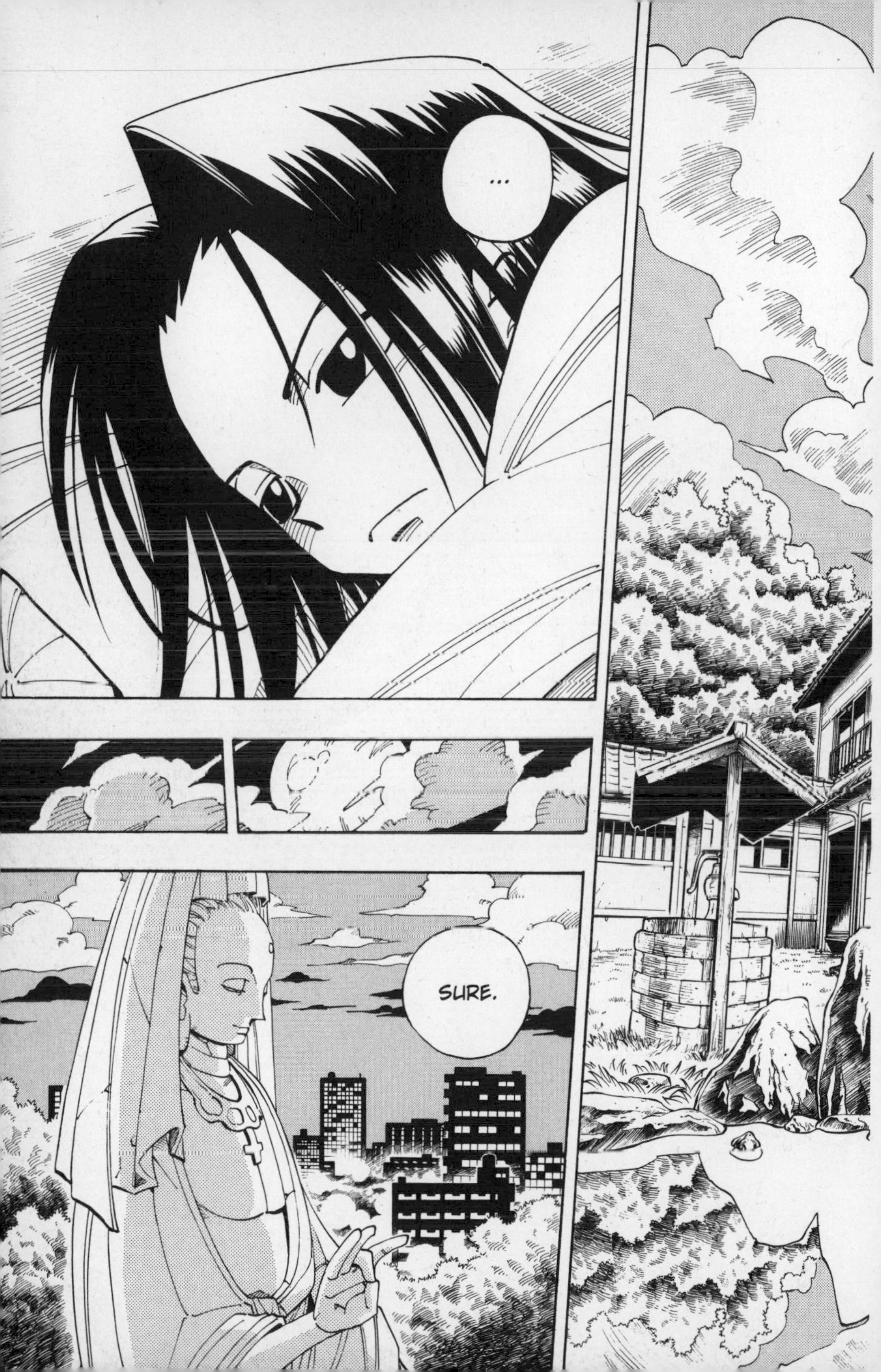
...
SURE.

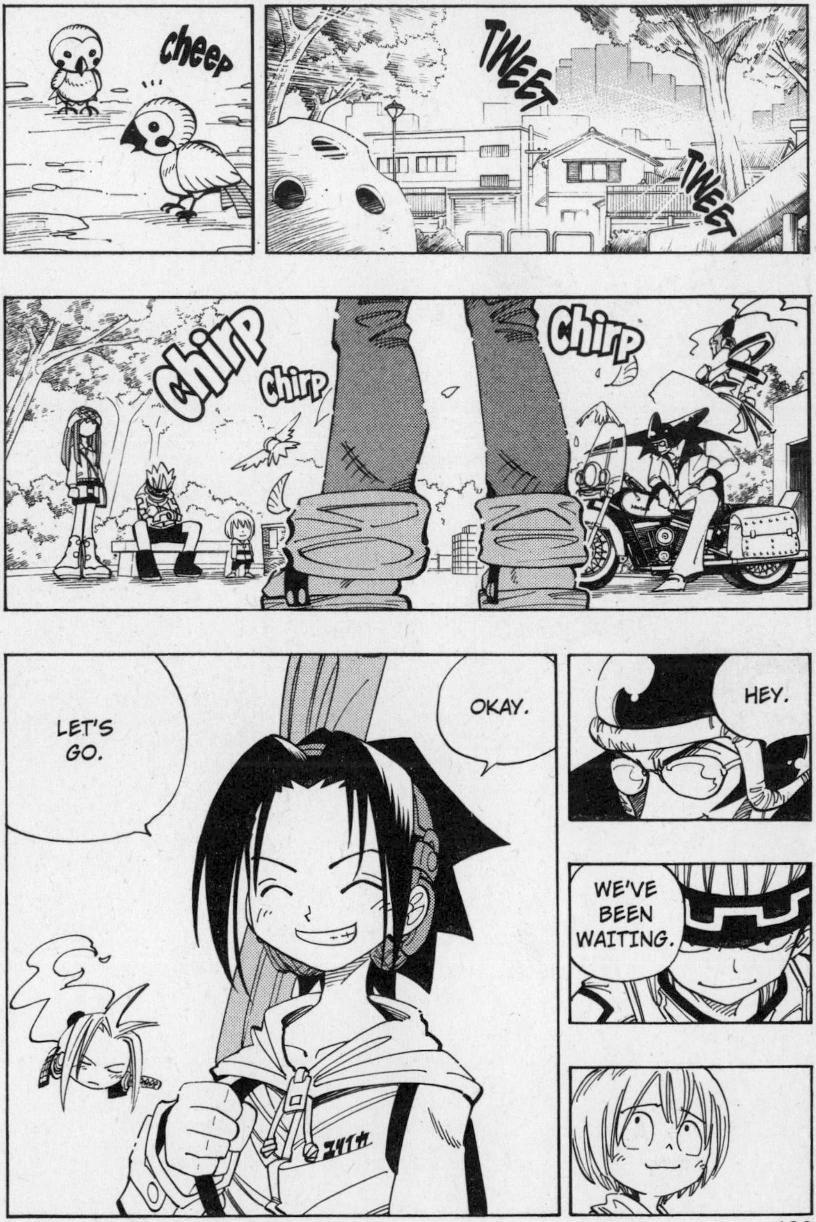
TWEET
TWEET
cheep
Chirp
Chirp
Chirp
HEY.
WE'VE BEEN WAITING.
OKAY.
LET'S GO.

READ THIS WAY

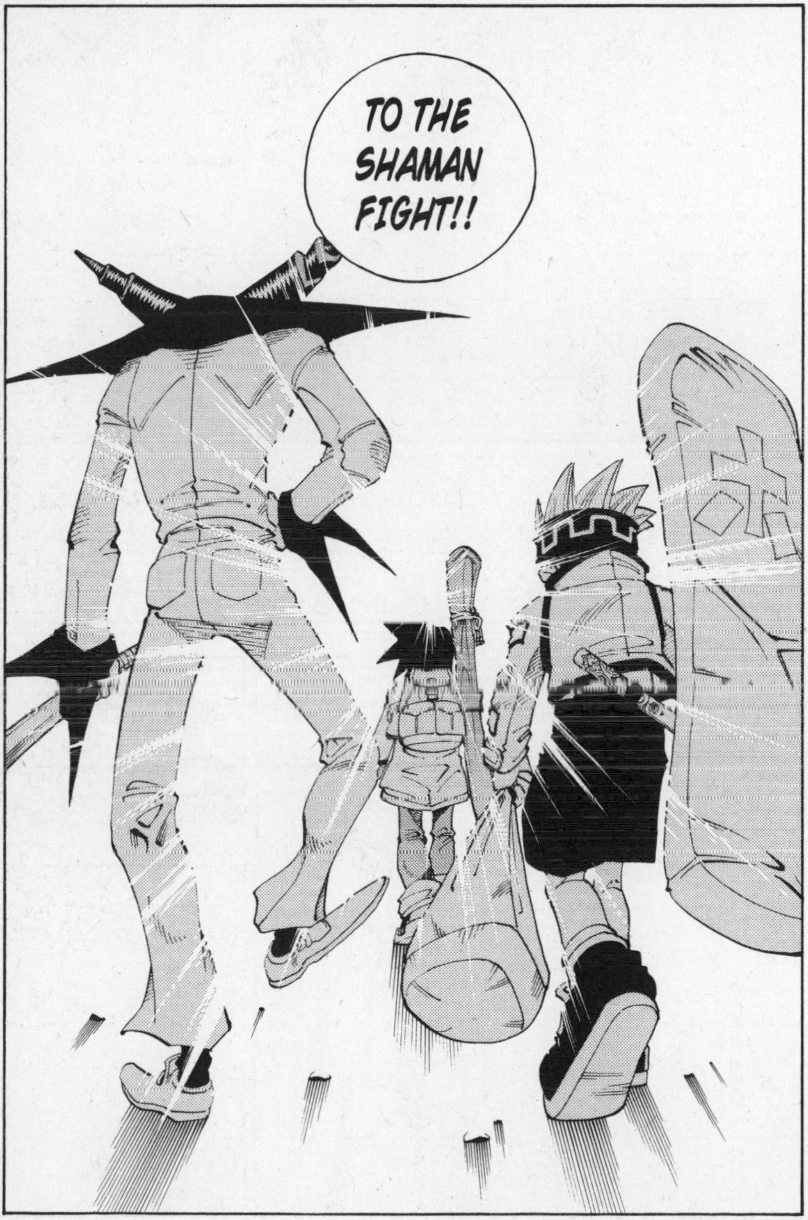
TO THE SHAMAN FIGHT!!

## SHAMAN KING CHARACTER FILE No.41

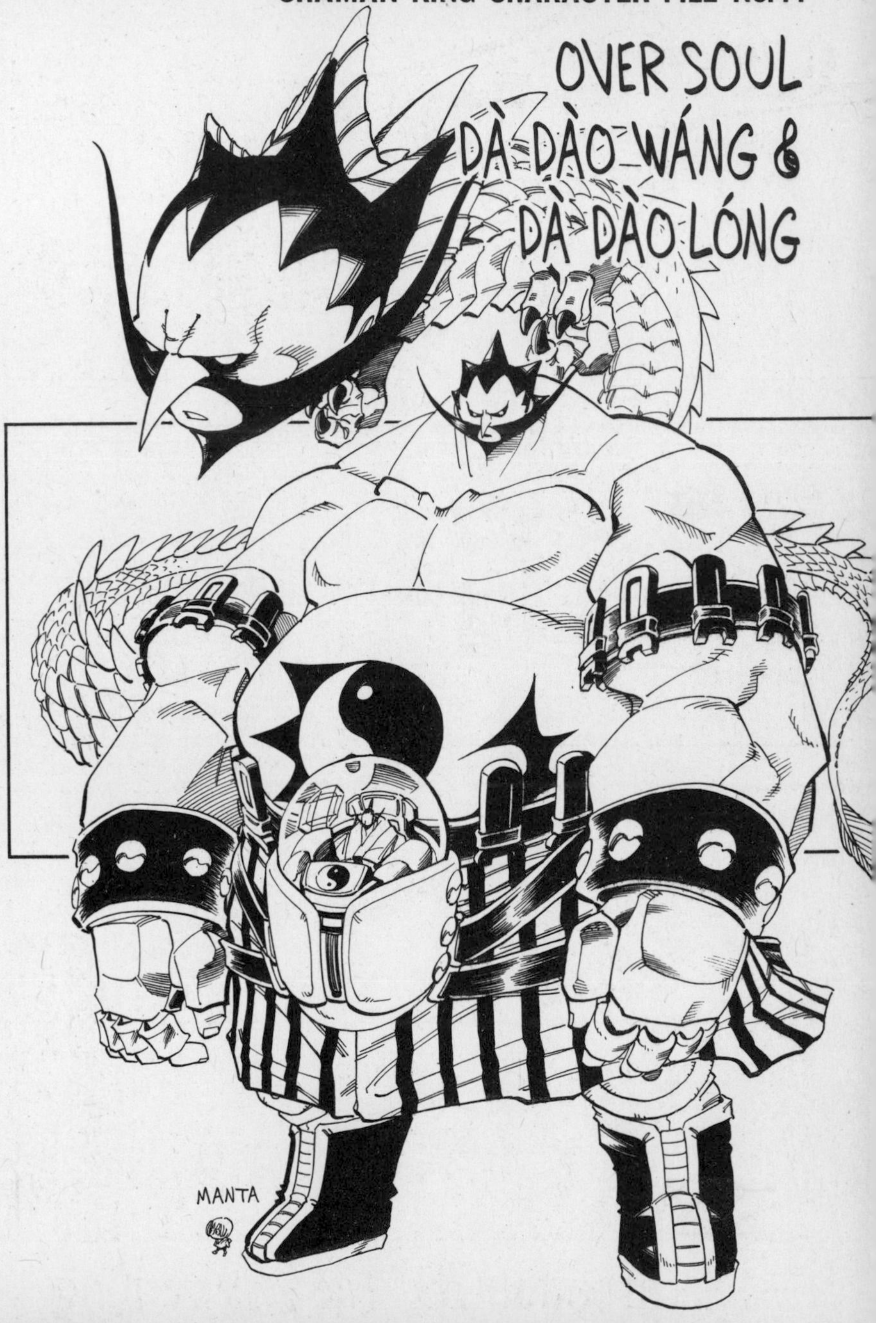
OVER SOUL
DÀ DÀO WÁNG &
DÀ DÀO LÓNG
MANTA

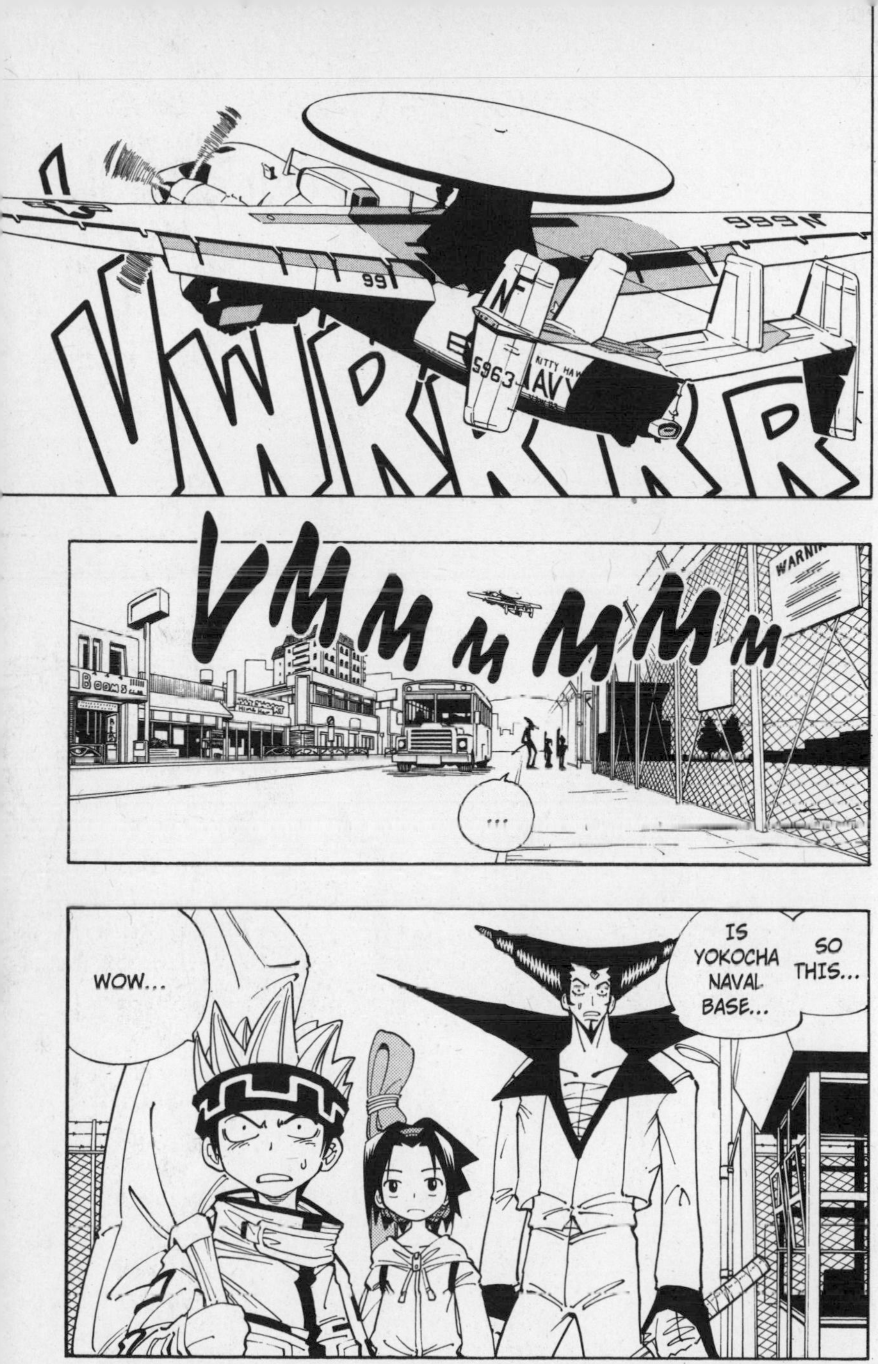
...
SO THIS...
IS YOKOCHA NAVAL BASE...
WOW...

# Reincarnation 78: The Future King

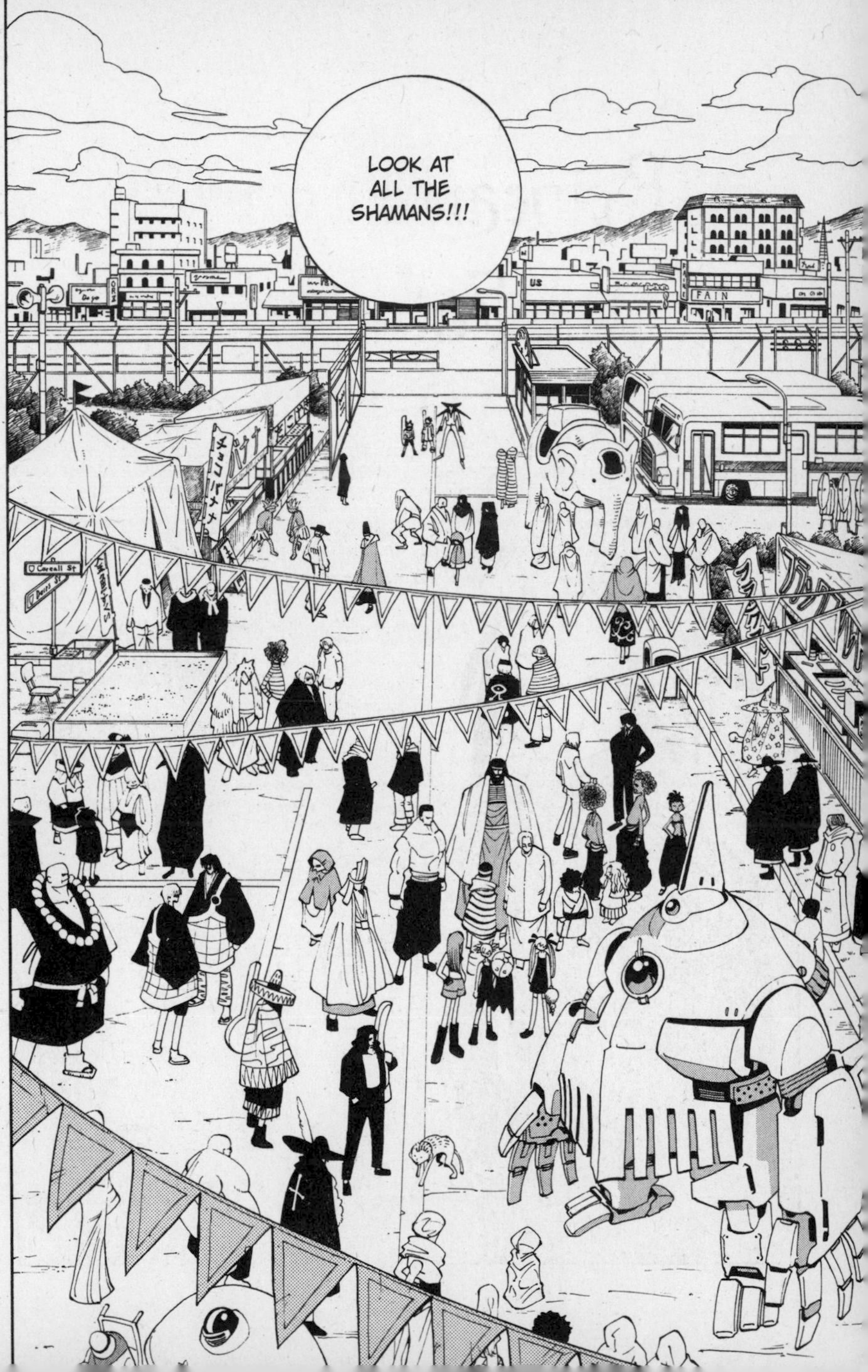
LOOK AT ALL THE SHAMANS!!!
FAIN
チョコバナナ

# Reincarnation 78: The Future King

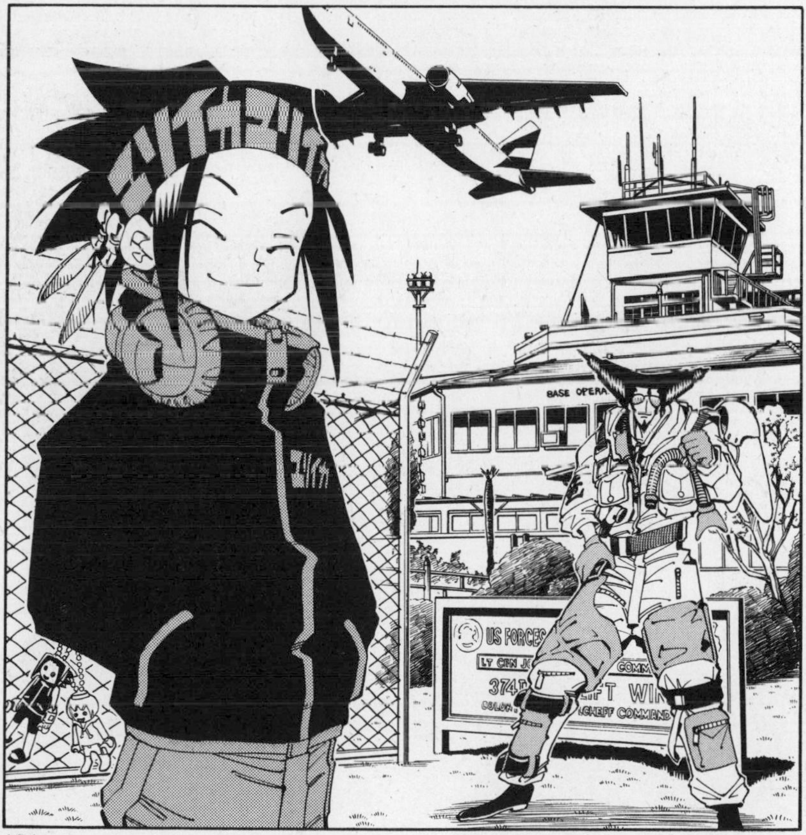
BASE OPERA
US FORCES

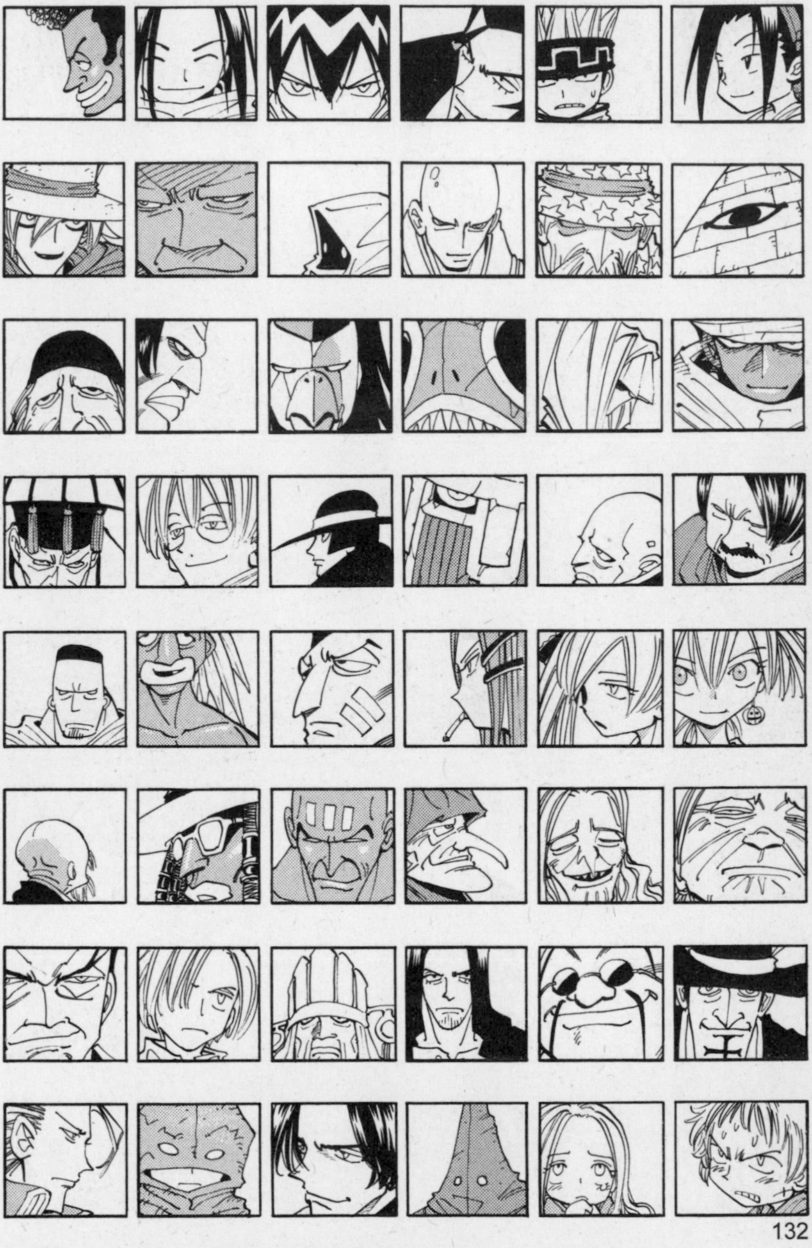

READ THIS WAY

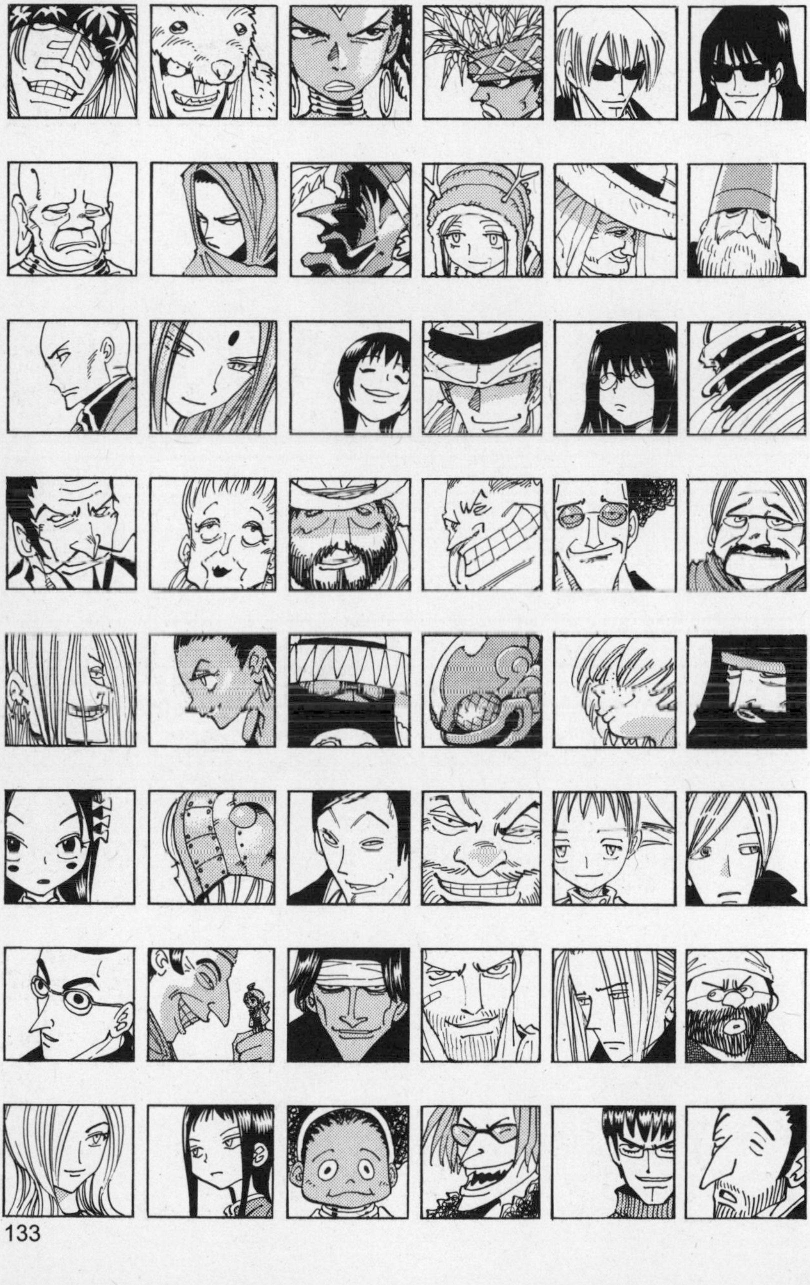

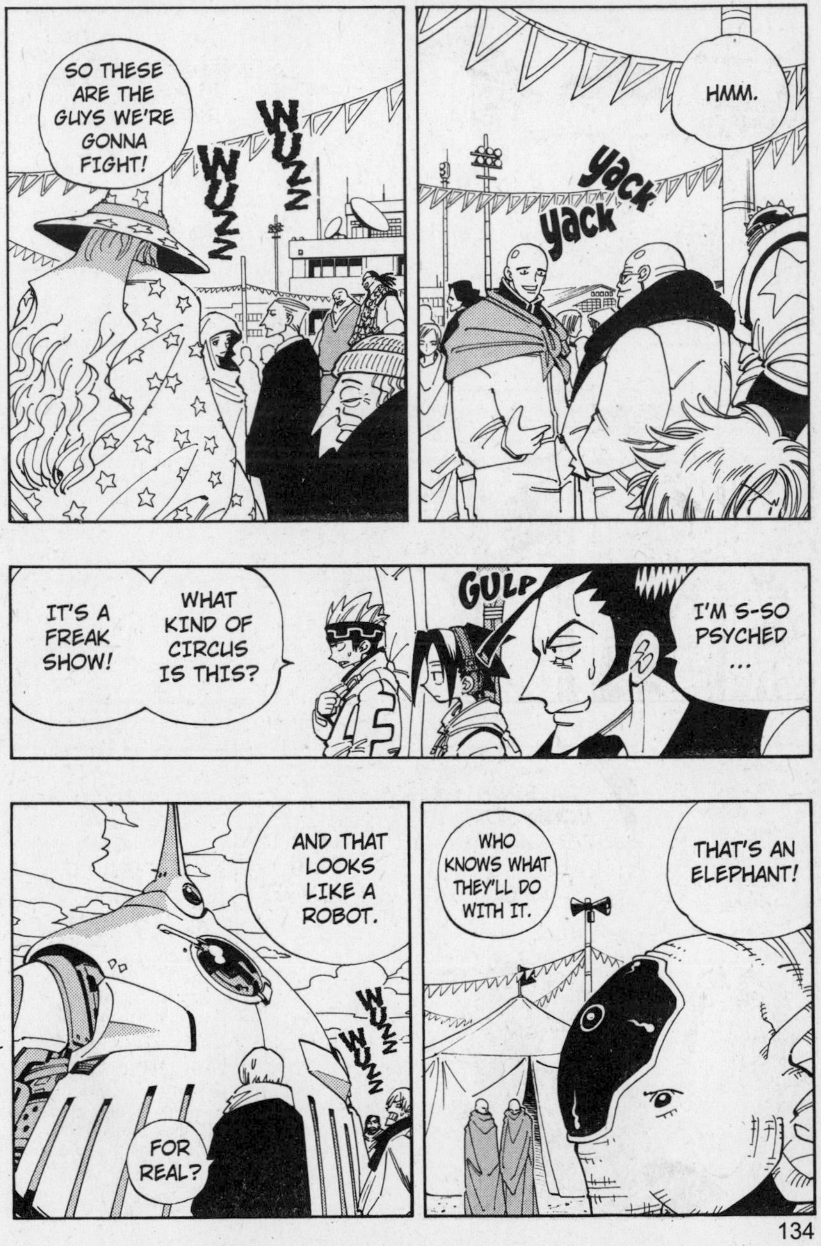
HMM.
YACK YACK
SO THESE ARE THE GUYS WE'RE GONNA FIGHT!
WUZZ WUZZ
I'M S-SO PSYCHED ...
GULP
WHAT KIND OF CIRCUS IS THIS?
IT'S A FREAK SHOW!
THAT'S AN ELEPHANT!
WHO KNOWS WHAT THEY'LL DO WITH IT.
AND THAT LOOKS LIKE A ROBOT.
WUZZ WUZZ
FOR REAL?

READ THIS WAY

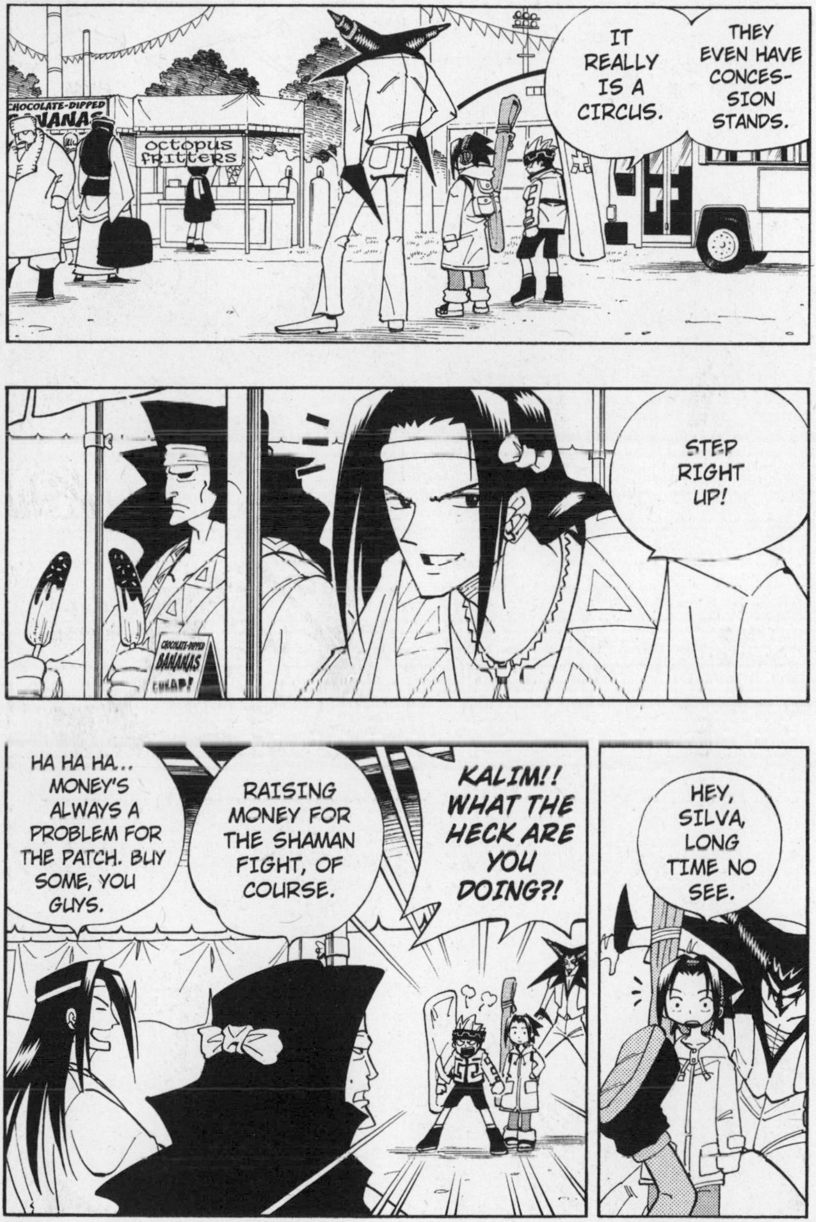

THEY EVEN HAVE CONCES-SION STANDS.
IT REALLY IS A CIRCUS.
CHOCOLATE-DIPPED BANANAS
octopus fritters
STEP RIGHT UP!
CHOCOLATE-DIPPED BANANAS CHEAP!
HEY, SILVA, LONG TIME NO SEE.
KALIM!! WHAT THE HECK ARE YOU DOING?!
RAISING MONEY FOR THE SHAMAN FIGHT, OF COURSE.
HA HA HA... MONEY'S ALWAYS A PROBLEM FOR THE PATCH. BUY SOME, YOU GUYS.

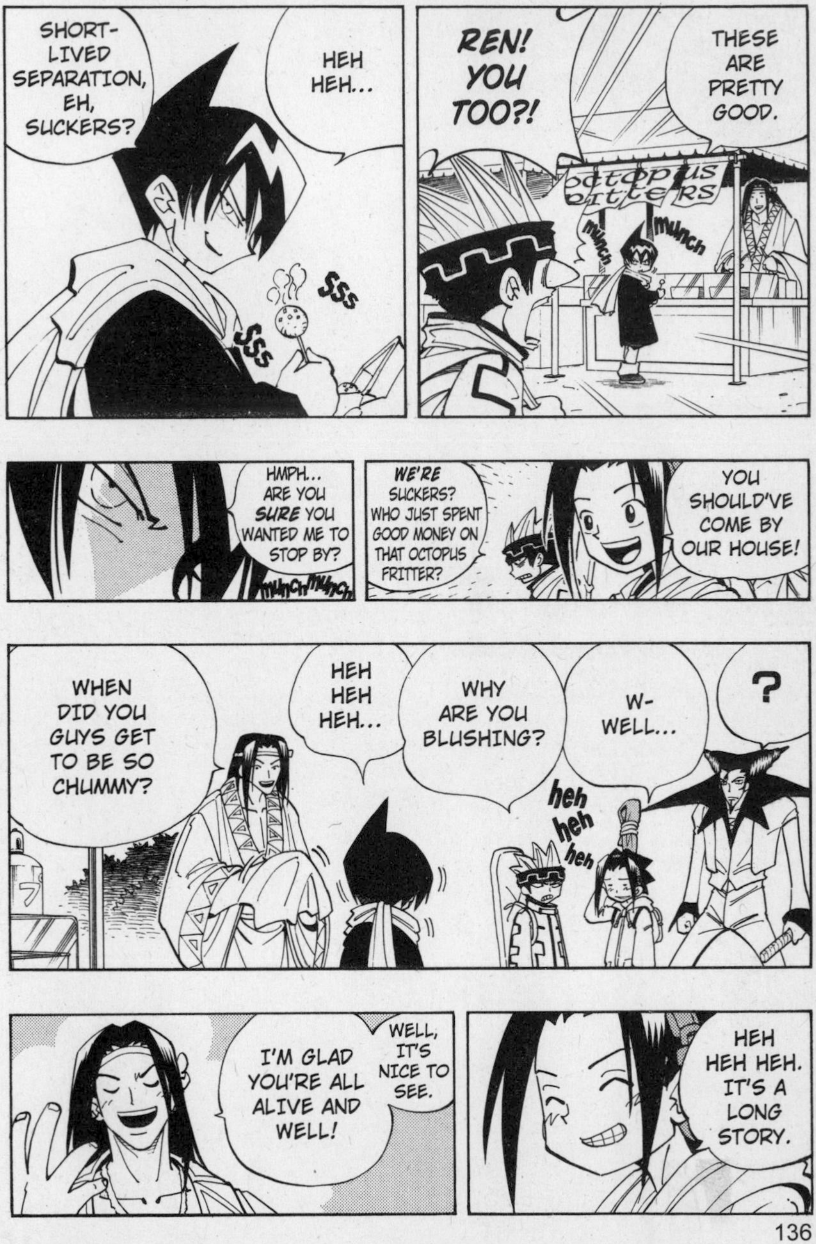
THESE ARE PRETTY GOOD.
REN! YOU TOO?!
munch
munch
HEH HEH...
SHORT-LIVED SEPARATION, EH, SUCKERS?
sss
sss
YOU SHOULD'VE COME BY OUR HOUSE!
*WE'RE* SUCKERS? WHO JUST SPENT GOOD MONEY ON THAT OCTOPUS FRITTER?
HMPH... ARE YOU *SURE* YOU WANTED ME TO STOP BY?
munch munch
?
W-WELL...
WHY ARE YOU BLUSHING?
heh heh heh
HEH HEH HEH...
WHEN DID YOU GUYS GET TO BE SO CHUMMY?
HEH HEH HEH. IT'S A LONG STORY.
WELL, IT'S NICE TO SEE.
I'M GLAD YOU'RE ALL ALIVE AND WELL!

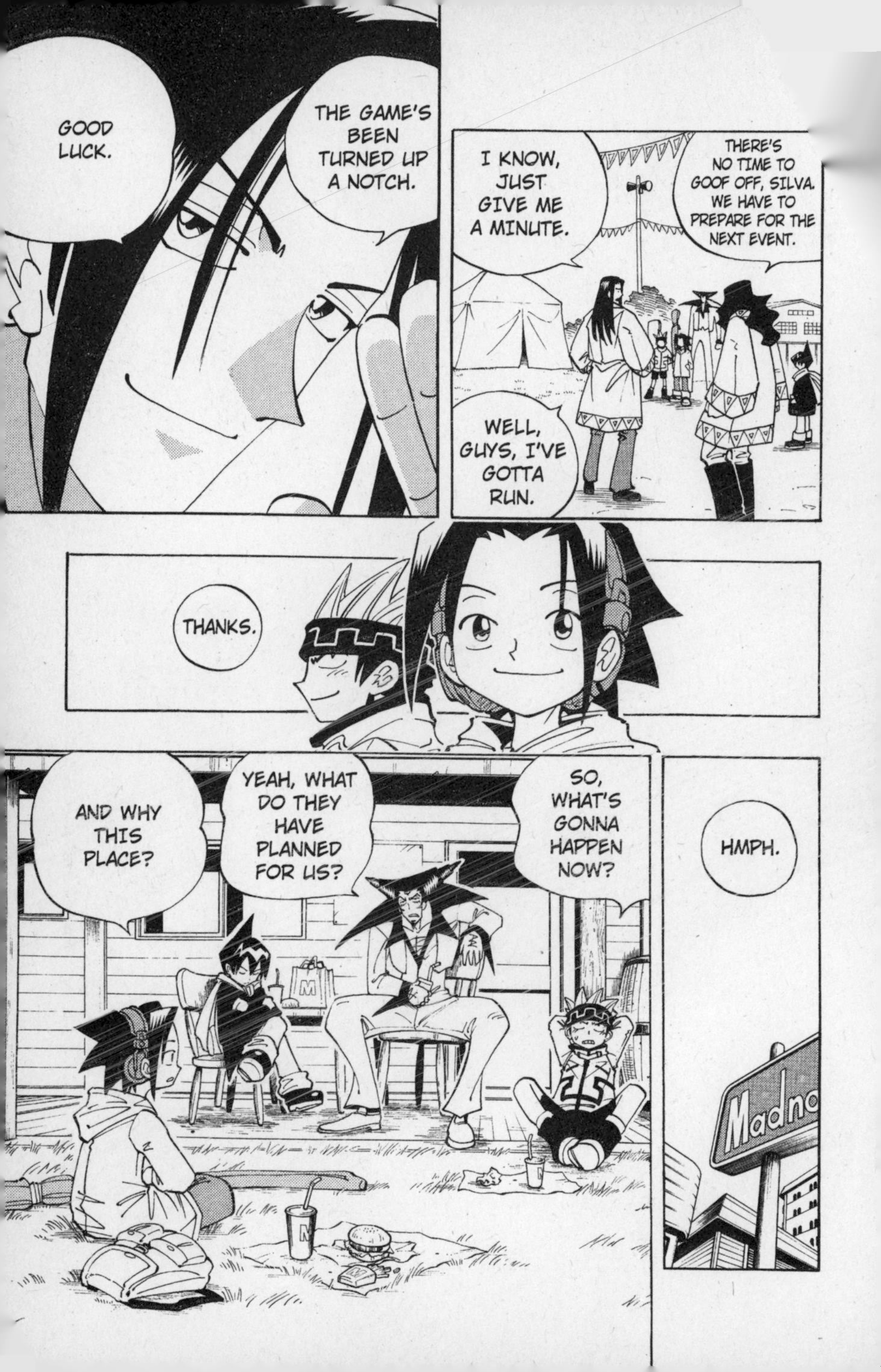
THERE'S NO TIME TO GOOF OFF, SILVA. WE HAVE TO PREPARE FOR THE NEXT EVENT.
I KNOW, JUST GIVE ME A MINUTE.
WELL, GUYS, I'VE GOTTA RUN.
THE GAME'S BEEN TURNED UP A NOTCH.
GOOD LUCK.
THANKS.
HMPH.
SO, WHAT'S GONNA HAPPEN NOW?
YEAH, WHAT DO THEY HAVE PLANNED FOR US?
AND WHY THIS PLACE?

WHY...
THIS BASE?
WE'LL HAVE TO FIGURE IT OUT.
HMM...
AMATEURS.
WARNING

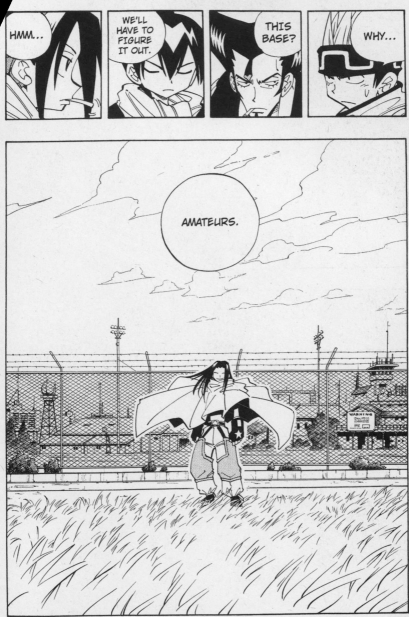

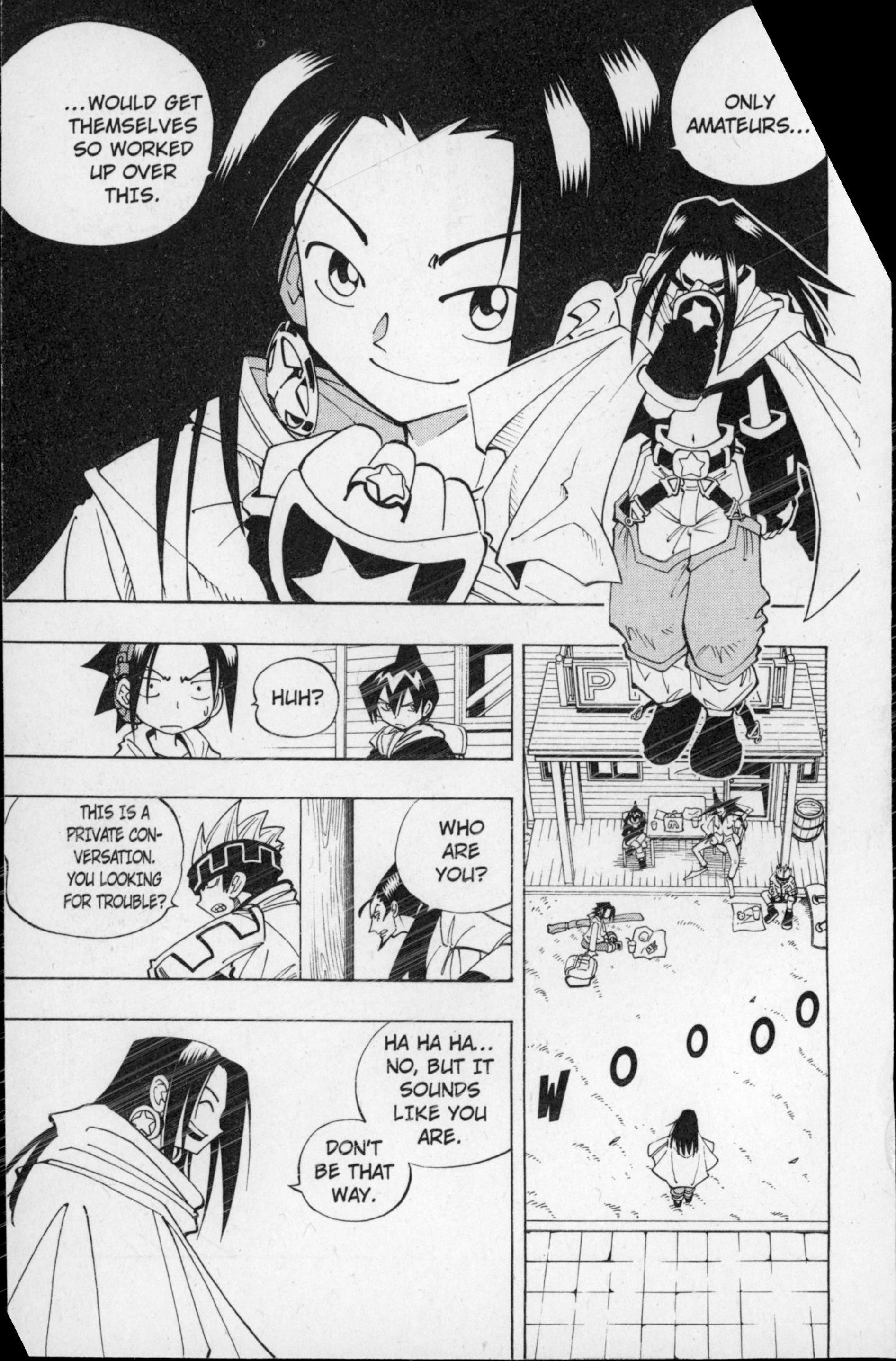
ONLY AMATEURS...
...WOULD GET THEMSELVES SO WORKED UP OVER THIS.
WOOOOO
HUH?
WHO ARE YOU?
THIS IS A PRIVATE CON-VERSATION. YOU LOOKING FOR TROUBLE?
HA HA HA... NO, BUT IT SOUNDS LIKE YOU ARE.
DON'T BE THAT WAY.

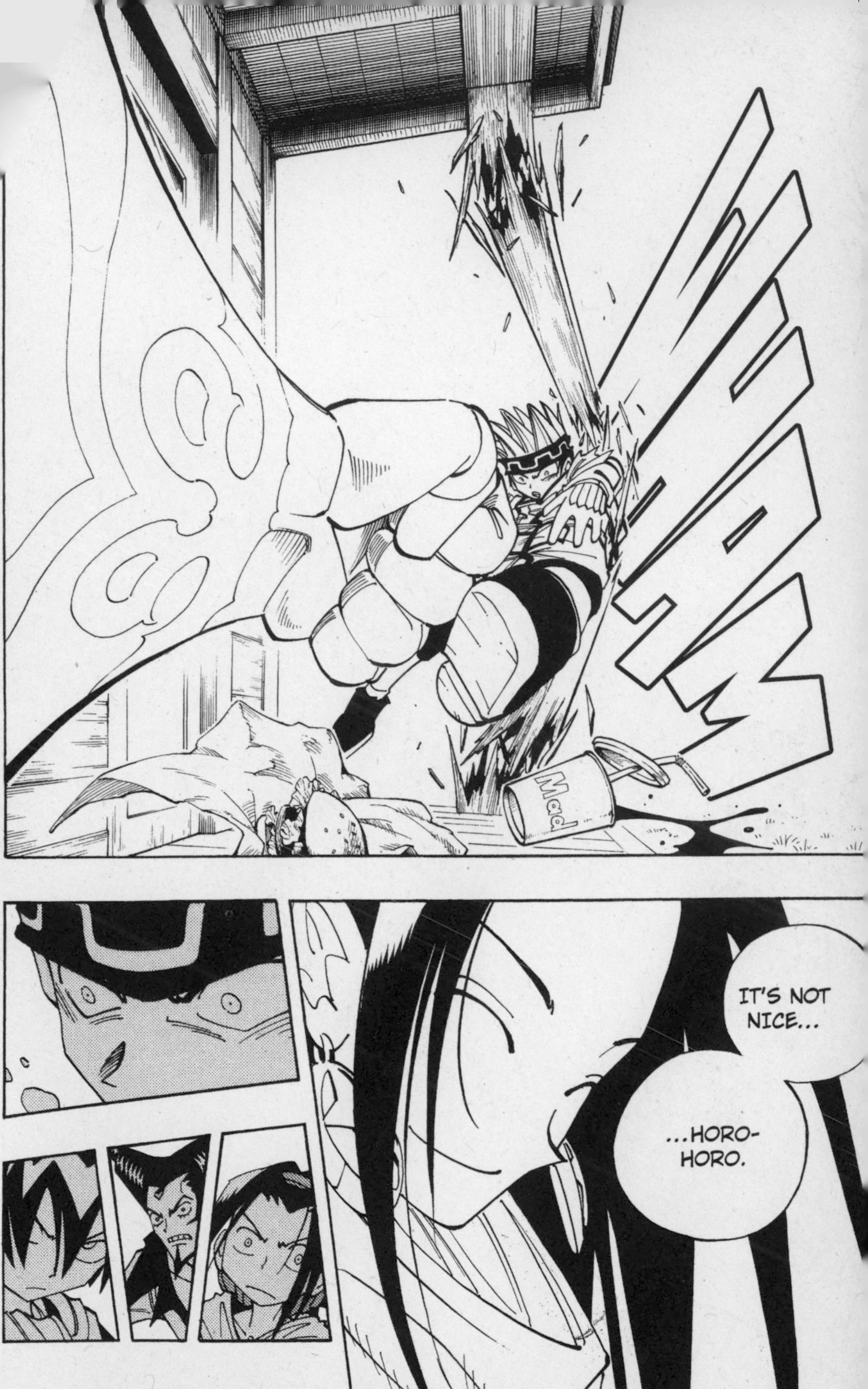
Mad
IT'S NOT NICE...
...HORO-HORO.

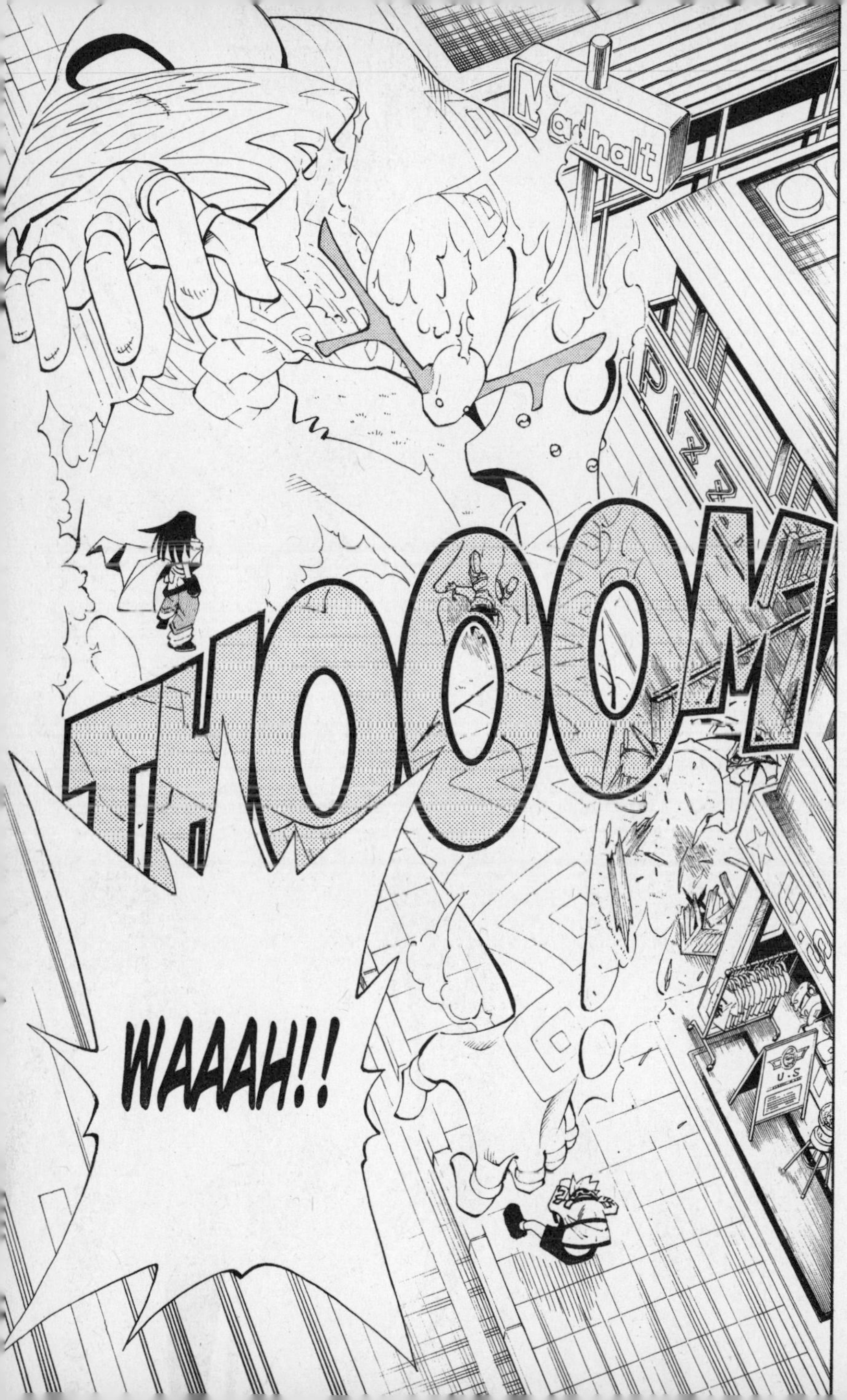
Madnalt
THOOOM
WAAAH!!

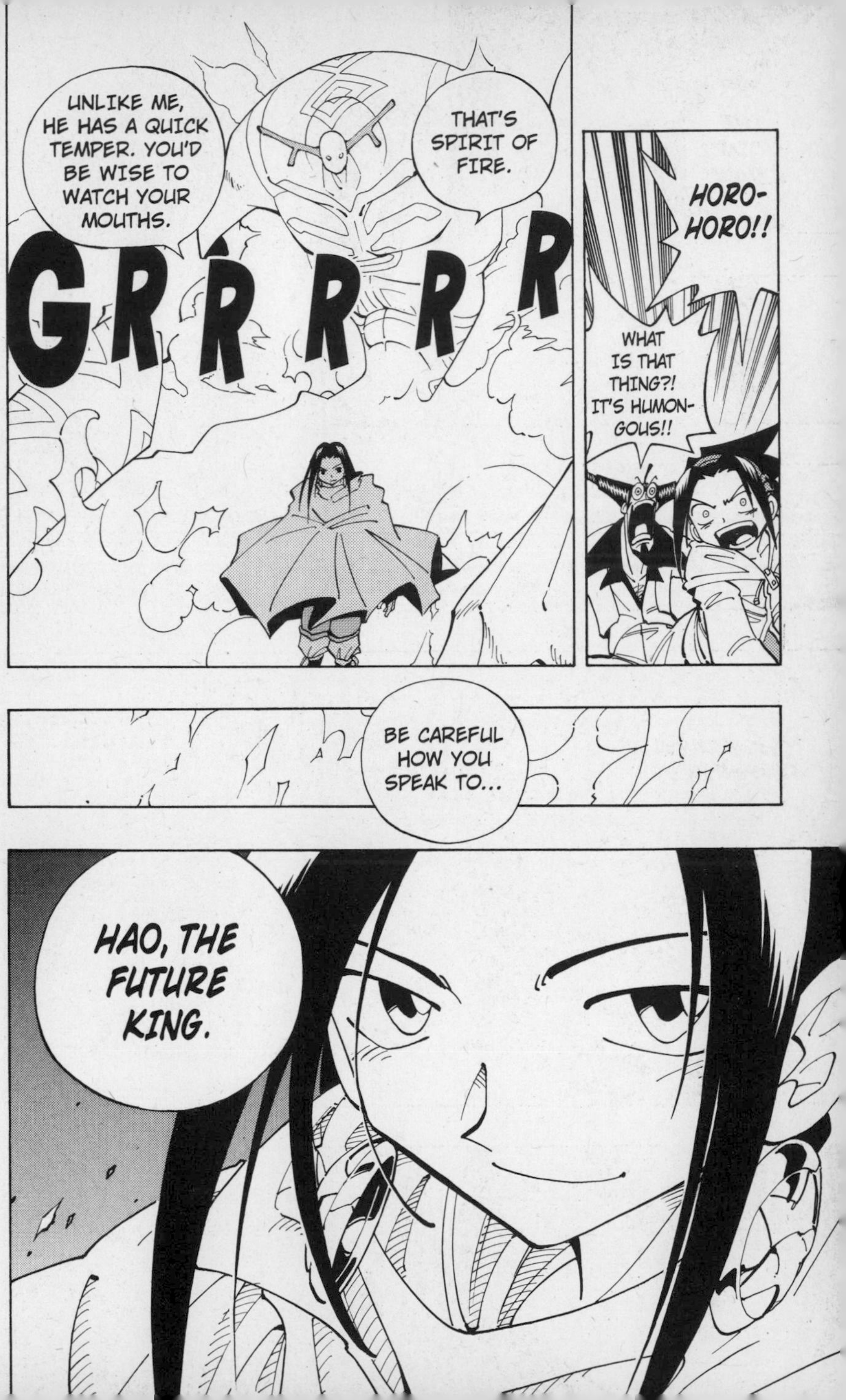
HORO-HORO!!
WHAT IS THAT THING?! IT'S HUMON-GOUS!!
THAT'S SPIRIT OF FIRE.
UNLIKE ME, HE HAS A QUICK TEMPER. YOU'D BE WISE TO WATCH YOUR MOUTHS.
GRRRRR
BE CAREFUL HOW YOU SPEAK TO...
HAO, THE FUTURE KING.

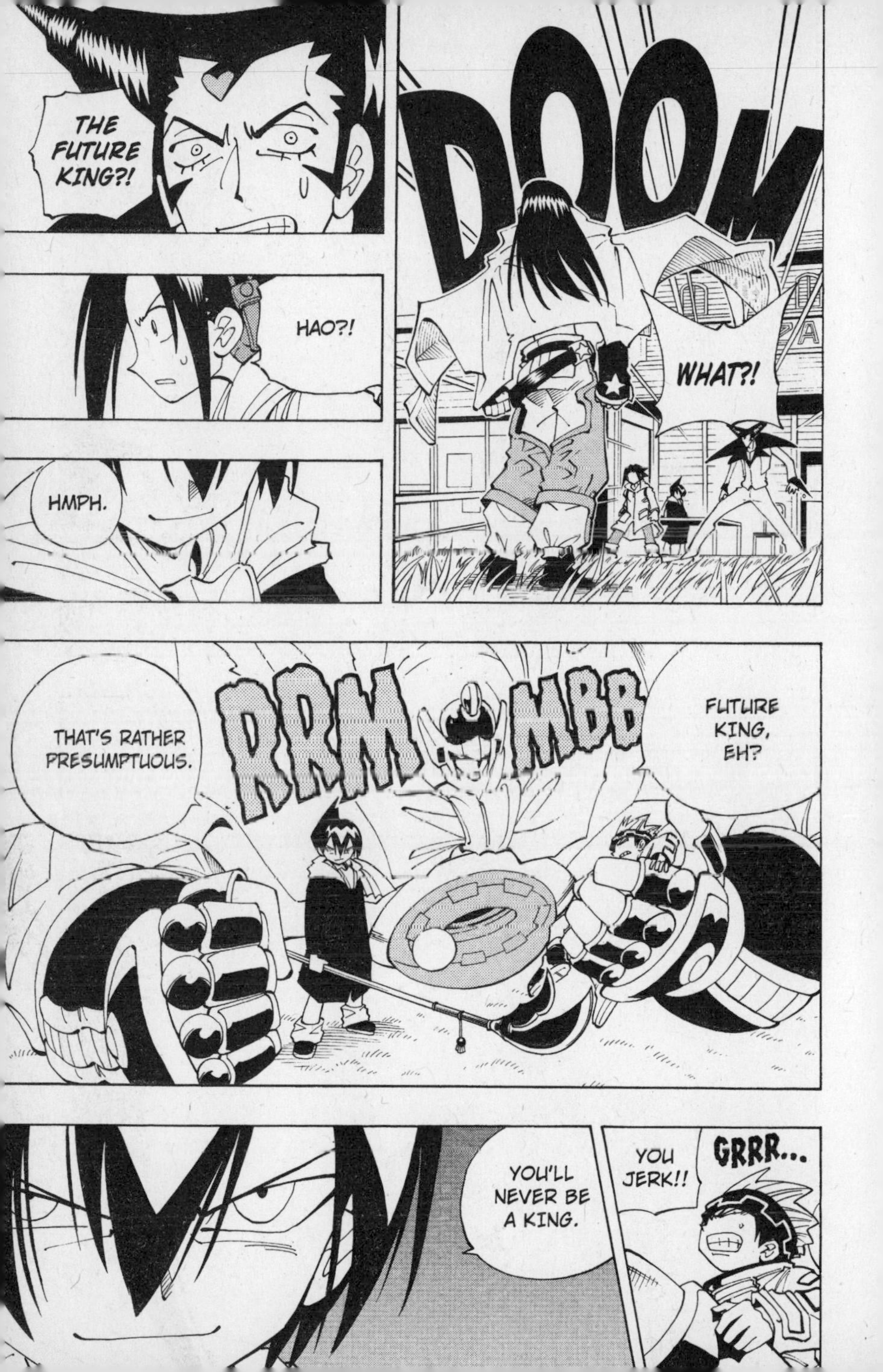
DOOM
WHAT?!
THE FUTURE KING?!
HAO?!
HMPH.
FUTURE KING, EH?
RRMMBB
THAT'S RATHER PRESUMPTUOUS.
GRRR...
YOU JERK!!
YOU'LL NEVER BE A KING.

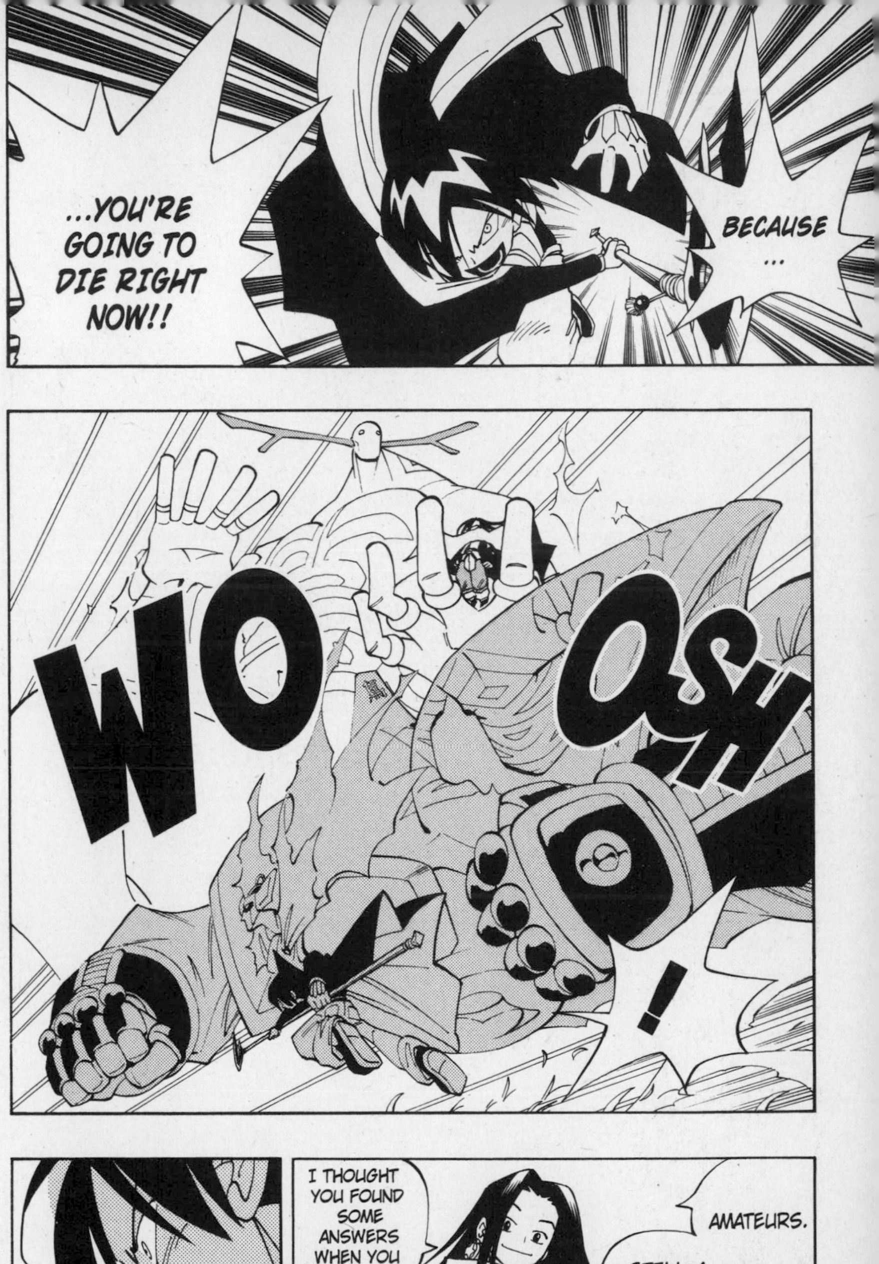
BECAUSE ...
...YOU'RE GOING TO DIE RIGHT NOW!!
WOOSH!
AMATEURS.
STILL A HOTHEAD, EH, REN?
I THOUGHT YOU FOUND SOME ANSWERS WHEN YOU WENT HOME.

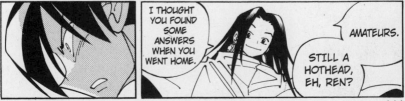

READ THIS WAY

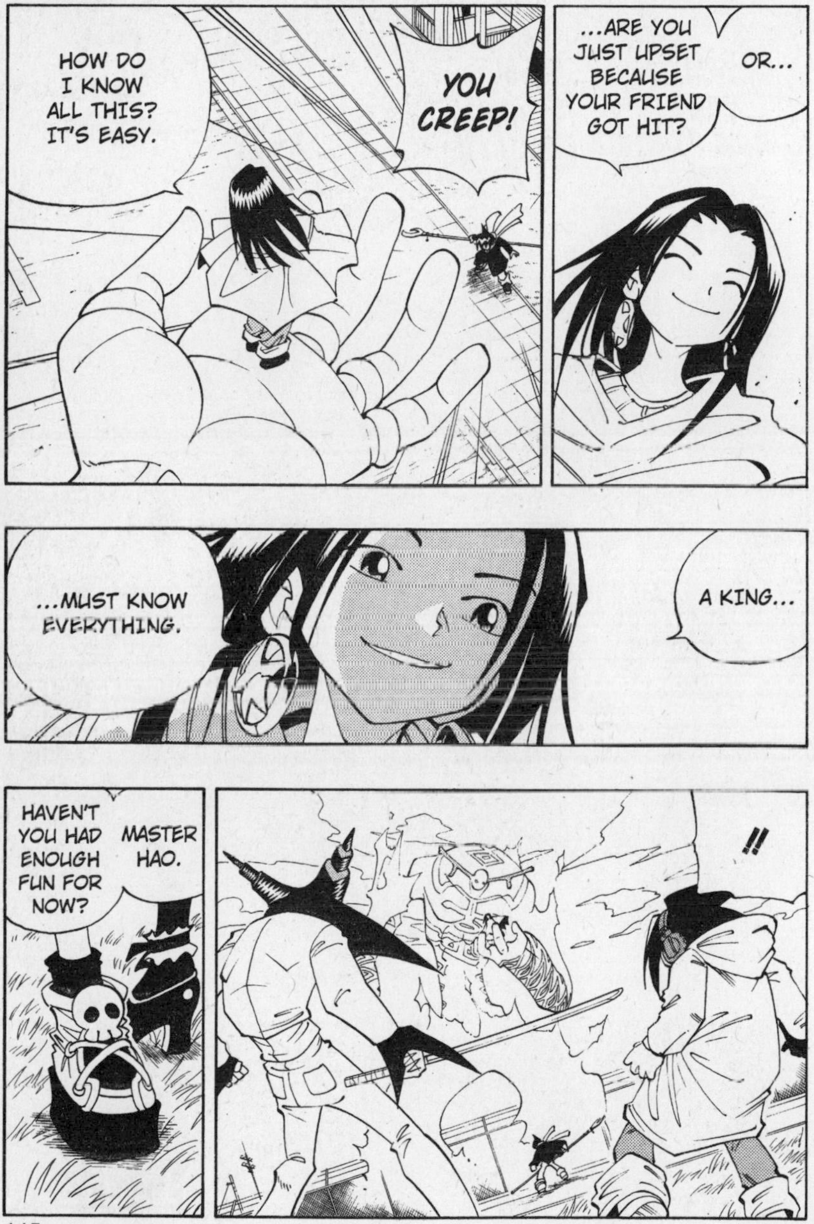
OR...
...ARE YOU JUST UPSET BECAUSE YOUR FRIEND GOT HIT?
YOU CREEP!
HOW DO I KNOW ALL THIS? IT'S EASY.
A KING...
...MUST KNOW EVERYTHING.
!!
MASTER HAO.
HAVEN'T YOU HAD ENOUGH FUN FOR NOW?

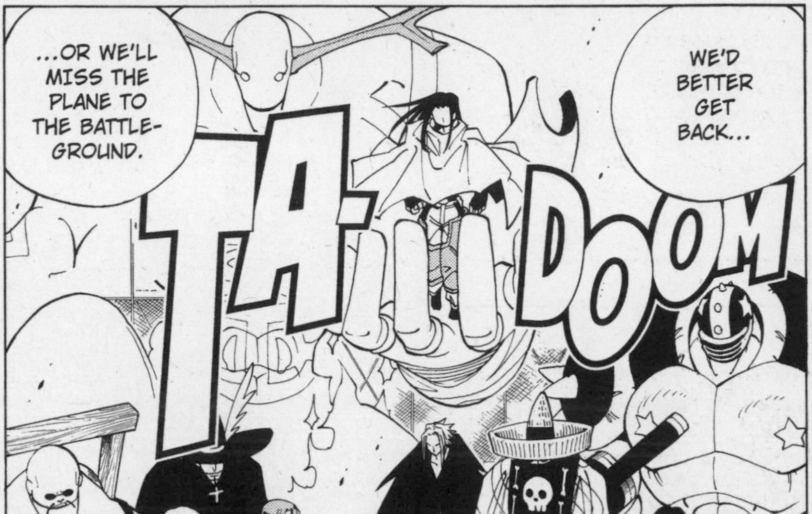
WE'D BETTER GET BACK...
...OR WE'LL MISS THE PLANE TO THE BATTLE-GROUND.
TA-DOOM

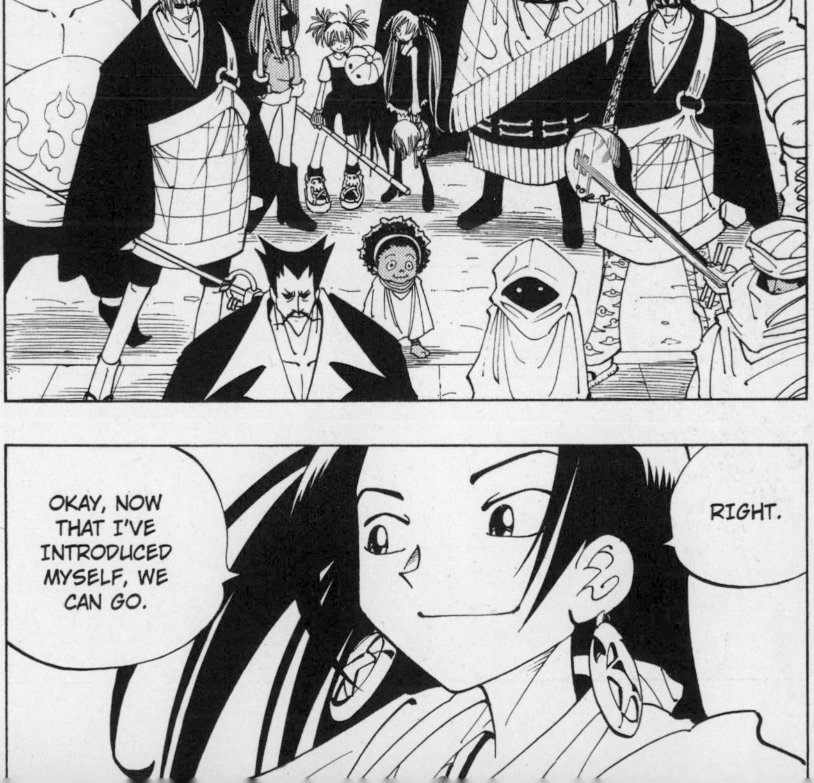
RIGHT.
OKAY, NOW THAT I'VE INTRODUCED MYSELF, WE CAN GO.

READ THIS WAY

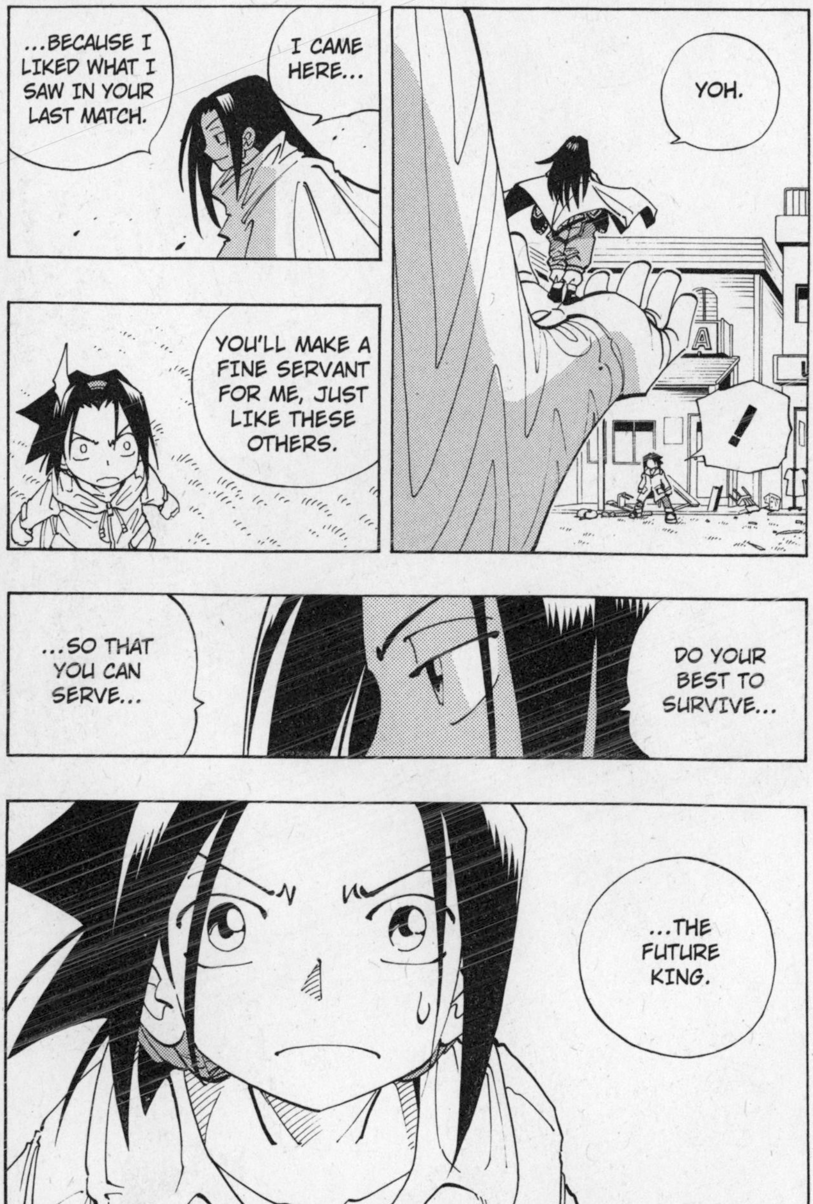
YOH.
!
I CAME HERE...
...BECAUSE I LIKED WHAT I SAW IN YOUR LAST MATCH.
YOU'LL MAKE A FINE SERVANT FOR ME, JUST LIKE THESE OTHERS.
DO YOUR BEST TO SURVIVE...
...SO THAT YOU CAN SERVE...
...THE FUTURE KING.

# Reincarnation 79: Patch Airlines

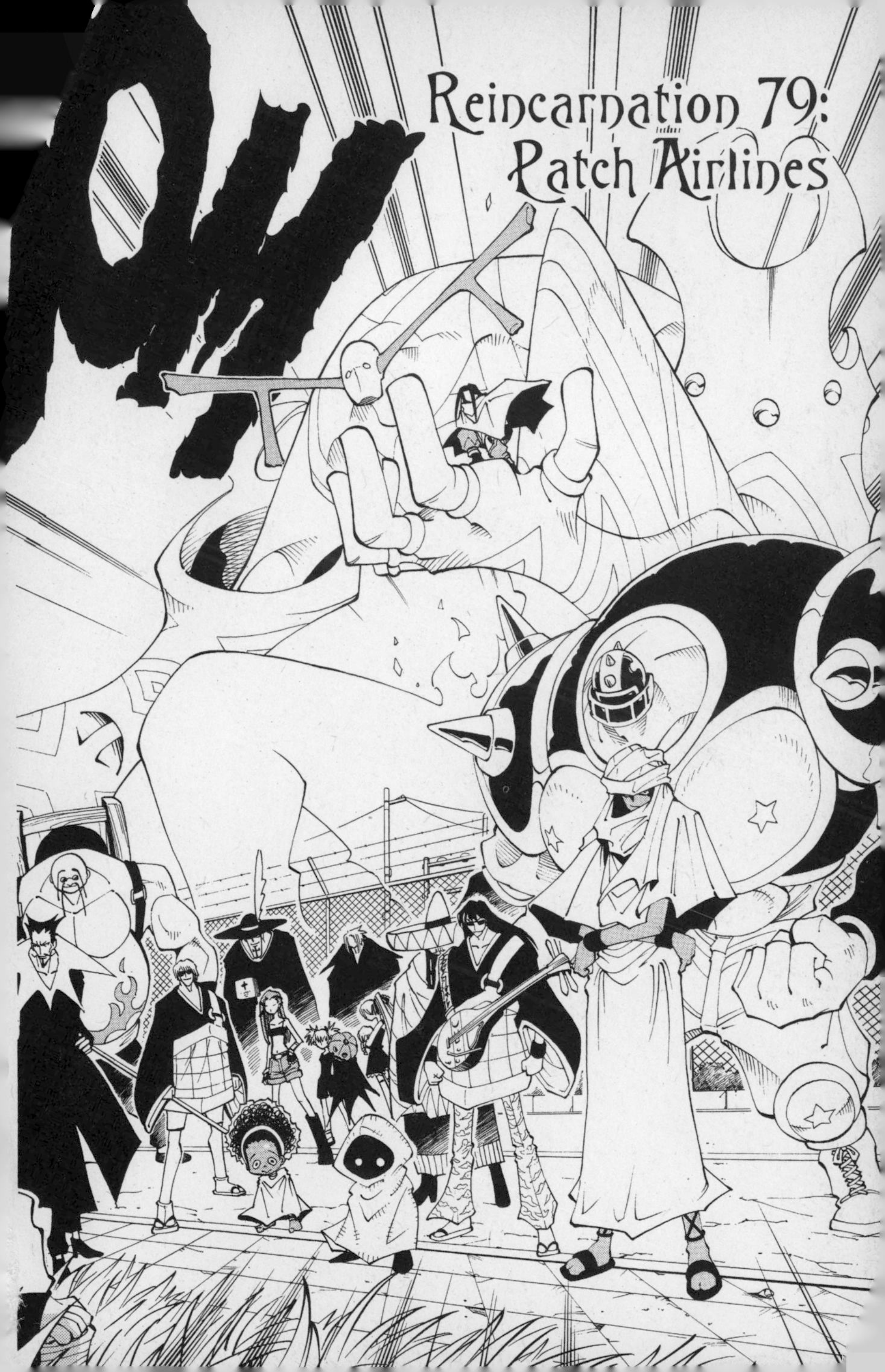

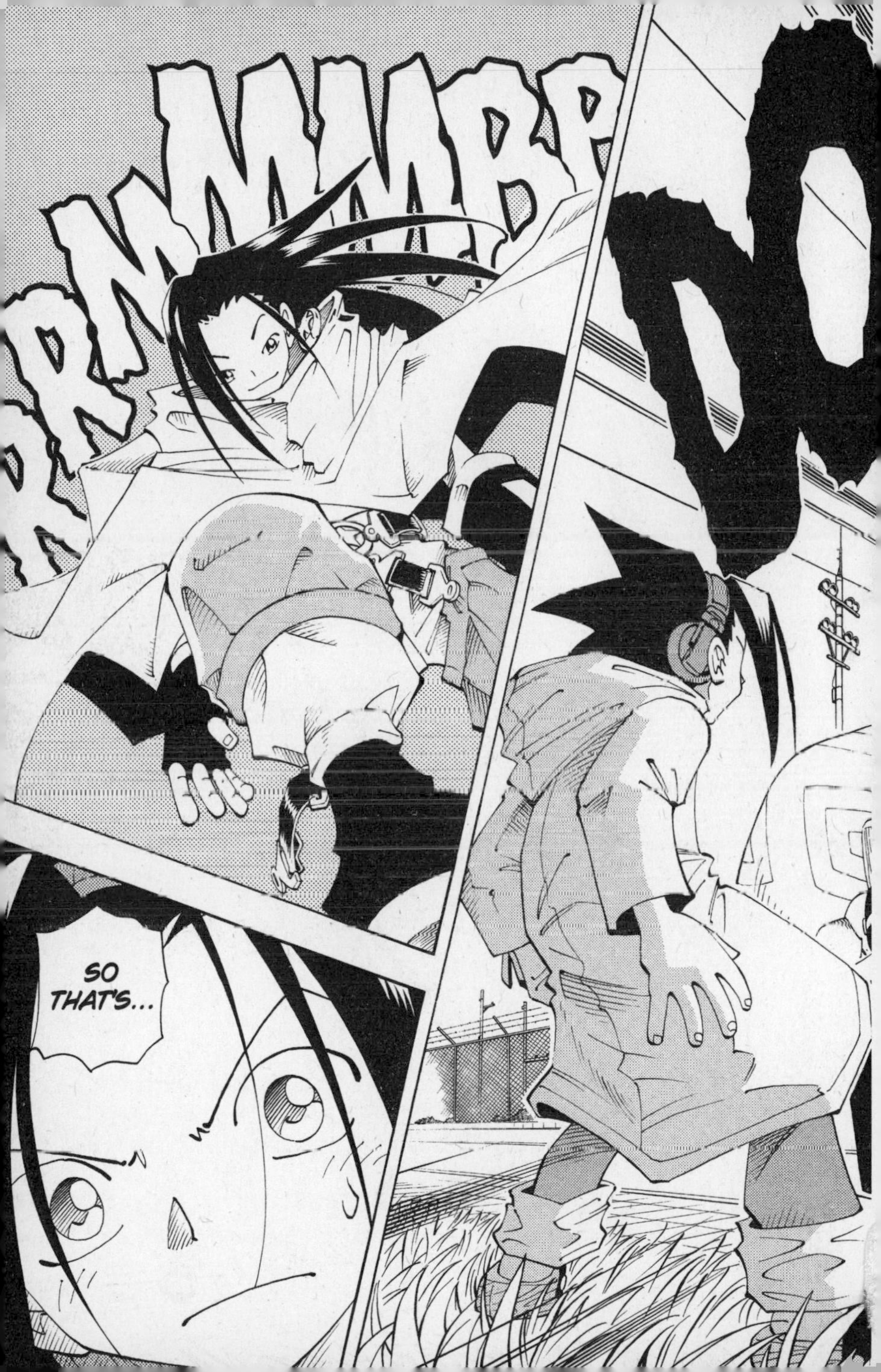
SO THAT'S...

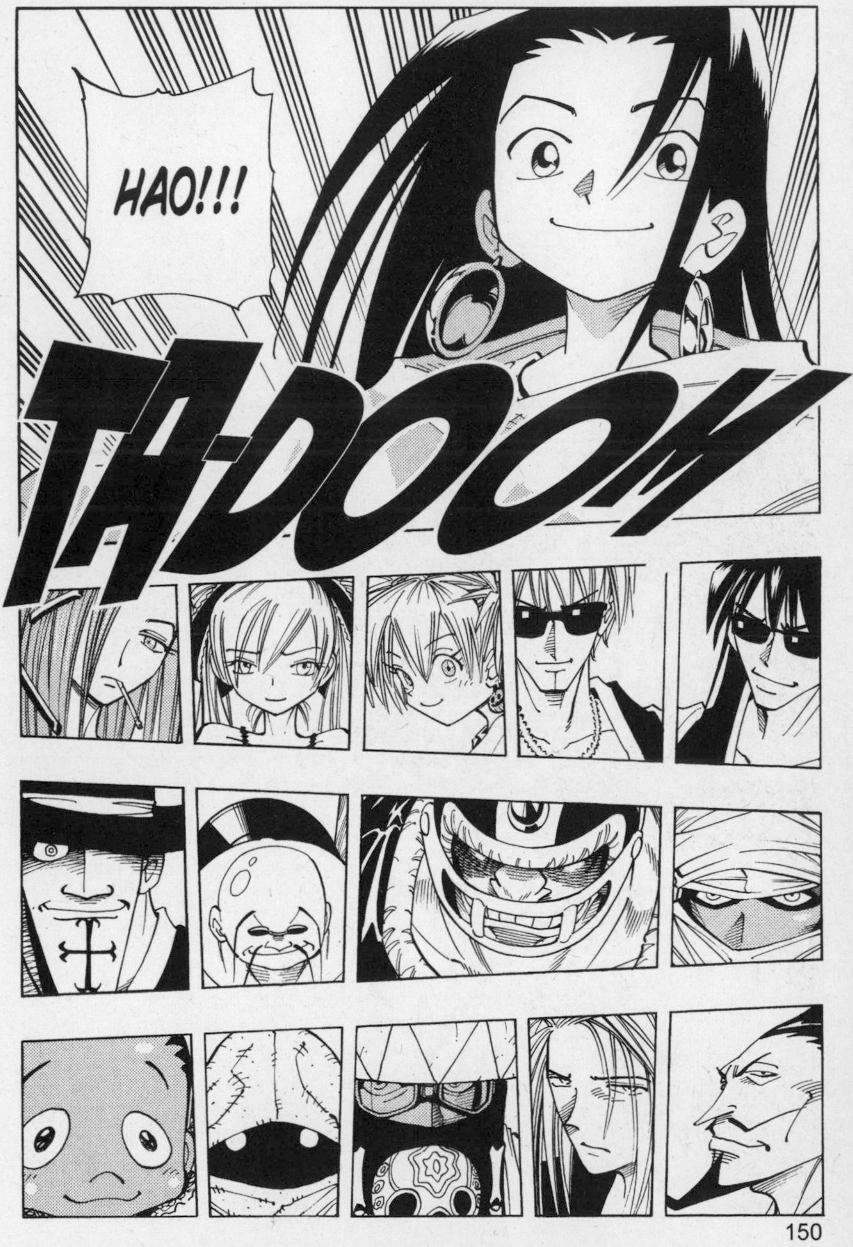
HAO!!!
TA-DOOM

# Reincarnation 79: Patch Airlines

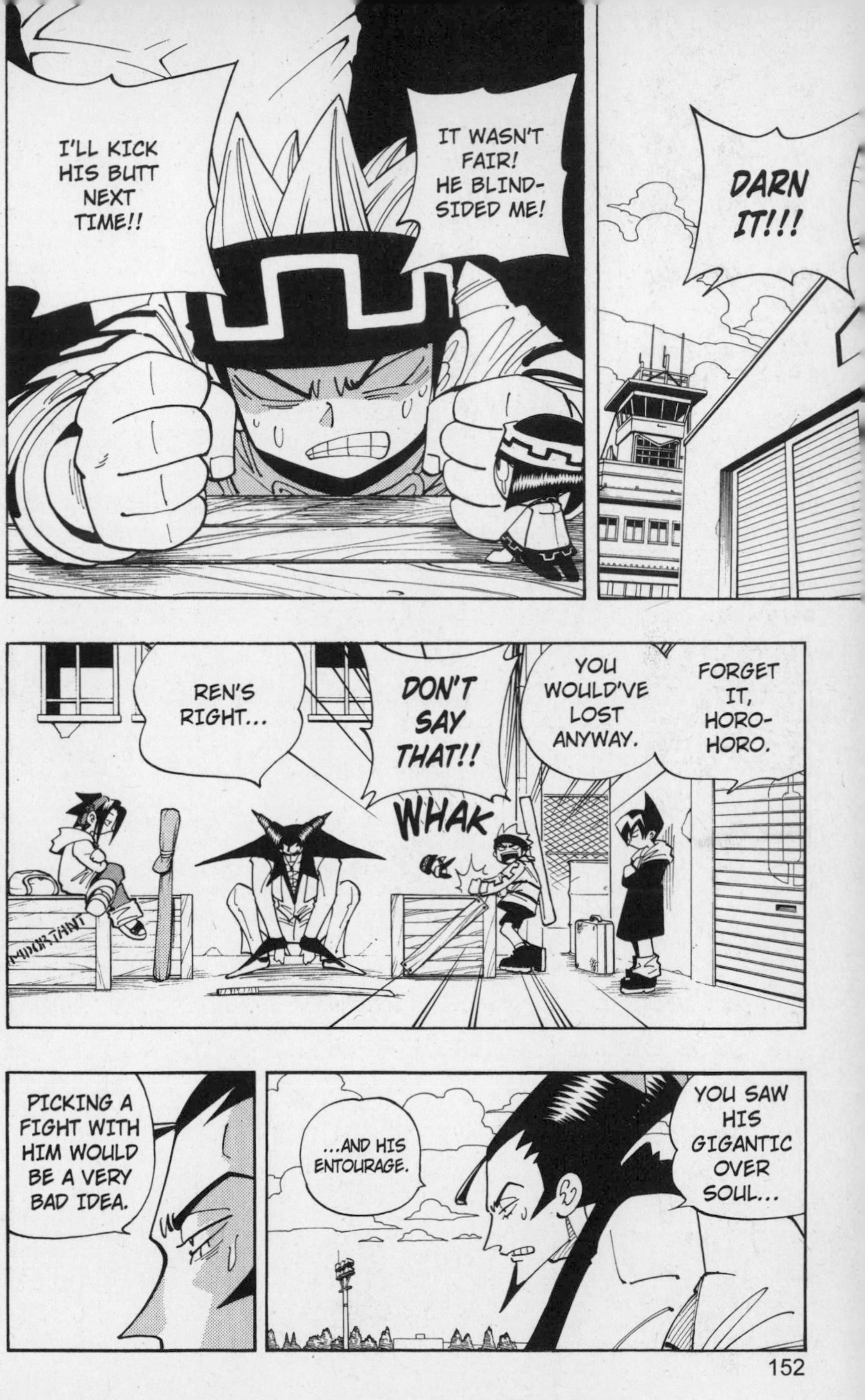
DARN IT!!!
IT WASN'T FAIR! HE BLIND-SIDED ME!
I'LL KICK HIS BUTT NEXT TIME!!
FORGET IT, HORO-HORO.
YOU WOULD'VE LOST ANYWAY.
DON'T SAY THAT!!
WHAK
REN'S RIGHT...
YOU SAW HIS GIGANTIC OVER SOUL...
...AND HIS ENTOURAGE.
PICKING A FIGHT WITH HIM WOULD BE A VERY BAD IDEA.

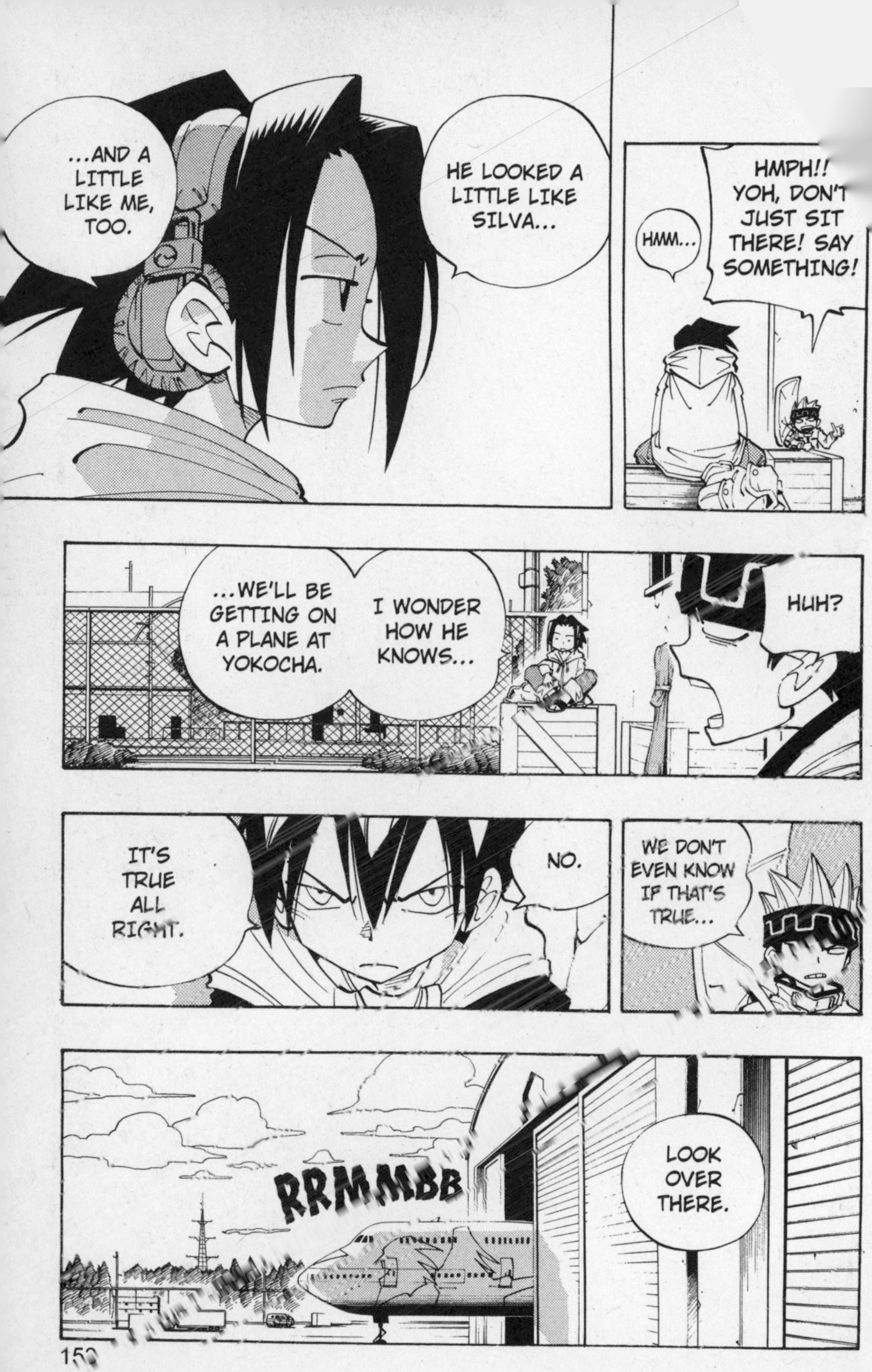
HMPH!! YOH, DON'T JUST SIT THERE! SAY SOMETHING!
HMM...
HE LOOKED A LITTLE LIKE SILVA...
...AND A LITTLE LIKE ME, TOO.
HUH?
I WONDER HOW HE KNOWS...
...WE'LL BE GETTING ON A PLANE AT YOKOCHA.
WE DON'T EVEN KNOW IF THAT'S TRUE...
NO.
IT'S TRUE ALL RIGHT.
LOOK OVER THERE.
RRMMBB

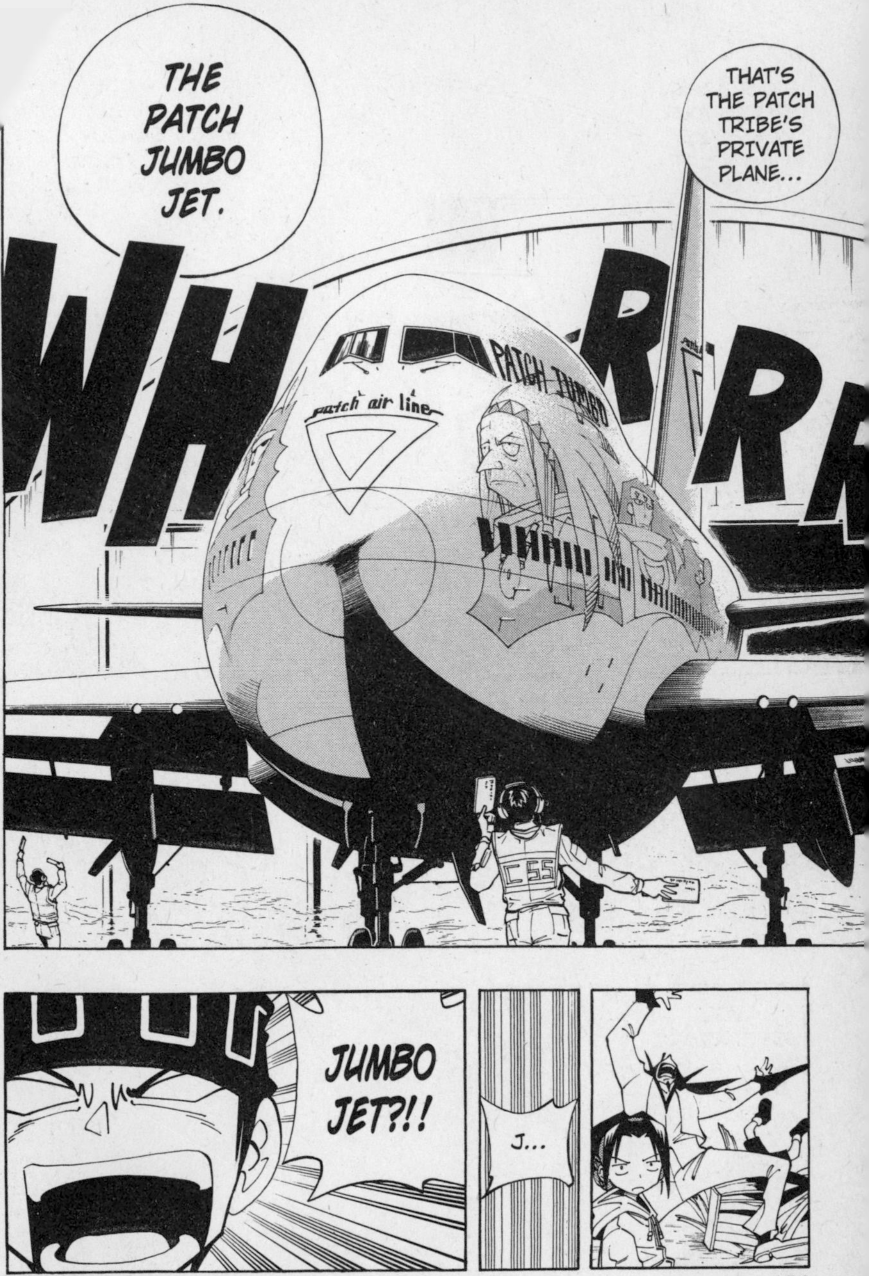
THAT'S THE PATCH TRIBE'S PRIVATE PLANE...
THE PATCH JUMBO JET.
WHRRR
PATCH JUMBO
patch air line
J...
JUMBO JET?!!

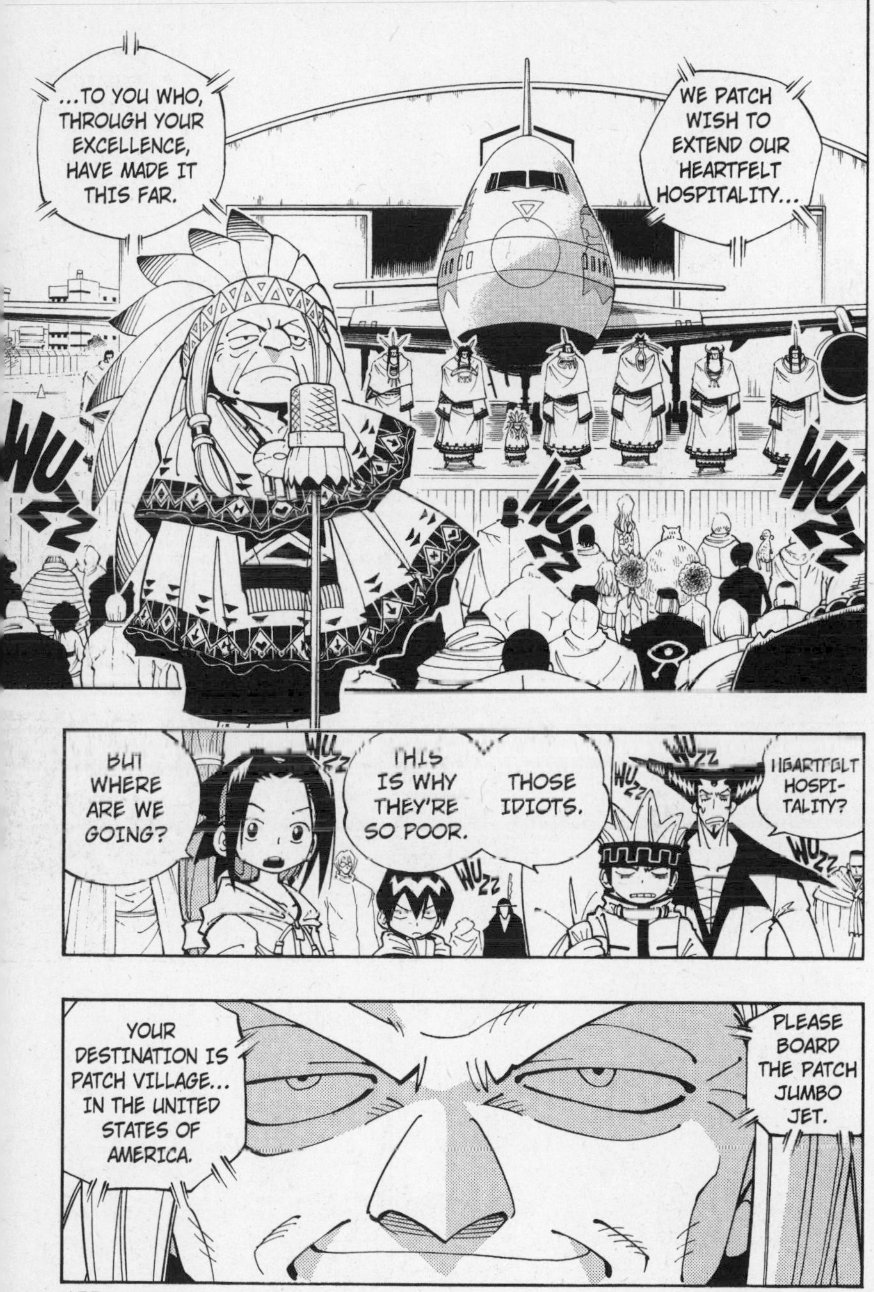
WE PATCH WISH TO EXTEND OUR HEARTFELT HOSPITALITY...
...TO YOU WHO, THROUGH YOUR EXCELLENCE, HAVE MADE IT THIS FAR.
WUZZ
WUZZ
WUZZ
HEARTFELT HOSPITALITY?
WUZZ
WUZZ
THOSE IDIOTS.
THIS IS WHY THEY'RE SO POOR.
WUZZ
WUZZ
BUT WHERE ARE WE GOING?
PLEASE BOARD THE PATCH JUMBO JET.
YOUR DESTINATION IS PATCH VILLAGE... IN THE UNITED STATES OF AMERICA.

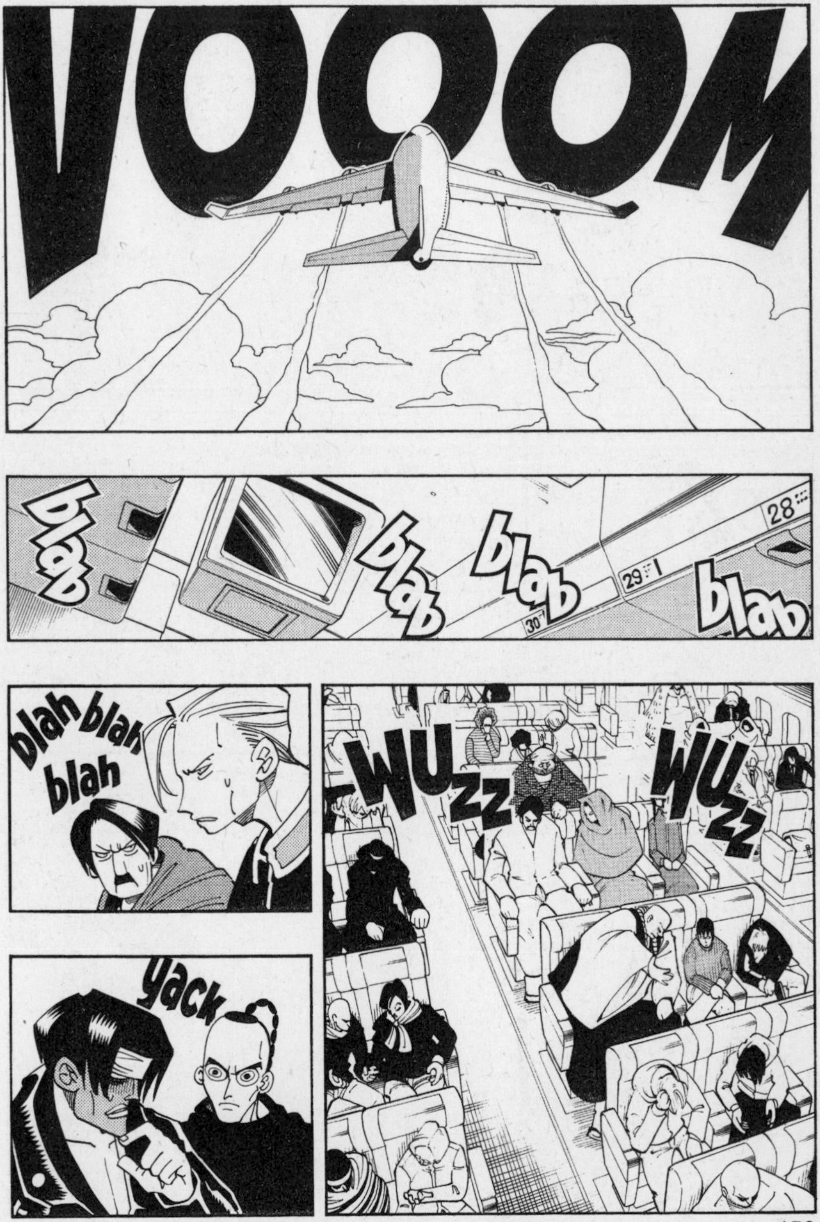
VOOOM
blab
blab
blab
blab
WUZZ
WUZZ
blah blah
blah
yack

READ THIS WAY

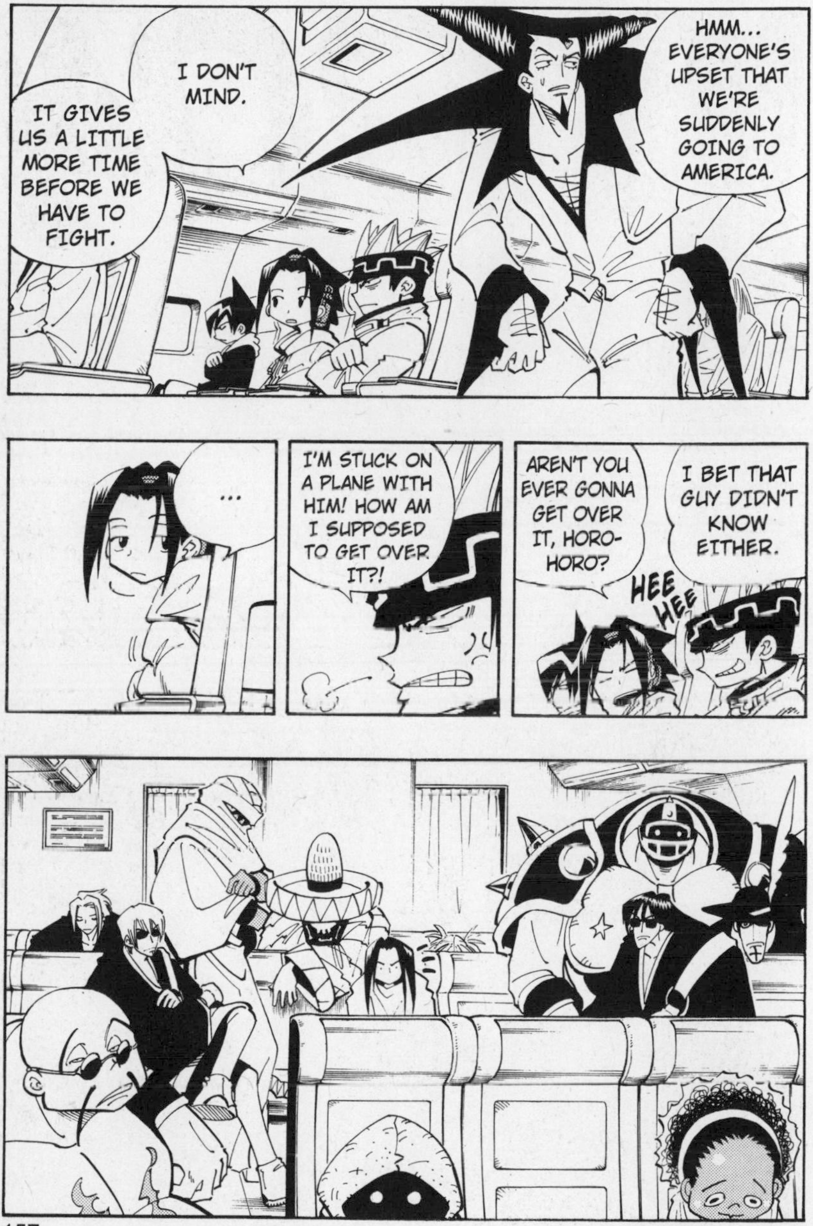

HMM... EVERYONE'S UPSET THAT WE'RE SUDDENLY GOING TO AMERICA.
I DON'T MIND.
IT GIVES US A LITTLE MORE TIME BEFORE WE HAVE TO FIGHT.
I BET THAT GUY DIDN'T KNOW EITHER.
AREN'T YOU EVER GONNA GET OVER IT, HORO-HORO?
HEE HEE
I'M STUCK ON A PLANE WITH HIM! HOW AM I SUPPOSED TO GET OVER IT?!
...

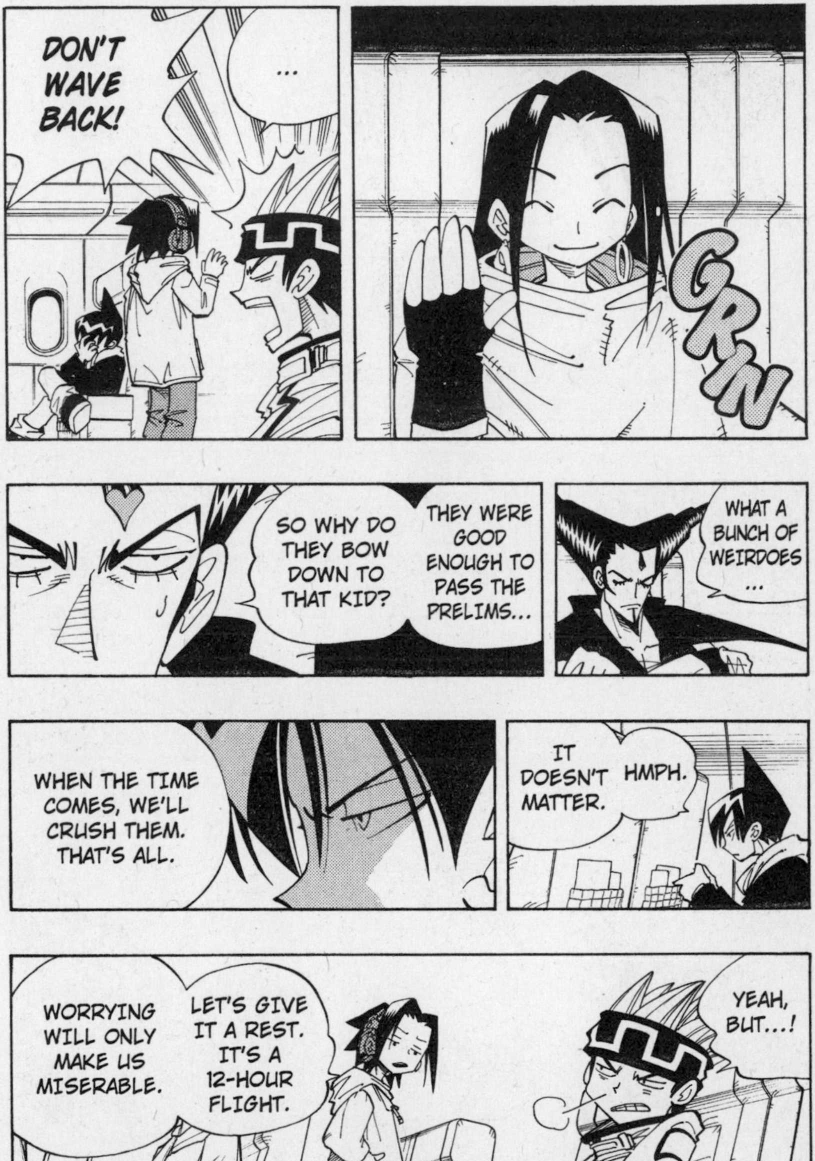
GRIN
...
DON'T WAVE BACK!
WHAT A BUNCH OF WEIRDOES ...
THEY WERE GOOD ENOUGH TO PASS THE PRELIMS...
SO WHY DO THEY BOW DOWN TO THAT KID?
HMPH.
IT DOESN'T MATTER.
WHEN THE TIME COMES, WE'LL CRUSH THEM. THAT'S ALL.
YEAH, BUT...!
LET'S GIVE IT A REST. IT'S A 12-HOUR FLIGHT.
WORRYING WILL ONLY MAKE US MISERABLE.

READ THIS WAY

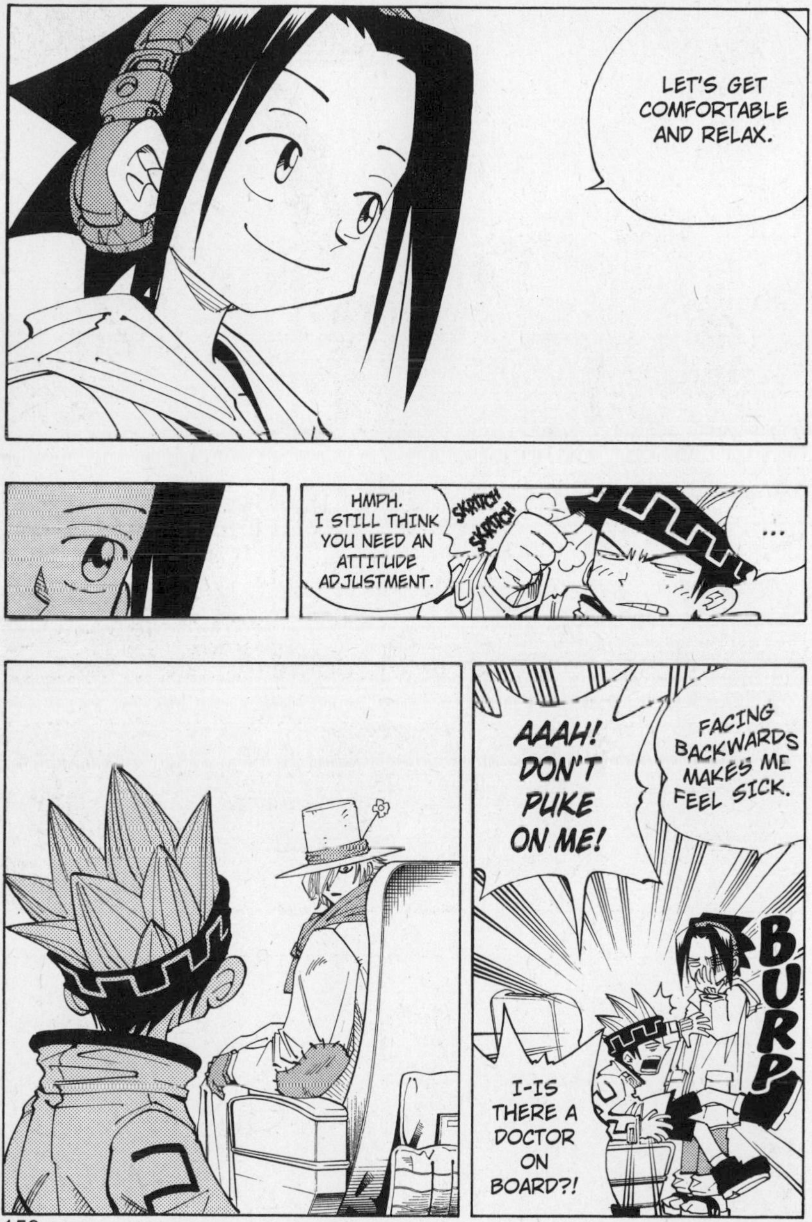
LET'S GET COMFORTABLE AND RELAX.
...
SKRITCH SKRITCH
HMPH. I STILL THINK YOU NEED AN ATTITUDE ADJUSTMENT.
FACING BACKWARDS MAKES ME FEEL SICK.
AAAH! DON'T PUKE ON ME!
BURP
I-IS THERE A DOCTOR ON BOARD?!

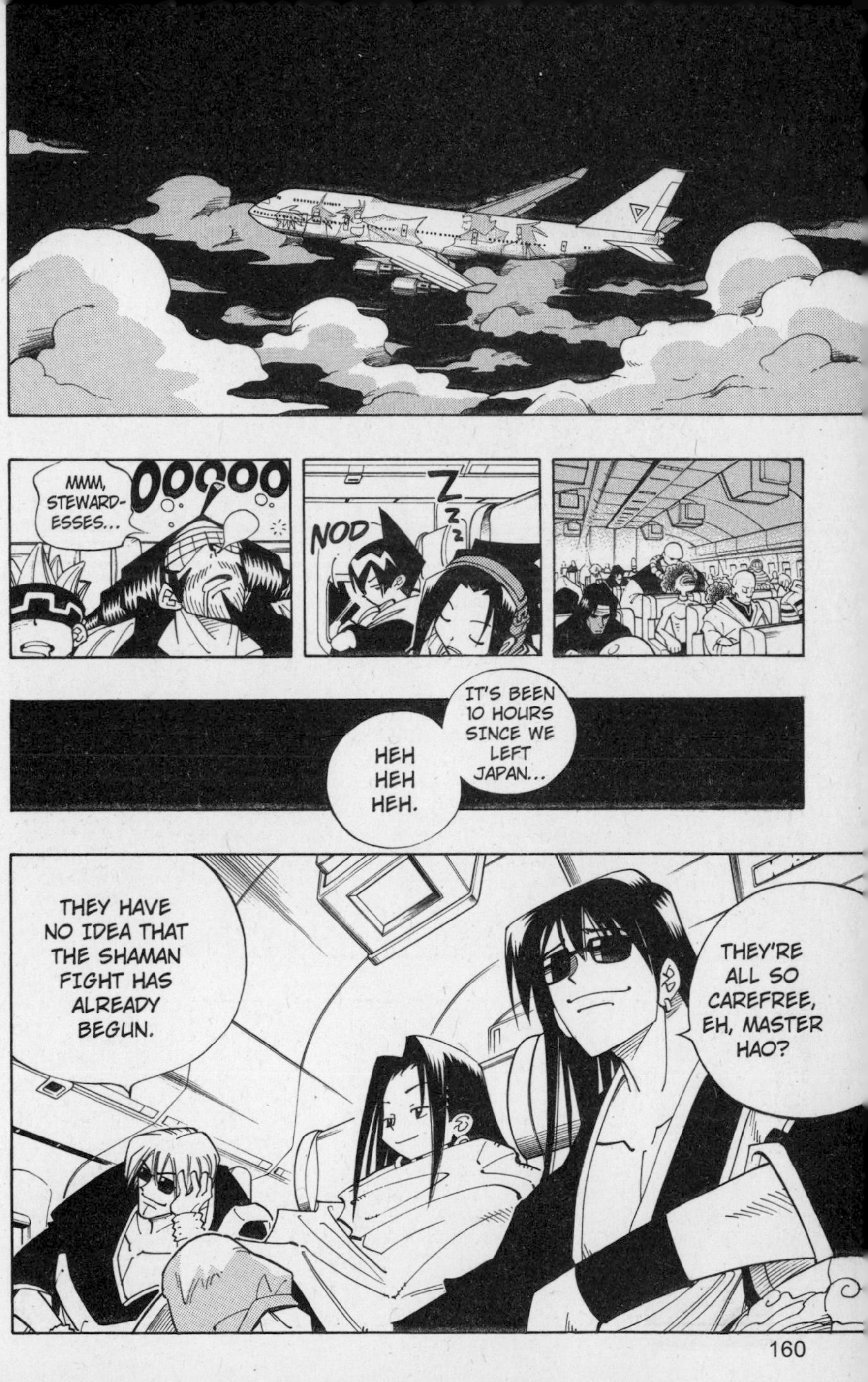
NOD
ZZZ
MMM, STEWARD-ESSES...
OOOOO
IT'S BEEN 10 HOURS SINCE WE LEFT JAPAN...
HEH HEH HEH.
THEY'RE ALL SO CAREFREE, EH, MASTER HAO?
THEY HAVE NO IDEA THAT THE SHAMAN FIGHT HAS ALREADY BEGUN.

READ THIS WAY

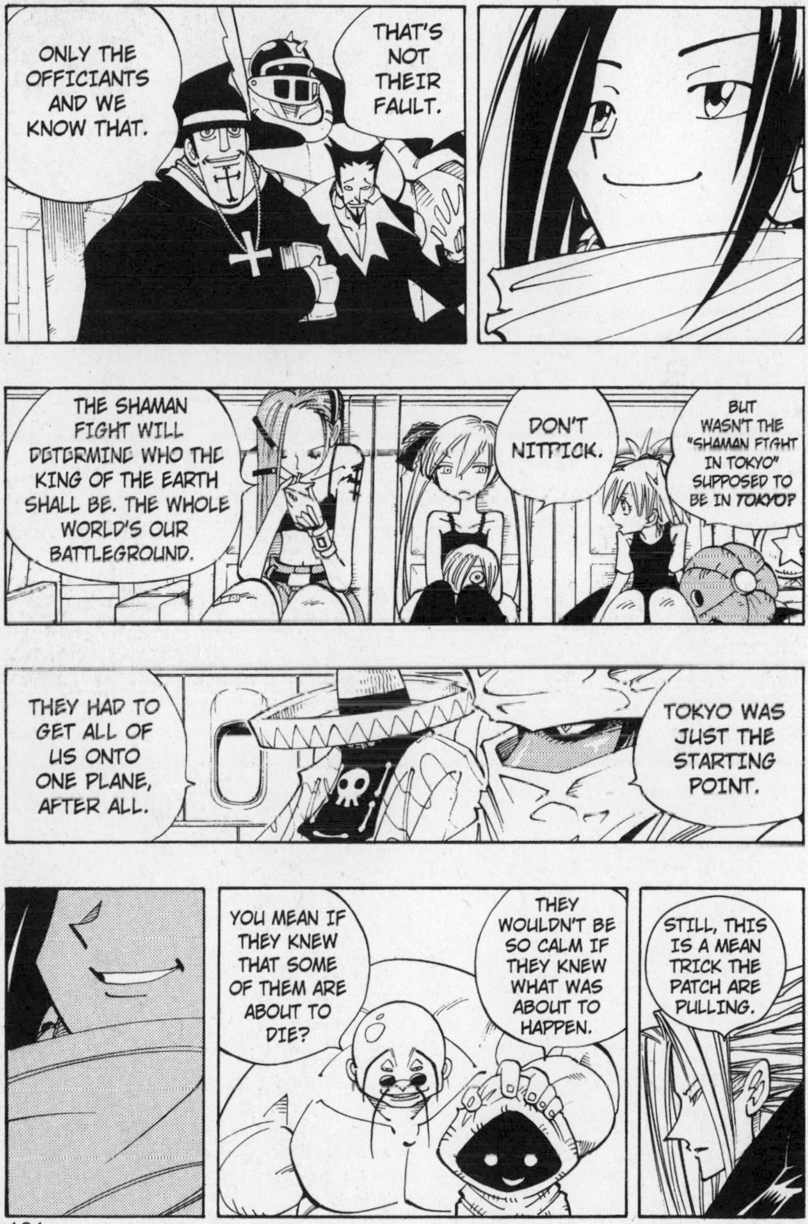
THAT'S NOT THEIR FAULT.
ONLY THE OFFICIANTS AND WE KNOW THAT.
BUT WASN'T THE "SHAMAN FIGHT IN TOKYO" SUPPOSED TO BE IN *TOKYO*?
DON'T NITPICK.
THE SHAMAN FIGHT WILL DETERMINE WHO THE KING OF THE EARTH SHALL BE. THE WHOLE WORLD'S OUR BATTLEGROUND.
TOKYO WAS JUST THE STARTING POINT.
THEY HAD TO GET ALL OF US ONTO ONE PLANE, AFTER ALL.
STILL, THIS IS A MEAN TRICK THE PATCH ARE PULLING.
THEY WOULDN'T BE SO CALM IF THEY KNEW WHAT WAS ABOUT TO HAPPEN.
YOU MEAN IF THEY KNEW THAT SOME OF THEM ARE ABOUT TO DIE?

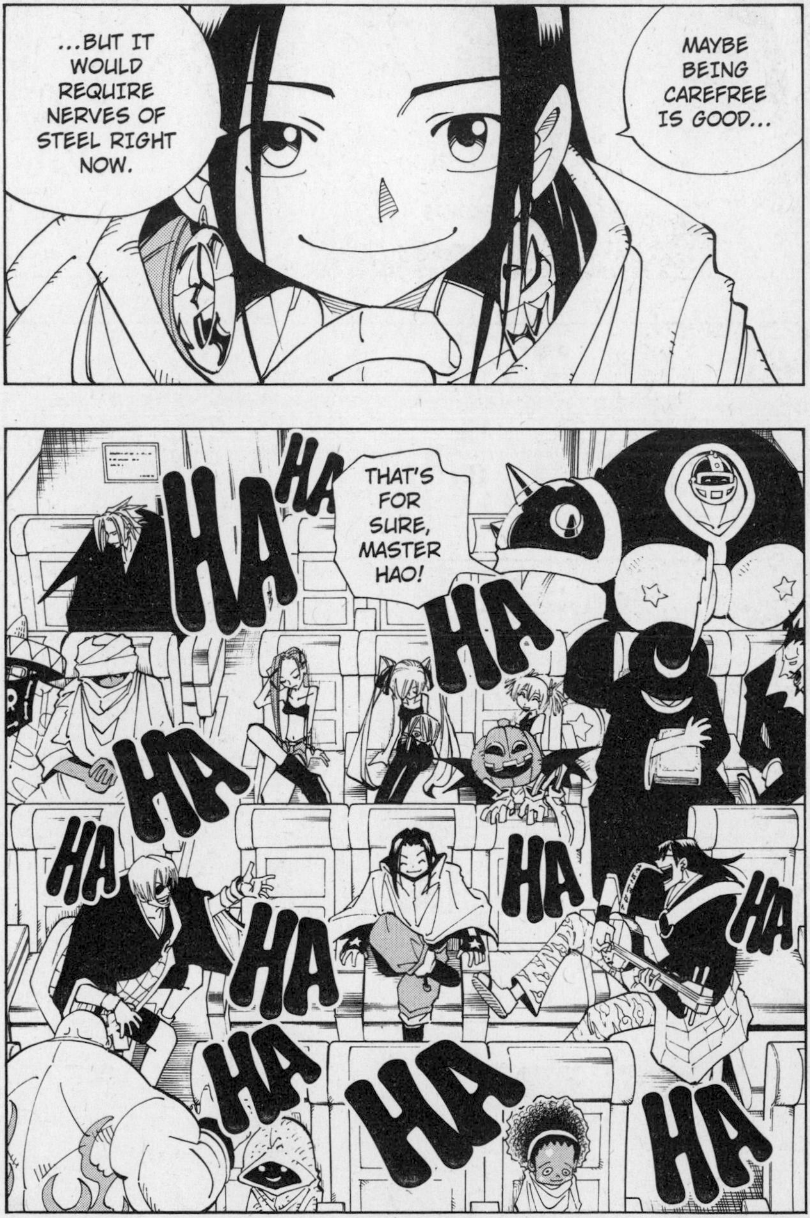
MAYBE BEING CAREFREE IS GOOD...
...BUT IT WOULD REQUIRE NERVES OF STEEL RIGHT NOW.
HA HA HA
THAT'S FOR SURE, MASTER HAO!
HA HA HA HA HA HA HA HA HA HA

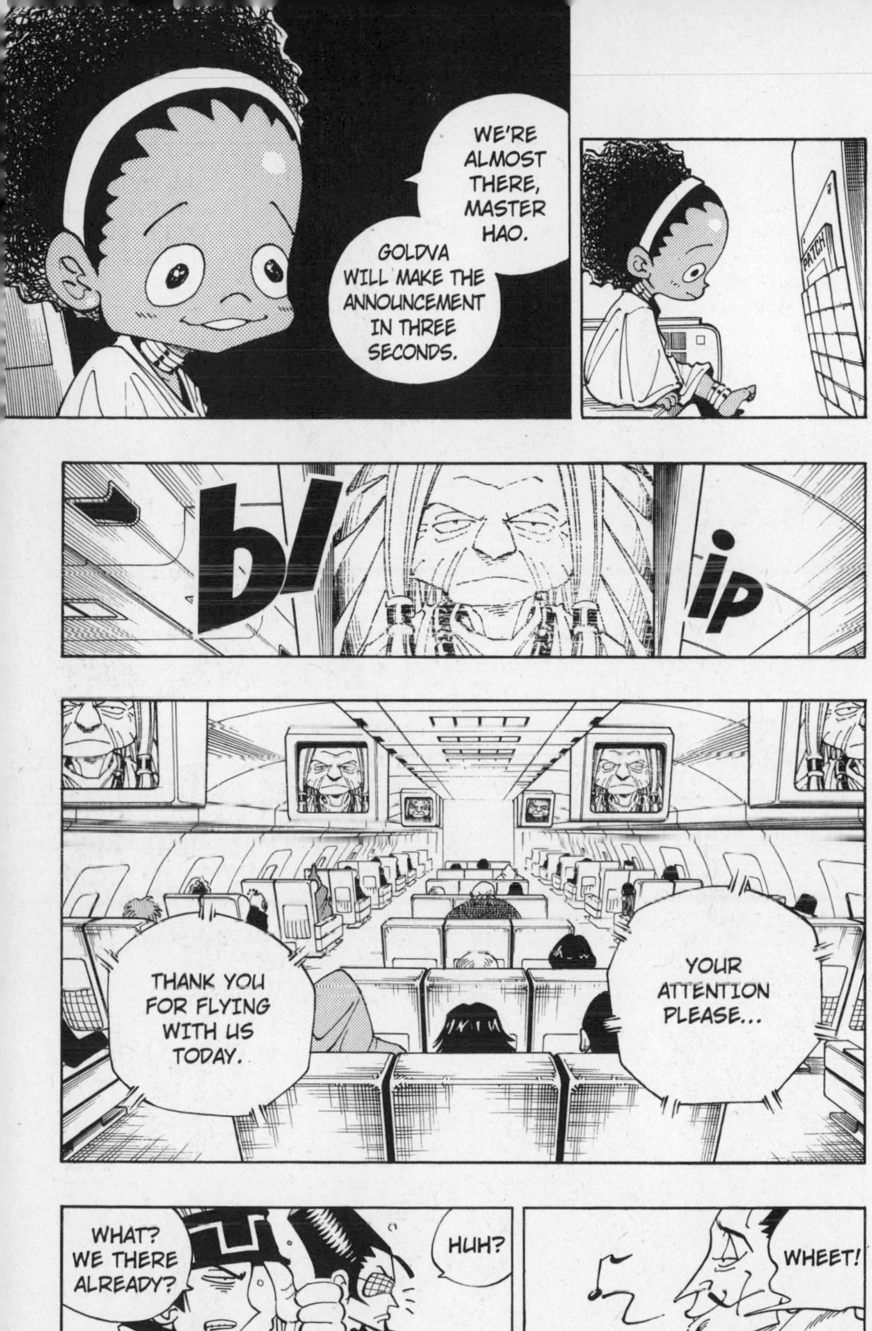
WE'RE ALMOST THERE, MASTER HAO.
GOLDVA WILL MAKE THE ANNOUNCEMENT IN THREE SECONDS.
blip
YOUR ATTENTION PLEASE...
THANK YOU FOR FLYING WITH US TODAY.
WHEET!
HUH?
WHAT? WE THERE ALREADY?

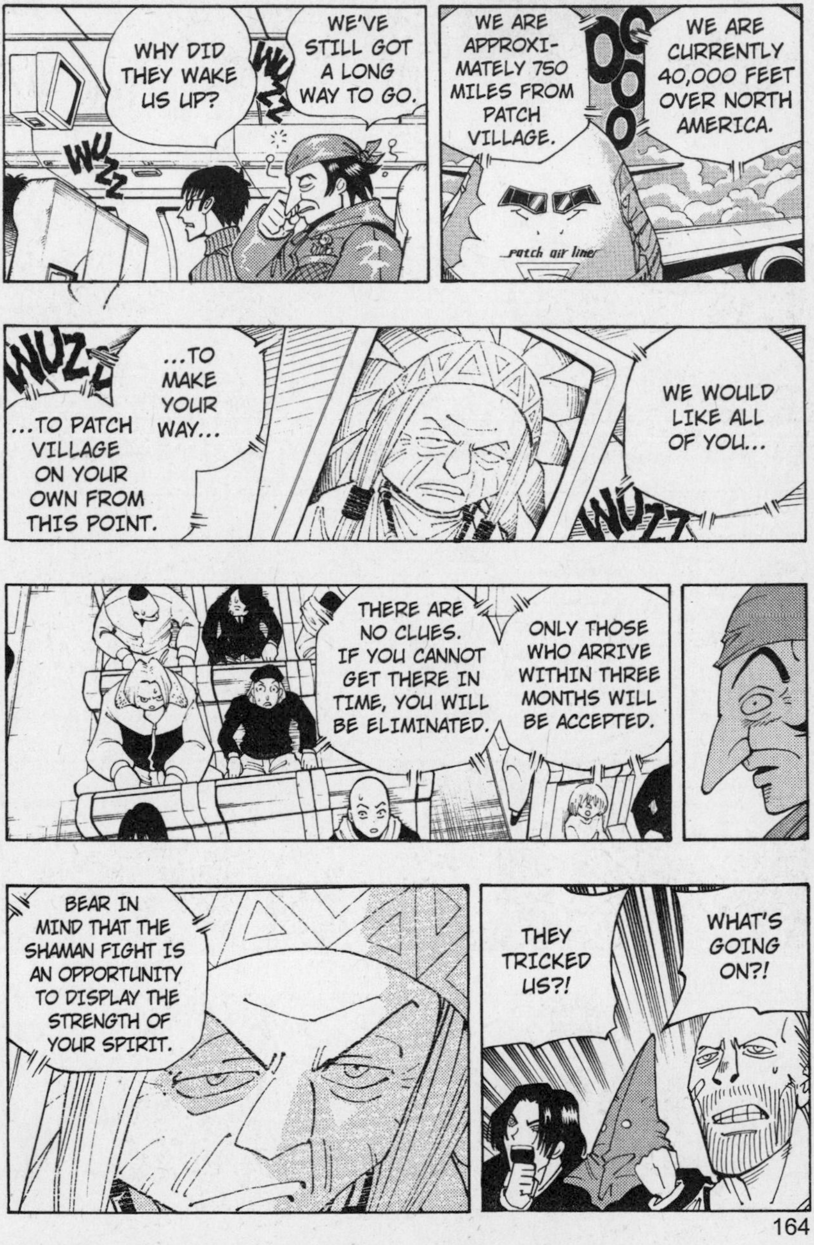
WE ARE CURRENTLY 40,000 FEET OVER NORTH AMERICA.
WE ARE APPROXI-MATELY 750 MILES FROM PATCH VILLAGE.
patch air line
WE'VE STILL GOT A LONG WAY TO GO.
WUZZ
WHY DID THEY WAKE US UP?
WUZZ
WE WOULD LIKE ALL OF YOU...
WUZZ
...TO MAKE YOUR WAY...
...TO PATCH VILLAGE ON YOUR OWN FROM THIS POINT.
WUZZ
ONLY THOSE WHO ARRIVE WITHIN THREE MONTHS WILL BE ACCEPTED.
THERE ARE NO CLUES. IF YOU CANNOT GET THERE IN TIME, YOU WILL BE ELIMINATED.
WHAT'S GOING ON?!
THEY TRICKED US?!
BEAR IN MIND THAT THE SHAMAN FIGHT IS AN OPPORTUNITY TO DISPLAY THE STRENGTH OF YOUR SPIRIT.

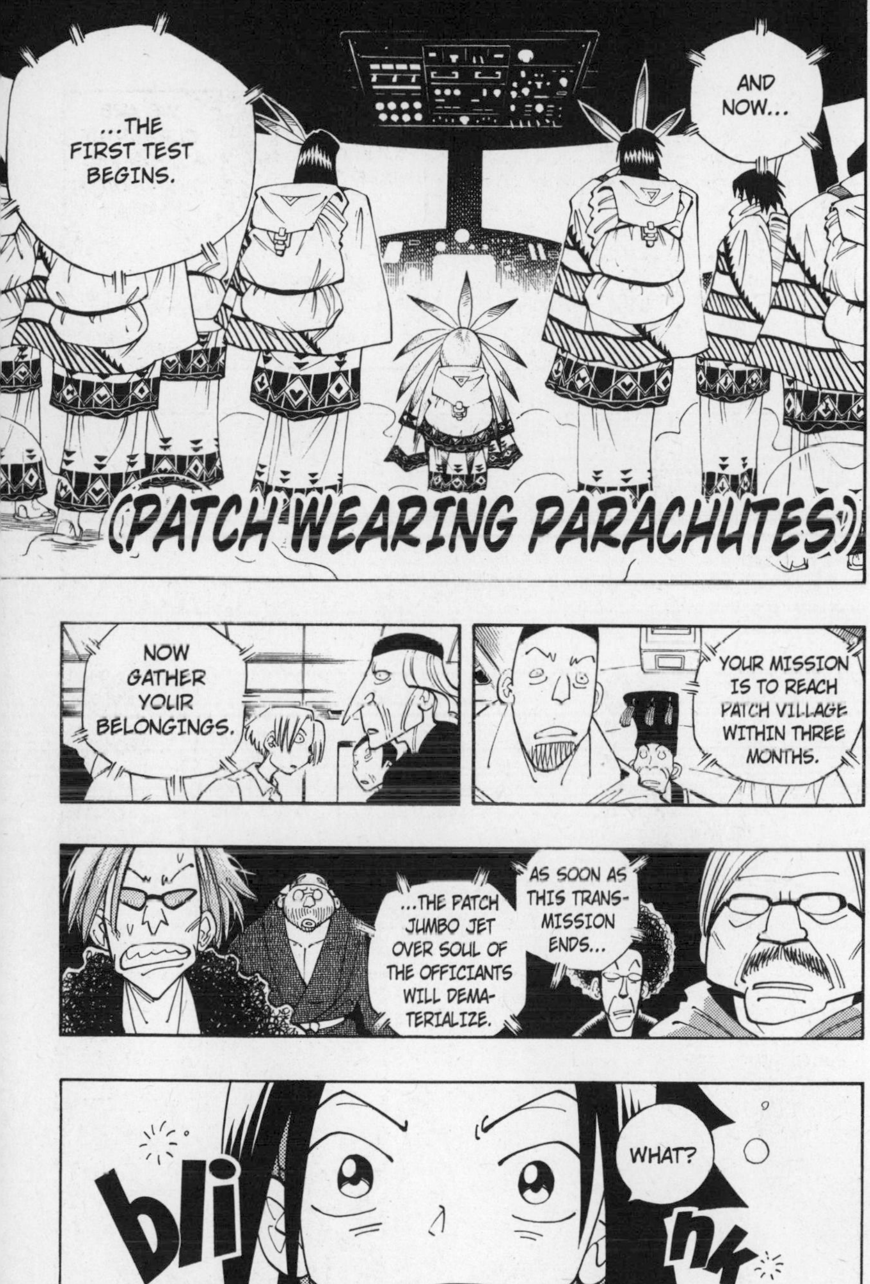
AND NOW...
...THE FIRST TEST BEGINS.
(PATCH WEARING PARACHUTES)
YOUR MISSION IS TO REACH PATCH VILLAGE WITHIN THREE MONTHS.
NOW GATHER YOUR BELONGINGS.
AS SOON AS THIS TRANS-MISSION ENDS...
...THE PATCH JUMBO JET OVER SOUL OF THE OFFICIANTS WILL DEMA-TERIALIZE.
WHAT?
blink

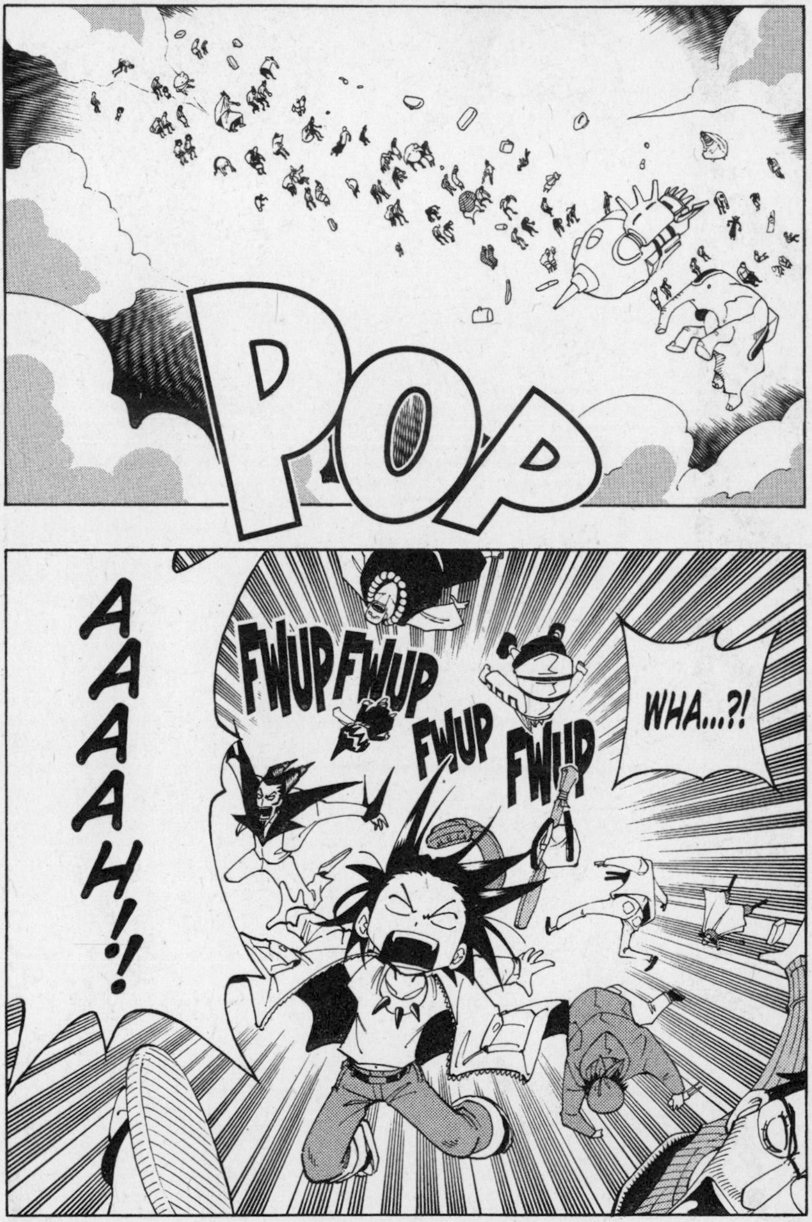
POP
WHA...?!
FWUP FWUP
FWUP
FWUP
AAAAH!!

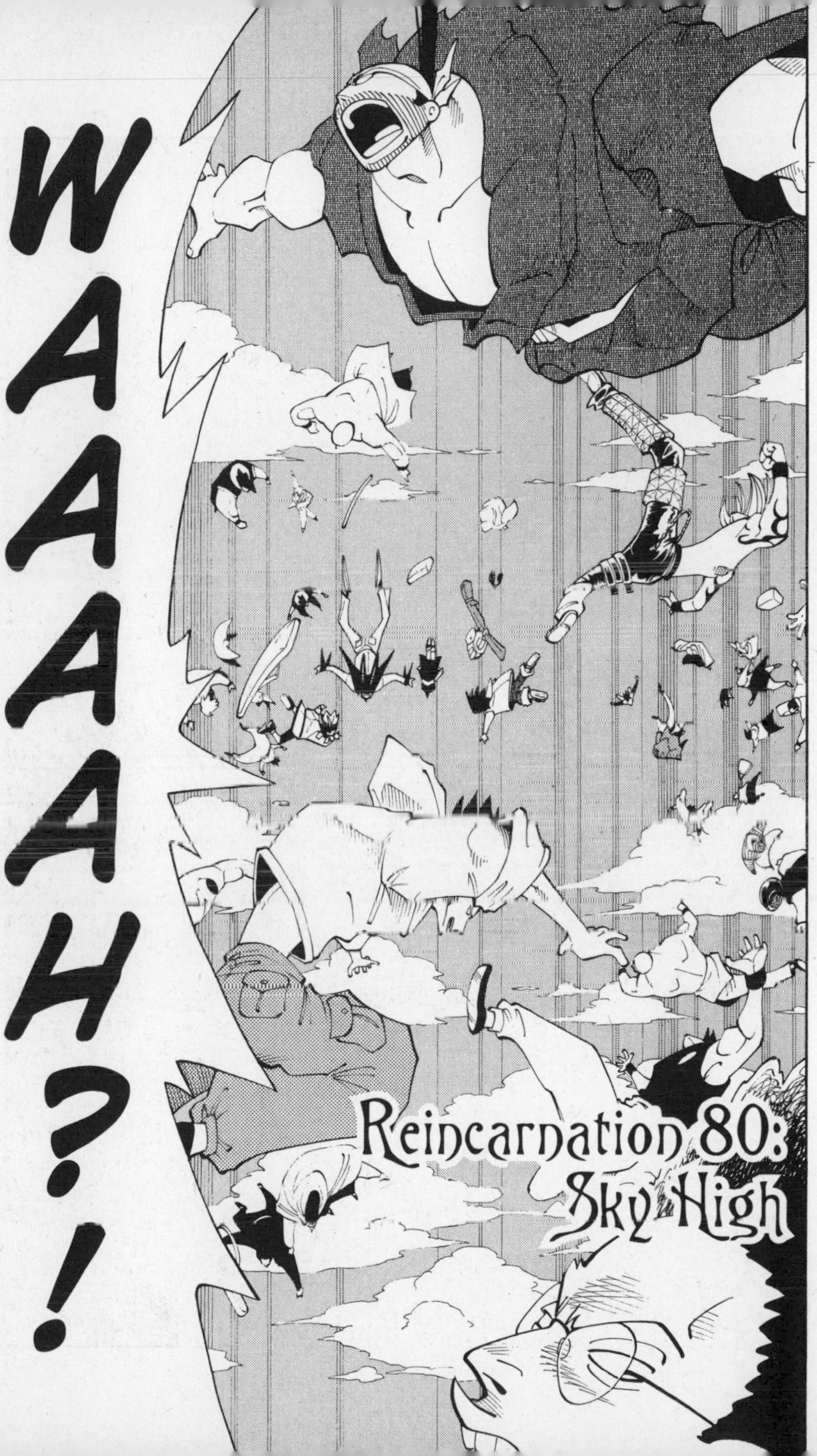
WAAAAH?!
Reincarnation 80:
Sky High

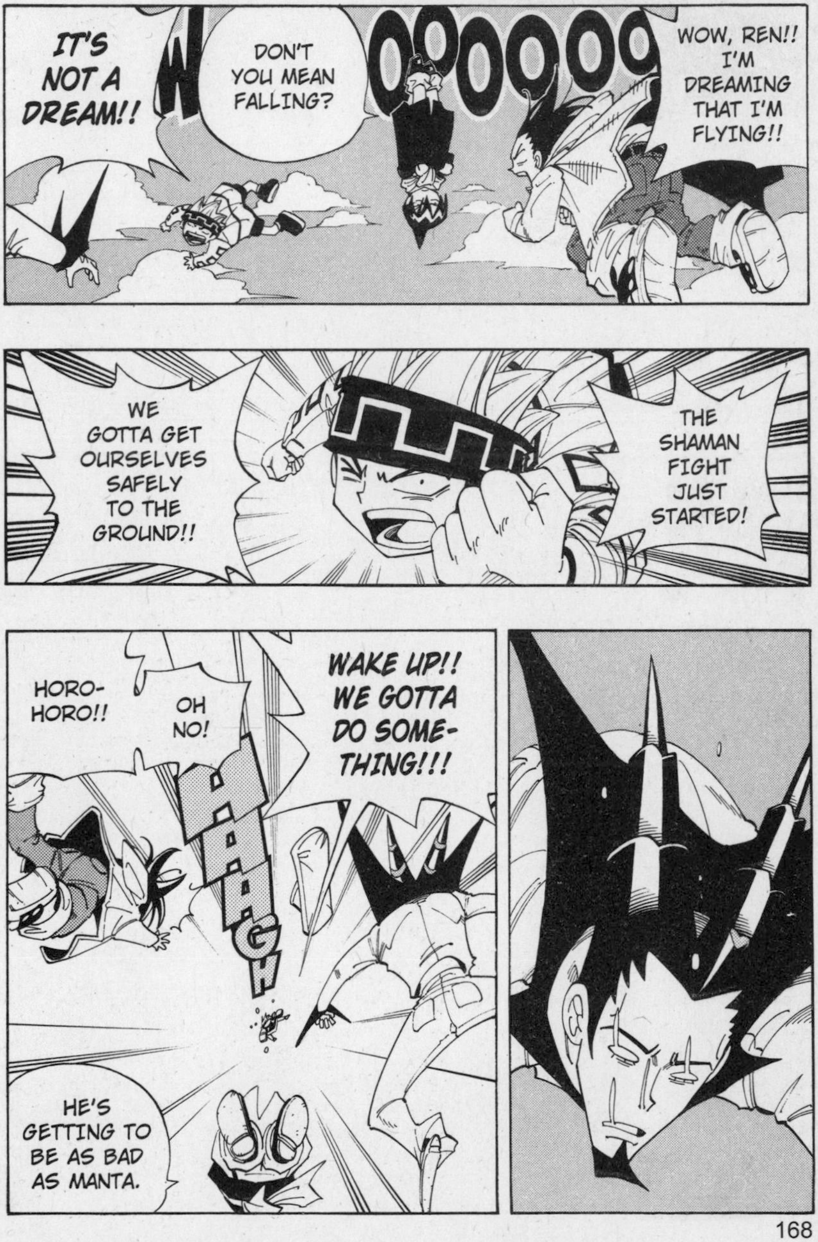
WOW, REN!! I'M DREAMING THAT I'M FLYING!!
WOOOOOO
DON'T YOU MEAN FALLING?
IT'S NOT A DREAM!!
THE SHAMAN FIGHT JUST STARTED!
WE GOTTA GET OURSELVES SAFELY TO THE GROUND!!
WAKE UP!! WE GOTTA DO SOME-THING!!!
OH NO!
HORO-HORO!!
HAAAGH
HE'S GETTING TO BE AS BAD AS MANTA.

# Reincarnation 80: Sky High

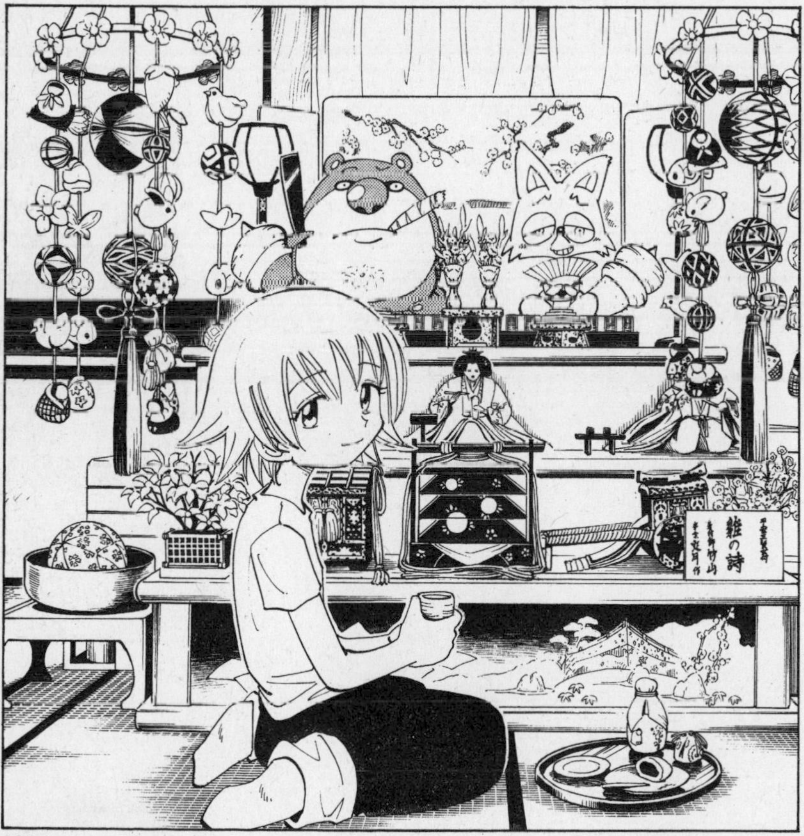
雛の詩

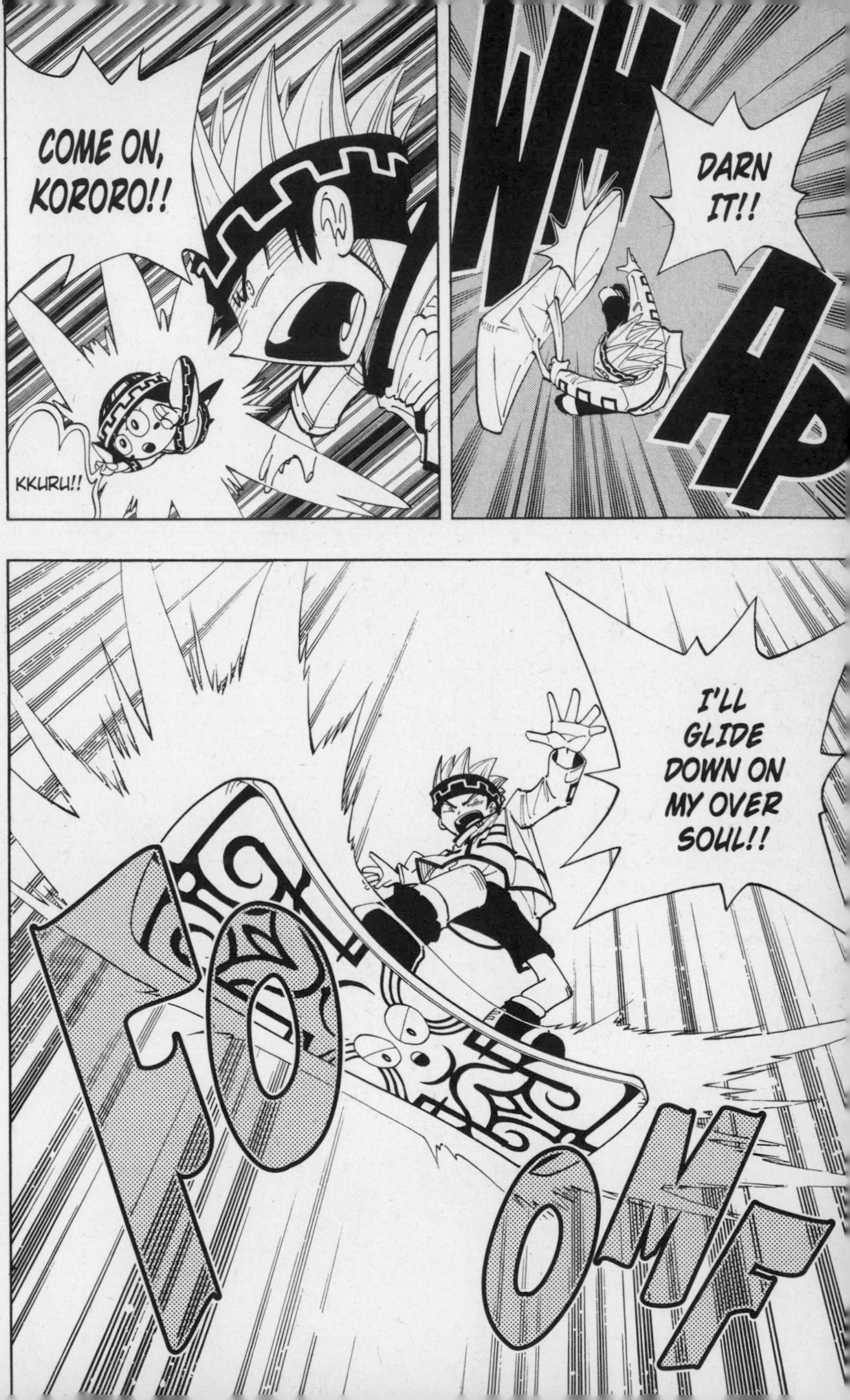
WHAP
DARN IT!!
COME ON, KORORO!!
KKURU!!
I'LL GLIDE DOWN ON MY OVER SOUL!!
FOOMF

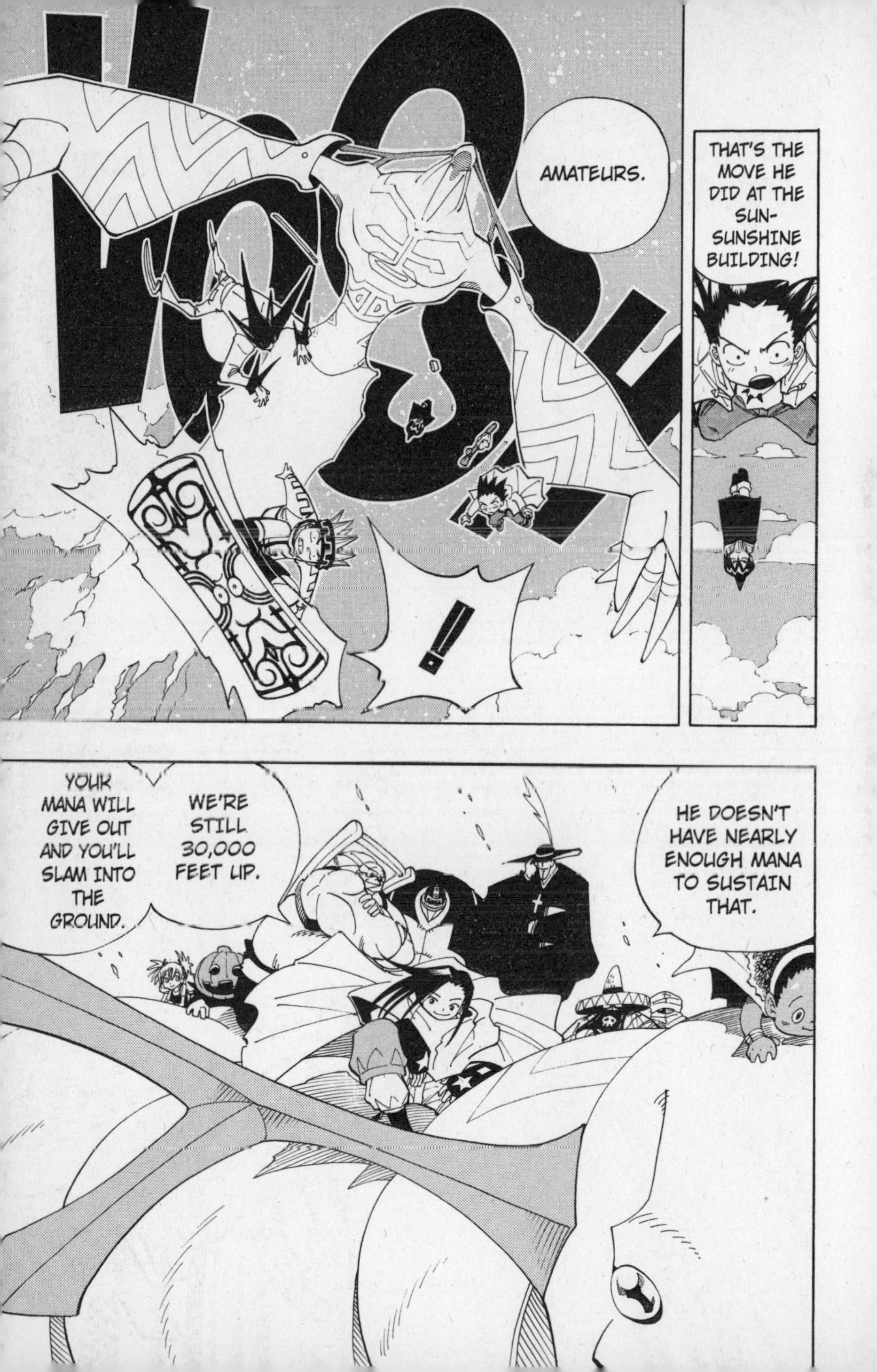
THAT'S THE MOVE HE DID AT THE SUN-SUNSHINE BUILDING!
AMATEURS.
!
HE DOESN'T HAVE NEARLY ENOUGH MANA TO SUSTAIN THAT.
WE'RE STILL 30,000 FEET UP.
YOUR MANA WILL GIVE OUT AND YOU'LL SLAM INTO THE GROUND.

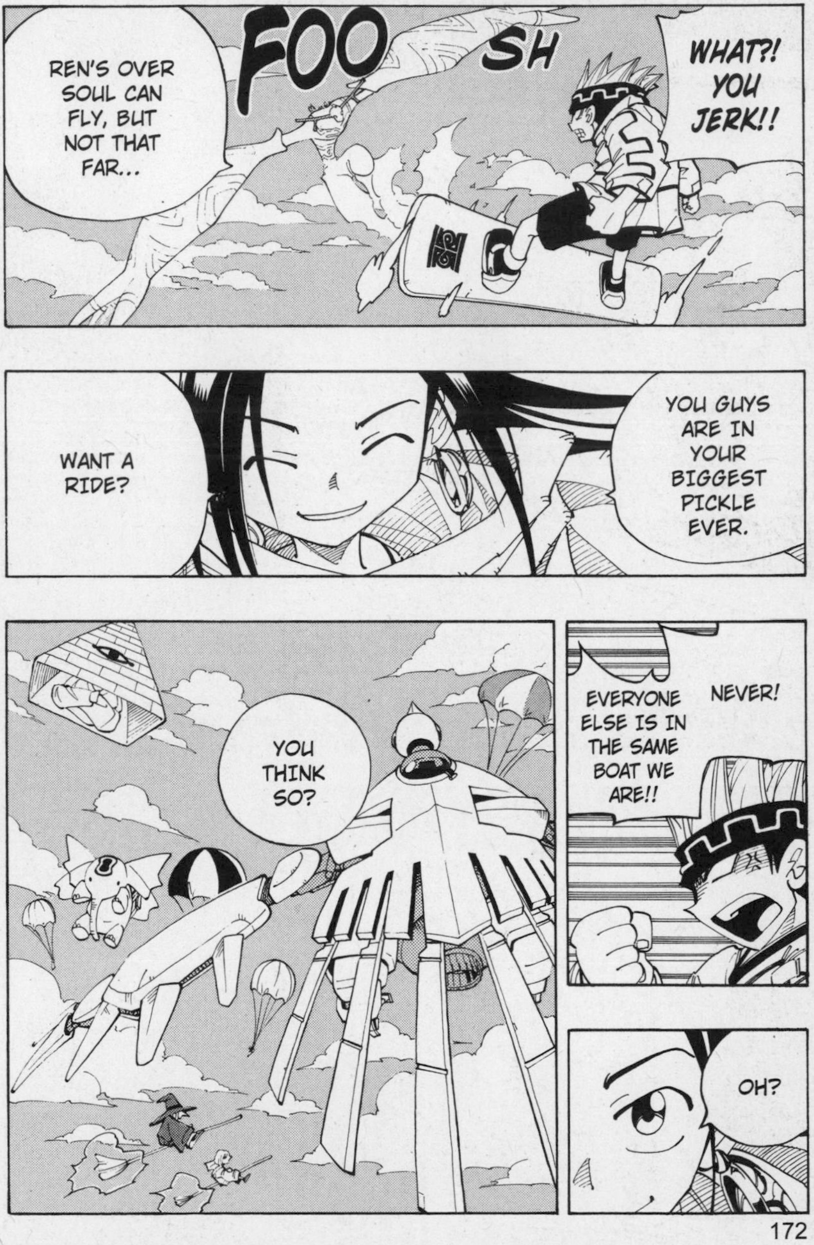
WHAT?! YOU JERK!!
FOOSH
REN'S OVER SOUL CAN FLY, BUT NOT THAT FAR...
YOU GUYS ARE IN YOUR BIGGEST PICKLE EVER.
WANT A RIDE?
NEVER!
EVERYONE ELSE IS IN THE SAME BOAT WE ARE!!
OH?
YOU THINK SO?

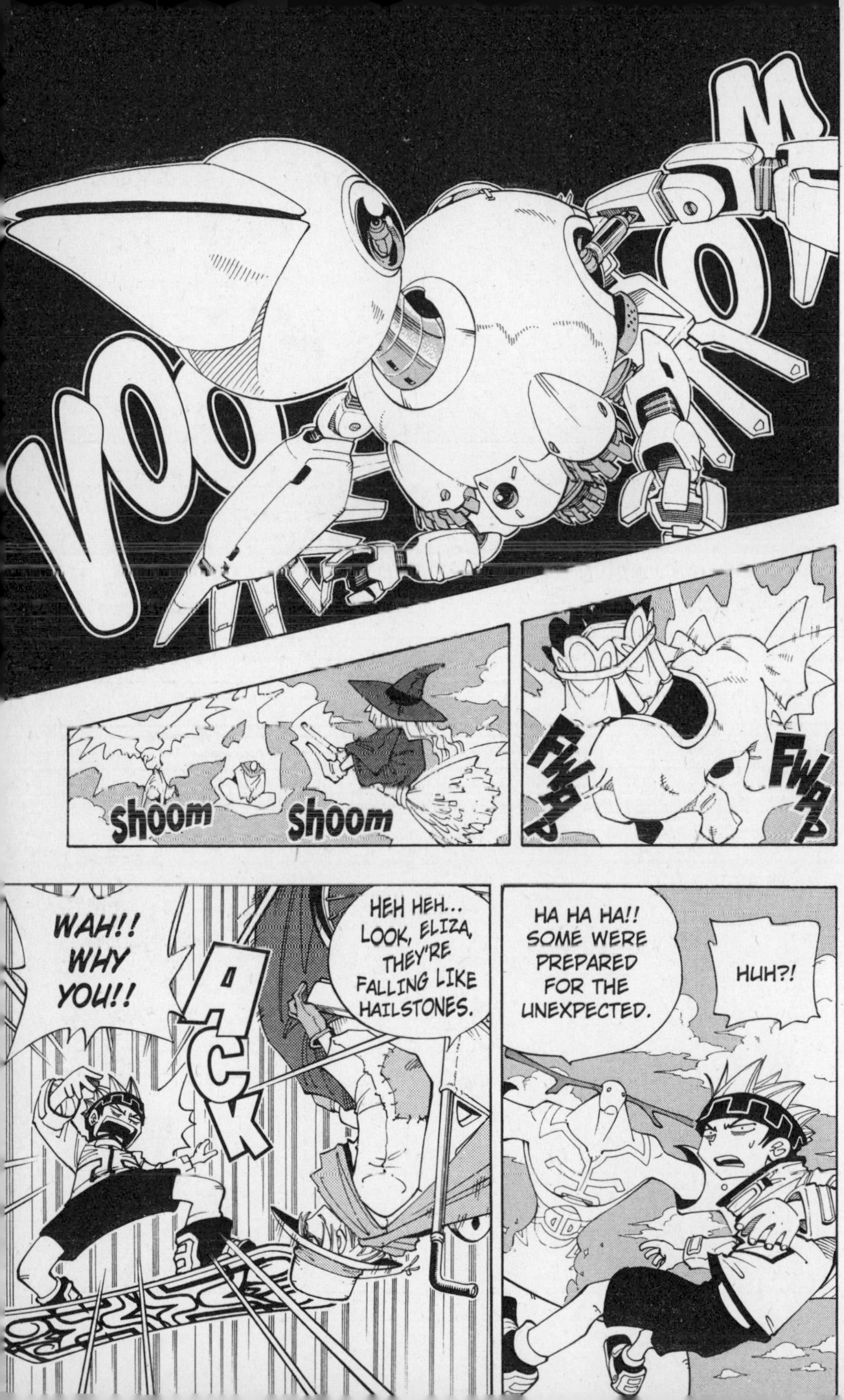
VOOOOM
FWAP
FWAP
shoom
shoom
HA HA HA!! SOME WERE PREPARED FOR THE UNEXPECTED.
HUH?!
HEH HEH... LOOK, ELIZA, THEY'RE FALLING LIKE HAILSTONES.
ACK
WAH!! WHY YOU!!

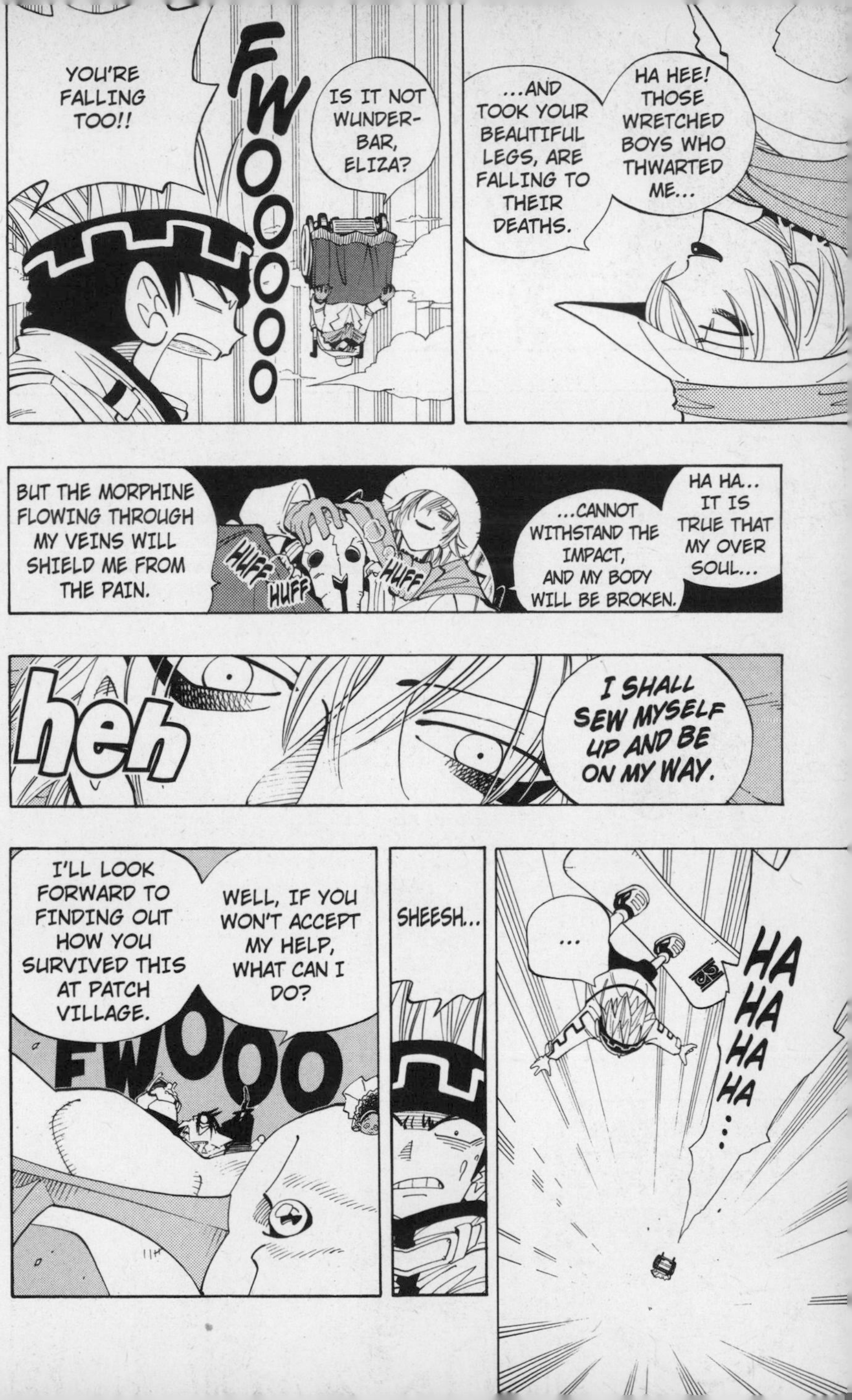
HA HEE! THOSE WRETCHED BOYS WHO THWARTED ME...
...AND TOOK YOUR BEAUTIFUL LEGS, ARE FALLING TO THEIR DEATHS.
IS IT NOT WUNDER-BAR, ELIZA?
FWOOOOOO
YOU'RE FALLING TOO!!
HA HA... IT IS TRUE THAT MY OVER SOUL...
...CANNOT WITHSTAND THE IMPACT, AND MY BODY WILL BE BROKEN.
HUFF HUFF HUFF HUFF
BUT THE MORPHINE FLOWING THROUGH MY VEINS WILL SHIELD ME FROM THE PAIN.
I SHALL SEW MYSELF UP AND BE ON MY WAY.
heh
...
HA HA HA HA HA...
SHEESH...
WELL, IF YOU WON'T ACCEPT MY HELP, WHAT CAN I DO?
I'LL LOOK FORWARD TO FINDING OUT HOW YOU SURVIVED THIS AT PATCH VILLAGE.
FWOOO

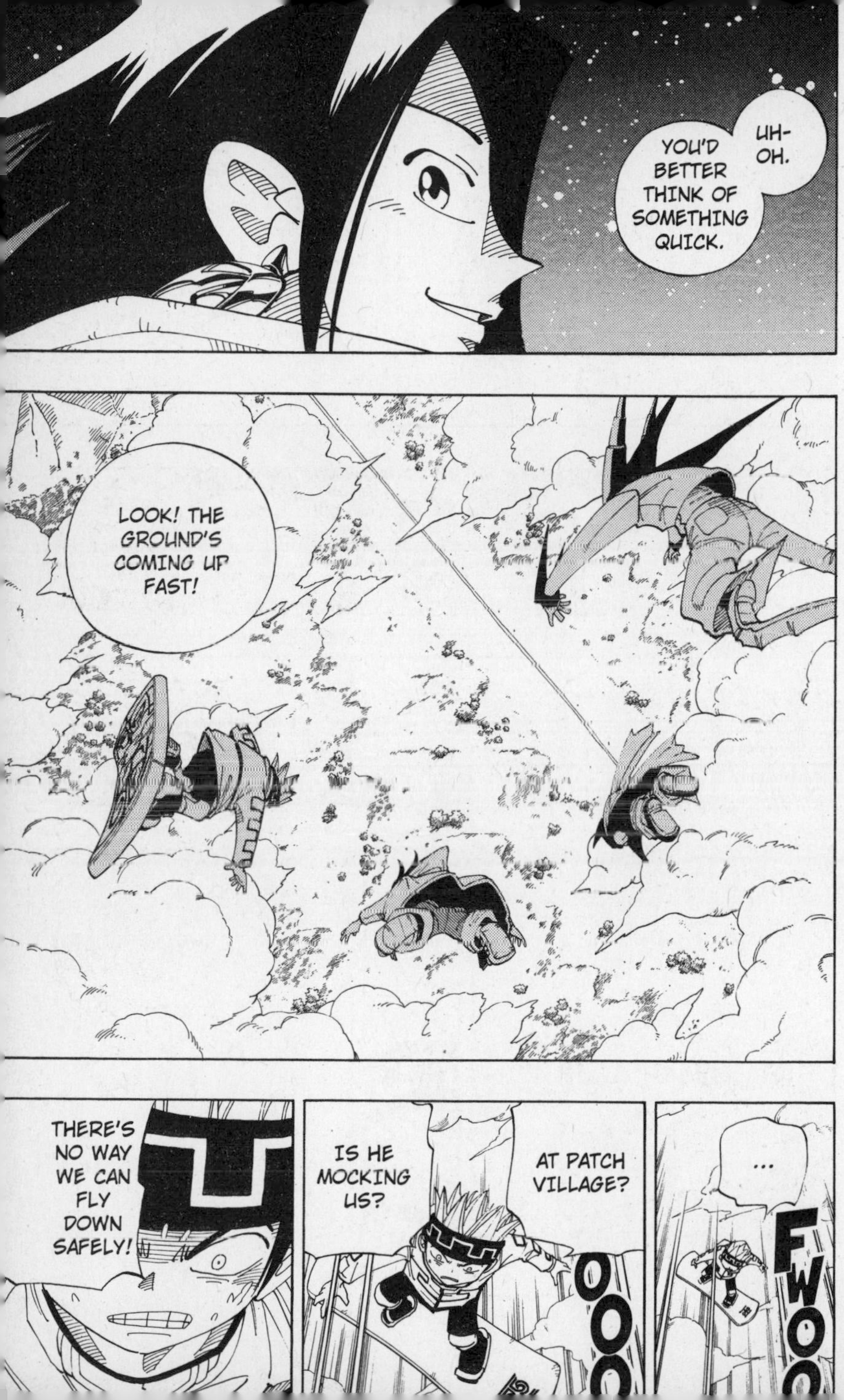
UH-OH.
YOU'D BETTER THINK OF SOMETHING QUICK.
LOOK! THE GROUND'S COMING UP FAST!
...
FWOO
AT PATCH VILLAGE?
IS HE MOCKING US?
OOO
THERE'S NO WAY WE CAN FLY DOWN SAFELY!

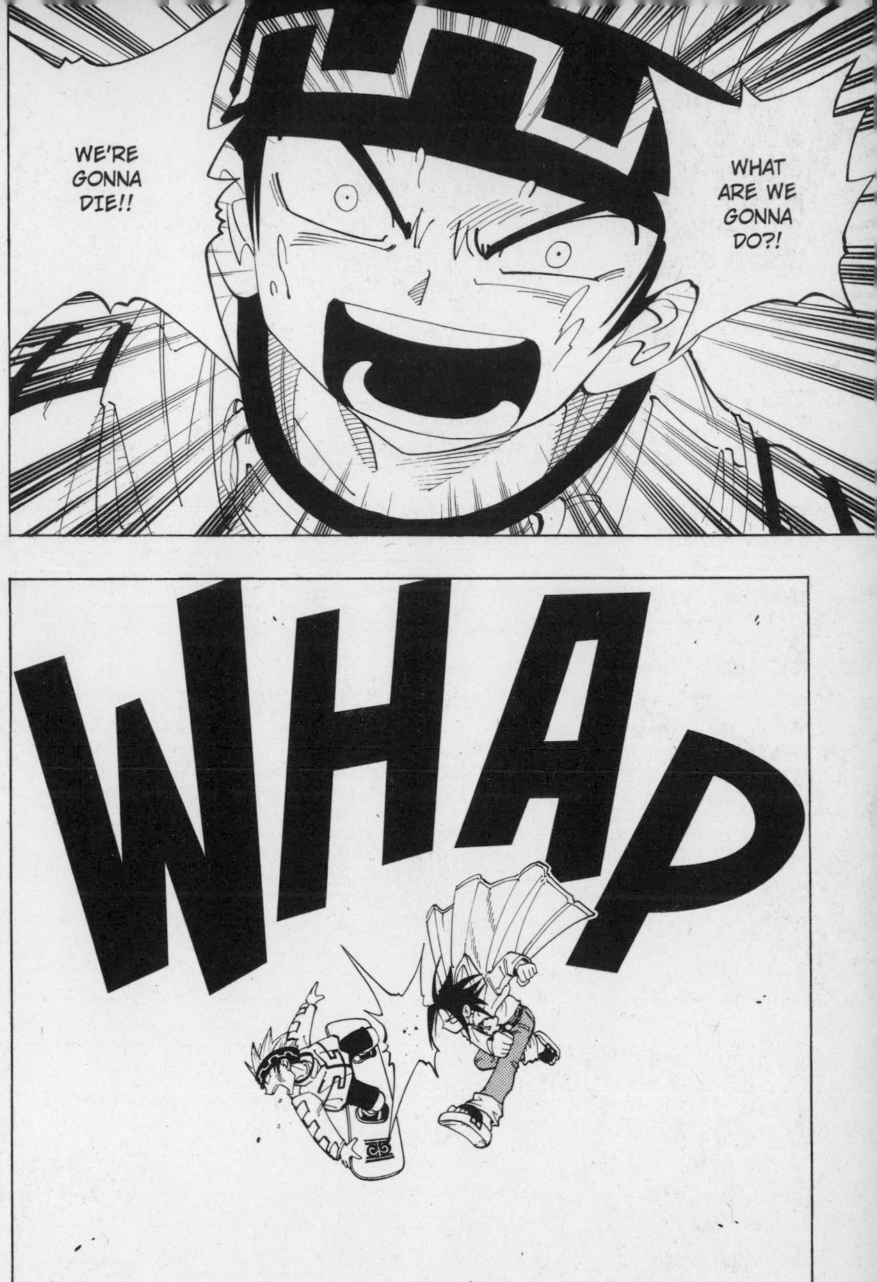
WHAT ARE WE GONNA DO?!
WE'RE GONNA DIE!!
WHAP

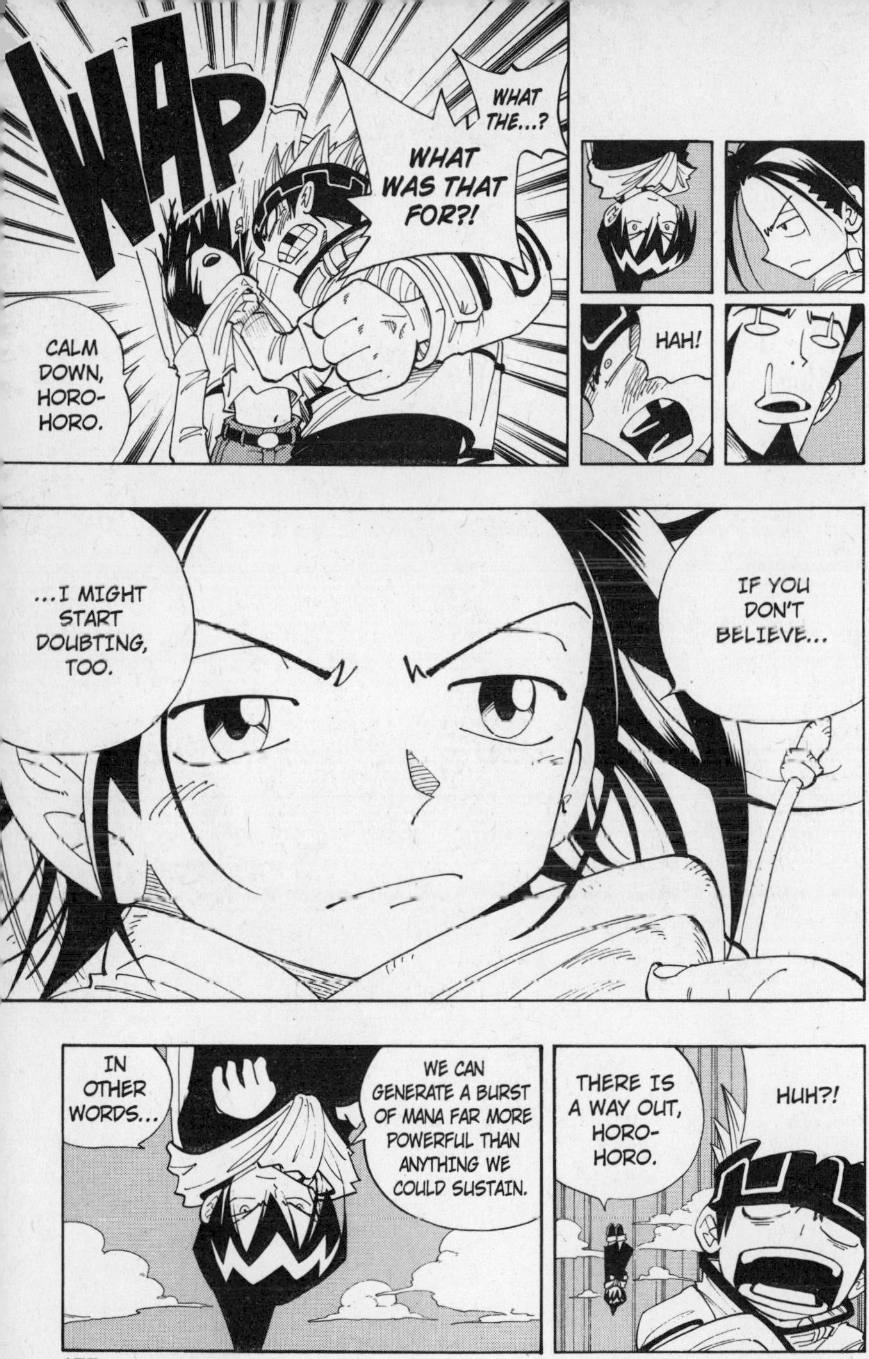
HAH!
WHAT THE...?
WHAT WAS THAT FOR?!
WAP
CALM DOWN, HORO-HORO.
IF YOU DON'T BELIEVE...
...I MIGHT START DOUBTING, TOO.
HUH?!
THERE IS A WAY OUT, HORO-HORO.
IN OTHER WORDS...
WE CAN GENERATE A BURST OF MANA FAR MORE POWERFUL THAN ANYTHING WE COULD SUSTAIN.

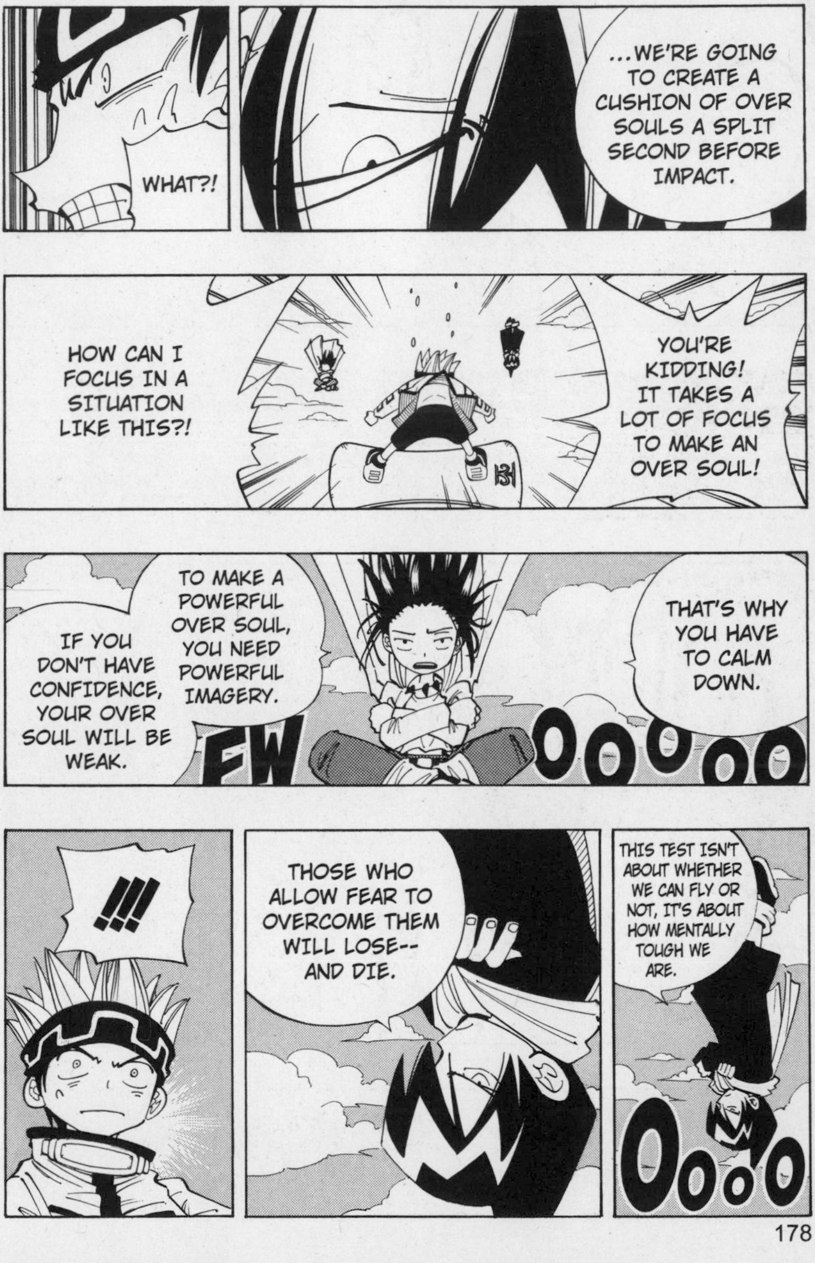
...WE'RE GOING TO CREATE A CUSHION OF OVER SOULS A SPLIT SECOND BEFORE IMPACT.
WHAT?!
YOU'RE KIDDING! IT TAKES A LOT OF FOCUS TO MAKE AN OVER SOUL!
HOW CAN I FOCUS IN A SITUATION LIKE THIS?!
THAT'S WHY YOU HAVE TO CALM DOWN.
TO MAKE A POWERFUL OVER SOUL, YOU NEED POWERFUL IMAGERY.
IF YOU DON'T HAVE CONFIDENCE, YOUR OVER SOUL WILL BE WEAK.
FW
OOOOO
THIS TEST ISN'T ABOUT WHETHER WE CAN FLY OR NOT, IT'S ABOUT HOW MENTALLY TOUGH WE ARE.
OOOO
THOSE WHO ALLOW FEAR TO OVERCOME THEM WILL LOSE-- AND DIE.
!!!

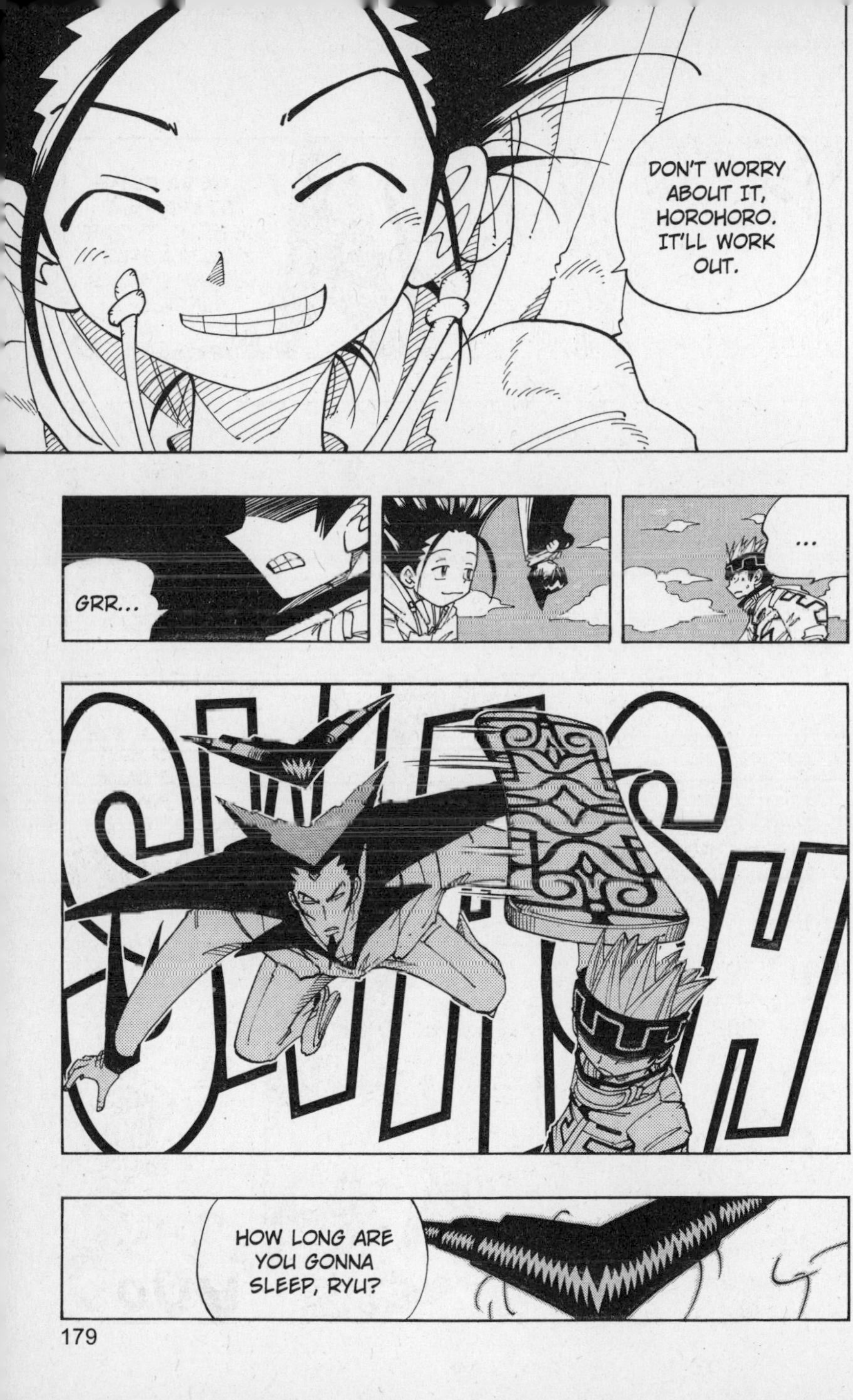
DON'T WORRY ABOUT IT, HOROHORO. IT'LL WORK OUT.
...
GRR...
HOW LONG ARE YOU GONNA SLEEP, RYU?

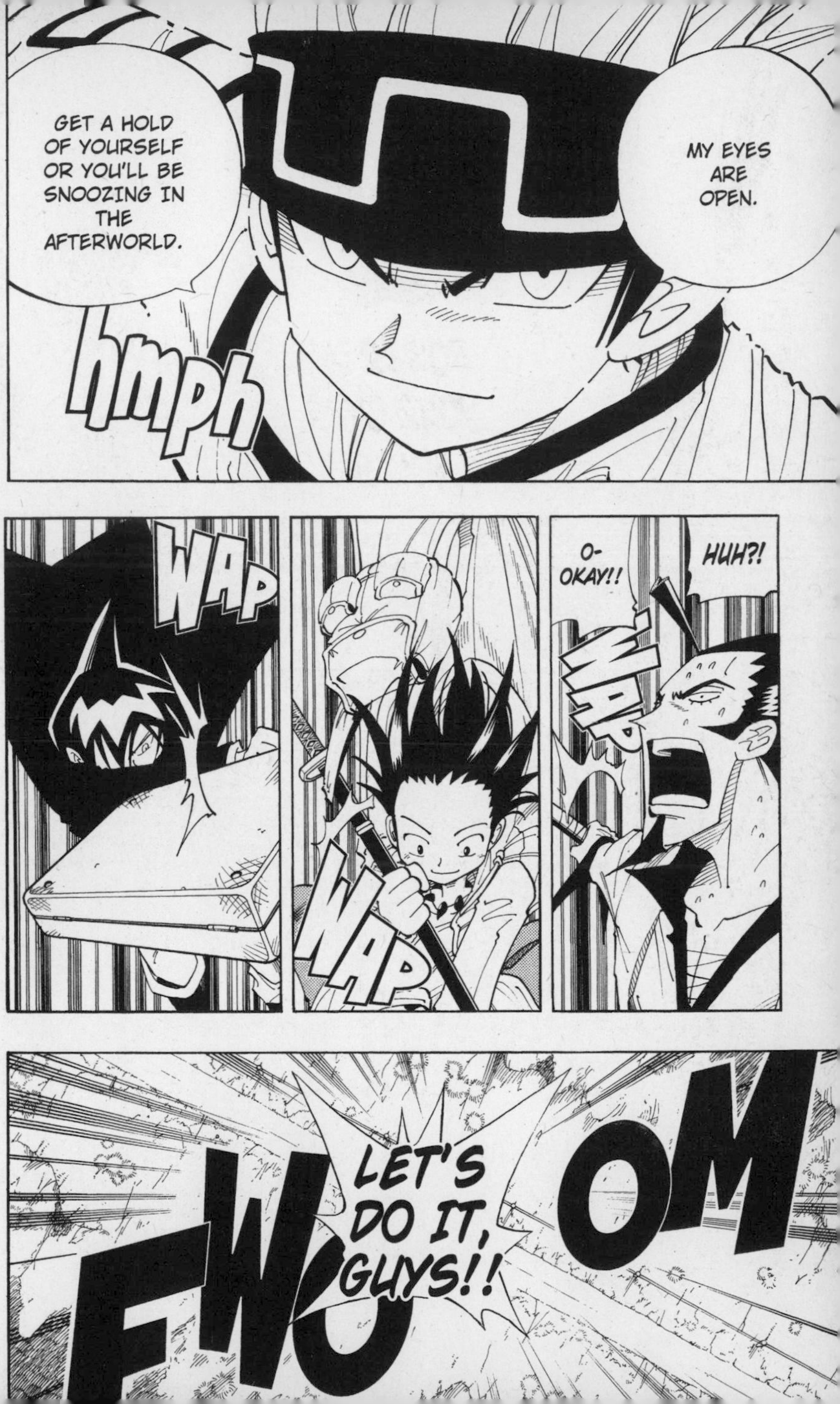

MY EYES ARE OPEN.
GET A HOLD OF YOURSELF OR YOU'LL BE SNOOZING IN THE AFTERWORLD.
hmph
HUH?!
O-OKAY!!
WAP
WAP
WAP
FWOOM
LET'S DO IT, GUYS!!

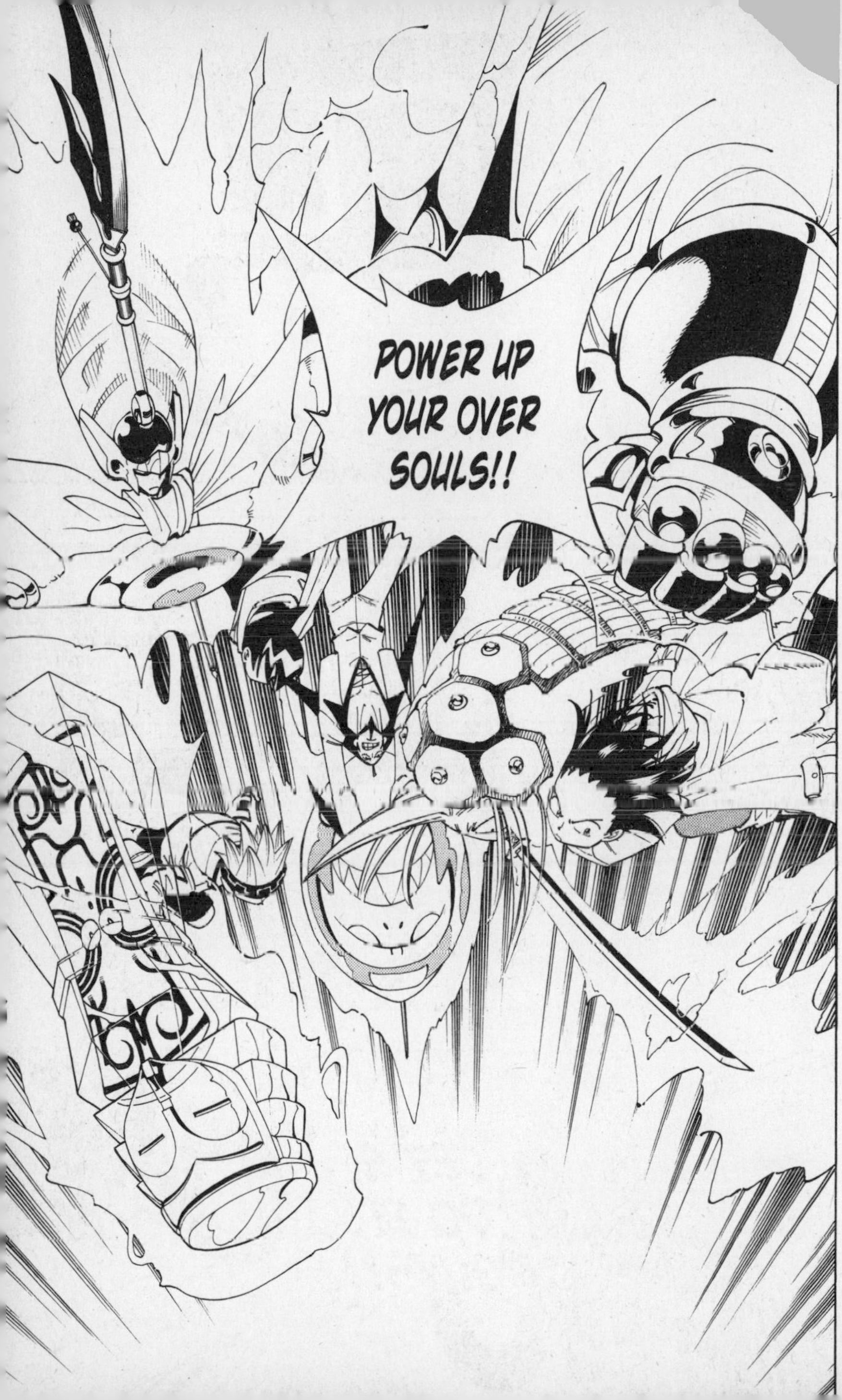
POWER UP
YOUR OVER
SOULS!!

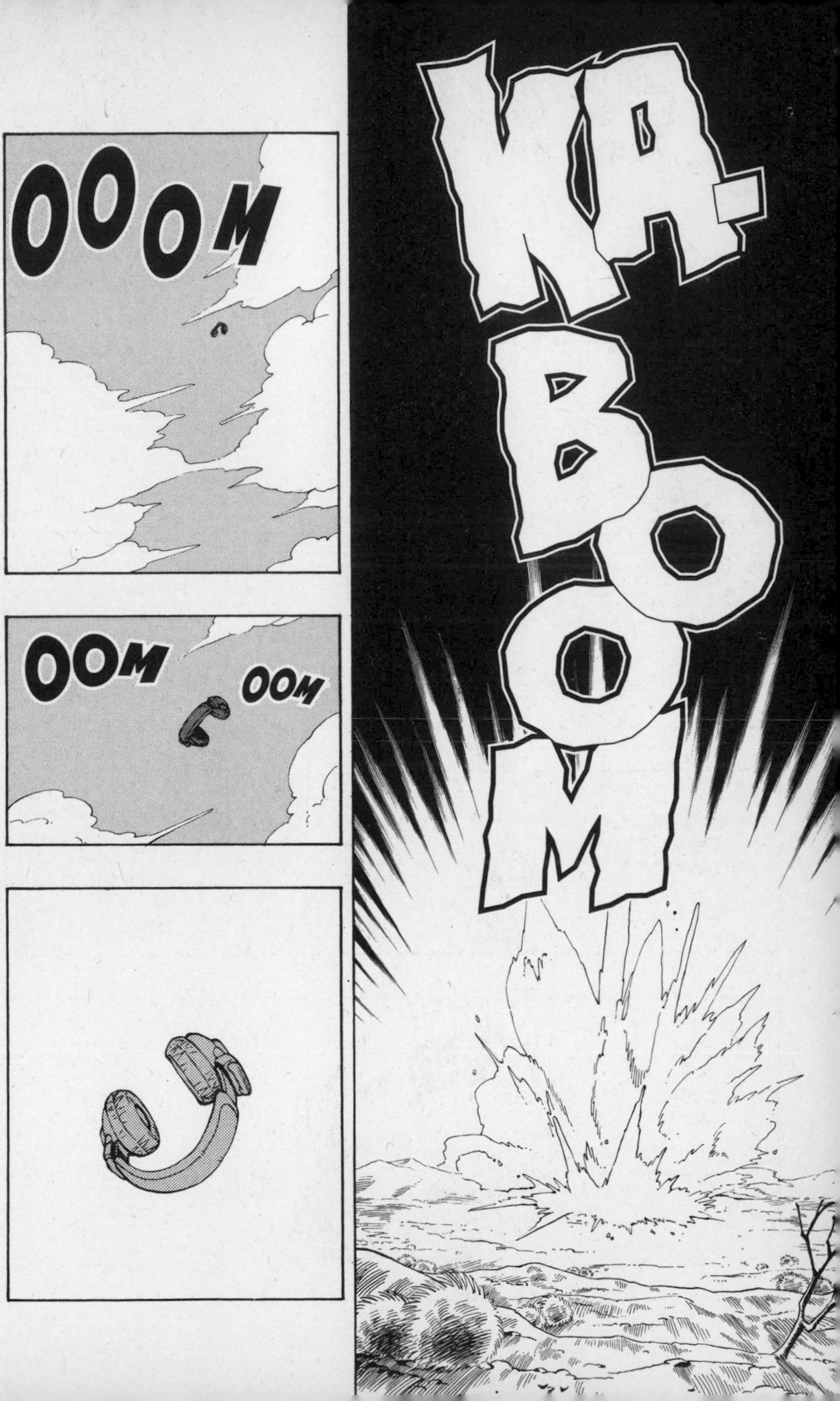
KA-BOOM
OOOM
OOM
OOM

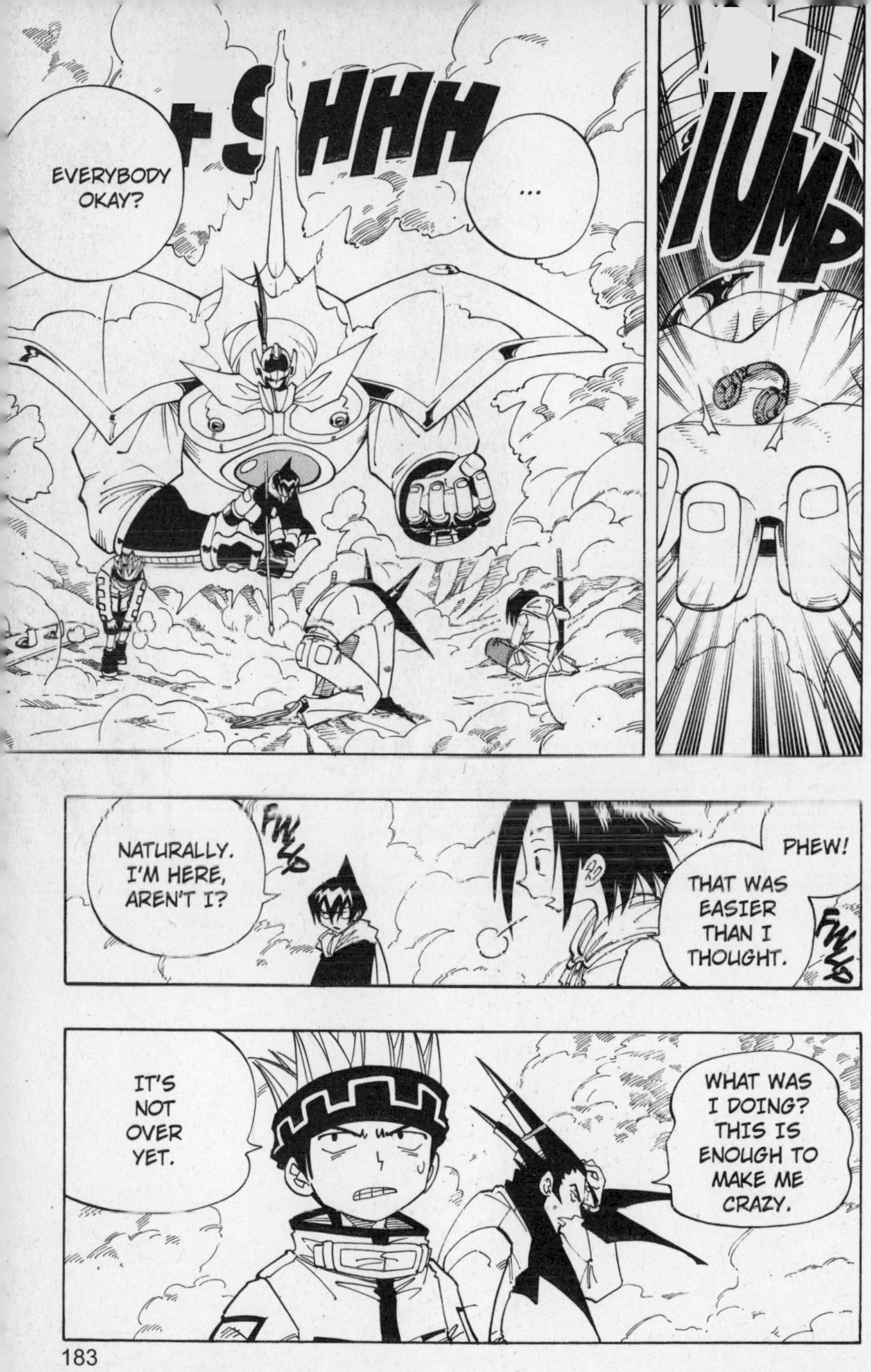
UMP
SHHH
...
EVERYBODY OKAY?
PHEW!
THAT WAS EASIER THAN I THOUGHT.
NATURALLY. I'M HERE, AREN'T I?
WHAT WAS I DOING? THIS IS ENOUGH TO MAKE ME CRAZY.
IT'S NOT OVER YET.

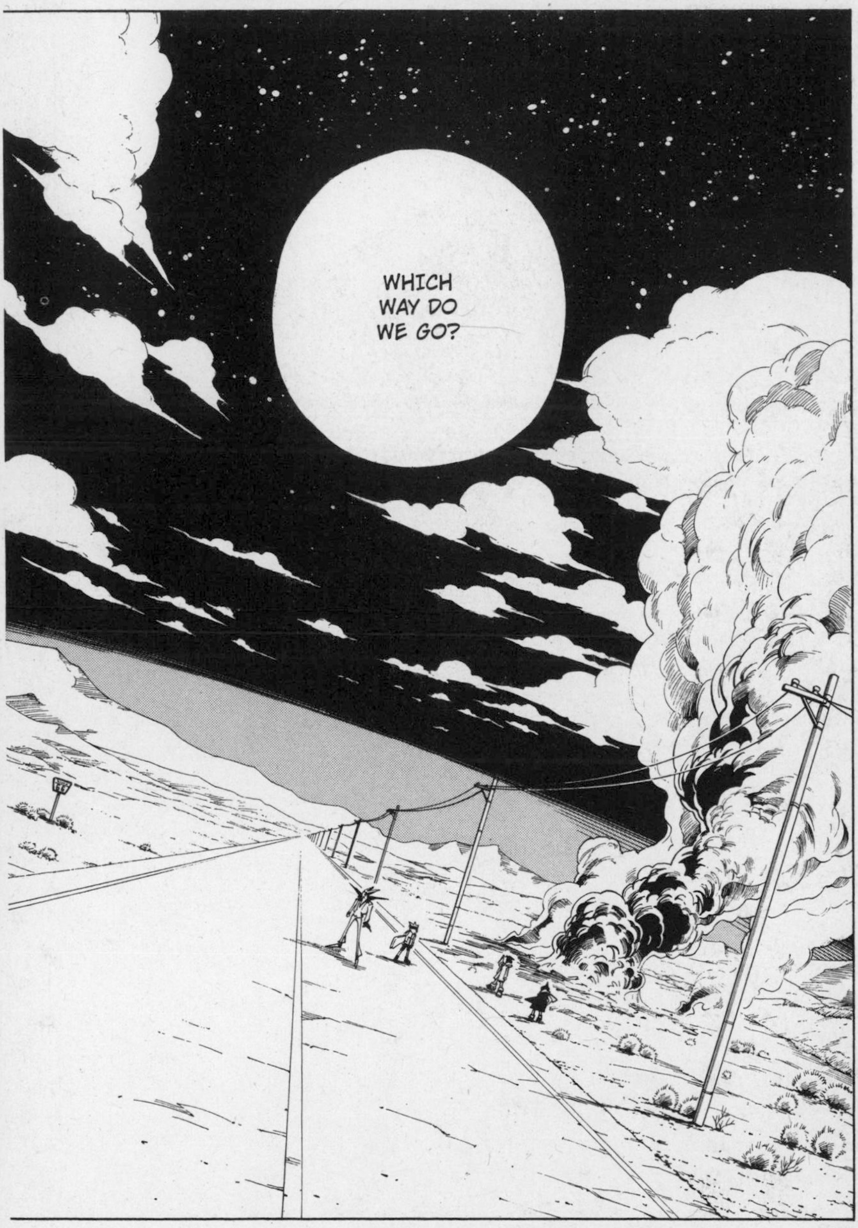
WHICH WAY DO WE GO?

READ THIS WAY

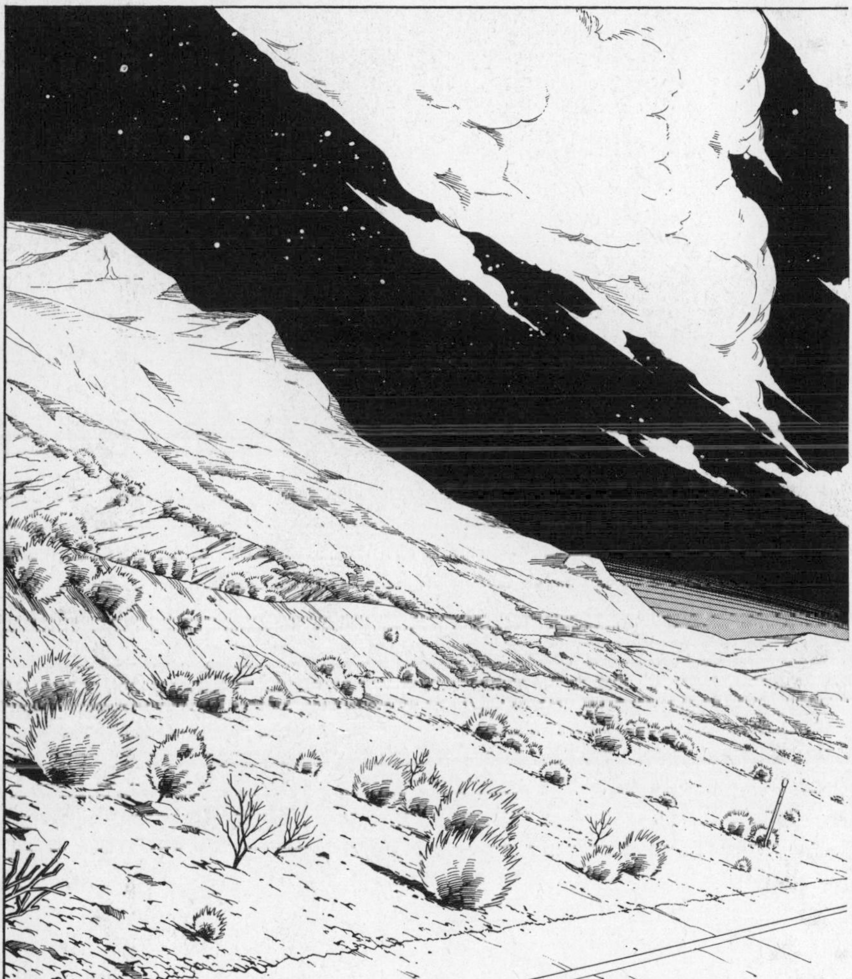

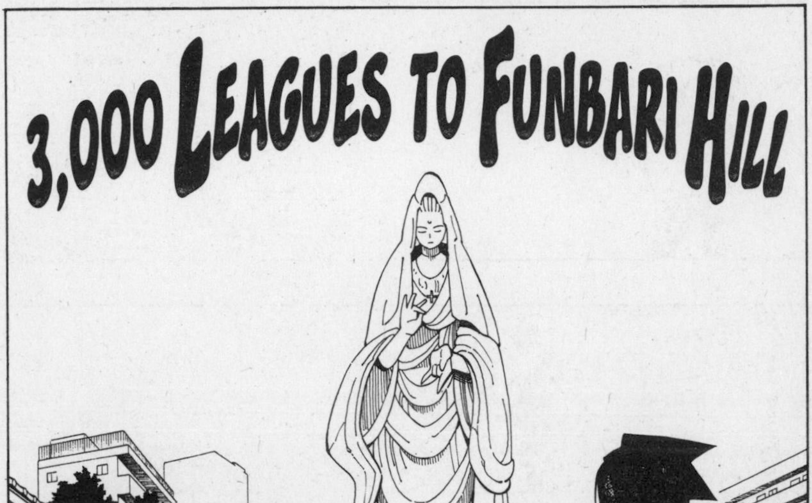
3,000 Leagues to Funbari Hill

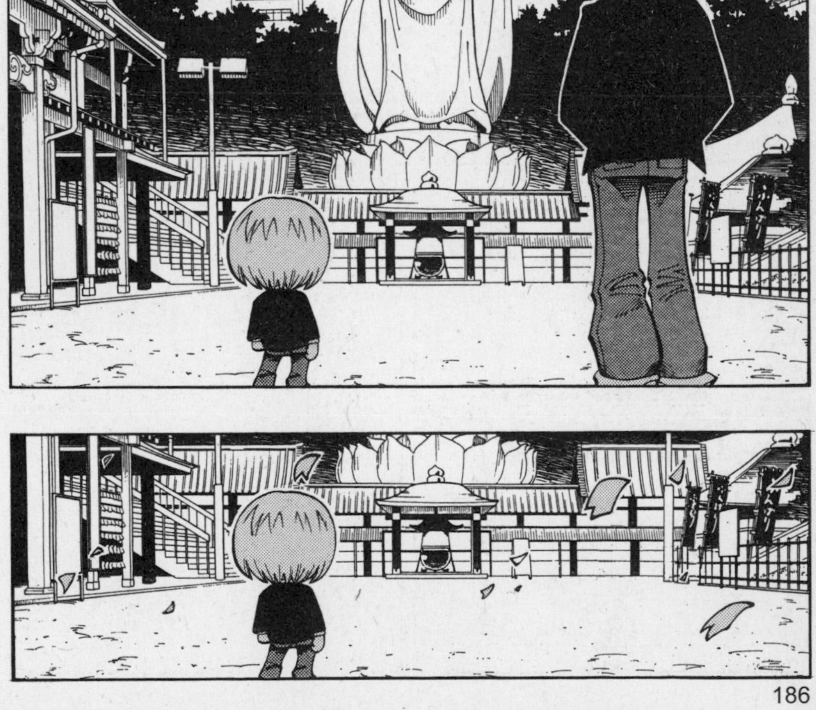

READ THIS WAY

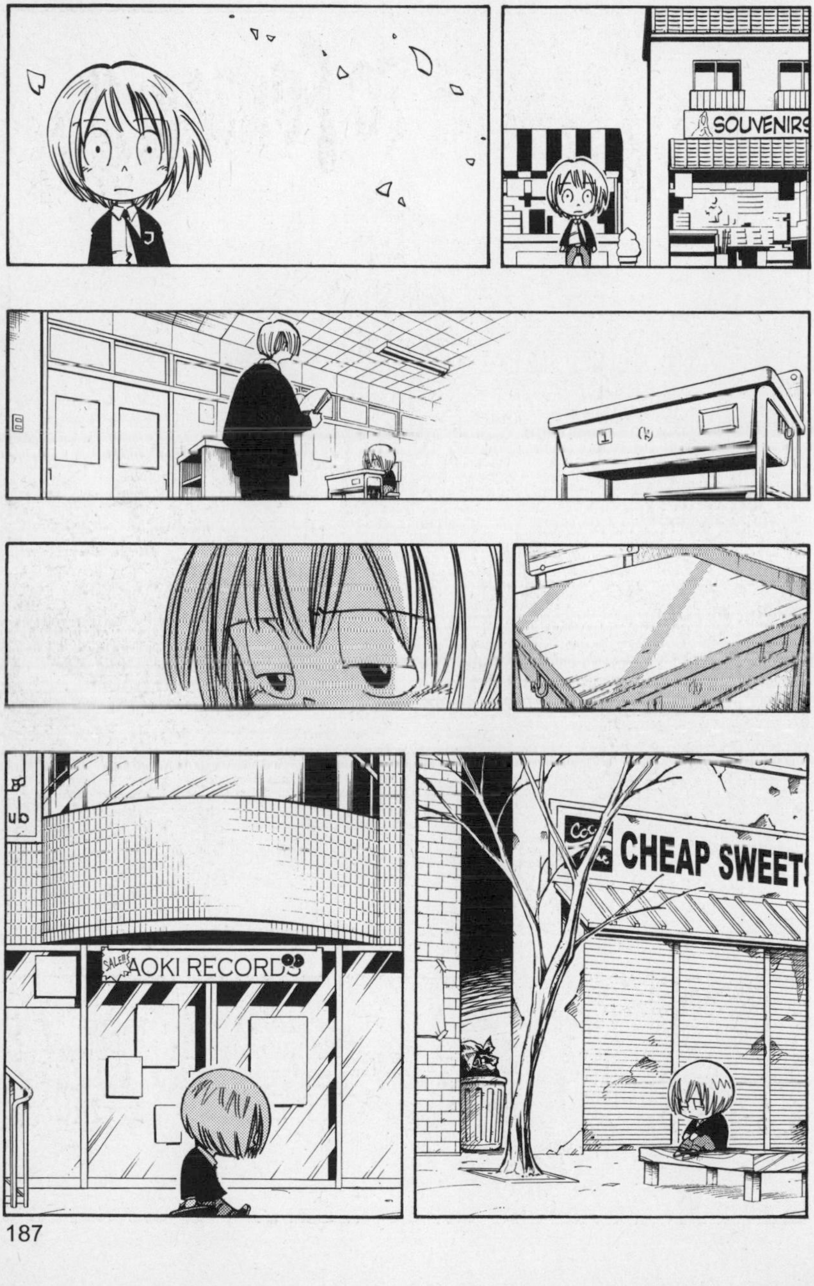
SOUVENIRS
CHEAP SWEETS
SALE!!!
AOKI RECORDS

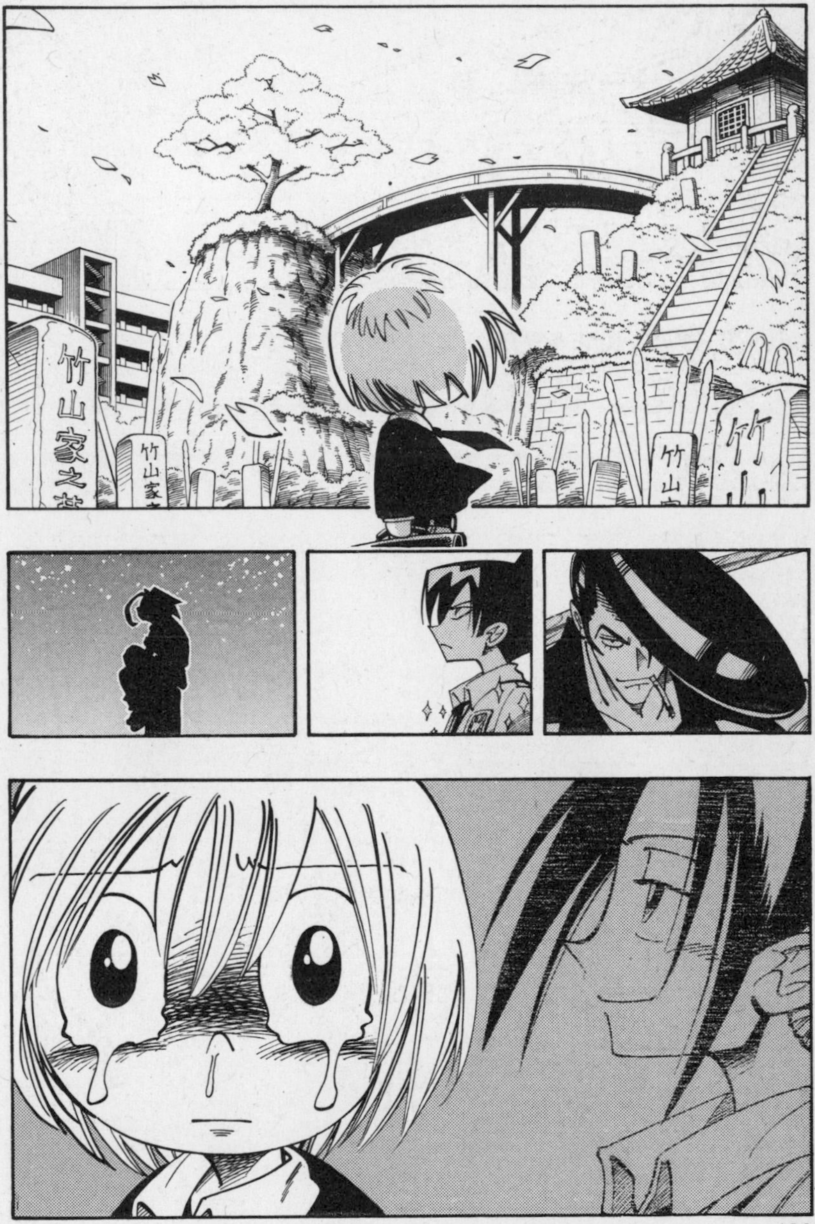
竹山
竹山家
竹山家之

READ THIS WAY

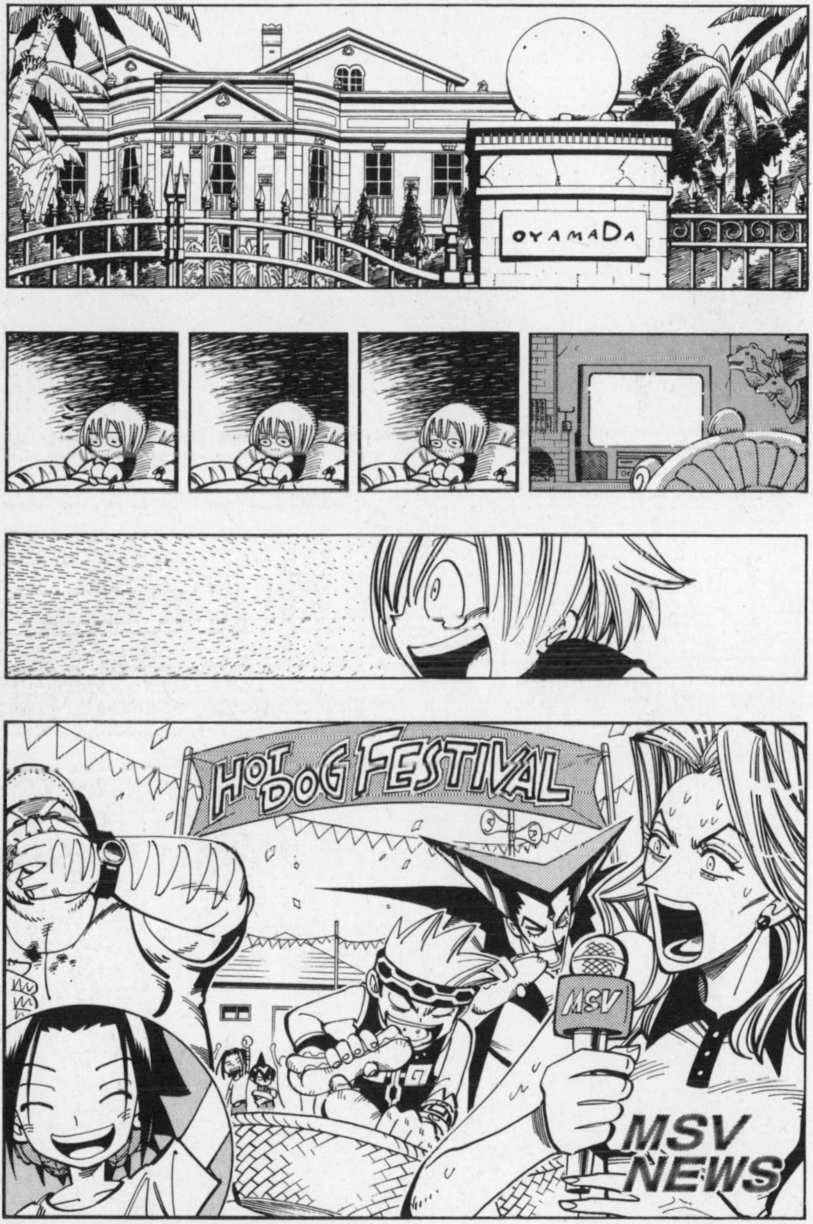
OYAMADA
HOT DOG FESTIVAL
MSV
MSV NEWS

 FUNBARI STORIES: END.

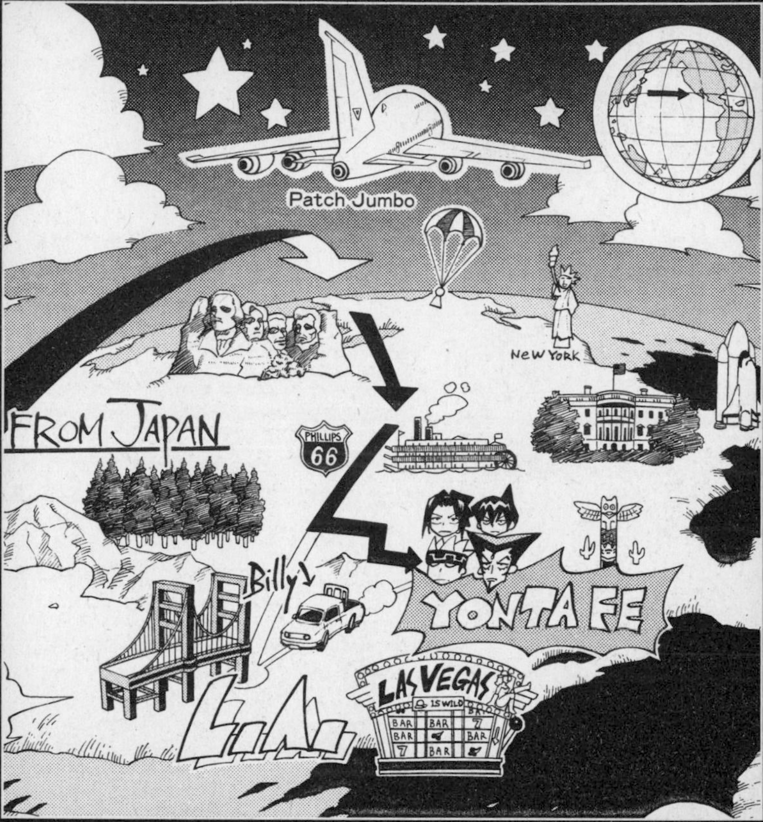
Patch Jumbo
NEW YORK
FROM JAPAN
PHILLIPS
66
Billy
YONTA FE
LAS VEGAS
15 WILD
BAR
BAR
7
BAR
BAR
7
BAR
L.A.

# IN THE NEXT VOLUME...

The shamans get their kicks on Route 66?! Yoh and the others survived their sudden descent from 40,000 feet, so they're now safely on the ground...in the middle of nowhere! How will they make it to the Patch Village in time for the Shaman Fight? Then, a mysterious Native American shaman says that the Patch are evil and threatens to kill anyone who aids the Patch in their plans... Can Yoh and his friends overcome this new roadblock?

***AVAILABLE SEPTEMBER 2006!***

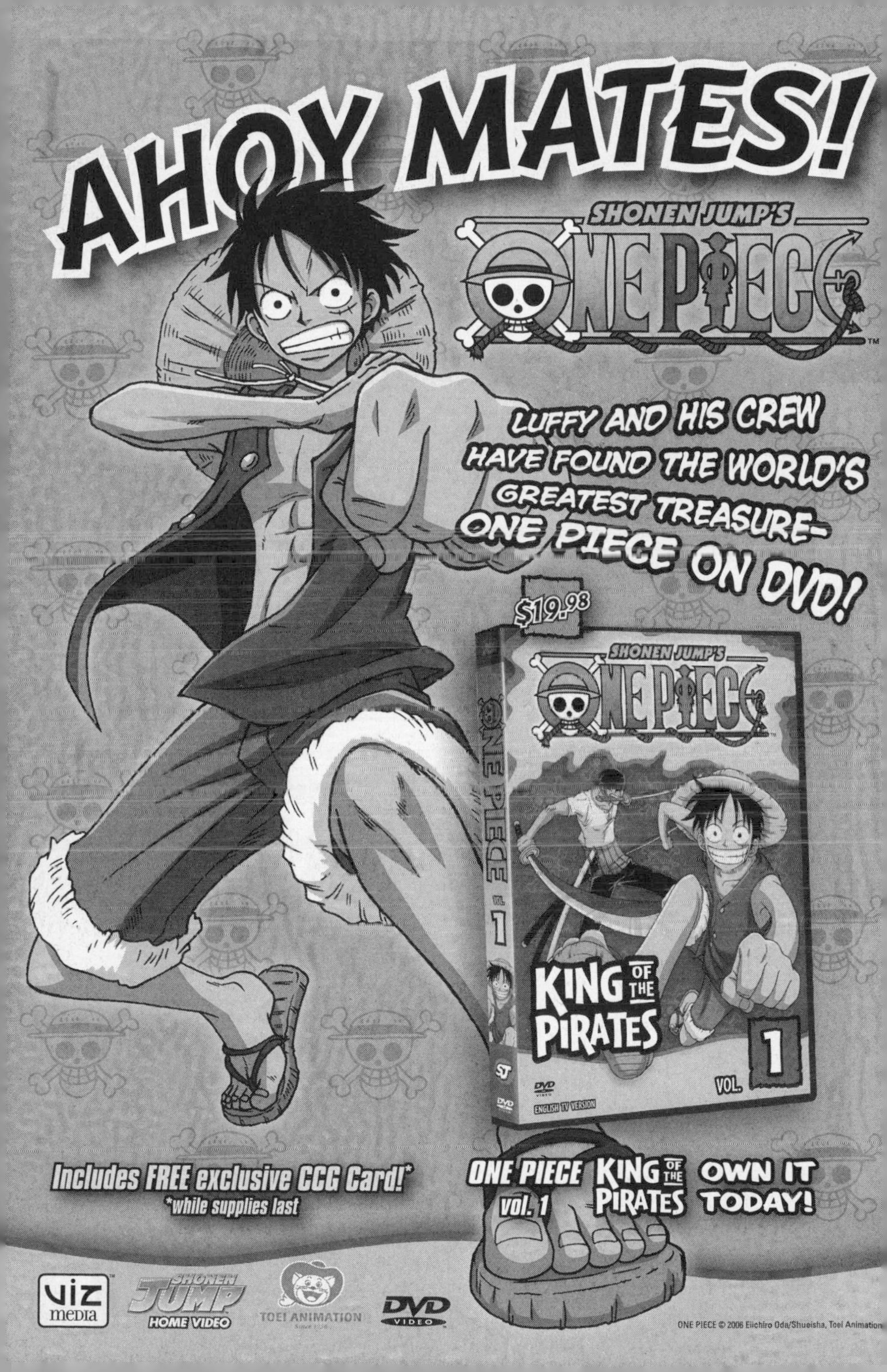

AHOY MATES!
SHONEN JUMP'S
ONE PIECE
LUFFY AND HIS CREW HAVE FOUND THE WORLD'S GREATEST TREASURE- ONE PIECE ON DVD!
$19.98
SHONEN JUMP'S ONE PIECE
KING OF THE PIRATES
VOL. 1
ENGLISH TV VERSION
Includes FREE exclusive CCG Card!*
*while supplies last
ONE PIECE vol. 1
KING OF THE PIRATES
OWN IT TODAY!
viz media
SHONEN JUMP HOME VIDEO
TOEI ANIMATION
DVD VIDEO
ONE PIECE © 2006 Eiichiro Oda/Shueisha, Toei Animation

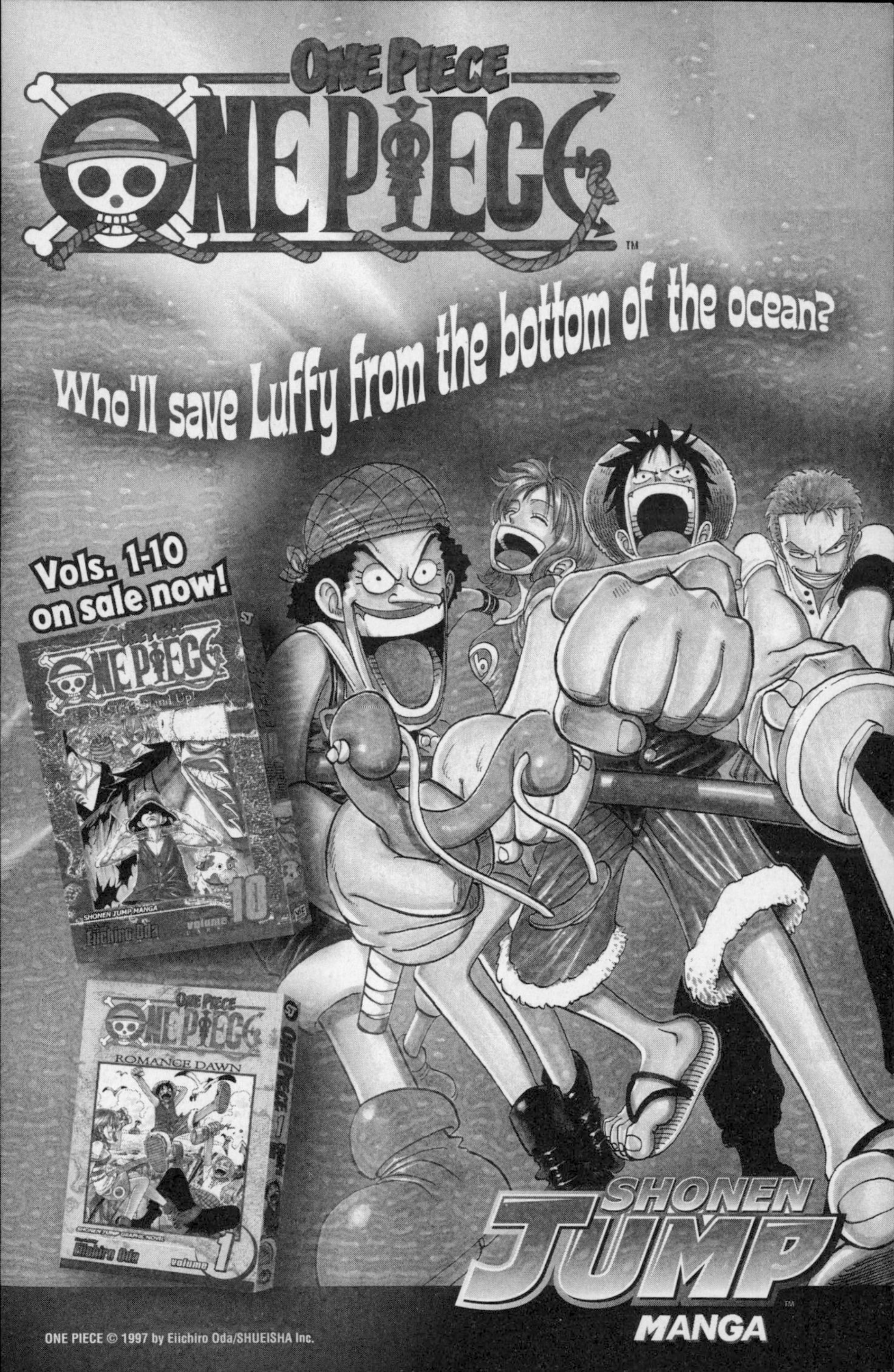
ONE PIECE
ONE PIECE™
Who'll save Luffy from the bottom of the ocean?
Vols. 1-10 on sale now!
ONE PIECE
SHONEN JUMP MANGA
Eiichiro Oda
volume 10
ONE PIECE
ROMANCE DAWN
SHONEN JUMP GRAPHIC NOVEL
Eiichiro Oda
volume 1
SHONEN JUMP™
MANGA
ONE PIECE © 1997 by Eiichiro Oda/SHUEISHA Inc.

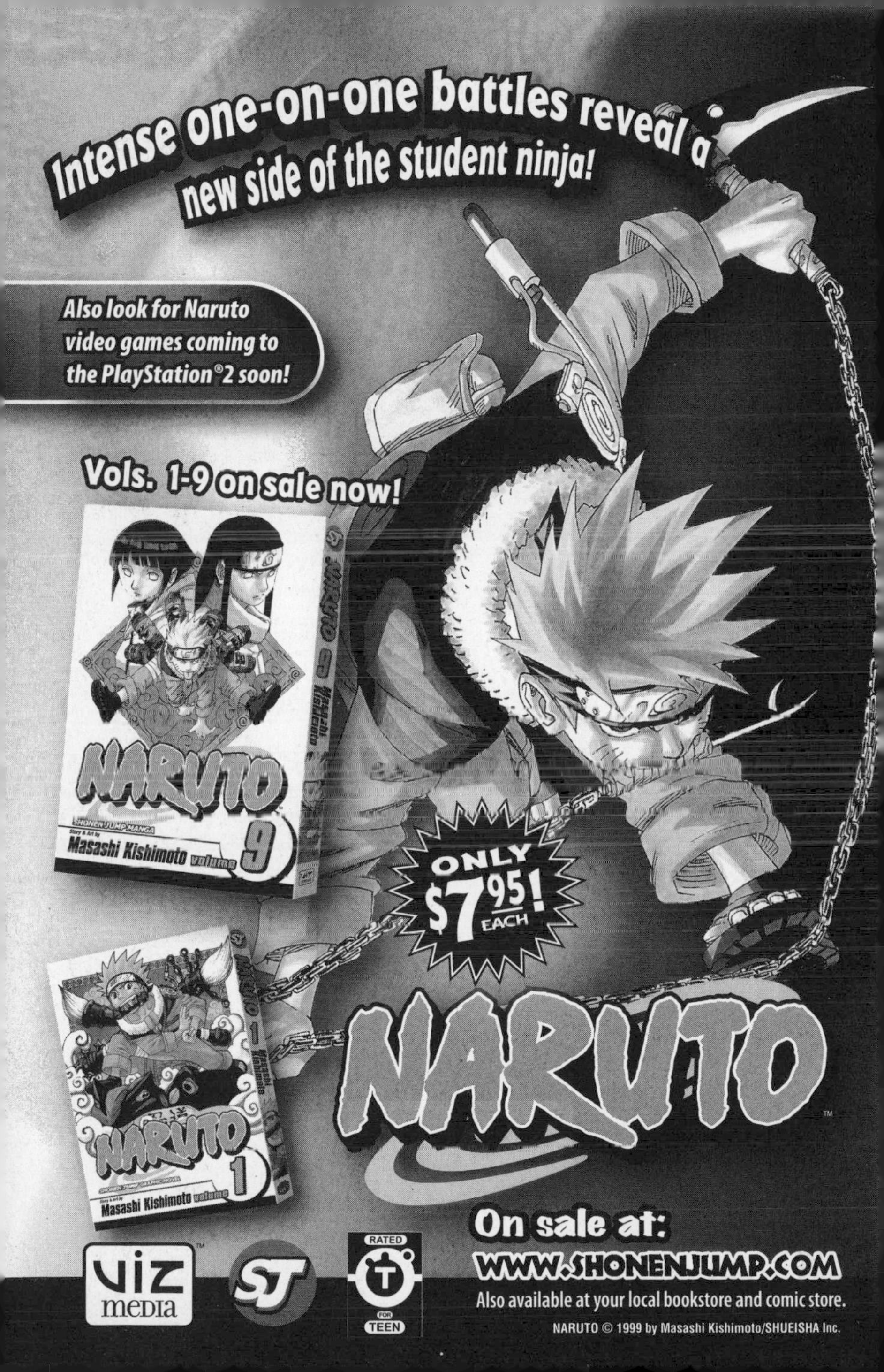

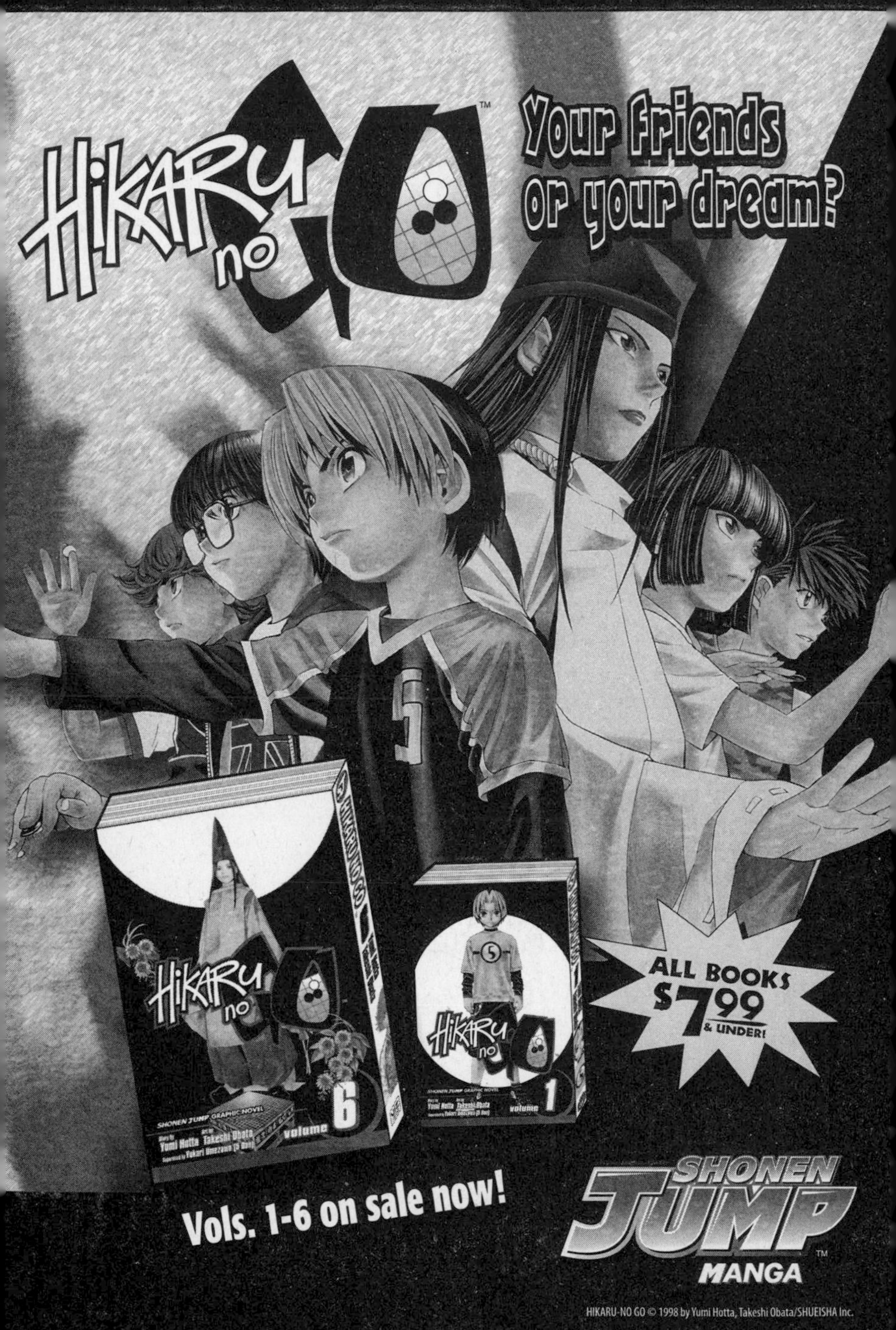

HIKARU no GO™
Your friends or your dream?
HIKARU no GO
SHONEN JUMP GRAPHIC NOVEL
volume 6
HIKARU no GO
volume 1
ALL BOOKS $7.99 & UNDER!
Vols. 1-6 on sale now!
SHONEN JUMP™ MANGA
HIKARU-NO GO © 1998 by Yumi Hotta, Takeshi Obata/SHUEISHA Inc.

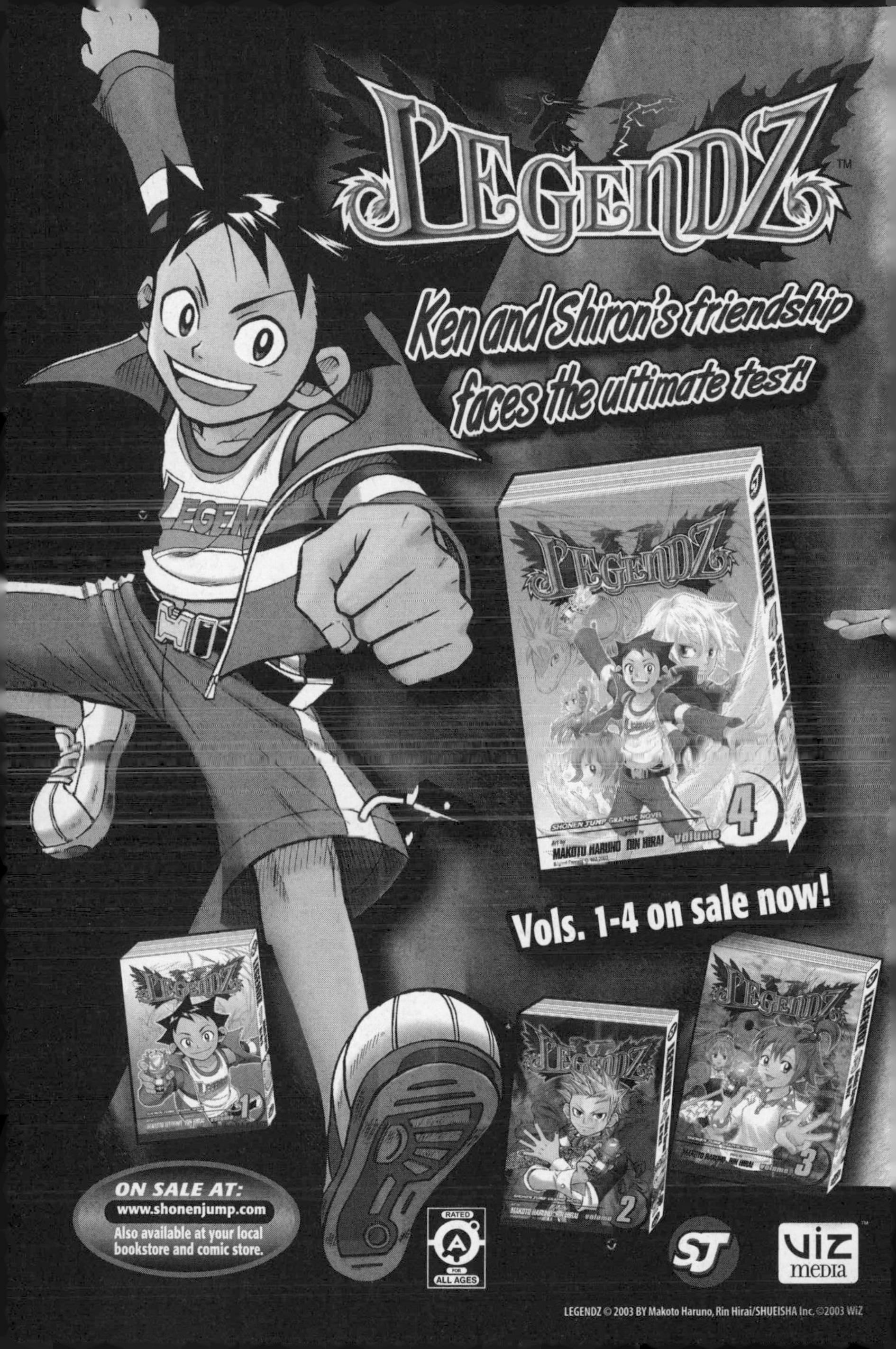
LEGENDZ™
Ken and Shiron's friendship faces the ultimate test!
Vols. 1-4 on sale now!
ON SALE AT:
www.shonenjump.com
Also available at your local bookstore and comic store.
RATED A FOR ALL AGES
SJ
VIZ media
LEGENDZ © 2003 BY Makoto Haruno, Rin Hirai/SHUEISHA Inc. ©2003 WiZ

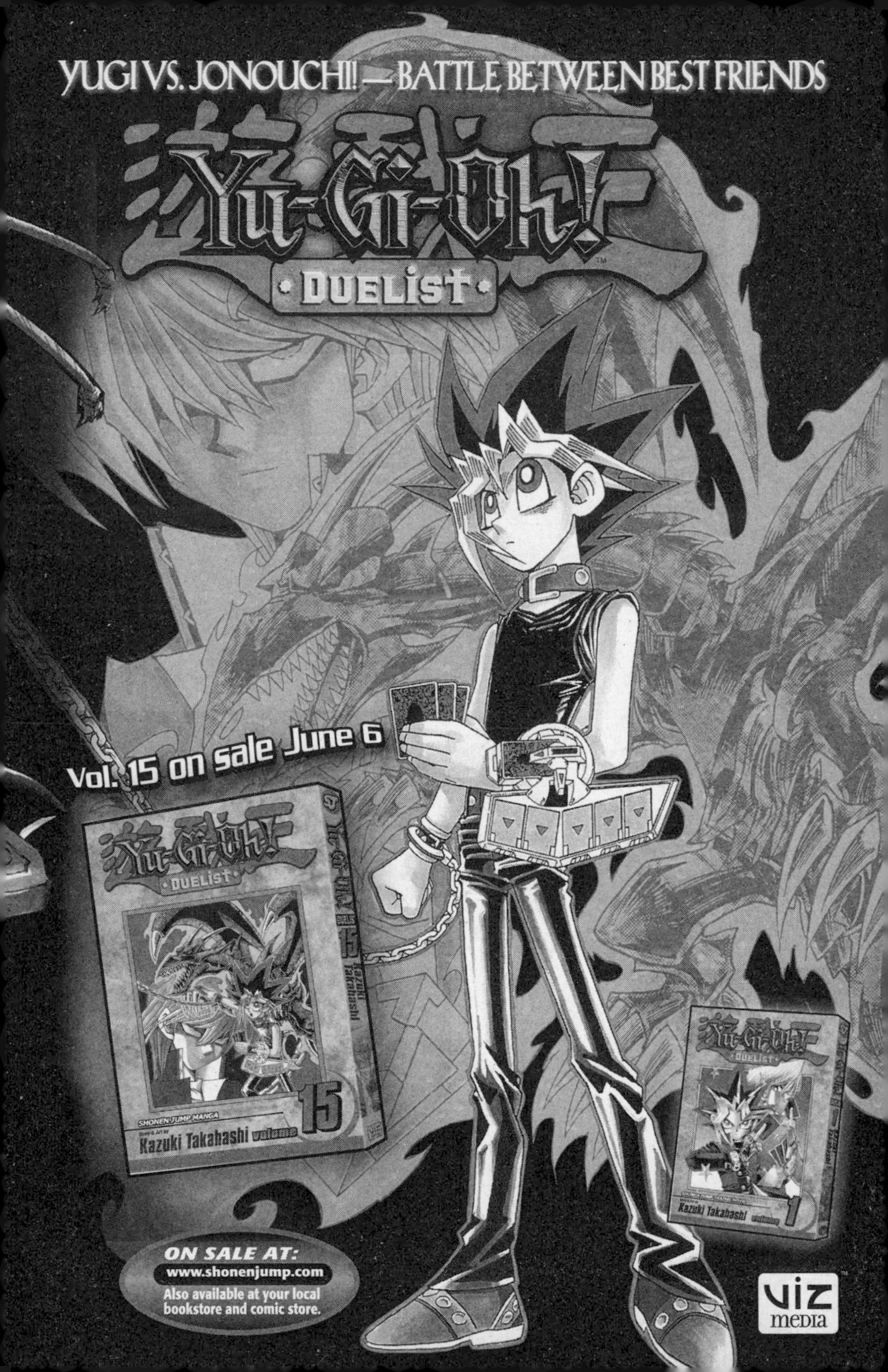
YUGI VS. JONOUCHI! — BATTLE BETWEEN BEST FRIENDS
Yu-Gi-Oh!
DUELIST
Vol. 15 on sale June 6
Yu-Gi-Oh! DUELIST
SHONEN JUMP MANGA
Kazuki Takahashi volume 15
Yu-Gi-Oh! DUELIST
Kazuki Takahashi volume 1
ON SALE AT:
www.shonenjump.com
Also available at your local bookstore and comic store.
viz media

# Tell us what you think about SHONEN JUMP manga!

Our survey is now available online.
Go to: **www.SHONENJUMP.com/mangasurvey**

# Help us make our product offering better!

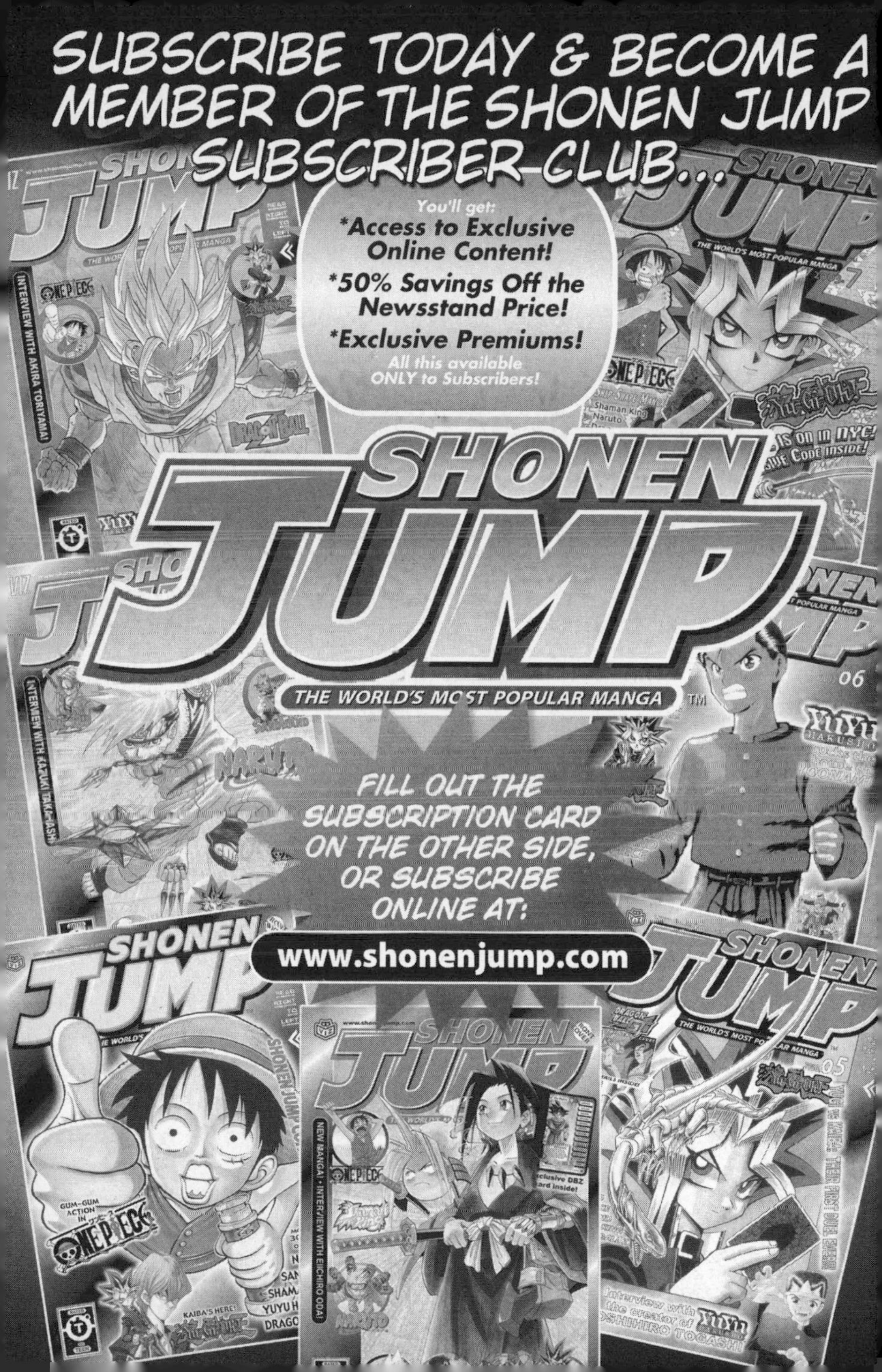
SUBSCRIBE TODAY & BECOME A MEMBER OF THE SHONEN JUMP SUBSCRIBER CLUB...
You'll get:
*Access to Exclusive Online Content!
*50% Savings Off the Newsstand Price!
*Exclusive Premiums!
All this available ONLY to Subscribers!
SHONEN JUMP
THE WORLD'S MOST POPULAR MANGA
FILL OUT THE SUBSCRIPTION CARD ON THE OTHER SIDE, OR SUBSCRIBE ONLINE AT:
www.shonenjump.com

# Save 50% off the newsstand price!

## SHONEN JUMP
### THE WORLD'S MOST POPULAR MANGA

**SUBSCRIBE TODAY and SAVE 50% OFF the cover price PLUS enjoy all the benefits of the SHONEN JUMP SUBSCRIBER CLUB, exclusive online content & special gifts ONLY AVAILABLE to SUBSCRIBERS!**

☑ **YES!** Please enter my 1 year subscription (12 issues) to *SHONEN JUMP* at the INCREDIBLY LOW SUBSCRIPTION RATE of $29.95 and sign me up for the SHONEN JUMP Subscriber Club!

**Only $29⁹⁵!**

NAME

ADDRESS

CITY                    STATE      ZIP

E-MAIL ADDRESS

☐ MY CHECK IS ENCLOSED      ☐ BILL ME LATER

CREDIT CARD:      ☐ VISA      ☐ MASTERCARD

ACCOUNT #                              EXP. DATE

SIGNATURE

**CLIP AND MAIL TO** →

SHONEN JUMP
Subscriptions Service Dept.
P.O. Box 515
Mount Morris, IL  61054-0515

Make checks payable to: **SHONEN JUMP.**
Canada add US $12. No foreign orders. Allow 6-8 weeks for delivery.

**P6SJGN**   YU-GI-OH! © 1996 by Kazuki Takahashi / SHUEISHA Inc.